KAUAI

Lehua Island

Ki'i

Paniau

Kiekie

Halulu Lake

Pueo Point

Nonopapa

Halalii Lake

NIIHAU

Kawaihoa Point

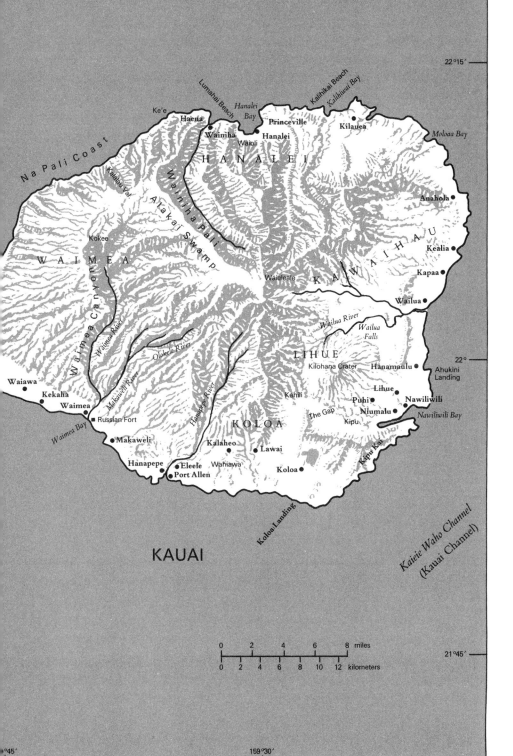

KAUAI

KAUAI

THE SEPARATE KINGDOM

EDWARD JOESTING

University of Hawaii Press

AND

Kauai Museum Association, Limited

First edition 1984
Paperback edition 1987
13 14 15 16 17 18   13 12 11 10 9 8

Library of Congress Cataloging-in-Publication Data

Joesting, Edward, 1925–1986
  Kauai : the separate kingdom.

  Bibliography: p.
  Includes index.
  1. Kauai (Hawaii)—History.   I.   Title.
DU628.K3J63   1984   996.9'41   84-16366
ISBN 0-8248-0943-2
ISBN-13: 978-0-8248-1162-4 (pbk)
ISBN-10: 0-8248-1162-3 (pbk)

All photographs are from the Kauai Museum unless otherwise indicated.

University of Hawai'i Press books are printed on acid-free paper
and meet the guidelines for permancence and durability of the
Council on Library Resources.

Designed by Roger Eggers
Printed by Sheridan Books, Inc.

www.uhpress.hawaii.edu

for
Juliet Rice Wichman
a distinguished woman
of Kauai

EDWARD JOESTING 1984

in memory of
Juliet Rice Wichman
from her many friends
and relatives

KAUAI MUSEUM ASSOCIATION 1988

Contents

A NOTE ON THE USE OF
THE HAWAIIAN LANGUAGE

Most of the Hawaiian words used in this volume will be familiar to those who have even a passing acquaintance with the Islands and their cultural traditions. Thus, italics and diacritical markings are used only where a word is introduced into the text, and at that point the meaning is given or can be inferred from the context. Thereafter, all common Hawaiian words are set in roman type, without macrons or glottal stops, and plurals are formed by adding *s*. Place names and personal names are spelled without hyphens and diacritics. The reader who desires a guide to the origin, meaning, and pronunciation of such proper nouns is referred to *Place Names of Hawaii* (M. K. Pukui, S. H. Elbert, and E. T. Mookini, 1974, The University Press of Hawaii) and *Index to "Ruling Chiefs of Hawaii" by S. M. Kamakau* (E. P. Sterling, 1974, Bishop Museum).

Preface

The task of writing the history of Kauai proved to be more than researching and organizing events, and drawing conclusions and relating them to the larger history of the Hawaiian Islands. With time it became clear that Kauai was a place distinct from the other islands. This added an unexpected and intriguing dimension to the writing of this book.

Kauai's distinctiveness, or separateness, in large part comes from its location. The whims of creation separated Kauai from Oahu by a wide and tempestuous channel and, of the major islands, it is the most remote. Although there was communication between Kauai and the other islands during ancient times, it was not as common as it was among the islands to the southeast. While these other islands were conquered and regained by a succession of rulers, there is no account of an enemy ever successfully invading Kauai. For generations, then, Kauai was an independent and isolated place.

Kamehameha I was not able to take Kauai by force and, although it became a tributary part of the Hawaiian kingdom, Kamehameha never set foot on Kauai. After the Kauai insurrection of 1824 had been put down and the northwest islands had been pulled into the kingdom, the memory of their independence continued to be an embarrassment to the heirs of the first Kamehameha. Consequently, little was written about the rebellion on Kauai, or about what happened to its people in the aftermath.

Those who first put the history of the Islands into written form—recording the ancient history that had been passed from generation to generation by word of mouth—these writers divided the Hawaiian Islands into two parts. The islands of Kauai and its small neighbor Niihau were called the leeward islands. All the islands to the southeast of Kauai were known as the windward islands. And so, from ancient times, Hawaii was divided into two parts. This distinction continued well into the nineteenth century.

Through the 1800s the leeward islands gradually and reluctantly became a part of the kingdom, drawn into the greater scheme of things through the search for economic well-being and through improved transportation. Economic well-being came with the development of the sugar business. Improved transportation came in the form of steamships, which finally came to Kauai on some sort of a schedule when the sugar industry made it economically feasible.

This book closes with the end of the nineteenth century, by which time the separateness of Kauai had all but disappeared. This ending was greatly speeded when Hawaii became a territory of the United States. That momentous event gently brought deep and far-reaching changes to the leeward islands. The twentieth century ushered in another era, which is not dealt with here. That story can best be told separately.

Into the narrative of ancient rituals and adventures, of isolation, the quest for power, and commercial struggles, I have endeavored to add something of the reality of the moment, what might be called "little things." By this means history escapes the dullness of a recitation and gains an urgency that can touch people across great spans of time.

Acknowledgments

This book was in preparation over a number of years and I am indebted to many persons for their assistance. My concern is that I might not acknowledge here all those who helped.

I owe my thanks to the staff of the Hawaiian and Pacific collections, Hamilton Library, University of Hawaii, with David Kittelson and Renée Heyum being of special help. The staff of the microfilm department at Hamilton Library was also helpful. The staff of the Hawaii State Archives, particularly Agnes Conrad, former state archivist, and Mary Ann Akao, assisted me in numerous ways.

Barbara E. Dunn of the Hawaiian Historical Society was always ready to assist, as were Lela Goodell and Mary Jane Knight of the Hawaiian Mission Children's Society. The staff of the Hawaii and Pacific Room at the main branch of the Hawaii State Library was helpful.

At the Bernice P. Bishop Museum, I am indebted to Kenneth Emory, Yosihiko Sinoto, Marion Kelly, and Cynthia Timberlake as well as Joyce Davis, formerly of the museum staff.

On Kauai I owe my gratitude to Robert Gahran, director emeritus of the Kauai Museum, who generously aided in a wide variety of ways from the beginning of the project. The staff of Grove Farm Homestead Museum is due my acknowledgment. The staff of the Kauai Public Library was always interested and helpful. Sophie Cluff added her support. Notes from the Catherine Stauder Collection at the Kauai Museum were of assistance.

This book was possible only because of the continuing assistance and confidence of Juliet Rice Wichman. Her deep knowledge and affection for Kauai were essential and her understanding of the difficulties of preparing a book such as this deserve my special thanks.

Others who contributed in various ways were Ruth Hanner, Alfons

Korn, Ella Wiswell, and the late Edith Rice Plews. John Charles aided particularly with the chapter on Russian activities on Kauai. Conversations with Mary Kawena Pukui were enlightening. O. A. Bushnell offered suggestions that are appreciated and valued.

Errors of fact, interpretation, of omission, and lapses in style are the responsibility of the author.

CHAPTER ONE

A Rippling on the Water

There is a rough plateau atop the island of Kauai and there is no other place like it in the world. Rising almost from the very center of the island, this mountain peak is 5,148 feet tall. At the top is a solitary, windy, rain-ravaged plateau. There is no doubt the mountain with its unique plateau of gullies and knolls dominates the island of Kauai. The mountain takes its name from a pond on the peak, Waialeale, a Rippling on the Water.

The ancient inhabitants of Kauai felt the mighty presence of this mountain, for they toiled to its peak and there constructed an altar to Kane. The chiefs, priests, and their retainers annually returned to pay their respects by making offerings to this powerful god. Kane was the god of living creatures, the spirit of living water, the god of sunlight, lord of the forests, and of all the creatures that dwelt in them. He was the leading god among the great gods.

The mountain peak of Waialeale is seldom seen from the rest of Kauai. Occasionally, at dawn, it may stand clear against a cloudless sky, but by early morning it is nearly always enveloped in a mantle of clouds. Kane, in his mountain height, prefers to remain aloof from all those about him.

The Hawaiians were sensitive to the world about them, to the hills, the streams, the trees, the seashore, the clouds. They chanted of these things, asking for protection, using them as symbols, or simply celebrating their beauty. These chants included the names of the familiar places about them. A chant of Kauai honoring Waialeale refers to Kawaikini, a nearby pinnacle, and to Alakai, the vast swamp on the northwest side of Waialeale:

> Beautiful is Kauai beyond compare,
> She sends forth a bud in the summit of Waialeale,

She flowers in the heights of Kawaikini,
Her strength radiates in awful splendor from the
    Alakai;
Though I weary, though I faint, she renews my
    strength in her soft petals.

To travel to the "bud in the summit of Waialeale" the chiefs, priests, and retainers very likely journeyed up the Wailua River. The first small portion of this pilgrimage might have been made by canoe to a point where the two branches of the river join. Here, some two miles from the sea, is a ridge called Kuamo'o-loa-o-Kane, or the Great-Ridge-Path-of-Kane. At this point the river is no longer navigable and the long walk would begin, following the north fork of the Wailua River, toward the cliffs that protected the place of Kane atop Waialeale.

These pilgrims followed the course of the river through the rolling lands of Wailua Valley, which cuts deep into the very heart of the mountain. On their journey inland the Kauaians saw those reassuring signs of nature that were significant parts of their lives. There was the *kōlea*, or Golden Plover, their brown backs spotted with gold, their spindly legs carrying them about as they nervously searched for insects. The Golden Plover is a part-time resident of Kauai. They live in Alaska and Siberia and after the mating season is over, they fly to the southern islands. When their plumage begins to return, they fly over 2,000 miles back to nest in the far north.

The procession of chiefs passed through groves of spacious *koa* trees, which the Hawaiians used for the hulls of their canoes. When a tree had been selected for a canoe hull, the workmen first watched for the coming of the *elepaio*, a useful bird, because when it alighted on a *koa* tree it searched for insects. If the bird soon flew away the Hawaiians assumed the tree was sound and not infected with damaging insects.

They passed various species of sandalwood trees. The trees did not stand out particularly with their slender gray trunks and the irregular shape of their branches. The leaves were oval or pointed depending on the species. Birds hovered about them when their flowers blossomed. Shavings from the inner heartwood of the tree, placed in the folds of *kapa*, barkcloth, gave fragrance.

The travelers passed stands of *'ōhi'a-lehua* and *lapalapa* trees. Foraging in these trees was the Kauai *'ō'ō*, a small, nearly black bird with a small cluster of yellow feathers above each leg. It responds to the human imitation of its loud mellow whistle. The Small Kauai Thrush, the *kāmaʻo,* about seven inches long, dark brown with grayish and white underparts, very sensitive to its environment, lives in isolated areas and depends on ohia-lehua forests for survival. It takes to the high branches of koa trees to sing its song.

And there is the Short Eared Owl, or *pueo.* These brown birds with yellow eyes, seen from sea level to the highest peaks, glide in wide circles looking for rats and insects. Some of the Hawaiians looked on the pueo as an ill omen, but others considered them to be a good sign and of assistance to humans.

As the Hawaiians marched on they came to another fork in the Wailua River. They again followed the northern flow of what now became a mere stream. They stepped from one moss-covered rock to another, sometimes wading through the cool waters of the stream itself. High, forest-covered ridges are on both sides and white clouds hurl past above, blown by strong northern winds.

Through dense groves of bamboo, mountain bananas, and thickets of ferns, species both large and small, the way becomes steep and laborious. The path upward could only be made by seizing branches of trees and undergrowth along the way. The way leads to the top of a mountain ridge that divides the present-day districts of Hanalei and Kawaihau. They ascended to the spine of this ridge at about the 2,300-foot level. The path along the spine is narrow with great drop-offs on either side.

Reaching this point in the journey had been a long, exhausting day's work. Camping on the ridge for the night was not uncommon.

In the morning, it was still a hard climb to the summit. The spine of the mountain is steep. The ground is slippery. Moss lies underfoot and sags from the limbs of trees. Branches ooze water when grasped. Rain fell in greater amounts as they ascended. At about an elevation of 3,200 feet the wearied travelers entered the first narrow, funnel-like end of the plateau on the northern end of Waialeale. The way still led upward nearly 2,000 feet to the altar of Kane, but experienced guides showed the way in a matter of several hours. Finally, over one more knoll, and the men and women who had come to pay honor to Kane were within sight of the altar.

Waialeale is not a flat area, but rather a series of shallow gullies and rises. The total space at the summit might be only six acres in size, but because of the terrain, the sweeping clouds, and the rain, it is easy to become disoriented and lost. It took little imagination on the part of the Hawaiians to see wisp-like figures loom and disappear. Often the range of vision is reduced to as little as ten feet.

The violent winds and moisture-heavy clouds that funnel up the valleys on the north side of Waialeale pass over some 2,000 miles of open ocean before hitting the land mass of Kauai. Sometimes one can be held up leaning full-weight into the wind, and sometimes one must squat down to avoid being blown over. The rain in the clouds is so heavy that it often drops before reaching the summit, and the ferocity of the wind rushing upward drives it straight up the valley walls, shooting above Mount Waialeale before falling to earth.

The ground of the summit of Waialeale is covered with black moss with lichen growing through the matting. Each step is into springy moss and mud, which squeaks under the pressure of the human foot. In the sheltered gullies a variety of rare plants grow, many found nowhere else in the world. There is a species of tiny violet, a diminutive aster bush, a geranium with dwarfish silver leaves, and a lily with silver, sword-like foliage. Everything that grows on Waialeale is of miniature size, trees reduced to bushes, and bushes to a fraction of their normal size.

Along the very edge of the precipice, which drops off some 2,500 feet into the valley on the north, grow large-leafed 'ape'ape plants. Growing on the precipice allows drainage; otherwise they would drown in the ooze of Mount Waialeale.

But the weary chiefs, their priests, and attendants had made the pilgrimage for one purpose—to honor and please Kane. As they approached the altar that had long ago been built to him, they chanted in his praise and of his power. This was a time of great solemnity.

The altar was named Kaawako. The inner meaning of the name is lost and it is possible that in ancient times it was known only to an honored few, a secret meaning that could be comprehended only by an elite group. The altar stood 2 feet high, 5 feet wide, and 7 feet long. At the rear of the structure, standing on end, was a phallic stone. The altar was located between two knolls and was constructed of smooth lava slabs. It still remains to be seen today.

Nearby is an oblong pond that varies in size, but usually is about 30 feet wide and 40 feet long. It is shallow, about knee-deep. The pond gives the mountain its name, because the winds that constantly come howling from the north cause a rippling on the surface of the pond.

The natural flow of the water from the pond on Waialeale is into the deep valley of Wainiha on the north of Kauai. Either from a sense of appropriateness or practicality the Hawaiians dug a ditch from the eastern end of the plateau so the Wailua River could also claim this sacred place as its source. Waialeale is the wettest place in the world, with an average of 466 inches of rain a year.

On the western side of Mount Waialeale lies the Alakai Swamp. It is an area of slime, mists, sedges, disintegrating trees, rare plants, and birds. The Alakai is the great watershed of Kauai. From here drain the waters to fill many of the rivers and streams that flow through the lowlands and which irrigated the fields of the ancient Hawaiians. The farmers gave thanks to Kane for providing them with "living water."

If for a moment the clouds and rain clear, the panoramic view from the top of Kauai is incredible. To the southwest lies the island of Niihau. To the north is the vast openness of the ocean, stretching unbroken to Alaska and the Aleutian Islands. To the south are the mountains of Kapalaoa and Kahili, and then, on the horizon to the southeast, the bluish-gray outline of Oahu may be visible. To the east, the Kauaians could look down upon the expansive valley of Wailua and see the way they had come on their journey to the summit.

The lower portion of the Wailua River, that portion where the waters flow into the Pacific Ocean, was one of the most desirable places to live in ancient Hawaii. It had been chosen as the capital by kings and was the home of the high chiefs of Kauai. Together with Waialua, on Oahu, it was considered to be one of the two most sacred areas in all the Islands.

Wailua Nui Hoano, or Great Sacred Wailua, was the name given to the ocean-bordered portion of this expansive valley. The sacred section extended inland for some two miles on the southern side and three miles on the north. The heart of this area is the present course of the Wailua River, although in the days of the kings and high chiefs, two rivers emptied into the ocean along this shore. In modern times the two rivers have joined into one.

The stone remains and ancient tales of Wailua are so numerous and varied that it is hard to sort them out. And it is difficult to set a date when Wailua Nui Hoano assumed its dominating importance. The ancient significance of Wailua is shown through the legends of men who sailed there and back again to Tahiti before the thirteenth century. Other legends talk of the frequent journeys of people from the other islands to Wailua. It was a famous place throughout Hawaii as well as in parts of Central Polynesia.

Within a small area Wailua offered most of the good things the ancient Kauaians desired. There was fresh water in abundance, and the ground was fertile, ideal for taro, yams, and bananas. The *kou* tree gave shade, its trunk often carved into bowls. The coconut tree was a source of food, utensils, and fiber. There were many bushes bearing the small yellow *'ilima* flowers used for *lei,* or wreaths. Varieties of red and white sugarcane were used by religious *kahuna,* or priests, as love potions. White sugarcane was used by the Kauaians in medicinal preparations. The ocean offered fish and other forms of seafood. It is little wonder that the rulers of Kauai, at some very early time, decided that Wailua was the most fitting place to establish their capital. It was a garden of plenty.

The white-capped ocean beyond the sandy beach was called Kaohala, The Thrust Passing, perhaps referring to Wailua's fame as a place to surf. Here the combers surge onto the beach, one behind the next. In ancient times both men and women of chiefly rank enjoyed surfing here.

Wailua Nui Hoano was reserved for the *ali'i,* or chiefs, of Kauai. A commoner could come into this domain only at the desire of the alii. Of such exalted rank were many of these chiefs that a commoner had to prostrate himself completely, face to the ground, if he came within sight of such a glorified person.

When a high chief returned from a journey, he was met in the surf by men who bore the canoe, with the chief aboard, to his dwelling and set him down at the entrance. The landing place where the canoes came ashore was the beginning of the path of the chiefs. This path ran upward through the lower part of Wailua, following close to the north bank of the present river.

The part called Wailua Kai, Wailua by the Sea, the small area at the mouth of the river and inland for a short distance, was a place where the ponderous and sacred ceremonies and rituals were performed, essential to the dignity and order of ancient Kauai. On both the north and south banks of the Wailua River are the stone ruins of the places where these ceremonies were conducted.

On the southern shore of the Wailua River, behind the place where the salt spray drifts upward from the collision of ocean on black lava rocks, was an enclosure that included a *heiau,* or temple. It was called Hikina a ka lā, Rising of the Sun, because the rays of the morning sun rising from the eastern sea came full against the stone structure. It was a large structure, 395 feet long, 80 feet wide at the front, or north end, and 56 feet wide at the rear. The walls of the enclosure were 8 to 11 feet thick and 6 feet high.

The walls of Hikinaakala were formed by great slabs of rock set on end in a double row, with the space between filled in with stones. The interior was paved throughout and divided into three sections. In the middle section were a number of graves, reported to be an entire family who had desecrated the structure by living and cultivating land within the walls.

Part of the interior of this structure is thought to have been a *pu'uhonua,* or a place of refuge. This was an enclosed place where a person who had committed a crime could find protection if he could elude his enemies and reach the safety of the walls. The person remained within the shelter of the walls for several days, performed certain rites prescribed by the priests, and then was free to leave without any punishment being dealt him. During war it was a place of safety.

Now the bare remains of this once great heiau have nearly disappeared. Today the casual observer would probably do little more than pause at this place where a grand structure once rose like a fortress, and where the salt mist still drifts upward from the sea. It is said that on the nights once designated for Kane, the sounds of a drum and a musical bow, strummed, can still be heard here.

Another heiau stood several hundred yards to the west, slightly back from the banks of the Wailua River. It was 273 by 324 feet in size. In its days of use there was an altar in the middle of this enclosure around which was a stone platform where people sat while ceremonies took place. The outer walls were 7 to 10 feet high and about 13 feet thick. It was called Malae and its remains are the largest of any heiau on Kauai.

At the entrance of the river are eight boulders deep in the channel mouth, and their existence is part of the voluminous mythology of Wailua. The demigod Maui, among his various escapades, chose to draw all the Islands together into one land mass. To do this he had to catch a giant fish called Luehu, but the fish avoided all of Maui's efforts.

Finally, Maui's mother told him that whenever he and his eight brothers put to sea to search for Luehu, the nine mud hens living in Wailua signaled the great fish by building a fire. Maui carved an image of himself and placed it in the canoe. When the mud hens saw the canoe depart, apparently with the usual nine men aboard, they started a fire to warn Luehu. Maui hid in a taro patch near Holoholoku and, seeing the fire, jumped from his hiding place, and caught a mud hen. He forced the hen to disclose how to make fire and thus was able to confuse the great fish he sought.

Then Maui and his eight brothers set out again. Before leaving Wailua, however, Maui was warned by his mother not to pick up a gourd canoe bailer that he might find floating on the ocean. But when the bailer appeared, bobbing on the sea, Maui picked it up and put it behind him in the stern of the canoe. He ordered his brothers not to look back at him under any circumstances. This time they succeeded in catching the great fish.

Luehu pulled Maui and his canoe around the Hawaiian Islands, wrapping the fishline around the Islands and drawing them together with its great strength. The only two islands that actually touched were Kauai and Oahu. The point of land on Kauai that touched Oahu was near Nawiliwili Bay, and on Oahu it was Kaena Point, nearest Kauai. As the canoe was pulled close to the shore of Oahu, a throng of people gathered and shouted, apparently at the great happening. But as the canoe came closer, Maui's eight brothers realized that the crowd was shouting in admiration of a beautiful woman. At once the eight brothers turned, looked back, and saw that the gourd bailer had turned into a beautiful woman. At that moment Luehu escaped from Maui's line and the two islands drifted back to their original positions.

Maui returned to Wailua. His brothers had disobeyed his orders, and so he turned them into stone and sank them in the mouth of the river. The eight boulders remain there still. At Kaena Point there is a rock called Pohaku o Kauai, Rock of Kauai. It was a piece of Kauai that became stuck on Oahu when the two islands touched.

On the north side of the Wailua River is a pool where legend says King Kaumualii, the last king of Kauai, used to swim. Nearby are a few rocks, once part of a small heiau for the ceremonial use of the king. Across from this was a coconut grove, now long gone, which was the area of the residence of Kaumualii.

A short way up the path of the chiefs is a place of immense impor-tance to all Kauai royalty. Beneath a cliff are the Birthstones, two large pieces of smooth stone. One supported the back of the woman and the second was where she spread her legs while giving birth. Adjacent to these stones was a grass house where the expectant mother would stay until the moment the birth was imminent. Near the Birthstones is a long flat slab of stone, set over the remains of a sacrificed dog. This was a sign that the place was *kapu,* forbidden. A commoner touching or stepping over the stone slab would be killed. Only at Wahiawa on Oahu can a similar place be found.

It was essential that all kings of Kauai be born on the Birthstones. Kaumualii had been born there. When chiefly ranks became diminished for some reason, the king selected women of common birth to deliver children at the Birthstones. Legend says such a child would be a chief. An ancient chant reinforces this idea. Holoholoku is the place name of the area where the Birthstones and the nearby heiau are located.

> The child of a chief born at Holoholo-ku is a
>   high chief;
> The child of a commoner born at Holoholo-ku
>   becomes a chief also;
> The child of a high chief born outside of Holoholo-
>   ku is no chief, a commoner he!

Yet another important ritual had to be followed. Once the child was born, the umbilical cord was wrapped in kapa and wedged into a crack in the rock cliff behind the Birthstones. Pebbles or small stones might help secure the little package. The umbilical cord was a symbol of a connection with the past. It was believed that if the cord of the child was eaten by a rat the child would grow up to be a thief. If it was not eaten it was a propitious sign for the future of the newborn alii.

One legend states that the newborn child was carried upward along the path of the chiefs to a boulder that stood on the ridge overlooking the river. As the kahunas walked in measured step they chanted of the arrival of a new chief. They then struck the Bellstone with a rock in a certain way so that the sound would travel up and down Wailua Valley and so everyone within hearing distance would know that a new chief was among them.

Near the Birthstones, but closer to the river bank, is a ridge known as Ka Lae o ka Manu, The Crest of the Bird. Below the ridge was Holoholoku heiau, 24 by 40 feet, much smaller than the others, but of great significance. It was a heiau of human sacrifice, and each month on a designated night a sacrifice had to be made. The altar was set against a cliff that rises upward on the western end. The entrance to the heiau was through a low passage, 20 inches high and 32 inches wide, only large enough for a person to crawl through. It is said to have been the oldest heiau on Kauai.

The walls stood some 5 feet high and within them, as well as on the ground inside the heiau were bits of coral that had been brought with seawater when the priests performed their rites of purification. The heiau is Tahitian in design, an indication of that influence during later migrations to the Islands.

Within the walls of the heiau was the grass-thatched house of the priest, with a floor paved with smooth, river-worn pebbles. Also within the walls were images of gods, with Ku, the stern and powerful deity who oversaw the sacrifices, being dominant. An oracle tower was built over the sacrificial stone and would have been made of ohia poles. Atop this tower the kahuna would commune with the gods, and from it would be hung the body of the person who had been sacrificed. Often the victims were prisoners taken in war, but if none were available, the kahuna would select a person and his executioner would strangle the unfortunate one secretly at night. The body would hang from the oracle tower until morning, when it was placed on the sacrificial stone. After the flesh had fallen from the corpse the bones were buried on the southern bluff that led down to the Wailua River.

The people of Kauai found symbolism in the physical configuration of a place or an entire landscape, and they bestowed names on the land in harmony with its use and location. This was particularly true in Sacred Wailua. The Crest of the Bird, Ka Lae o ka Manu, might have been thought of as the crest or the comb of a fighting cock. The crest atop a warrior's helmet might have had the same meaning, a symbol of importance and domination.

The Crest is the beginning of a rising ridge that runs along the north bank of the Wailua River. Where the ridge becomes higher it is called Kuamoʻo, the Spine of the Lizard. The Wailua River, running close by, is the fluid that flows in the spine.

The heiau at The Crest of the Bird was a much feared place, but it also was famous in the history of Hawaii because, according to legend, here the first large drum was introduced from Tahiti. These drums were made from hollowed coconut logs and were covered with taut sharkskin. Eventually they were used in all human sacrifice heiaus and to accompany the hula throughout the Islands.

The legend of the drums begins with Moikeha, one of the earliest voyagers to Wailua from Tahiti. In Tahiti, Moikeha lived with a lovely woman by the name of Luukia, by whom he had a son, but a jealous suitor convinced Luukia that Moikeha was making fun of her to others. Believing these lies, Luukia had herself bound in cord from her waist to her thighs so that Moikeha could no longer have intercourse with her.

Luukia refused to tell Moikeha the reason for her action and he sailed away from Tahiti together with his priest, navigators, sailing masters, and attendants. Moikeha landed at night on the beach at Wailua and it was not until the next morning that the people of the valley saw his double-hulled voyaging canoe on the beach with the kapu sticks in the sand before it, denoting that a chief was aboard.

Among those who came to look were the two daughters of the king of Kauai. Both fell in love with Moikeha, who was a handsome man with dark-reddish hair. The newcomer was taken to the king, eventually married both daughters, and had five sons by the two women over the years. When the old king died, Moikeha became ruler of Kauai.

However, Moikeha longed to see the son who had been born of Luukia in Tahiti, and decided to test his five Wailua sons to determine which one would be sent to Tahiti to bring back the child he had not seen for many years. Moikeha stood on one bank of the Wailua River and his five sons on the other. He ordered each to make a miniature sailing canoe from a broad ti leaf and, setting it on the water, to try to direct his canoe between Moikeha's spread legs on the opposite bank. Kila, the youngest son, was the only one to accomplish this feat and so he was selected to undertake the mission.

Kila succeeded in finding his half-brother and in the process he met Luukia, the mother of the boy he came to carry back to Kauai. Kila also took revenge on the enemies of his father in Tahiti. The jealous suitor, who had caused so much anguish to Moikeha, suffered a special, slow death. Kila ordered his men to hold him down in the bottom of his canoe and urinate on him. After two days and one night the captive drowned.

In Tahiti Luukia came to Kila in the middle of the night. The cords that had bound her were undone and, in the words of the translator of the legend, "Then they gathered up the fine strands of thought, indulging love's desire, and braided the lehua wreaths in dreamland, after which Luukia went her way. Later she became wholly Kila's."

Kila's half-brother was to have a profound effect upon the Hawaiian Islands. He was reported to have introduced the sharkskin-covered drum into the sacrificial heiau on the hill called The Crest of the Bird, overlooking the Wailua River.

Farther up the Wailua River, on an imposing flat site, is a famous and unusual heiau, called Poliahu. It is built high above the banks of the river, commanding a view of the lands below and the ocean beyond. In clear sight, across the river, is Malae heiau. It is believed there was some connection between these two temples. Both were supposed to have been built by the Menehune, a people of legend, who formed a long line and passed the rocks for these structures all the way from Makaweli, on the west side of Kauai, to Wailua.

Poliahu is not an ordinary heiau and is something of a mystery. It was devoted to the interests and affairs of the gods, demigods, and highest alii. No mere mortal was allowed to go there. Legend says deities gathered at Poliahu once a month, on the night of Kane. While the common people dared not venture near the heiau they could see the glimmer of lights and hear the beat of the drums and the applause and loud laughter of the gods.

The ancient people of Kauai and Niihau believed their islands were the children of the gods. As the gods dwelt in the sky they bore children who fell into the sea and became Kauai and Niihau. Geologists take a somewhat different view. They believe the leeward islands were born far below the surface of the sea. Some 15,000 feet down, on the floor of the ocean, there was movement in the upper mantle of the vast Pacific plate, or perhaps a fissure or deep trench opened up. Through this opening in the ocean floor poured forth an incredible volume of lava, pushing upward against the tremendous weight of the sea. As soon as the first upheaval took place the destructive forces of the sea were at work, eroding the lava that was rising from the blackness of the ocean depths. But the pressures continued and the mass of lava worked upward over eons of time. For periods of time the eruptions stopped, only to begin once more.

No human eye was there to see, but at last the islands of Kauai and Niihau pushed through the blackness of the sea and into the sunlight. They were sterile piles of black lava, still hot with the fires from far below. Pillars of steam ascended into the skies.

When this happened most of the land masses of the earth had already taken shape, for the Islands are latecomers in the geology of the world. With the appearance of the Hawaiian Islands the seemingly endless horizon of the north Pacific was broken, with new land now standing some 2,000 miles off the North American coast.

Kauai and Niihau are the most northwestern of the major islands of the Hawaiian chain. Kauai is fourth in size among the Islands, some 555 square miles of land. Its neighbor island, Niihau, 17 miles to the west and slightly to the south, comprises 72 square miles of land. At some time, perhaps millions of years ago, Niihau was larger and closer to Kauai and the channel between the two islands remains relatively shallow. Most of the surface portion of Kauai is estimated by geologists to be about 5.6 million years old, although minor eruptions occurred at later times. The basic shape and size of the island was set by the initial eruption.

Kauai comes closer to being round than any other island of the group. It is 33 miles from west to east and 25 miles from north to south. The reason for this near roundness is that Kauai is essentially the result of one enormous volcanic mountain from which lava flowed downward in all directions. Its center was Mount Waialeale. This volcano has a volume of about 1,000 cubic miles and its top is somewhere between 10 and 12 miles in diameter. It is the largest shield volcano in the Hawaiian Islands.

The center of this caldera has never been located, because it is filled with lava and ash nearly to its brim, and centuries of exceedingly heavy rainfall have produced such heavy growth that exploration can be done only with the greatest difficulty and some hazard. There were other volcanic outcroppings also, minor by the standards of Waialeale. The flatlands of the Lihue and Haupu areas and some of the land built up along Na Pali, the northern coast, were the work of later volcanic activity.

A collapse in the shield took place in an area called Makaweli, on the southwestern side of the island, but this was later filled by additional flows from above. The belated lava flows reached all the way to the sea. At Lihue and nearby Haupu are the only flank calderas known in Hawaii.

While Kauai is considered the oldest of the major islands, it is possible that eruptions were taking place on Oahu at the same time. Some believe that the small island of Niihau might have broken the surface of the ocean before Kauai. Exact ages and the sequence of eruptions are speculative and a definitive answer will probably never be forthcoming. But most scientists believe that Kauai was the first of the major islands to reach the approximate shape that it has today. The geology of the island is extremely complex because areas that had previously been eroded were covered by later lava flows.

One of these sets of eruptions is called the Koloa volcanic series, which broke out at numerous places on the eastern half of the island. Another eruption, but not as extensive, took place about five miles south of Mount Waialeale. The Koloa volcanic series scattered from about forty vents and covered what is now the entire floor of the

Lihue basin. It is estimated that the last flows on Kauai took place 1.5 million years ago. The Koloa flow built a broad and relatively level flat area over about one-fifth of the island, from Koloa to Kapaa.

Like all the islands of Hawaii, Kauai has been relentlessly buffeted by the elements of wind, rain, and wave. Na Pali coast is a classic example of the effects of these destructive natural forces. A million or more years ago the mountains on this northern part of the island ran smoothly in a gentle slope into the sea. Ocean waves traveling the 2,000 miles from the north battered the coast without ceasing. Rain on the mountains poured down rivers of water that cut knife-like into the porous slopes, opening areas that were then more easily eroded by the pounding seas. The never-ceasing destruction took its toll. The smooth mountain sides of Na Pali were gradually undercut by wave action, until great areas of earth fell off into the ocean, creating low cliffs that in turn were undermined, and more of the gentle slopes reeled into the sea. That Na Pali mountains originally sloped gradually into the sea has been demonstrated by drillings along its shores. These corings have shown a layer of boulders, followed by silt, and then a solid bed of basaltic rock, the original lava base that formed the graceful descent of northern Kauai into the sea. The process has continued over the centuries and persists today, making Na Pali one of the most rugged, spectacular, and wildest beauty spots in all the Islands. The cliffs fall 2,500 to 3,000 feet downward, to where crashing waves continue to batter the land.

To the northwest of Kauai lie numerous shoals, pinnacles, and atolls, too small or barren to support a human population for any length of time. In the southeast are the other high, large islands of Oahu, Molokai, Lanai, Maui, and Hawaii. The islands to the northwest of Kauai are geologically older and those to the southeast are younger.

The first men and women who made Kauai their home must have been astonished by the great diversity in the landscape they beheld. The lowland slopes were dry and barren. The high mountains were wet and green with growth. Over the centuries seeds and spores had been carried by wind currents and by birds, who also brought insects in their feathers, and by floating debris washed onto the shore from distant lands. One new species of plant or insect might have arrived every 10,000 or 20,000 years.

The fringing reefs surrounding sections of Kauai were built up over very long periods of time. Coral reefs, formed by marine animals that extract calcium carbonate from seawater and deposit it as a growing "skeleton," can grow and exist only in warm seawater. Seldom will reef corals grow at depths of more than 200 feet or at temperatures below 73 degrees Fahrenheit. One of the best developed of living reefs in the Hawaiian Islands runs along the north shore of Kauai from Kalihiwai Bay to Haena.

The first settlers found fresh water—more than could be used—and wood for canoes and housing. Within the reefs women and children could find a wide variety of seafood for a wholesome diet. There were dry areas of sand, such as Mana, where the heat is intense, but where one can always regain the warmth absent in colder and wetter regions. The settlers found room and abundance for all. It was a place of natural richness beyond imagination.

Where did the inhabitants of Kauai and the other Hawaiian Islands come from? Most authorities agree that the first settlers came from the Marquesas Islands, some 2,400 miles to the south. Why they sailed into unfamiliar seas is not known, but among the possible reasons might be wars, or because a lesser chief wanted to found a kingdom where he would be supreme. It seems likely that over-population, and, therefore the specter of starvation could have forced migrations.

There are no coral reefs in the Marquesas, thus eliminating that calm area of water with its variety of seafood. Level land is rare. Valleys are deeply cut into mountains, and some can only be entered from the sea. In ancient times houses were built near any place where food could be grown. Although water was plentiful, the sun touched the narrow floors and sides of many valleys only briefly each day. On some smaller low islands there were times of drought. Among those who lived in the deep damp valleys with a minimum of sunlight, arthritis was a common malady, as is shown in skeletal remains.

E. S. Craighill Handy, an authority on life in the Marquesas during ancient times, wrote that "the density of the population in the Marquesas was equal to the maximum that could be supported by agricultural and fishing industries of the primitive order practiced by the natives."

It is little wonder the Marquesans became one of the most ruthless races in all of Polynesia. Men and women were often tattooed bluish-black from hairline to toe in an attempt to appear fierce. The men carved whale-tooth discs to set in their ears, and the weight stretched the lobes to their shoulders. Sometimes a human skull dangled from cords tied to a warrior's loincloth.

In the midst of this hunger and savagery some Marquesans thought there must be a better place in which to live, and they sailed forth in search of that hoped-for home. Because so many islands were peopled from the Marquesas Islands they have been called the dispersal center of Eastern Polynesia.

The date of arrival in the Hawaiian Islands of these Polynesians from the south has not been established, except within very broad bounds. All the Hawaiian Islands were occupied between A.D. 500 and 1200, with A.D. 850 being a generally accepted date. Results of radiocarbon dating have varied so widely that archaeologists are hesitant to give anything but a generalization.

And where had the Marquesans come from before occupying the Marquesas Islands? The peoples of the Polynesian Triangle, which extends from New Zealand in the west, to lonely Easter Island in the east, and to the Hawaiian Islands at the northern apex, are grouped together because of similarities in customs and language. The Marquesas are on the eastern fringe of this triangle, but their language, like that of the rest of Polynesia, bears many root words that come from the Indonesian language. A few root words can be traced to the Malayan, Chinese, and Formosan languages. Indonesia was once a divided but great trading nation, and merchants of Persia could understand enough Indonesian to conduct trade for the valuable spices and other goods found there. The thousands of Indonesian islands were referred to by their ancient inhabitants as "Our Earth and Water." The settling of Indonesia goes so far back that it is lost in obscurity.

Excavations in Melanesia indicate that certain designs used on ancient pottery in those islands are essentially those used as designs in Western Polynesia. Other similar investigations are being pursued in Thailand. Eventually the origins of the Polynesians might be pushed back to a more western place and an earlier date. If evidence ties Polynesian culture with the more western of the Asian countries, the assumption would be that some group of people traveled eastward, perhaps forced from place to place by local inhabitants until they reached Indonesia, where they set forth on their great ocean explorations. In the course of centuries of wandering they must have intermarried with many peoples en route, thus producing, in the end, the Polynesian race.

Some of those who learned their seamanship in the waterways of Indonesia and then decided to depart apparently went east into Polynesia, while others sailed west. In the Republic of Malagasy, long known as Madagascar, off the east coast of Africa, the culture clearly indicates

Indonesian-Polynesian influences as well as African influences. Again, some root words are distinctly connected with Indonesian words. Another connection with Southeast Asia and much of Oceania is the use of the outrigger canoe, a type of craft found only in these two areas of the world. Certain methods of farming and fishing were also similar to those practiced in Indonesia and Polynesia.

The people who settled the Marquesas Islands were among the first to travel so far east. Settlement of their islands is estimated to have been during the first 300 years after Christ. It appears they came from either Tonga or Samoa, far to the west. In about A.D. 600 the Marquesans settled Tahiti. Thus at one time the populations of these islands were of the same people. At a later date, another group of Polynesians settled nearby Raiatea. Raiateans soon came to dominate Tahiti and other islands, establishing themselves as the heart of Central Polynesian culture.

When the Polynesians sailed north toward Hawaii, they came in double-hulled voyaging canoes. While there is no detailed knowledge of the type of canoes the Polynesians used for long voyages, some impressive remains attest to their ability as canoe builders. The remains of an ocean-going canoe, wooden planks about 40 feet long, were unearthed in the Society Islands some years ago. Holes had been drilled along the top of the gunwale so that wash-strakes could be lashed on with sennit, setting the sides higher, and giving additional protection in the open sea. The first Westerners to discover the Marquesas were the Spanish in 1595, and the navigator on that voyage described a double-hulled canoe. Such canoes carried a triangular or claw-shaped sail, with the mast stepped forward of amidships. The largest canoes were capable of holding forty to fifty paddlers.

Those ancient Polynesian sailors had none of the navigational equipment common today. Yet they made long voyages over the open sea well before Western man was willing to sail beyond the sight of land. They sailed by the stars, by the currents, and by the winds. Sailors were bred with a sensitivity to the sea and it became their natural element. In spirit the seamen were one with nature, considering the elements about them as their friends. Their ability as sailors was phenomenal.

There is no evidence of a mass exodus from the Marquesas northward. Perhaps a single canoe or several canoes carried the first immigrants. In the course of time, craftsmen came bringing their various skills. All the kinds of plants and animals that had been important in their old homes eventually were carried to the north. Among these importations were taro, used to make the staple food *poi*, ti plants, sugarcane, wild ginger, the bottle gourd, the candlenut tree, two kinds of mulberry plants, bamboo, turmeric, arrowroot, several varieties of yams, and the breadfruit tree. They also brought the hog, dog, and jungle fowl, and the rat probably came as a stowaway. Since the climate of their new home was similar to that of the Marquesas, plants and animals flourished.

Travel between Hawaii and the Marquesas took place, probably luring other adventurous persons northward. Under ideal conditions the course from Hawaii south, with favoring winds and currents, would carry a canoe to the Marquesas, but a slight variation would bring the sailors into the vicinity of Tahiti. It seems likely the Tahitians learned of Hawaii in this way for, in about A.D. 1,000, they too sailed for the Hawaiian Islands. The Tahitians came in voyaging canoes up to 100 feet in length, with the advantage of a protective shelter on the platform between the hulls, where a fire could be built on a base of earth.

Then, for reasons unknown, the voyages between the northern and southern islands ceased. Tradition tells us that one of the last important persons to arrive in "Burning Hawaii," as these volcanic islands were called in the south, was a priest named Paao.

Paao was disturbed by the fact that the alii were intermarrying with commoners. To him this was an untenable situation. He returned to Tahiti and brought back to Hawaii a highborn chief, who married and through his children helped to re-establish the respect due high lineage. To strengthen the dignity of these chiefs Paao reportedly established a new design for heiaus, instituted the custom of human sacrifice, and initiated the draping of a long red-feather girdle on a new king at the time of his investiture.

During the era when Tahitian-Hawaiian ties were waning, about A.D. 1275, the Crusades were coming to an end in the Middle East, Dante was writing *The Divine Comedy*, and Kublai Khan had extended the frontiers of his empire throughout China and all the way to the Pacific Ocean. It would still be 200 years before Christopher Columbus sailed forth into the Atlantic. On Kauai, a civilization had been established that would change little in its religion, social organization, or material culture for 500 years.

CHAPTER TWO

There Were a People Called Menehune

O n Kauai there is evidence of ancient connections with the southern islands of Central Polynesia not found on the other islands of Hawaii. That these differences existed on Kauai for so long after communications with Central Polynesia had ceased is a manifestation of the isolation of Kauai from the rest of the Hawaiian Islands. Differences are seen in the stone implements that were once used on Kauai, in styles of heiaus, in language, and in the stories of the Menehune. Long considered a mythical people of Kauai, in reality the Menehune were a distinct people of an ancient time.

Among the stone implements common to the Kauaians were two types of poi pounders restricted almost exclusively to that island. Pounders were used to mash the corm of the taro plant into poi, the staple food of the Hawaiians. The two Kauai types are the ring and stirrup pounders. The stirrup pounder has an indentation that allowed the user to hold the implement more firmly while pounding the corm of the taro plant. The ring pounder has a hole cut through the stone so that it could be grasped firmly. The poi pounder common to all the Hawaiian Islands has a single round handle and a flared, circular pounding surface. Most pounders stand about nine inches high.

A discovery of significance was made in recent years on the island of Uahuka in the northern Marquesas when an "ancestor" stirrup pounder was discovered there. It is estimated, through radiocarbon dating, that it was in use at sometime between A.D. 600 and 1300. This type of pounder has been found only on Uahuka and Kauai and thus links these two distant islands.

There are also connections between heiaus, or temples, on Kauai and in Central Polynesia. Much work remains to be done on heiaus in order to understand the reasons for the many styles of construction. The heiaus of Kauai, such as the one at Waimea drawn by John Webber of James Cook's expedition, and the Poliahu heiau at Wailua, bear strong resemblances to those in Central Polynesia. Upright slabs of stone were used in these heiaus as well as in heiaus on the small islands of Necker and Nihoa, northwest of Kauai. The long, narrow heiau is also a distinctive Kauai style.

And there is the matter of language. The Reverend William Ellis, who was proficient in Tahitian and helped to establish Hawaiian in written form, noticed a distinct pronunciation difference between Kauai and the rest of Hawaii. He wrote, ". . . but it is remarkable that in their language they employ the *t* in all those words in which *k* would be used by the natives of the other islands." Abraham Fornander, writing in the late 1870s, noted that the *l* and *k* differentiation in speech had been evident as recently as fifty years previous.

Another example of surviving ties with Central Polynesia are the tales of a group of people called the Menehune, whose home was on Kauai. In recent times the Menehune have been thought of as a group of mythical people, small in stature, who performed prodigious feats of construction during the night. It seems likely, however, that Menehune was the name given by the Tahitians to the early settlers of Hawaii who had come from the Marquesas.

There is a logical process in the evolution of the name. In their homeland the Tahitians had once been known as Manahune, a slight dialectical variation of Menehune. They bore the name with honor until Tahiti was conquered by warriors from Raiatea, when it took on a very different meaning. Manahune became the name for a commoner and a term of derision. In the Hawaiian Islands, seizing the positions of leadership, the Tahitians labeled the original settlers Menehune, a repetition of what the Raiateans had done to them.

The following Tahitian mele is in disdain of the Manahune.

> Go to the mountains where you belong,
> Far, far away up there;
> Far away where the red skies lie,
> Away to the road of separation,
> Far away to the clustering yellow bamboos,
> Torch-fisher of the nato of Motutu,
> Picker of eels,
> Thou art the grandchild of the mountain,
> Thou slave of the Arii!

The Marquesans had no such word as Manahune in their vocabulary. In the Marquesas the word for commoner was *makaainana,* which became the accepted word in Hawaii for a commoner, or a person who tended the land. The name Menehune seldom appears in the writings of early Hawaiian historians (none of whom were Kauaians) who wrote down the things they had been told about their ancestors before the arrival of the first Westerners. The idea of a physically small race of people caught the imagination of Westerners and they made them into a colorful, romantic, and mysterious group of men and women who lived in the deep valleys and far up the mountain slopes.

One of the reasons for the growth of the Menehune myths might have been the questions of early Westerners who were curious about various structures on Kauai and other islands. In explanation a Hawaiian might well have answered "Oh, they were built by the Menehune," meaning they were built by the common people of generations past.

The Menehune came to be regarded as a physically small, muscular, broad, and strong race of people. William Hyde Rice described the work of the mythical Menehune.

> They were credited with the building of many temples, roads, and other structures. Trades among them were well-systematized, every Menehune being restricted to his own particular craft in which he was a master. It was believed that they would work only one night on a construction and if unable to complete the work, it was left undone.

The mythical Menehune worked with great diligence, often forming lines many miles long, as with Malae heiau at Wailua, passing rocks from hand to hand across the whole diameter of Kauai. The construction of Alekoko fishpond at Nawiliwili is also credited to the Menehune. One of their most unusual accomplishments was the building of a ditch to divert water from the Waimea River to irrigate dry lands to grow taro. Part of the walls of this Menehune Ditch are still visible, an example of cut-and-dressed stone, rare in the Hawaiian Islands.

The number of Menehune on Kauai in ancient times was said to be enormous. A population of 500,600 has been mentioned, of which 160,000 were women. In addition, there were some 20,000 boys and girls up to the age of seventeen. They grew taro, bananas, yams, and ferns, and fished in the lagoons and sea to sustain themselves.

Mythology gives several ways in which these people came to Kauai.

Some sources say they came on a cloud of three levels, which landed on Kauai. Some say they arrived on a floating island. Another theory is that once a great continent in the Pacific extended all the way from New Zealand to the Hawaiian Islands. The Menehune crossed over this land mass and settled on Kauai, although they traveled back and forth to New Zealand. Eventually the ocean rose, and only the major islands that still exist were left above sea level. After this, the Menehune remained on Kauai.

At last the king of the Menehune decided there was too much intermarriage between Menehune men and Hawaiian women. The race was becoming impure. The king gathered the Menehune together, organized them into divisions, and ordered them to leave their Hawaiian wives behind. They then set sail to seek new lands in which to settle. The stone structures on the small northwestern islands of Necker and Nihoa indicate that some people stopped there for a period of time. These islands would be capable of sustaining only a very small population.

Perhaps the last mention of the Menehune—and one of the most intriguing—is contained in an article written by John M. Lydgate. He stated that in the very early 1800s a census was made on Kauai. In an upper section of Wainiha Valley, on the north coast of Kauai, sixty-five persons described their nationality as Menehune.

The tales of Menehune had their beginnings in fact. The idea that they were small might have referred not to their physical size, but to their small importance in the social system after the Tahitians came. Of all the human skeletons uncovered over the years on Kauai, there are no known remains of a physically small people. There were a people called Menehune, but they were not small in stature.

Another important fragment of evidence linking Kauai directly with Central Polynesia concerns winds and currents. During certain seasons of the year, winds and currents will carry a sailing vessel from the Marquesas to the north and slightly east, until it reaches the vicinity of the equator where it will be carried farther north and slightly west. It would not have been unusual for a voyaging canoe, propelled by winds and currents, to bypass the southern Hawaiian Islands and land on Kauai.

Captain James Cook experienced such winds and currents in 1778, and finding it impossible to reach the island of Oahu, he went with the winds and currents and reached Kauai. In more recent times, in 1925, Commander John Rodgers was forced to land a Navy seaplane on the ocean east of Maui. He drifted northwest on the currents and was finally rescued off Kauai. It is likely, then, that canoes traveled directly to Kauai from the South Pacific.

Some distinguished Polynesian authorities have long sensed a particularly strong connection between southern Polynesia and Kauai. In 1893 Dr. Nathaniel Emerson, a medical man by profession and a Hawaiian scholar by avocation, summed up the situation.

> It is a matter of observation that only on the island of Kauai both the special features of its spoken language and the character of its myths and legends indicate a closer relationship to the groups of the southern Pacific, to which the Hawaiian people owe their origin, than do those of the other islands of the Hawaiian group.

The social organization of ancient Kauai was a highly stratified and rigid system. People led essentially the same lives as their ancestors had for generations past. The system was enforced by *kapu* (taboo), a series of forbidden activities which mostly affected commoners. The kapu system provided the laws that held the social system of ancient Hawaii together. Breaking a kapu had serious consequences. It was kapu for women to eat certain foods, for men and women to eat together, or for a commoner to touch the food of a chief or to enter his house.

In the early years following first settlement it appears that the rule of chiefs and enforcement of kapus were less strict than in later times. Probable reasons for this were a comparatively small population and the vastness of the land. With time the increased population made changes necessary and the social structure as remembered from their distant and crowded homelands was more firmly enforced.

Kauai and all the islands were ruled by chiefs who in theory were of the highest lineage through both mother and father. Such a person became the *moi,* the king or sovereign. The sovereign owned all the land and all that came from it. He held the power of life and death over all the people in his domain.

If a chief and chiefess were both of very high and equal rank, children born of them were *ali'i kapu,* or sacred chiefs. If a brother and sister born from such a union were united in an "arched marriage," their children, in turn, would be of *pi'o* rank, of such high lineage that they were gods, above all law. Other chiefs and retainers could only converse with such sacred ones at night. A chiefess of this sacredness, Kaapuwai, married Kaumeheiwa, who was a king of Kauai. Kaapuwai was the daughter of Peleioholani, an eighteenth-century ruler of Oahu who often resided on Kauai.

There were other chiefs of varying rank, depending on their lineage. These chiefs were at the command of the king and served him in any way he wished, and in turn, were served by lesser chiefs. Certain chiefs were put in charge of land districts. In return for the right to use a section of land, a chief owed the king not only his total loyalty, but also provided him with food, mats, canoes, soldiers in time of war, and all the other things the king might wish. Lesser chiefs did the same for those to whom they were beholden.

The king of Kauai surrounded himself with high chiefs at his place of residence, or capital, at Wailua. Customarily they acted as his advisers. Often an ambitious chief, not trusted by the ruling chief, was kept at court so his activities could be watched.

Over the generations there were unions between those of chiefly rank and commoners. The children of such unions were generally found among the ranks of commoners, but there were notable exceptions. Umi a Liloa, a powerful chief of the island of Hawaii, had a commoner as a mother. The same was true of Manokalanipo, a ruler of Kauai who had common blood in his veins, as did the chief Puwalu of Niihau.

The lineage, or rank, of a chief dictated the amount of kapu he possessed. One class of chiefs, for example, possessed the *kapu moe,* which required all commoners and chiefs of lesser rank to prostrate themselves whenever such an exalted person appeared. Even in marriage, rank could not be ignored. If a chief and a chiefess of unequal rank married, the one holding the higher degree of kapu expected the spouse to adhere to the kapu rituals. Children born of such a union would fall into a class between the rank of the mother and father. Needless to say, the determination of rank became difficult after generations had passed.

Certain foods were kapu during a particular time of year. A bay or a section of land might be declared kapu. No person except a higher chief could break such an order. Usually there was a practical reason for this. It was a matter of conservation. A bay might have been depleted of its sea life and so needed time to replenish and become again a valuable source of food. Forests might have been over-cut and trees become few in number. In order to allow saplings to grow tall, a kapu would be put on the land. With the growing trees, birds would return to the forest, assuring a supply of colorful feathers for the adornments of the chiefs. The *kapu* system was a wise and necessary way in which the resources of nature could be replenished and life preserved.

The sovereign and many chiefs of high rank kept two important advisers near them at all times. One was called *kalaimoku,* the administrator who oversaw the efficient workings of the government. The second adviser was a *kahuna nui,* a priest who advised the king or high chief concerning the propitiousness of undertaking any important task, such as an ocean voyage, waging of war, or entering into an alliance. When advice was needed, a kahuna nui went to the heiau and with proper reverence and perfection performed the required rituals. Then he would commune with the gods and give to his king the opinion that had been transmitted from on high.

The kahuna nui was of chiefly rank. He oversaw the proper performance of the rituals due the gods. He was greatly feared because he had tremendous power, dealing with things unseen. This exalted position was often hereditary, with some families becoming well-known throughout the Islands over generations of time.

There were various kinds of kahunas, some of whom were prophets, both men and women, generally not of chiefly rank. Their duty was to foretell the important events of the future, such as the overthrow of a government, the death of a king, the presence of good or evil, an increase in population, and the sources from which blessings could be obtained.

The term kahuna was a broad one, meaning a person very skilled in a certain occupation. A canoe builder, an expert in spear throwing, a person who could select proper sites for construction, and those who were expert carvers or house builders were kahunas. They were not of chiefly rank, but they were respected and above the common people.

The common people made up the great mass of the population. They performed the chores that made the entire system work. They farmed the land and fished the seas. They made kapa, cloth, out of the pounded bark of bushes and trees. In time of war they were the bulk of the army. These common working people were called *maka'āinana,* sometimes termed "the reddened men," because they toiled long in the sun. In the end the well-being of each kingdom was in their hands, as they were the ones who provided the rulers with the necessities of life.

Beneath all others was a class of outcasts, or untouchables. They were called *kauwa* and they sought lives of isolation because, as a despised class, they could be abused by all others at will. They were often selected as human sacrifices, and they were buried alive next to chiefs. It was unthinkable that a person of chiefly rank had a kauwa in his ancestry. If such a secret were discovered, that chief would be laid before his master and his eyes scooped out.

This stratified class system was strongly enforced in ancient Hawaii. While there were instances of a talented commoner rising to the kahuna class, or a warrior chief rising in rank through his fighting ability, such instances were rare. It was a stratified social structure in which people lived out their lives in the condition into which they were born and into which their forebears had been born. It was dangerous to think in any other way.

For the most part life was full of hazards, because of the large number of kapus that surrounded the lives of commoners. The usual penalty was death, either by strangulation, by the club, or by being burned or baked in an *imu,* an earth oven, "until the body grease dripped." If the crime had been a particularly grievous one, the body of a culprit might be dragged along the paths as an example to others.

What sort of crimes brought on such retribution? If a commoner or a lesser chief did not observe the days designated to the gods, he was guilty, and members of his family unit could also be destroyed. If the shadow of a commoner fell across the person of a high chief or across his shadow, the penalty was death. If a commoner passed beyond the crossed kapu sticks of a chief, it meant death. When rituals were being conducted in a heiau, a person who interrupted the perfection of the ceremonies through the slightest disturbance might be executed.

The only recourse a commoner or lesser chief had was to go to a high chief and present his grievances or simply plead for mercy. The high chief was judge and jury, and by his word a man lived or died. Along with the planting, fishing, and many other chores required to maintain a tolerable life, commoners needed great doggedness and a resignation to their position in order to survive.

And what of the chiefs? As in all civilizations since men and women first gathered to live in groups, there were thoughtful and protective chiefs and cruel and indolent ones. There were times when the patience of the commoners finally ran out and they would no longer tolerate an evil ruler. In such instances chiefs were killed by their subjects, although such drastic action was rare.

Lives might be spared by a ruling chief who had the authority to invoke an edict called *kānāwai aliʻi.* This authority was used in time of war, which in ancient Hawaii was usually a matter of total annihilation of the enemy by the victors. Not only were soldiers slain in pitched battle, but the remnants of the fleeing army were pursued and as many killed as could be found. Although women, children, and old people often hid in caves or fled to a place of refuge, any who were found were killed. Some warriors were made captives and kept for human sacrifices.

Kānāwai ali'i was put into effect at some ancient time by Kukona, king of Kauai. The island was threatened by Kalaunuiohua, who had conquered all the islands except Kauai. The invading force was defeated in the channel between Oahu and Kauai. When the issue was no longer in doubt, Kukona ordered his forces to stop the slaughter. The invaders were taken as prisoners to Kauai. Eventually Kukona allowed the invaders to return to their homes, and years of peace followed.

Such rulers were highly regarded by their subjects. They were trusted and their assistance was sought to settle differences among the commoners. They were looked to for protection and help because they placed value on human life. Commoners did their bidding with eagerness and more willingly fought for them in battle. They were the finest examples of the ancient rulers.

Although authority lay completely with the chiefs, an intelligent ruler well understood that he needed assistance and at least a degree of good will from the commoners. A chief who wanted to gain the cooperation of his subjects avoided situations that would result in commoners breaking the kapus and suffering the bitter consequences. Thus, a *kapu moe* chief, before whom commoners were required to lie face down, customarily sent retainers ahead who shouted *"Kapu moe!"* so that persons would be warned of his coming. Many ranking chiefs seldom ventured forth from their dwellings except at night, because their mere presence could bring about such grave consequences. In reality some sort of compromise had to be made if society was going to function at all. A reasonable chief would try to avoid circumstances that endangered commoners, and in return commoners were expected to respond to the demands of the chiefs.

The class system of Kauai had many parallels with the feudal system of medieval Europe. There was, however, one important difference. On Kauai, as on the other islands of Hawaii, commoners did not belong to the land. If a commoner was unhappy with his situation under one chief, he was free to leave and establish himself in the domain of another. This practice was not uncommon, although those who too often switched allegiance were considered unstable and difficult.

Commoners and alii were expected to follow certain customs concerning children. If the firstborn of a couple was a boy he was reared by the grandparents on his father's side. If the firstborn was a girl she was reared by the grandparents on the mother's side. Older people were generally entrusted with passing on customs, traditions, and the ways of their station to the young. If a man and woman had several children and their relatives or close friends had none, they would give a baby to such a childless couple. Younger children were subservient to older children.

Certain rituals were required following birth, such as secreting the umbilical cord, making proper offerings, and the giving of prayers at a heiau. A boy might be taken from his mother at birth, or as late as the age of three, to eat with the men in their eating house. It was, of course, kapu for male and female to eat in one another's presence. If custom was followed a young boy was circumcised, which called for additional rites. The rituals were less elaborate with commoners than with alii.

The rites necessary after the death of a chief were strict. A corpse was a kapu thing. With the exception of the family, if people were in a house when someone died, they immediately left. The family was considered defiled and could not enter another house, eat of the food of others, touch anyone, or do any work. Friends of the deceased could sit before the house and wail, but dared not enter. If the person had been much loved the corpse might be disemboweled, the cavity filled with salt, and the body kept in the house for several days.

But there came a time when the body had to be buried. A rope was tied around the knees and neck and pulled tight until the knees touched the chest. Then the body was wrapped in kapa and placed in a cave or a pit in the ground. After this was done, all those who had been involved with the dead person bathed and seated themselves before their house. A *heiau kahuna*, or *kahuna pule heiau*, was sent for to perform the rites of purification. He said a prayer, which included responses from those sitting before him. Then the kahuna sprinkled seawater, seaweed, and turmeric on the people and the act of purification was over. The kapu lasted for another day or two if the dead had been a commoner.

Such funeral proceedings might also be followed after the death of a skilled craftsman. Rites varied greatly, depending on the rank of the deceased. In the case of a commoner, with little or no time or means of payment for the services of others, the corpse might be stretched out in a sandhill grave and purification ceremonies conducted by a kahuna.

In the case of a high chief the rituals became complicated, often frenzied, took longer periods of time, and could involve many of the people under his rule. Persons close to the deceased wailed and knocked out teeth, and burned or tattooed themselves as a visible and lasting public sign of their grief. The remains of a high chief might be tied in a sitting position and placed in a wickerwork container. Or his bones might be cleaned of flesh and bound with wicker. It was essential that the bones should not be desecrated in any way, such as being carved into fish hooks. For this reason the remains of a chief would be carried away secretly, often at night, and hidden in a cave in some inaccessible place. The kapu period following the burial of a high chief might last for ten days.

With a high chief would be buried his "death companions," persons who had been close to him in life, such as his advisers. Long and intimate associates of a high chief deemed it an honor to be his death companions and to share his burial cave. During the days following the death of a high chief some of those who had been his subjects engaged in a prolonged orgy. All sense of law seemed lost. Sexual activity ran at passion fever, property was unsafe, and a kind of madness continued, until exhaustion brought with it some sense of order.

Telling tales about gods and goddesses and the mere mortals who came into contact with them was a favorite pastime. Together with sports, the hula, and the chanting of *mele,* this was a major recreation for the Kauaians. Their stories were full of magic, of heroic deeds, of love and retribution. These tales were told and re-told as they were passed from one generation to the next.

One of the favorites in ancient Kauai was the story of Pele, the fire goddess, her sister Hiiaka, and a handsome man named Lohiau. When Pele became a young woman she asked permission of her parents to travel. This was granted and she set out on her adventures with a younger sister, who had been born into the world in an egg. Pele hid the egg under her arm until it was time to be hatched.

Pele was a beautiful woman whose back was as straight as a *pali.* Her charm and beauty were astounding. Pele was searching for fire in the earth, and where she could find fire, she would live. She started her quest on Niihau where she became a friend of the queen, but digging in the earth she could find no fire. Assuming her spirit body, Pele crossed to Kauai.

On Kauai Pele quickly traveled along Na Pali coast on the north shore of the island. As darkness fell she heard hula drums beating, and following the sounds she came to an enclosure where people were gathered for sport. The place was Haena and among those present was Lohiau, king of Kauai, a young and handsome man. Pele immediately decided she would seek him as her husband.

When Pele entered the enclosure all the people stared at the beautiful stranger and then crowded about her. Lohiau bade the people stand back and was surprised when the unknown woman asked to become his wife. He consented only when he was convinced that Pele was a mortal woman and not of the spirit world.

Pele told Lohiau she could not live with him until she had found a suitable place for them to dwell. She searched in the earth of Haena hoping she would find fire, but neither near the sea nor in the mountains did she have success. Traveling as far as Koloa she was still unsuccessful, and she decided to leave Kauai and search the islands to the southeast for the place she would call home. She tried, but still without success, to dig for fire on Oahu, Molokai, and Maui. She wept and longed for Lohiau.

Finally, at Kilauea, on the island of Hawaii, Pele discovered fire. This, she decided, would be her long-sought home. Her home would be large enough to include all her brothers and sisters. It was at Kilauea that Pele, the goddess of fire, transformed the egg, carried with her through her journeys, into her younger sister Hiiaka. The brothers and sisters lived happily in Kilauea, but Pele yearned for Lohiau.

It was decided that Hiiaka should go to bring Lohiau to Pele. The younger sister was concerned about making the trip alone, but Pele promised that she would meet a companion who would accompany her to Haena. Before Hiiaka departed, Pele warned her not to kiss Lohiau. As Hiiaka entered the forest above Hilo, she met a woman who was expert at making leis from lehua blossoms, and this woman traveled to Kauai with Hiiaka. The time allotted for the journey was forty days.

Despite many delays and attempts to thwart their way, the two women persisted in traveling toward Kauai. Only because of the supernatural powers of Hiiaka were they able at last to reach Haena.

Kilioe, the sister of Lohiau, was the first to see them approaching. Kilioe was the mistress hula dancer and teacher on Kauai. It was Kilioe who broke the sad news. In a mele, she related the death of Lohiau to Hiiaka and her companion.

Hiiaka was not easily discouraged. Seeing the spirit of Lohiau soaring over the peaks behind the sea, she went in pursuit, finally capturing the spirit in a flower. She then slowly worked the spirit back into the dead king, who had been buried above the wet cave that Pele had dug earlier in her search for fire. Lohiau returned to life. When Kilioe saw that he was alive again she beat the drum to let the people know the joyful news. By now much more than the allotted forty days had elapsed.

Hiiaka, together with her companion, set forth for Hawaii with Lohiau. At the rim of Kilauea crater Hiiaka sent her companion to tell Pele of their coming. As Pele approached, Hiiaka was overcome with emotion for Lohiau and she threw her arms about him and kissed him. Pele thought Hiiaka had done this to mock her, and in great wrath she ordered the destruction of Lohiau. He was immediately covered with lava.

Two brothers of Pele, arriving from a foreign land, saw the body of Lohiau bulging through the lava, and again brought him back to life. They carried him to Kauai where, in hiding, he watched games being played at Kapaa. In the meantime Hiiaka had returned to Kauai and also was watching the games. Lohiau sang the songs the two had composed when they traveled to Hawaii together and hearing these, Hiiaka discovered him amidst the folds of kapa where he was hiding.

And so, at last, Hiiaka and Lohiau were united and lived happily at Haena for many years.

Like many of the mythological stories on Kauai, the tale of Pele, Hiiaka, and Lohiau does have a foundation of substantial physical evidence. In Haena, where the coastal plain narrows to an end and there are only sheer cliffs beyond, are the remains of a stone wall. On the flat area formed by the wall stood the house of Lohiau. Only the discerning eye would realize that once this overgrown area of level land, reaching out from the mountainside, was the site of a house. Nevertheless, it is still known today as the house of Lohiau.

The house site looks toward the beach of Ke'e, where a broad strip of sand borders on a green-blue lagoon, protected against the wild ocean by a reef. Near this beach camped the persons who aspired to become professional in the hula. They came here from all the Islands for intense training under the scrutiny of their teachers. Just as Kilioe was the mistress teacher of her day, successive generations after her have followed in the same tradition. The school was maintained through generations by strict teachers who demanded not only the highest performance in dancing and chanting, but also discipline in the personal lives of their pupils.

Past the curve of sand and a hundred yards beyond the house site of Lohiau the sandy shore gives way to boulders. Fifty yards beyond the sand and to the left, built upon the boulders, is a heiau. It is probably the most famous of its kind, if not unique among all the Islands in its purpose. Those who came here learned the ancient art of communicating, through the dance and chant, the loves, beauties, adventures, passions, loyalties, and treacheries of times past.

Up from the water-splashed rocks is a boulder named after that teacher of ages ago, Kilioe. In and around this boulder were secreted the navel cords of children of the neighborhood, wedged into crevices with small sticks and closed over with stones.

On the boulders that rise between the ocean and the cliff are the remains of the heiau Ka ulu a Paoa, which can be translated as "the protection of Paoa." Paoa was a hula master and a friend of Lohiau. It is a dizzying experience to stand on the first terrace, looking at the shades and tints of blue that spread to the horizon, and then to turn and raise your eyes upward, to the infinite shades and tints of green on the imperious pali. The white clouds race through the sky with enormous speed, propelled by the trade winds off the northern sea.

On this first terrace, which is paved with flat stones as large as 2 by 3 feet in size and a foot thick, stood either a house or were planted the bases of wooden images. Perhaps both occupied a section of this terrace. On the eastern end of this terrace is a refuse pit where the decomposed remains of offerings were thrown. There is a narrow middle terrace and next to the refuse pit stood an oracle tower. Midway along the upper terrace stood a platform about 10 feet long and 18 inches high.

A short distance behind the heiau was the dancing pavilion and shrine of Lohiau. There was a sloping terrace in front, and behind the main terrace was the *hālau,* or long hall, in which the hula was performed. The halau consisted of a thatched roof area, which probably ran the entire 100-foot length of the upper terrace. It had been built with care and ceremony. A high propriety of demeanor was maintained in the halau. Certain foods were kapu and there was no rudeness of talk.

The upper terrace was a shrine as well as a dancing pavilion and before this shrine the dances were performed. The shrine was dedicated to Laka, the patron deity of the hula. Here were placed the flowers and leaves of many special plants, including *lehua* and *maile,* the *palapalai* fern and the *'ie'ie* vine, *lama* and ginger, the *'ākōlea* and *laua'e* ferns, *pili* grass, and branches from the koa, breadfruit, and *kukui* trees. Each plant had a symbolic meaning. The breadfruit signified growth. *Pili* means to cling, and so the grass signified the wish of the students to have the wisdom of the hula cling to them all the days of their lives.

The gathering of the forest greenery was done with ceremony and reverence. The gods and goddesses who protected the forests might not approve of the taking of their vines and branches, and a mele was chanted to let all know why the greenery was being collected.

> In the forests, on the ridges
> Of the mountains stands Laka;
> Dwelling in the source of the mists.
> Laka, mistress of the hula,
> Has climbed the wooded haunts of the gods,
> Altars hallowed by the sacrificial swine,
> The head of the boar, the black boar of Kane.
> A partner he with Laka;
> Woman, she by strife gained rank in heaven.

The rules during the time of training were very strict. A pupil could only share his or her food with other members of his class. Certain foods were kapu, such as sugarcane, taro tops, certain types of seaweed, and squid. If such foods were eaten the knowledge of the hula would flee from the student. Sexual intercourse was prohibited during the time of training. Fingernails could not be cut, nor hair trimmed, and men could not shave. Yet each day the pupils had to bathe and change their clothes. From the days of the building of the altar until graduation, the greenery remained fresh because Laka was there. After the graduation ceremony, the leaves and blossoms became brown and fell away.

A test is said to have been given to determine if all the rules of training had been kept. Students swam from the sandy beach to the rocks before the heiau. This was not a long or difficult swim, but it could be dangerous, for it was believed that a shark lurked within the reef. It would attack only those who had not strictly followed the rules laid down by the master teacher.

Men and women dressed alike, wearing either the *pāʻū,* or skirt, or the *kīkepa,* which came up to the underarm and was knotted on the opposite shoulder. The apparel was donned, and the seashell anklets and leis were fastened, while chanting. The distinctive color of the Haena school was yellow, although when a dance was done in honor of the fire goddess Pele, the color worn was red.

Chanters as well as dancers perfected their art at Ka-ulu-a-Paoa. Chanters came here to receive the most advanced training. They walked toward the heiau across the water-smoothed boulders at the edge of the sea, and as they approached the heiau they chanted their mele, competing against the pounding of the ocean on the shore and the sound of the wind. Into the twentieth century, after the heiau had long fallen into disrepair, a certain select few still came to test their skills. One such person was Mary Kawena Pukui. She was brought to the heiau at Haena by her teacher. As she approached the renowned ruins of Ka-ulu-a-Paoa she was given her test as she chanted:

> Laka dwells in a beautiful forest,
> Standing above at Moohelaia,
> An ohia tree standing up Maunaloa,
> Love to you, O Kaulana-ula.
> Here is the voice, a gentle voice,
> A gentle chant of affection to you, O, Laka,
> Laka, inspire us.

Like many before her, Mary Kawena Pukui did not pass the examination. She suffered from an asthmatic condition and her voice did not carry loudly enough above the noise of the sea and wind.

The hula master of ancient times would select those pupils who had passed the examinations and deny the privilege of graduation to those who had not met the high requirements demanded by Ka-ulu-a-Paoa. A time of feasting, hula, and chanting of name songs followed for those who had passed the tests. Families and friends gathered from all places on Kauai. Canoes swarmed the beach at Keʻe and for ten days there were celebrations.

One of the most impressive celebrations was fire-throwing from a nearby steep mountain named Makana, meaning a gift or a reward. Men would climb this mountain, nearly 1,600 feet tall, with spear-like shafts of *hau* and *pāpala* wood that had been dried for six to eight months in preparation. The trail upward was treacherous and in at least one place it was so windy and precipitous that the men clung, facing the mountain, as they sought secure footing to go ahead. The wooden shafts were lashed to their backs.

After dark, the tinder-dry shafts were lighted and hurled from the peak of the mountain toward the sea. The glowing firebrands would sail on the prevailing winds, sometimes gliding into the sea, sometimes falling on the beaches below. The fire burned through the inner sections of the shafts and flamed backward, leaving a trail on the night air. Canoes waited in the sea and people crowded the beaches to watch the spectacle of the falling flames. When chiefs graduated from Ka-ulu-a-Paoa, firebrands were also hurled from a mountain next to Nuololo Valley, miles farther up Na Pali coast.

It was a time of great high spirits, of gratification over success. There were no dark fears of human sacrifices, or retaliations for evils done. It was a joyous time for the graduates and for all those who came to celebrate the very important occasion.

CHAPTER THREE

"Their Hospitality and Generosity Were Unbounded"

Even as the people of Kauai continued to honor their gods and implore their assistance, to periodically plant and harvest, to wage war and seek peace, two ships were sailing up from the south, bearing crews of white men who would change the lives of the Kauaians forever.

The ships were the *Resolution* and the *Discovery*. They were under the command of Captain James Cook, a renowned and austere English explorer who had made two previous voyages into the Pacific. The orders from the British Lords of the Admiralty for the voyage were very clear. Cook was to find the Northwest Passage that supposedly linked the Atlantic and Pacific oceans across the top of the North American continent. Parliament had added incentive to the orders of the Admiralty. To the first English expedition to make the discovery would go the huge sum of 20,000 pounds.

The *Resolution* and *Discovery* sailed from England on 12 July 1776. On the passage down the Thames to the Deptford Yard, where Cook received his provisions, they passed a fleet of ships making ready to take supplies and reinforcements to battle the revolutionists in the American colonies. Cook sailed around the southern tip of Africa, passed to the south of Tasmania, on to New Zealand, and eventually to Tahiti, an island he knew well from previous explorations.

In December 1777 Cook sailed north, relieved to put Tahiti astern. He was behind schedule, there had been trouble with the Tahitians, and his seamen were growing too fond of the cheerful, willing island women. Cook missed most of the Line Islands, but at daybreak on 24 December he sighted an atoll to the northeast. The two ships spent several days there, including Christmas, and so the atoll was named Christmas Island. Cook was impatient to move northward. He would not have remained so long except that the fishing was good and the turtles were plentiful—he took some 300—and so was able to replenish his food supplies. He did not expect to see land again until he reached the Northwest Coast of America, so all added supplies were salted down and gratefully stored aboard.

James Cook's sailing plan was simple enough. He would sail north from the Society Islands until he caught westerly winds to speed him on. He knew Spanish galleons sailed with these winds to reach the shores of North and Central America.

A week after leaving Christmas Island turtles and birds were seen, signs of land. On 18 January he saw high land to the northeast, but winds and currents kept him away. He stood to the north and again sighted land. He reached the southeast coast of the island of Kauai on the afternoon of 19 January 1778.

Only briefly did Cook wonder whether this island was inhabited. Soon, as he coasted, canoes came out to the ships and the people traded pigs and sweet potatoes for nails. Cook was surprised that the people in the canoes spoke a language similar to that of Tahiti. Some Hawaiians ventured on board the ships, and, although they seemed startled by what they saw, they freely attempted to take away with them any metal items they could carry.

The *Resolution* and *Discovery* stood off-and-on along the west coast of Kauai. James Cook put Lieutenant John Williamson in command of three armed boats and sent him to search for an anchorage and a source of fresh water. At one place, as Williamson came through the breakers to beach his boats, a group of Hawaiians rushed into the sea, either to help the sailors or to steal metal objects. Williamson, unnerved, pulled a pistol and shot a Hawaiian dead. When Cook learned of this incident he was furious.

The Hawaiians had no written language, and in attempting to spell Hawaiian words as he heard them from the inhabitants, Cook wrote of Kauai in his journal as Atoui, and Niihau, he spelled Enecheeou. He named the whole island group the Sandwich Islands, after his patron, Lord Sandwich. These names, with variations for individual islands, stayed in use by future explorers for many years.

On 20 January, Williamson found Waimea, the name given to a bay, a river, a valley, and a village. The two vessels dropped their anchors in the black sandy bottom offshore. Before them was a wide, slow-flowing river that emptied across a dark gray sandbar into the sea. Cook went ashore immediately and the Hawaiians prostrated themselves as they would before the highest alii.

The next day Cook, William Anderson the surgeon, and the artist

John Webber walked up Waimea Valley, and again the people threw
themselves to the ground as the three appeared. The little party
reached a heiau, which included an oracle tower, carved images, sacred
buildings, a drum house, and graves. Webber made a drawing of the
heiau and also one of the village. Cook's crew was busy filling water
casks and trading with the Hawaiians for pigs and plantains, bartering
nails for food supplies. The Hawaiians had a knowledge of the importance of metal and eagerly sought these objects in trade for provisions.

Eighty-eight years after the arrival of the *Resolution* and *Discovery* a
Hawaiian historian, Samuel M. Kamakau, wrote what he had been
told about the reactions of the people of Kauai to the arrival of the
Westerners. Kamakau's observations are interesting because of the
details they include. Looking at the ships from the shore, one Hawaiian asked another, "What are those branching things?" Another
answered, "They are trees moving about on the sea." A kahuna
declared that one of the ships could certainly be nothing other than the
heiau of the god Lono. Kamakau wrote, "The excitement became
more intense, and louder grew the shouting."

Those who went aboard the ships saw many wonderful things. The
amount of iron amazed them. They thought the men who wore tricornered hats had tricornered heads. Cook gave one chief a knife and
the chief named his daughter "Changed into a Dagger." Those who
smoked pipes "breathed fire from their mouths," and were given the
name "Lono of the Volcanic Fire." The Hawaiians were sure the *Resolution* was indeed the floating heiau of their god Lono, who had disappeared across the horizon long, long before.

The thing the Hawaiians wanted most was iron. One chief, unable
to restrain himself, picked up all the objects of metal he could easily
collect and threw them overboard into his canoe. Before the chief
could get away he was shot and killed by an English guard. The
Hawaiians called the death-dealing instrument a "water squirter,"
because the smoke reminded them of water squirting through
bamboo.

James Cook soon learned that the calm waters of Waimea Bay were
deceptive. Strong currents and quickly shifting winds made the
anchorage hazardous. Of the two weeks he spent off Kauai he was
able to go ashore only three times, and out of fourteen attempts, on
only three occasions was he able to hold anchorage at Waimea. At
night the winds and currents carried them to sea, and the next day was

spent in trying to beat back to the bay. The supplies he could take on were thus limited, so he sailed for the small island of Niihau to the west.

Still eager for supplies, Cook was able to get a party of men ashore on Niihau, headed by Lieutenant Gore. Gore could not secure water on that dry island, but he did barter for a supply of salt and yams. The surf rose and Gore and twenty men had to stay on shore for two nights and one day. When they did come out to the ships, most of the supplies were lost in the tumbling surf.

That was bad enough, but James Cook wrote in his journal a sad line, "the very thing happened that I had above all others wished to prevent." Cook was referring to the spreading of venereal diseases among the Hawaiians, something he had tried to avoid. Venereal diseases were unknown to the Polynesians until the coming of Western man. The crew of Captain Samuel Wallis, who discovered Tahiti in 1767, had infected the population of that island. Cook's ships had been overrun by women at Tahiti, undoubtedly increasing the virulence of the diseases among his crew.

The pay book of the *Resolution* showed that 66 men of a total crew of 112 had venereal diseases. The actual number was undoubtedly greater, because many men would show no outward signs of these maladies. Off Kauai, Cook had ordered men who were known to have "the venereal distemper," as he called it, to remain aboard ship, and no man was to spend the night ashore. The severe punishment for breaking this order was flogging. On Niihau his orders could not be enforced. When Cook reached the island of Hawaii a year later signs of venereal diseases were already apparent in the Islanders. In but a year's time, they had spread through the entire Island chain.

On Niihau Cook moved his ship to another anchorage, got his men aboard, and presented a Niihau chief with goats and pigs, as well as seeds for melons, pumpkins, and onions. He signaled the *Discovery* to follow, and on 2 February the expedition sailed for the north. It must have been a melancholy time for James Cook. He had not acquired the desired supplies, time had been lost, and he was sure that his crew had infected the Hawaiians with venereal diseases. Now he was headed for the icy reaches of the north. Fearnought jackets and trousers had already been issued to his crew for the cold weather ahead. Cook himself suffered from rheumatism from the waist down, and often could hold no food in his stomach.

The search for the Northwest Passage was probably the most trying experience ever endured by Cook. He sailed up broad inlets, thinking they were channels into the Bering Sea, but they proved to be only inlets. He felt his way through the Aleutian Islands and sailed through fog and freezing weather northward. The rigging hung with icicles, the ships leaked, and the snow had to be pushed off the decks every several hours. At last James Cook could proceed no farther. Above the Arctic Circle the ships came to a solid wall of ice and there was no way through.

Pumps were manned nearly continuously during the voyage south. The rigging, which had been wet and frozen for months, was unsafe. James Cook ordered a return to the Sandwich Islands where he hoped to repair his ships, relax his men, and take on supplies. For nearly two months the English explorer searched Island shores for an acceptable harbor. Finally, on 17 January 1779, he anchored in Kealakekua Bay on the island of Hawaii.

The Hawaiians and English got along well, supplies were furnished in abundance, repairs went ahead, and it appeared that fortune had at last smiled upon James Cook. When provisioning and repairs had been completed he ordered anchors upped. They sailed north, but the strong winds that sweep around the north point of the island of Hawaii suddenly struck and the mainmast of the *Resolution* split. There was no choice. He returned to Kealakekua Bay.

The reception this time was not as gracious. The bay had been placed under kapu, undoubtedly because it had been overused during the month of Cook's anchorage. The mainmast was unstepped and floated ashore to be repaired. The Hawaiians were hostile and numerous disputes took place. At dawn, 14 February 1779, it was found that the *Discovery*'s cutter, which had been tied to her stern at night, had been stolen. Cook went ashore with nine marines to make a hostage of the king until the boat was returned, and through a series of unfortunate incidents the English and the Hawaiians clashed. In a brief skirmish, only seconds in happening, James Cook and four marines were killed.

The Hawaiians regretted the circumstances that had caused the death of a man they considered to be a god. They fretted about future vengeance. The English were silent, shocked, and, at first, hostile. They grieved over the fateful wind that had split the mast and forced them to return to Kealakekua Bay. Into the bay were dropped the remains of Captain James Cook, one of the most humane of all explorers and probably the finest navigator the Western world had ever known.

After the death of James Cook, Charles Clerke assumed command and the vessels sailed northward among the islands of Hawaii, seeking again the anchorage off Waimea. In the words of Cook's renowned biographer, J. C. Beaglehole, Clerke "Obviously . . . must make for Kauai, where he hoped also for yams, good keepers at sea; and having got rid of all his women on Oahu, lest they should talk too much of Hawaiian misfortune, he was at the old anchorage in Waimea Bay on 1 March, prepared for a stay of some days."

At Waimea, Clerke was at first met with hostility, but this soon changed. He was disappointed by the scarcity of yams but pleased with the amount of pork he obtained and the ready supply of salt, needed for curing the meat. During a week at Waimea a number of chiefs came aboard and discussed the entangled political affairs on the island. The two ships then sailed for Niihau, where Clerke encountered mostly bad weather and the supply of yams fell short of expectations. After another week of sailing off-and-on he departed to the north to again search for the elusive Northwest Passage.

Instead of traveling to the Pacific Northwest Coast as Cook had done, Clerke sailed for Kamchatka, the Russian peninsula reaching down toward Japan from the north Asian continent. Here Charles Clerke anchored his battered ships in the harbor of Petropavlovsk. The town was supposed to be fortified, but its forces consisted only of a handful of scurvy-ridden soldiers who had suffered through a miserable winter made more awful by a smallpox epidemic.

The governor, a Major Behm, resided on the western side of the peninsula. He came overland to visit Clerke with supplies of flour, beef, and tobacco. Major Behm turned out to be an intelligent and helpful man. When Clerke learned that Behm was about to return to St. Petersburg, he decided to entrust him with Cook's journal, some important charts, and a variety of other reports. Behm would see to their being forwarded to the Lords of the Admiralty in London via the British ambassador in St. Petersburg.

It was a calculated risk. Behm had inspired great confidence in Clerke, and the English captain knew that after another voyage into the Arctic his ships might not survive the long trip to England. Charles Clerke was also a very ill man, dying of tuberculosis, often confined to his cabin for days at a time. He lived long enough to endure the dangers of the Arctic in his futile quest for the Northwest

Passage. Returning south, however, Clerke died on 22 August 1779, within sight of Kamchatka, and was buried at Petropavlovsk. From there the English ships proceeded around Africa to the yards at Deptford on the Thames.

Thus the Russians were the first Europeans to know of Cook's death and of his discoveries in the Pacific, including the Hawaiian Islands. A detailed report on these events was written by Peter Simon Pallas of the Imperial Academy at St. Petersburg before Cook's journal ever reached the British Admiralty. The Russians were interested in Pacific exploration, already being involved with the Russian American Company in Alaska.

An unexpected result of the Cook expedition was the discovery by the English of sea otters and seals in the Pacific Northwest. They took aboard some furs of these animals, and as they turned homeward along the coast of Asia the vessels stopped at Macao. Here they found that the Chinese were obsessed with the furs, and the English sold them at enormous prices. The prospect of such staggering profits made it difficult for the British officers to prevent mutiny and desertion among their crews. Once back in England, word of these trade possibilities spread rapidly. This was to have a profound effect on the Hawaiian Islands.

After the final departure of the *Resolution* and *Discovery* from the Hawaiian Islands, several years passed before an expedition could be launched to exploit the promising fur trade between the Pacific Northwest and China. Then in 1786 two ships, both under the command of men who had sailed with James Cook, made their appearance off the coast of Kauai. In command of the expedition was Nathaniel Portlock, on the *King George,* with George Dixon as captain of a smaller vessel, the *Queen Charlotte.* They had rushed back to the Pacific to seek the profits the fur trade promised. En route to China the Hawaiian Islands were ideally located as a place to rest and take on supplies of water, food, firewood, and salt.

Portlock and Dixon stopped at Oahu, obtained some provisions, and then sailed on to Kauai, which they would visit twice in 1786 and again in 1787. Ever since the death of Cook the Hawaiian Islands had been thought of as being filled with a murderous, cannibal population. The journals of both Portlock and Dixon indicate, however, that they felt less tension on Kauai than on the islands to windward. George Dixon wrote on returning to Waimea in 1786:

On our asking for water, they presently brought us some very excellent, indeed the best by far we had hitherto met with. . . . Cocoa-nuts we found in the greatest plenty; the settled price for them was five an eight-penny nail. The sugar-cane was exceeding fine, and equally cheap. The taro here by far the finest of any we met with, and very plentiful; we commonly got fine roots for an eightpenny or tenpenny nail. This island produces no yams, and very little, if any bread-fruit.

The next year Dixon returned to Waimea. As he walked along the shore, he looked up the valley and reported it "entirely planted with taro; and these plantations are laid out with a great deal of judgment."

Captain Dixon noted that trenches brought fresh water from the Waimea River to the fields, that raised footpaths intersected the various fields, and that the houses, on higher ground than the fields, were often surrounded by mulberry trees, the bark of which was used to make kapa, or barkcloth. Dixon paid the residents of Waimea a high compliment:

. . . at present I shall close the subject, by observing that whether we regard the sound judgment and (I had almost said scientific) skill with which these grounds are laid out, or the close attention and unremitting diligence shewn in their cultivation, in either of these points of view, they would reflect credit even on a British husbandman.

Nathaniel Portlock was no less impressed, but he wrote it in more general terms:

. . . it is not in my power to give half the praises that are due to these people, from the king to the tow-tow; their attention and unwearied industry in supplying us with everything in their power was beyond example; their hospitality and generosity were unbounded; and their eagerness to do us acts of kindness was amazing.

The first Christmas to be celebrated on Kauai took place at Waimea aboard the ships of George Dixon and Nathaniel Portlock. Each captain reported on the occasion in his log. It was 25 December 1786 and Dixon ordered special fare for his men. A pig was brought from shore and roasted, and sea-pie, a mixture of meat and vegetables covered with crust, was made, a favorite and special dish for men at sea. The day's ration of rum was mixed with coconut milk.

Captain Dixon recorded in his journal, "This being Christmas, that season of the year so universally convivial throughout the civilized world, we spend out our time as agreeably, and with plenty of good cheer as we could procure." About the punch he noted, "Perhaps it pleased more on account of its novelty than from any other circumstance."

Aboard the *King George* Nathaniel Portlock wrote that he had gone ashore the day before and had passed out small presents to women and children. On Christmas morning, a high chief, Kaiana, "came off in a long double canoe and brought me a present of some hogs and vegetables, which I received and made him a return that pleased him very much." The people of Kauai certainly knew nothing of such customs, but gifts were indeed exchanged during this first Christmas on Kauai.

Also in 1787 the *Nootka,* a vessel of British registry, stopped at Waimea on her way to Canton. John Meares was the master, and he thought the people of Kauai were more than generous and kind. "They received us with joy—and saw us depart with tears." Meares, as other captains after him, was besieged by men and women who wished to sail with him. They wanted to see the wonderful world beyond their islands, and some offered to pay for the privilege of going to sea. Most of the Hawaiians wanted to see England, because that was where the earliest ships had come from. Meares took only one person with him. He reported in his journal, "Among the numbers who pressed forward with inexpressible eagerness to accompany us to Britannee, Tianna [Kaiana] a chief of Kauai . . . was alone received to embark with us, amid the envy of all his countrymen."

It was little wonder that John Meares chose Kaiana. The Kauai chief was reported to have been a handsome man, over six feet tall and—as later events would prove—he was a shrewd, winsome person capable of playing whatever role would benefit him. Kaiana never got to England, but in Canton he became a favorite among the members of the British trading colony. He adopted Western dress and had his portrait painted by an English artist.

Kaiana's trip was full of adventure. In Canton he came upon a Hawaiian woman named Wainee, who had gone aboard an earlier ship as a servant to the captain's wife and, becoming ill, had been left in Canton. Kaiana stayed with the British colony in Canton after Meares sailed and finally was carried to the Pacific Northwest by another fur-trading captain. Kaiana insisted that he take Wainee back to her homeland, but she did not survive the voyage and was buried at sea. From the Northwest Kaiana sailed back to the Islands with Captain William Douglas in 1788.

During his time in Canton, Kaiana was able to purchase, through the generosity of his English hosts, hatchets, knives, saws, cloth, carpets, bars of iron, and a considerable amount of chinaware. The most prized things he secured, however, were muskets and ammunition. The Hawaiians on all the islands sought weapons with the hope of gaining superiority over neighboring chiefs and those on other islands. On nearing home, Kaiana became concerned that perhaps his enemies were in power on Kauai and, stopping at the island of Hawaii, he learned that this was indeed the case. Captain Douglas left Kaiana on Hawaii, where he became a chief under Kamehameha. His end would finally come when he deserted Kamehameha and joined the army on Oahu; he was killed when that island was overrun by Kamehameha.

William Douglas had more than his share of troubles on his visits to the Hawaiian Islands. In 1789, while gathering provisions at Waimea, one of his seamen, Jones, got into a fight while filling water casks ashore. Aboard ship Captain Douglas ordered him punished, but Jones climbed the foretop ladder to escape and armed himself with a loaded blunderbuss, kept there in case of attack by the Islanders. After Douglas fired one shot over the seaman's head and threatened him with the other barrel, he came down and was given the choice of accepting punishment or being left ashore. Jones, probably surprised at being offered a choice, without hesitation chose to be put ashore.

Others of Douglas' crew found the Islands a more attractive place than the forecastle of the ship *Grace,* and three deserted at Niihau after unsuccessfully trying to set the vessel afire. Douglas got two of the deserters back again, but the third could not be found. Captain Douglas also left two crew members on Kauai to search for and collect sandalwood.

A year later, in 1791, Captain John Kendrick, in command of the *Lady Washington,* left three men on Niihau with instructions to sail to Kauai to look for pearls and sandalwood. Although nothing came of these particular attempts, the beginnings of what would eventually become Hawaii's first important export commodity, sandalwood, can be traced to these early years.

Sandalwood might first have been taken aboard sailing vessels as firewood, and its value to the Chinese discovered only accidentally after ships reached Canton to trade for Chinese goods. The early evidence is cloudy. One report, given to Captain Joseph Ingraham by Isaac Ridler, a deserter from the American merchant ship *Columbia,* was that a cargo of sandalwood had been taken aboard at the island of Hawaii in 1790. In 1815, Captain Amasa Delano recalled seeing in

Canton "more than thirty tons of what was called sandal wood," which he said came from the Hawaiian Islands.

Sandalwood was highly prized by the Chinese. It was made into boxes, chests, and ornaments, used as a perfume, in cosmetics, and in medicinal preparations, and burned on religious and ceremonial occasions. No sandalwood grew in China and for generations it had been imported from India. The Chinese wanted few things from the Western world, mainly furs, and they wanted Spanish gold pieces in payment for the goods they sold. Thus the discovery of their desire for sandalwood was a great boon for impoverished American traders, seeking to recoup losses suffered during the American Revolution. In turn, traders took tea and chinaware to be sold in the United States and England.

There are many species of sandalwood and some are not as fragrant as others. Early wood sent to China was of the wrong species and was not acceptable to the merchants in Canton. Because of this the Chinese looked upon sandalwood from Hawaii with skepticism and apparently little trade took place for a number of years. It took some years to learn what the Chinese wanted and to establish a satisfactory trade.

The perfume from sandalwood comes from the oil in the heartwood of the tree. The tree grows slowly, reaching maturity in about forty years. Since the wood nearest the root has the greatest fragrance, trees were dug out of the ground. This lower trunk was the most desirable, and much of the rest of the tree was discarded or used as firewood. Harvesting sandalwood was a very wasteful operation.

The sandalwood trade was in a state of flux for a time, because of the poor reputation of Hawaiian wood in comparison with wood from other Pacific islands and from India, but after 1805 the possibility of trade was being considered by Boston trading companies. In 1807 the prominent Boston firm of J. and T. H. Perkins wrote to their Canton correspondent, suggesting future trade in "Sandal wood &c from Canton to the Islands, & direct back as long as Vessels & Crew's will hold together." It is not certain whether the islands referred to by Perkins were only the Hawaiian Islands, but the company's ships did touch at Kauai. J. and T. H. Perkins was one of the first companies to realize that sandalwood could be a separate trade, divorced from the fur trade with its base in the far-off Pacific Northwest Coast of America.

George Vancouver, who had been with James Cook as a midshipman on his second and third voyages into the Pacific, arrived in the

Islands in command of his own expedition in 1792. His orders were twofold. In the Pacific Northwest he was to regain property that had been seized by Spaniards, and he was to complete the charting of the Northwest Coast, a chore started by Cook.

Of lesser importance, he was instructed to winter in Hawaii and to chart the Islands during his visits. Captain Vancouver had good reason to be wary of the Hawaiians. During a clash preceding Cook's death, he had been badly beaten by Hawaiians at Kealakekua Bay. The captain now stayed briefly at Kealakekua Bay, where he met Kaiana. The much-traveled chief wanted firearms, but Vancouver had decided to avoid dealing in weapons and gave him none.

Vancouver sailed northwest in the *Discovery,* making no prolonged stops until he came to Waimea, arriving at daybreak on 9 March 1792. His supply ship, the *Chatham,* was slower and arrived at noon. Perhaps remembering Cook's difficulty in holding his anchorage at Waimea, Vancouver ordered cables be put out, both bow and stern, in the sandy bottom. The captain went ashore and reported in his journal that he was met with "distant civility."

Vancouver's assessment not notwithstanding, the local chief had placed a kapu on two houses near the shore, one for the use of officers and the other for marines. Stakes were driven in the ground along the Waimea River and to the beach, a sign to the Hawaiians to stay out of the area.

Perhaps this thoughtful act on the part of the chief somewhat eased the apprehensions of the captain, because he walked up Waimea Valley for a distance and admired the well-kept fields of the farmers. He also noted the "excessive wantonness" of the women. This was much worse, he thought, than when he had been at Waimea with James Cook, and he concluded that it must be the "result of civilized" people.

Vancouver met the three men who had been left by Captain John Kendrick in October 1791 to search for sandalwood and pearls. Their names were Rowbottom, James Coleman, and John Williams, and apparently they had accomplished little, having gone instead into the service of chiefs. Rowbottom could not have eased Vancouver's anxieties when he warned the captain to be on the lookout, because the Kauaians might attack if they thought they might be successful.

Further concern arose when the chief produced four letters that had been left with him by captains who had recently visited Waimea. The chief, of course, could not read and thought the letters were in his praise, but in fact they warned captains to be very careful in dealing with the local chiefs. Vancouver read them with care and told the chief that he should show them "to the commander of the next and every other vessel that might arrive at Kauai, which he promised to do."

Then even more upsetting events took place. James Coleman came aboard to announce that the prince of the island would come to Waimea, visiting Vancouver the next day at noon. The prince did not appear. Then the surf rose and Lieutenant Peter Puget and the marines, who were customarily ashore only during the day, could not get back aboard ship for the night. Vancouver saw fires burning on the hills behind Waimea, and thought they might be signals to bring warriors to attack his ships. He ordered two launches to stand by outside the surf through the night, ready to give assistance if the men ashore needed it. The night passed without incident.

The next day Vancouver ordered Puget to come through the surf at all cost, and he did so in a Hawaiian double canoe. The English lost two muskets, three axes, a saw, and several other tools, but the men made it safely to the ship. Fires continued to burn on the hills and still the prince did not appear. Later the Kauaians returned a musket they had retrieved.

The prince was apparently in Waimea, but he would not come aboard the flagship unless hostages were left on shore during his visit. Vancouver agreed, and two sailors stayed ashore while the prince and retinue were aboard.

The prince was Kaumualii, about twelve years old, Vancouver estimated. The English captain was much taken with the prince. He considered Kaumualii cheerful, friendly, and bright. Apparently Vancouver felt much relieved. The prince wanted to be called King George, after the English sovereign, and he was addressed as such by the three Western sailors living on the island. With the prince came a number of chiefs, along with the regent, a man named Inamoo. Kaumualii was destined to play a significant role in the events of Kauai and all the Islands.

As usual, the chiefs who came on board with the prince wanted firearms, because their enemies on the other islands had obtained them from traders. Vancouver continued to be firm. He declared that he would not give them such "engines of destruction." But he did give the prince two goats, a male and a female, and three geese. That night Vancouver put on a fireworks display for the benefit of the prince and all the population on shore.

Vancouver was also well aware of the possible importance of sandalwood. In March 1792 he noted in his journal,

Previously to the departure of Rowbottom and Williams, they informed me, that their captain had conceived that a valuable branch of commerce might be created, by the importation of the sandalwood of this country into India, where it sells at an exorbitant price; that, in the fur trade immense profits had been gained, insomuch that it was expected not less than twenty vessels would, on these pursuits, sail with their captain [Kendrick] from New England, and that they were desired to engage the natives to provide several cargoes of this wood, which is easily procured, as the mountains of Attowai [Kauai] as well as those of Owhyee [Hawaii], abound with the trees from which it is produced; though we were not able to procure any of their leaves, to determine its particular class or species. The wood seemed but slightly to answer the description given of the yellow sandal wood of India, which is there a very valuable commodity, and is sold by weight.

Vancouver had taken on such supplies as he could secure at Waimea, and on 14 March he upped anchors and sailed for Niihau, where he secured a supply of yams. Three days later he sailed for the Pacific Northwest, to carry out the orders of the Admiralty in connection with the Spanish seizures, and to continue charting the coast.

By October Vancouver had peacefully settled the return of property that the Spanish had seized from the English. Several days before he was to move down the Pacific coast and cross to Hawaii, an English merchant vessel, the *Jenny,* put in at Nootka. Its captain, James Baker, requested that Vancouver take two girls he had aboard and return them to the Hawaiian Islands. Baker said the girls had been hidden aboard the *Jenny* without his knowledge before leaving Niihau. George Vancouver obliged and took them aboard.

In early October 1792 Vancouver sailed southward, charting the coast as he went. At an unnamed Spanish settlement in California the captain took the two young women ashore, where they had the opportunity of riding horses. It must have been an exciting adventure for them, because horses had not as yet been introduced into the Hawaiian Islands. The two-ship expedition reached Monterey, farther down the California coast, charting as they went. Vancouver remained in Monterey for two months. Very likely the reason for this long stay was that the two women passengers were taken seriously ill and the considerate captain did not want to put to sea until they were well.

George Vancouver took on cattle and sheep to leave in the Islands and departed on 13 January 1793 for Hawaii. By 12 February he was sailing along the coast of the island of Hawaii, making several stops before dropping anchor at Kealakekua Bay. He was much impressed with Kamehameha and spent considerable time discussing affairs with the high chief. The attention the captain paid to Kamehameha and the advice and aid he gave him did much to enhance that warrior-chief's prestige throughout the Island chain.

But Vancouver was still leery of the Hawaiians. At Kealakekua Bay he laid down strict rules for the conduct of his crew and of those Hawaiians who came aboard. He was particularly concerned about the former Kauai chief, Kaiana. He thought Kaiana wanted to seize the *Discovery,* and on one occasion ordered his crew to assemble on deck in a show of force.

Sailing northwest, the captain anchored at both Maui and Oahu, his men mapping the islands as they proceeded to Kauai. Crossing the channel to Kauai, the *Discovery* sighted canoes headed for Oahu in search of Kaeo, the father of Kaumualii. In a canoe were the leg bones of two chiefs who had been the leaders in an uprising against Inamoo, the regent. Although the two chiefs and five warriors had been killed, Vancouver learned, Inamoo and his followers had suffered no casualties. The uprising had been against Inamoo, not Kaumualii, the young and future king he held in trust.

From earlier visits to Kauai, both the visits with Cook and his own of the previous year, Vancouver knew that the high chiefs of Kauai made their homes in Wailua Valley on the eastern coast of the island. Landing at Wailua was hazardous and there was no safe anchorage, so Vancouver studied the shoreline and saw three rivers emptying into the sea, two at Wailua and one at Kapaa. He wrote that this was "the most fertile and pleasant district of the island" and "the principal residence of the king."

Toward the end of March 1793, the two ships sailed for Waimea. George Vancouver had told the high chiefs who came aboard at Wailua that he was sailing for Waimea, and so gave the Kauaians several days' head start to arrive there, saving him valuable time. With high chiefs available, decisions could be reached quickly and orders passed on to the people.

Vancouver needed only minor provisions, because Kamehameha had supplied him well with pigs and other necessities in return for Vancouver's friendship and advice. The main purpose of the captain's visit was to fill his water casks and to add a few more supplies. Also important was returning the two girls he had carried from the Northwest to their homes on Niihau. Gaining the supplies was relatively easy, but he learned that there was a drought on Niihau and so left his two young charges at Waimea, receiving the promise that they would each be given a tract of land and looked after by the local chief. With these assurances, he stopped briefly at Niihau and once again sailed for the Northwest Coast of America.

In early January 1794 Vancouver was again back from the Northwest and briefly anchored in Hilo Bay. With Kamehameha aboard, he sailed to Kealakekua Bay. At Kealakekua the captain ordered his carpenter to lay the keel for a thirty-six-foot vessel, to be named the *Britannia*. During Vancouver's stay on Hawaii, Kamehameha ceded the island to Great Britain, with the details of the cession being somewhat obscure. The offer was never acted upon by the English parliament, but the fact that it was tendered made the influence of Great Britain and of Kamehameha all the greater throughout the Islands. Clearly, Kamehameha was Vancouver's favorite among Hawaiian chiefs.

Again sailing northwest, George Vancouver completed his mapping of the Hawaiian Islands on the way. To finish this task he had to sail around the north coast of Kauai, a difficult task, which he accomplished during March 1794. Again he anchored at Waimea, mainly to be sure that the two girls he had brought there on his last visit had been properly cared for. While away from the Islands the girls had become used to Western dress and food, and Vancouver was concerned about their welfare. Nevertheless, he found they were doing very well and so continued on, sailing around Niihau. He then moved southward, toward the Straits of Magellan, and home to England. He had mapped much of the Pacific Northwest Coast and completed the first mapping of the major Hawaiian Islands, and he had also secured the English property from the Spanish. His mission had been successfully completed.

George Vancouver was a man of contradictions. As a captain in the British Royal Navy he was a stern taskmaster. There was a high sense of discipline aboard his ships, enforced by the possibility of a flogging for those who failed to follow orders in a lively manner. Although he had been beaten as a midshipman by the Hawaiians and was cautious of them, he tried earnestly to be the great conciliator and attempted to persuade the high chiefs of the Islands to cease warring against each other. He had real affection for the Hawaiian people, as witnessed by the concern he felt for the two girls from Niihau.

On his return to England Vancouver retired to his country house. A bachelor his whole life, he suffered much during his last voyage into the Pacific, very likely from a hyperthyroid condition, and was constantly under the care of the ship's surgeon. He died before he had finished editing the journals of his last voyage.

George Vancouver, more than any other man, drew the Hawaiian people toward Great Britain. Kaumualii wanted to be called King George, after the British monarch, and he named a son George to help perpetuate the memory. The British flag flew before Kaumualii's residence for some time, and on the island of Hawaii the same flag flew at the residence of Kamehameha.

In February 1796 William Robert Broughton reached Waimea. He found Kauai in a state of turmoil and war. One chief had taken Waimea, although his hold on the district seems to have been anything but firm. This warrior chief came on board the *Providence,* Broughton's flagship, but when he saw a fleet of canoes heading toward the bay he hurriedly set out for shore. Kaumualii was in one of the canoes and he spent the night aboard the *Providence,* while Broughton tried to act the role of peacemaker, without success. After the Hawaiians disembarked from the *Providence* Broughton sailed for the Northwest.

By the end of July of the same year, Broughton was back at Waimea to fill his casks, but was told he would have to pay for the water. He sent an armed force ashore and took what he needed. Two days later he sailed for Niihau to collect a supply of yams. A man from Kauai said he would see that supplies were sent over from his island, and some did arrive. In the meantime, Broughton sent three marines, a mate, and a botanist ashore on Niihau. They set up camp to search for provisions, but had little success.

At about 11:00 A.M. on 30 July 1796, noticing that most of the canoes had left the shore, Broughton sent up a signal for the five men to return to the ship. A boat went in to get them, but before they could come in close enough they heard shots. The men ashore had been attacked by the Hawaiians. The little party of Englishmen retreated into the surf, but two of the marines died at the hands of the Hawaiians. The three others barely made it to the boat. The bodies of the marines were recovered, but they had been stripped of their equipment. The Hawaiians danced in joy, showing off their spoils, but they were careful to stay out of range of Broughton's guns. Broughton ordered other marines ashore to burn all property within a mile of where the incident had taken place.

During this ill-fated event we hear the last of the two girls brought back to Kauai from the Northwest by Vancouver. Broughton had carried the two girls with him to Niihau, one with her baby. They were terrified by the violence, but the husband of one had been a leader in the attack on the marines, and the girls decided they wanted to stay on Niihau. Broughton put them ashore and gave them letters addressed to any passing captain so that they might be transported back to Kauai if they so wished.

CHAPTER FOUR

"Is It Face Up or Face Down?"

The political situations on Kauai and the other islands were confusing and intertwined until 1795, when Kamehameha I finally brought all the Hawaiian Islands except Kauai and Niihau under his control. To understand the events that took place on Kauai, it is necessary to know the persons on the other islands who affected events.

In the year 1786 the dominant man in the Hawaiian Islands was Kahekili, king of Maui and Oahu. Kahekili's half-brother was Kaeokulani, known as Kaeo, king of Kauai and Niihau. The island of Hawaii was divided among three ruling chiefs who warred constantly against Kahekili, with much of the conflict centering in the Hana district of Maui.

Wars had raged for many years, with chiefs on the same island fighting each other, and with forays back and forth between various islands. By 1786 two things had happened. There was a general exhaustion of nearly all combatants and second, Western man had come, with his impressive weapons of destruction, and the rulers realized whoever could obtain the largest number of these weapons would have a tremendous advantage over others.

From the time of Captain Cook's visit to Kealakekua Bay, when local chiefs tried to persuade Lieutenant James King to desert and remain as a high chief, the captain of nearly every ship in Hawaiian waters was beseeched for arms, and crew members were approached to come ashore and become important persons in the service of some chief. When Captain Clerke returned to Waimea in 1779, some of his men were invited to desert and enjoy the good life of Kauai. Chiefs constantly implored Vancouver for weapons during his travels through the Islands, but Vancouver always refused, saying they were the property of his king and not his to give away.

In 1790 Captain William Douglas had left two men on Kauai to search for sandalwood, and a year later Captain John Kendrick left three men on Kauai for a similar purpose. These three men, and perhaps those of Douglas, soon joined the entourages of chiefs. Douglas also traded firearms for supplies, and though we do not know how many other merchant-captains did so, this was the easiest way to obtain provisions because weapons were what Hawaiians coveted most. The race for accumulating arms—as well as for white men to show them how to use these guns and cannons—went on with a vengeance. Captain Broughton had found that men on Niihau would kill in order to get the equipment of the marines he had sent ashore.

In 1790 the relative peace of the years since 1786 was shattered when Kamehameha, one of the three ruling chiefs of Hawaii, saw an opportunity to invade Maui, with Kahekili being on Oahu at the time. Kamehameha swept through Maui, Lanai, and Molokai, where he took Keopuolani, a girl of very high chiefly rank, under his protection. She would later become one of his wives and the mother of Liholiho and a younger son, both of whom would become kings of the Hawaiian Islands. It was also from Molokai that Kamehameha sent for the famous prophet Kapoukahi from Kauai, then living at Waikiki, to inquire what he must do to conquer all the Islands.

But Kamehameha's own island was still far from being under his control and his arch rival, the ruling chief of Ka'ū named Keoua, ravaged much of that island, including Kamehameha's domains. Kamehameha hurried home to try to recapture his lands and put an end to resistance on Hawaii. Keoua and Kamehameha fought bitter battles, without either gaining the upper hand.

Meanwhile, Kahekili and his half-brother Kaeo, king of Kauai, retook the islands of Molokai, Lanai, and Maui. And in 1791 they attacked the island of Hawaii, each side making use of its stock of wonderful new weapons. Off the northeastern coast of Hawaii the two fleets met and fought the sea battle that came to be called the battle of the red-mouthed guns. Kaeo and Kahekili suffered defeat and withdrew.

Kamehameha now turned to follow the advice of the Kauai prophet, Kapoukahi, and built a great heiau at Kawaihae on the west coast of the island of Hawaii. When it was completed he sent several of his chiefs to visit Keoua. They invited the rival chief to come to Kawaihae and counsel with Kamehameha. Some say that Kamehameha suggested they talk about ruling the island jointly, some believe it was simply to talk of peace. Others believe that Keoua knew that death awaited him and traveled by canoe with those who would normally be his death companions.

A great mass of his Ka'ū subjects followed Keoua to Kawaihae. When his canoe touched the sandy beach below the newly completed heiau, a high chief of Kamehameha, named Keeaumoku, ran forward and threw his spear at Keoua. The ruling chief of Ka'ū was killed together with all in his canoe except for one man. Kamehameha then declared the kapu, *kānāwai ali'i,* thus saving the many subjects of Keoua from slaughter. The body of the ruling chief was carried to the heiau and placed on the altar. With Keoua's death the whole island of Hawaii belonged to Kamehameha.

Keeaumoku was the father of perhaps the most famous of all the women of Hawaii. Her name was Kaahumanu. She was born in a cave on the ocean side of a high cinder cone in the Hana district of Maui, and as an infant she was carried to the island of Hawaii. She endured the wars that raged there, and at about the age of sixteen, she became a wife of Kamehameha. In determination and shrewdness she was a match for Kamehameha. In future years she would play a role in the destiny of Kauai.

Kamehameha had had little success against Kahekili and made no great attempt to conquer Maui while Kahekili was in residence. But he did continue to strengthen his arsenal of weapons, to seek the service of Westerners, and to build his navy, which consisted of double-hulled war canoes and a few Western vessels. In 1794 Kahekili died at Waikiki on Oahu and his kingdom of islands was left to Kalanikupule, one of his sons, and to Kaeo.

Kaeo wished to return to Kauai. Stopping at Oahu he sensed that his warriors were restless, and fearing rebellion he engaged in battle with Kalanikupule. Kaeo's forces held the upper hand until they advanced to the area of Pearl Harbor, where there were three foreign ships. Volunteers from these ships rowed in close to the shore in a small boat and poured murderous fire into the ranks of Kaeo. Kaeo and many of his troops were killed.

It was now time for Kamehameha to make his move. His forces quickly overran Maui, Molokai, and Lanai. From Molokai, Kamehameha invaded Oahu. The tired forces of Kalanikupule fought one decisive action in Nuuanu Valley, where they were soundly defeated. Kalanikupule wandered about the mountains, but finally was captured and offered as a sacrifice. By the middle of 1795 Oahu had succumbed, and by October of the same year Kamehameha was gathering his armies and navy to capture his last prize, the islands of Kauai and Niihau.

The historian James Jarves reported that Oahu endured much during this period. "The island was suffering all the miseries of protracted warfare; provisions were exceedingly scarce; many natives had starved to death, and some had been burnt alive by their chief for stealing food to supply their famishing families." This was a common occurrence during periods of warfare. There were probably more casualties among non-combatants than among the soldiers. Jarves continued, "War, famine, pestilence and oppression, with all the attending evils of an unsettled community, told heavily upon the nation."

After the conquest of Oahu Kamehameha was spurred on to invade Kauai for yet another reason. The brother of the sacrificed king of Oahu, several lesser chiefs, and an undetermined number of warriors had succeeded in fleeing to Kauai, where they had been given protection. Captain Charles Bishop, an English merchant-sailor who was in Hawaii in 1796, reported on the recent events. "Immediately on the King being in full possession of Woahoo [Oahu], in a Council of war, it was resolved to Attack Attooi [Kauai] for giving refuge to Tom hoa moto [the brother of the last Oahu King]." Captain Bishop later continued, "It Seems his chiefs are averse to Attacking Attooi, but the King tells them it was THEIR advice he took the Islands and now by HIS advice they SHALL take Attooi and Oneehehow [Niihau]."

The respected adviser John Young was among those who opposed Kamehameha's wish to invade Kauai. John Boit, captain of the *Union,* talked with Young in October 1795. He recorded Young's feeling in his journal.

Young seem'd to wish that Tamaa-maah [Kamehameha] would give up the thoughts of attacking Atooi. As he seem'd to be fearful that the Owhyhee chiefs would get worsted, for that there was a considerable number of Bottanay Bay gentry at the last mentioned Isle of Atooi, who in all probability would fight desperately . . . . I rather think that ye Botany men would fight desperately for ye generality of ye convicts sent to Botanay are desperate fellows. Young did not rightly know what vessel had left them at Atooi but he said that he heard it was an American ship that brought them.

When Charles Bishop arrived at Kauai he wrote, "This island is the Pleasentest by far we have seen but [it is] now torn to Pieces by the distractions and civil War reigning at this time." When Kaeo was killed, a son of his, a chief named Keawe, decided to ignore his father's wishes that Kaumualii become king. Keawe warred against Kaumualii, and had the upper hand when Bishop was at Kauai in March 1796, although the final outcome had not yet been determined. In speaking with Keawe, Bishop reported:

> He told me he meant to join Tim Himy Haw [Kamehameha] if he came down to that Island before he had conquored King George [Kaumualii], but should he be Successful before he came He purposed opposing the King of Owyhyhee with the whole Force of the Island. On his leaving us, the most grateful Present I could make him was a Quantity of Powder and Ball in return for several large Hogs and Yams &c.

Keawe had triumphed by July of 1796, and he kept Kaumualii under house arrest. But Keawe soon died and Kauai and Niihau were for the first time under the rule of Kaumualii, who was approximately sixteen years old. It now fell upon the shoulders of the new king to lead his people in their efforts to remain free of the ambitions of Kamehameha. This was to become one of the most dramatic episodes in the history of the Hawaiian Islands.

Kaumualii probably possessed the highest lineage of any chief in all the Islands. His grandfather, Kekaulike, had been the warrior-king of Maui. Kekaulike had harassed the island of Hawaii and died on Maui in about 1736. Kaumualii's father was Kaeo, a high chief of Maui, who was a half-brother of Kahekili. His mother was Kamakahelei, a descendant of the early rulers of Oahu who became the hereditary ruling chiefess of Kauai. Kamakahelei was described by Surgeon Ellis of Cook's expedition as "short and lusty . . . and very plain with respect to person," but she was much more than those words would imply.

Kamakahelei was of the highest rank. Her prestige was further enhanced by her possession of a powerful prayer called Aneekapuahi. We know little of this prayer except that it had something to do with fire or heat, and it was feared throughout the Islands. Upon his union with Kamakahelei, Kaeo peacefully became the king of Kauai.

With such a distinguished lineage it is no wonder Kaumualii looked upon Kamehameha as considerably beneath him in rank. Captain George Vancouver had once described Kamehameha to Kahekili, the uncle of Kaumualii, as a great chief. The Maui king had then set the captain straight on the matter in no uncertain terms. While Vancouver was referring to Kamehameha's ability as a warrior, Kahekili thought in terms of inherited rank.

Kaumualii was born in about 1780, according to the estimates of ship captains, beginning with Vancouver. Tradition tells us he was born at the Birthstones in Wailua Valley. We know little of his early years, except that he was dominated by Inamoo for some years and for a brief period of time was a prisoner of Keawe. We have no mention of his ability as a warrior. From the reputations won by his ancestors we could assume he would have been a fierce warrior, but his tests were not destined to come on the battlefield.

As Captain Bishop had reported, Kamehameha started making preparations for an attack on Kauai immediately after completing his conquest of Oahu. The fleet he assembled, the troops he gathered, and the supplies to arm and maintain them by far surpassed anything the Islands had ever seen. There were between 1,200 and 1,500 canoes, according to Western observers. The fleet was ready to transport about 10,000 soldiers, perhaps half of them armed with muskets. Kamehameha carefully followed all the religious practices expected by the gods, including the offering of human sacrifices.

According to Samuel Kamakau, the Hawaiian historian, Kamehameha's fleet sailed from the sandy beaches of Waianae, on the northwest shore of Oahu, in the spring of 1796. With him Kamehameha carried his trusted war god, Kukailimoku, who had served him so well in previous battles. The departure was at midnight, hoping to reach the area of Wailua on Kauai by daylight.

In the midst of the 60-mile-wide Kaieie Waho Channel, which separates Oahu and Kauai, a strong wind arose, endangering and capsizing some of the advance canoes. The canoes that came to their rescue were also swamped. The currents in the channel, always strong, became very confusing. Canoes sank, men drowned, and the whole fleet was in danger.

Kamehameha ordered his remaining canoes to return to Oahu. It must have been the most reluctant command he ever gave, but if he had not done so the entire fleet could have been destroyed. It was the greatest defeat Kamehameha ever suffered and thereafter the expedition bore the name of the channel, Kaieie Waho.

Strife-torn Kauai could have offered little resistance to the invasion armada of Kamehameha. Keawe had declared to Captain Bishop that he would join the forces of Kamehameha if he had not defeated Kaumualii by the time the invasion came, and in April 1796 the two were still battling for control of Kauai. If it had not been for the winds and currents of the wild Kaieie Waho Channel, Kauai would certainly have fallen to the forces of Kamehameha.

Following his defeat by the winds and currents, Kamehameha learned that a rebellion had broken out on the island of Hawaii. He returned to his home island and established his supremacy there. He remained for six years, attempting to consolidate his hold over the islands of his domain and to organize a workable government. But he had not forgotten Kauai and it was still his purpose to conquer the leeward islands, the last prize he wanted.

Kaumualii, a young man of sixteen or seventeen at the time of the first invasion attempt, took firm hold on his government on the death of Keawe. He knew of Kamehameha's determination to seize his kingdom, and he worked hard to secure arms and generally prepare for the defense of his island. But his resources were not as great as those of his opponent and he must have been well aware of this.

We know little of what was taking place on Kauai between 1796 and 1803. Kamehameha was at Lahaina on Maui, and in 1803 asked Richard J. Cleveland, supercargo aboard the *Lelia Byrd,* to carry a letter to King Kaumualii demanding that he acknowledge Kamehameha as his sovereign. The letter was delivered to a retainer of Kaumualii, but apparently was not answered. There were other communications between the two rulers. Captain William Shaler reported that Kamehameha "had sent an embassy" to Kauai to tell Kaumualii that he would be satisfied if Kaumualii would acknowledge him as sovereign and pay an annual tribute. Shaler reported "The latter [Kaumualii], not trusting implicitly to the declarations of his adversary, had detained his ambassadors on frivolous pretexts." Later William Shaler stopped at Kauai, met with Kaumualii, and described to him the armed forces that Kamehameha commanded.

In early 1804 Captain John Turnbull, an English merchant-sailor, came to Hawaii by way of Sydney and Tahiti. Stopping at Oahu, he arrived in time to see the vast preparations Kamehameha was making for the second invasion of Kauai. He told Kaumualii and his chiefs of these preparations and how advanced they were. The chiefs of Kauai, anxious and depressed, pleaded with Turnbull for arms and ammunition. Turnbull reluctantly but repeatedly refused.

Warnings concerning the might of Kamehameha caused Kaumualii to take another kind of action. He ordered some of the foreigners in his service to construct a small vessel in which he could escape if his defenses failed. The Kauai king reportedly would seek another island on which to live, or perhaps go to China. Captain Turnbull could not refuse to help in fitting out the little vessel.

Kaumualii was not totally engrossed in the defense of Kauai. Learning that John Turnbull had stopped at Tahiti, the Kauai king inquired after a man he had earlier sent there to select a wife suitable to his lineage and position. Turnbull reported he had met such a man and that he had come aboard intending to return to Kauai, but at the last moment had jumped overboard and swum to shore. Apparently the delights of Tahiti were too much to be given up. Turnbull had brought a Tahitian couple with him, and on Kauai the woman danced to the accompaniment of a hornpipe and a violin. It must have been a welcome diversion as the forces of Kauai awaited the forces of Kamehameha.

Before Kamehameha left Hawaii a prophet gained an audience with him and is supposed to have said, "Do not go on this expedition. Live here in Hawaii. There is food in the uplands, there is fish on the seacoast; heaven above, earth beneath." Kamehameha replied, "I shall not remain as you advise. I shall go." The prophet is then reported as saying, "A man-made canoe you have to sail away from Hawaii, but a god-made canoe it will be that brings you back again. . . ."

Kamehameha then consulted all the important hereditary religious kahunas to determine what rites he must perform en route to make sure that his expedition would be successful. He took a number of kahunas with him to point out the location and superintend the building of heiaus.

Kamehameha's fleet then moved to Maui, spending time at Lahaina where he met with Richard J. Cleveland, who carried a message from him to Kaumualii. Kamehameha remained for some time, gathering vast amounts of provisions of all kinds. Then he moved to Oahu, again gathering vast amounts of food for his troops and the hundreds of counselors and families of chiefs who accompanied him. While it was necessary to secure these provisions in order to maintain his army, it was also a premise of Kamehameha's that if he left an island nearly stripped of its food supplies, the people would concern themselves with mere existence and not have time to think of rebellion.

For the invasion of Kauai, Kamehameha had composed a *ho'ohiki,* or vow, undoubtedly to show his own determination and inspire his warriors: "Let us go and drink the water of Wailua, bathe in the water of

Namolokama, eat the mullet that swim in Kawaimakua at Haena, wreathe ourselves with the moss of Polihale, then return to Oahu and dwell there."

Kamehameha had indeed gathered a great force. Accounts vary somewhat, but it is agreed he commanded an army consisting of about 7,000 Hawaiian men and 50 Europeans. Most of these men carried muskets. He had eight cannons, forty swivel guns, and six mortars, together with a substantial amount of ammunition. In addition to a great fleet of double-hulled canoes, his navy comprised twenty-one armed schooners, a more potent fleet than his first armada.

The forces gathered, possibly in the area of Ka'a'awa, on the eastern shore of Oahu and final preparations were being made. It was here that disaster struck Kamehameha's forces once more. It came in the form of a devastating foreign disease called *mai 'ōku'u,* or squatting sickness. Most likely it was a typhoid-like fever.

Samuel Kamakau described the disease as follows:

> It was a very virulent pestilence, and those who contracted it died quickly. A person on the highway would die before he could reach home. One might go for food and water and die so suddenly that those at home did not know what had happened. The body turned black at death. A few died a lingering death, but never longer than twenty-four hours; if they were able to hold out for a day they had a fair chance to live. Those who lived generally lost their hair.

Kamehameha contracted the disease, but was one of the fortunate ones who survived. Many trusted counselors and chiefs, some of whom had served Kamehameha for twenty years or more, died together with their families. The destruction to his forces was greater than any he could have suffered in battle. His forces were so depleted, particularly through the loss of dedicated and trusted chiefs, that the idea of invading Kauai became an impossibility.

When Kamehameha heard that Keeaumoku was dying he rushed to his side. Keeaumoku was the chief who had thrown the first spear at Keoua when the Ka'ū chief stepped ashore to meet Kamehameha on Hawaii. Kamehameha asked of the dying man, "When you are gone will conspirators arise and take the kingdom from me?" Keeaumoku said the only one who might succeed was his daughter, Kaahumanu. Kamehameha therefore—concerned that some man might win her affections, and that this could result in rebellion—declared a law that any man who slept with Kaahumanu should be put to death. Kaahumanu had many relatives who were chiefs, and the danger lay in the possibility that they might join forces with her.

In 1804 Captain Urey Lisiansky, the Russian explorer who commanded a ship on an around-the-world exploring expedition, came to the island of Hawaii. He wished to visit with Kamehameha, but learning that he was on Oahu and that an epidemic was raging there, he bypassed that island and sailed for Kauai, reaching there on 19 June 1804. Kaumualii came aboard, anxious to hear any news about Kamehameha's activities. When he was told that an epidemic had spread among Kamehameha's troops, Kaumualii was elated.

Kaumualii declared he was determined to defend himself to the last. He said he had 30,000 warriors and Lisiansky assumed this meant all the people of his islands, although that figure would have exceeded even the population of Kauai and Niihau. The Kauai king had three cannons, forty swivels, and a sufficiency of powder and ball. Kaumualii asked for bar iron and paint to complete his escape vessel, but Lisiansky gave him none.

With this second disaster of the epidemic, Kamehameha must have pondered the words of the prophet who had beseeched him not to invade Kauai. He must have remembered that his trusted chiefs had warned him against his first attempt eight years earlier. He certainly knew the fate of the ambitious high chief from Hawaii, who, generations earlier, had attempted to invade Kauai but was defeated. The powerful prayer possessed by Kaumualii's mother would put fear and uncertainty in the heart of any mortal. Moreover, throughout the Islands Kauai was noted for the religious nature of its people often referred to as Kauai *pule oʻo,* Kauai of strong prayers. Certainly these things weighed on Kamehameha's mind, yet he remained determined that Kauai should come under his control.

The vast amount of arms and ammunition, particularly muskets, possessed by Kamehameha and Kaumualii is witness to the large number of sailing ships that visited the Hawaiian Islands in the 1790s and early 1800s. While there were some principled captains who would not deal in weapons, most were willing to supply the Hawaiians with anything they wanted.

The vessels that came were mostly American, with a lesser number being British. There were a few others, occasionally a Russian ship, a South American, or a European vessel. If it were not for a continuing series of wars fought by Great Britain during these years, the English very likely would have dominated Pacific trade. Many English merchant-captains had been ordered into the Royal Navy and were involved in the Napoleonic wars or with the revolt of the American colonies.

One reason for the large number of American ships in Hawaii was the desperate economic condition of the colonies at the close of the American Revolution. During the years of hostilities the New England merchant marine had been nearly annihilated. To rebuild the merchant fleets and their economy, shipyards sent new vessels down the ways and merchants sought places where they could trade. The profitable trade with England was gone—the British would not deal with their lost colonies. Trade with wartime ally France soon proved unsatisfactory. Finding little trade in Europe, the determined New Englanders looked to the far Pacific. They knew of the sea-otter furs on the Pacific Northwest Coast and the value placed on them by the Chinese. The voyage from New England to the Northwest Coast was ordeal enough, but the merchant sailors then had to sail across the Pacific Ocean to Macao, where they followed a ritual, laid down by the Chinese, to proceed up the Canton River to the city of Canton.

The Chinese took a dim view of the foreign devils who came to trade in the only port in China open to foreigners. What they wanted most were Spanish gold pieces in exchange for tea and chinaware, which were marketable items in New England. In their poverty the New England merchant-sailors could not pay for this merchandise in gold pieces, so they had to find items the Chinese would accept in trade. Initially, there were two things the Chinese wanted. Furs, and bêche-de-mer, a cucumber-like form of sealife found on reefs throughout the Pacific islands and considered a great delicacy by the Chinese.

The American merchants were so desperate, competing against each other as well as with English and Russian traders, that they exchanged firearms for furs with the Northwest Indians. This was a risky thing, since the Northwest Indians used the arms against other Indians as well as traders, including the Russian American Company settlements. This finally led to official diplomatic protests by the Russian government to the United States government.

After taking on furs in the Pacific Northwest and moving westward toward Canton, the Americans found the Hawaiian Islands a logical place to stop. The Islands were also a good market for firearms. The

Mount Waialeale is seldom seen, normally hidden beneath a cover of clouds. The mountain is the heart of Kauai and the ancient Hawaiians believed its topmost reaches were occupied by the god Kane. From the mountain heights radiate rivers that water all of Kauai.

This drawing was made in 1778 by William Ellis, surgeon's mate aboard James Cook's *Discovery*. The view is of Kipu Kai, near where Cook's ships first approached land along the south coast of Kauai. The drawing is considered the first of the Hawaiian Islands to be made by a Westerner. (Bishop Museum photo.)

This drawing of a heiau at Waimea was made by John Webber who was with Cook's expedition. It shows the appearance of a heiau before the coming of Western influences.

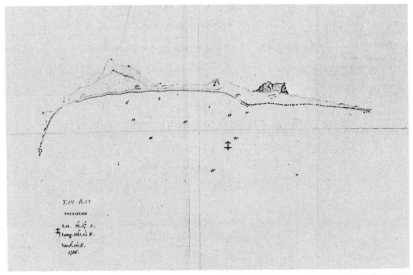

A map of Yam Bay and the island of Niihau appeared in Captain George Dixon's journal in 1788. For many years Niihau was called Yam Island by Western sailors because of the high quality of yams grown there. (Hawaiian Historical Society photo.)

Mercy Partridge Whitney was the patient wife of the Reverend Samuel Whitney. She lived in Waimea during all her years in Hawaii and noted in her journal many of the events that took place on Kauai. The Reverend Samuel Whitney was a quiet, tireless worker. His advice was sought by Hawaiians and foreigners in secular affairs, and his faithful efforts were highly regarded by his fellow missionaries.

Georg Scheffer's ambition was to establish a kingdom of his own in the Hawaiian Islands. Employed by the Russian American Company, his alliance with Kaumualii caused anxiety to Kamehameha I, but Scheffer's authority abruptly ended and he was forced to leave the Islands.

Herman Widemann is shown with his wife Mary Kaumana and two daughters
Emma and Martha. Widemann, a native of Germany, served as a judge on Kauai and
was active in the sugar business.

The Reverend Doctor James William Smith was the only medical doctor on Kauai
for many years. The needs of the sick and injured frequently sent him rushing to distant parts of the island. His congregation was at Koloa. It fell to his wife, Melicent
Knapp Smith, to offer hospitality to the wives and families of visiting whaling captains as well as to travelers who disembarked or departed from Koloa.

William Harrison Rice and his wife, Mary Sophia Hyde Rice, photographed
together, were stationed first at Hana on Maui and later at Punahou School. Rice left
the mission to become manager of Lihue plantation; he built the first irrigation system to carry water to the sugar fields.

The beautiful *Cleopatra's Barge*, renamed *Pride of Hawaii*, was the royal yacht of Kamehameha II. Kaumualii was whisked to Oahu aboard this ship after he was kidnapped in 1821. The yacht was later lost in Hanalei Bay.

Frederick Godfrey Wundenberg (left) was among the earliest German settlers on Kauai. He married Ann Moorea Henry and for a time ran Wyllie's sugar plantation at Hanalei. Later he moved to Honolulu where he managed the finances of the kingdom.

Annie Sinclair lived on Niihau where she was courted by Valdemar Knudsen. The youngest daughter of Eliza Sinclair, both she and her mother were known as intrepid horsewomen.

Valdemar Knudsen started a ranch and planted an orchard at Waiawa on the west side of Kauai. Norwegian by birth Knudsen was an avid botanist and ornithologist.

Steam engines made plowing easier. With the new method, a plow (shown on the right) was pulled back and forth between two steam engines by means of a cable wound onto a large circular drum beneath the boiler.

Plowing fields for planting sugarcane was terribly hard work requiring the use of many yokes of oxen. Special plows were built that could plow to the necessary depths.

Ox carts brought sugarcane to factories, such as this one at Lihue. Slow moving oxen limited the distance cane could be planted from the factory. The introduction of railroads meant faster transportation and new areas could be planted in cane.

Paul Kanoa served as governor of Kauai from 1846 until 1877. He performed his duties with authority. During Kanoa's time sugarcane emerged as the dominant commercial enterprise on Kauai.

Americans traded weapons for pork, fresh water, cordage made of *olonā* fiber, highly regarded by sailors, yams, and taro. Not the least of island products was salt. The Hawaiians had long been expert in making salt from seawater; it was in demand for preserving pork and, even more important, the precious pelts, during long voyages.

One of the major resources of the Islands was their supply of manpower. Visiting captains took on many Hawaiians as seamen because they quickly discovered that the Islanders were superb sailors. Captain Charles Bishop recorded in his journal that the ship *Mercury* arrived in Hawaii, probably in 1795 or 1796, and that, "Amongst the many difficulties this vessel has encountered in her lengthened Passage to this coast [is] the loss of most all the Crew at the Sandwich Islands." The desertion of the crew created a very serious situation for the vessel, on its way to the Northwest Coast.

Bishop wrote, "It was determined to seize some of the Islanders in place of the crew, and which they did confining them below till the Ship was out of sight of their Native Land—and these fine Fellows has been the Guard and Protection of the vessel at all Places while the others have been Employed in the trade." What the captain of the *Mercury* did not know at first was that the majority of the Islanders were pleased to go to sea and see the wonders of foreign places. The ocean was just as much a natural element of life for the Hawaiians as was the island land they walked upon. Journals of early captains contain numerous entries about Hawaiians who had jumped overboard and saved a New England shipmate who had fallen into the sea.

Among the Islanders Charles Bishop employed was a man from Niihau who apparently became the personal servant of the captain.

A youth who had rendered himself familiar by his great good humour was after much Solicitation received on board. His Sister (by no means an unhandsome young Woman) pressed much to accompany her Brother, and had actually got on board, and it was not without a Present and some harsh words we could Perswade her return to her canoe. Their Parting was like Brother and Sister. It was affectionate nor could they refrain from Tears. She continued to follow us 'till the Breeze Freshening they found the Ship haistily leaving them, when with seeming reluctance they paddled slowly back towards their Native Isle.

The pay book indicates that the Niihau boy served for some time aboard the *Nautilus*. His pay was $4.00 a month, and when he was finally discharged he was due $95.00. He took his pay in stores, cargo, and slops, the term used for clothing and other necessities aboard ship.

After failing for a second time to conquer the leeward islands by force, Kamehameha turned to other means to accomplish his objective. He still bought arms and ships and sought the services of foreigners who could help him, but not at the former frenzied pace. Undoubtedly, Kaumualii also continued to arm himself to the best of his ability. But the tone of relations between the two rulers was changing.

Kamehameha sent a chief, Kihei, to Kauai to discuss a basis whereby Kauai and Niihau could peacefully come under the rule of Kamehameha, but with Kaumualii retaining authority over his domains. Chief Kihei proved to be a poor choice. He became so enamored with life on Kauai that he decided to stay on the island and did not return to report to his king. Nevertheless, he did deliver Kamehameha's message, and in return Kaumualii sent Wahine to see Kamehameha. Wahine was treated well and sent back to Kauai, bringing the order that Kaumualii must go and see Kamehameha in person.

But Kaumualii was not ready to undertake such a trip, which would put him into the hands of his greatest enemy. He sent persons of greater importance than Wahine, including a high chief who was his closest friend, to meet with Kamehameha. The expedition consisted of eleven double canoes and nine single canoes carrying a variety of rich presents for Kamehameha. The fleet came to grief in the Kauai channel, and the only surviving canoe was washed ashore on Niihau.

The reports of ship captains, in addition to the flow of emissaries, must have impressed Kaumualii with the eventual futility of his situation. Kamehameha controlled all but the leeward islands, and numerous ships stopped at the ports he closely supervised. Some of these ships proceeded to Kauai, where Kaumualii and his chiefs were told of the power Kamehameha possessed and what a capable ruler he was. Whether Kamehameha intended it that way or not, it was an effective method of psychological warfare. And always behind the negotiations was the threat of still another invasion attempt.

Kaumualii sent his favorite nephew to visit with the ruler of the windward islands, but he did not prove to be a satisfactory substitute, and Kamehameha still insisted on meeting Kaumualii face-to-face. At last, in 1810, after some five years of negotiations, Kaumualii consented to go to Honolulu. Probably the man who did the most to convince him was Captain Nathan Winship, a New England merchant, who left his first mate on Kauai as a guarantee of the good will of Kamehameha. Kaumualii took with him his two leading war chiefs and priests who were learned in the prayers of old. They were attired in their long, colorful feather cloaks. Kamehameha came out with a fleet of canoes to meet him at Honolulu Harbor. The time was late March or early April. The historian Kamakau recorded what he was told took place:

> When Kamehameha and his chiefs came aboard in their feather robes, Ka-umu-aliʻi singled out the (ruling) chief and grasping his hand said, "Here I am; is it face up or face down?" Kamehameha disclaimed the inference, and the chief continued, "This is my gift at our meeting: the land of Kauai, its chiefs, its men great and small, from mountain to sea, all above and below, and myself to be yours." Kamehameha said, "I shall not accept your land, not the least portion of your domain. Return and rule over it. But if our young chief (Liholiho) makes you a visit, be pleased to receive him." Ka-umu-aliʻi answered, "We have met, and I am now returning." Kamehameha said, "Let us land; we have food and fish and wealth; better come ashore." Ka-umu-aliʻi and his wife Ke-kai-haʻa-kulou landed and all the chiefs and followers bestowed gifts upon them.

Most accounts of this face-to-face meeting tell of the wish of some chiefs to kill Kaumualii while he was in the grasp of Kamehameha. The plan was to poison him. Isaac Davis, a long and trusted friend of Kamehameha and one of his important advisers, learned of the attempt to be made and succeeded in preventing it. Kaumualii, hearing what lay in store, fled back to Kauai. Isaac Davis, in turn, was dead by poisoning in April 1810. It is not certain whether Kamehameha knew of the plot or not.

Kaumualii had learned of the plan to kill him from foreigners in Honolulu. As he sailed back to Kauai he must have thanked his gods and remembered the fate of another high chief, Keoua, who had gone to meet with Kamehameha and had fallen under the spear of a warrior. Kauai must have been a welcome sight for both Kaumualii and Captain Winship. Winship could regain his first mate, who certainly would not have survived if Kaumualii had not.

Captain Nathan Winship did not carry Kaumualii to Honolulu and then rush him back to Kauai simply as an act of kindness. There were important trade considerations involved. Winship together with his brother, Jonathan, and William Heath Davis, another New Englander, each captained vessels in Pacific trade. They had found that competing for furs with the Russian American Company and with other Americans at the Columbia River was ruinous, and they sought furs most successfully along the California coast. The Winships and Davis also had visions of gaining a monopoly on the sandalwood trade in Hawaii. By playing peacemaker between Kaumualii and Kamehameha, these three men hoped they could secure such a monopoly.

The years 1811–1812 marked the real beginning of the sandalwood trade with China. Clearly the early prejudices of the Chinese against Hawaiian sandalwood were being overcome. Where once Hawaiian wood had been considered inferior, it was now accepted. The plan of the three New Englanders seemed to be well on its way to success. They secured an agreement with Kaumualii and also with Kamehameha, but Kamehameha was dissatisfied with the returns from his first trading venture with Canton and backed out of the arrangement.

And yet the three captains might have been successful in the trade if it had not been for the coming of the War of 1812. While American merchant-captains were more numerous in the Islands than the English, the English still held great influence with the leaders in the Hawaiian government. Kaumualii was called George after the king of England and he gave his favorite son the same name. Kamehameha considered the Islands to be under the protection of England. His most trusted foreign advisers were Englishmen, the principal one being John Young. And the memory of Captain George Vancouver was fresh in the minds of many chiefs. Following threats by John Young of what would happen to those who cooperated with the enemies of Great Britain, Kaumualii also refused to deal in sandalwood with the Winships and Davis. The Winships sought more favorable trade conditions elsewhere, while William Heath Davis remained in the Islands as a trader for the rest of his life.

The War of 1812 brought a slowdown in trade. Tales of the destruction of the American merchant marine during the American Revolution had not been erased from the minds of New England captains, and many sat out this new war in the safety of neutral ports. For about three years the sandalwood trade declined, only to start again with new vigor after the war was over.

On Kauai, Kaumualii pondered his situation. He still ruled his islands even though they had officially become a part of Kamehameha's kingdom. The wish of some of Kamehameha's chiefs to poison him while in Honolulu had diminished whatever small trust he might have had in the windward chiefs. He sought some solution to his problems. In a moment of reminiscing he must have taken pride in the exploits of his warrior-ancestors who had conquered all the Islands except Hawaii. Kaumualii's distinguished lineage, so superior to that of Kamehameha, certainly bolstered his resolve through his whole life.

The years ahead would unfold happenings that not even the most talented of the Kauai storytellers would have been able to imagine.

CHAPTER FIVE

An Interesting Diversion

Kaumualii was left undisturbed on Kauai after promising allegiance to Kamehameha in 1810. Tribute had been pledged, but there are no details of the arrangements. Life for the people of Kauai and Niihau was peaceful, although commoners suffered much hardship. The chiefs demanded they cut sandalwood in the mountains and haul it to the shore, where it was loaded onto ships to be carried to China.

Peace, however, did not extend to the mind of Kaumualii. His feelings toward Kamehameha probably were a mixture of fear, disdain, and suspicion. While Kaumualii wished to be free of Kamehameha, the need for caution was obvious. Outright rebellion was absurd. Help from outside was necessary if he wished to achieve his goal, but where could he turn? The British openly backed Kamehameha. The Americans wanted sandalwood and supplies and it was not to their advantage to disrupt trade by siding with Kaumualii. The only other nation to have made an impression of strength in the Hawaiian Islands was Russia.

In 1804 Kaumualii's appeal to the Russian Lieutenant Urey F. Lisiansky had brought sympathy, but not help. In 1809 Lieutenant-Captain L. Hagemeister also refused Kaumualii's request for help. This disappointing lack of aid from the Russians undoubtedly hastened Kaumualii's trip to windward for his meeting with Kamehameha. Eventually, however, it was through the Russian American Company, with its Pacific headquarters in Sitka, Alaska, that Kaumualii would gain a fleeting and uneasy sense of freedom and power. Some background on Russian activity in the north Pacific, however, will be helpful in understanding the Russian role in Hawaii.

Russians—or explorers hired by the Russians—were curious about northeastern Asia and the American continent, wanting to know if the two were connected. As early as 1648 Simeyon Dezhnev had passed through what would become known as Bering Strait and into the Bering Sea. Dezhnev had discovered there was no land connection between Asia and America, but somehow his evidence was not believed or was lost.

In 1728 Vitius Bering, a Dane in the service of Russia, sailed the same area, but at no time coming or going did he sight the American continent through the fogs and mists. In June 1741 Vitius Bering tried again in the ship *St. Peter.* On this terribly trying trip he did see the American mainland, but did not go ashore. On his way south Bering was shipwrecked and died of scurvy. Those who survived constructed a small boat from the wreckage of the *St. Peter.* James Cook later used some of Bering's charts in searching for the Northwest Passage.

The greatest commotion involving Bering's second voyage did not result from his seeing the American continent, but rather from a book published by a German, George Steller, who was the naturalist aboard the *St. Peter.* In his book Steller gave the first descriptions of four previously unknown marine mammals—the fur seal, the sea otter, the sea lion, and the sea cow.

The revelation of the existence of these creatures in large numbers brought Russian trappers, hunters, and adventurers to the Aleutian Islands, to Alaska, and down the Northwest Coast of America. This influx of Russians occurred during the second half of the eighteenth century. Because of the profitable trade involved, the Russian American Company was founded. In 1790 Alexander Baranov was named manager of the Russian American Company and was also appointed governor of Russian America. The company was the agency of the Imperial Russian government in North America and was granted a monopoly on fur trading in 1799. Headquarters were situated at Sitka in Norfolk Sound.

The Russians would have preferred to keep the fur trade to themselves, but that was impossible for two reasons. First, they could not guard the extensive coast against all the English and Americans who wanted to hunt there. Second, and perhaps more important, the Russians received supplies on an irregular basis from ports far away. The headquarters of the company was in St. Petersburg, and supply ships sailing from the Baltic Sea took from nine months to a year to reach Alaska. The continuing question for the Russians was, could they survive until the next shipment of supplies came?

Reluctantly, Baranov was forced to deal with English and American vessels, trading furs as well as firearms for supplies. Firearms and ammunition apparently were among the few things in good supply among the Russians, because they were a necessity in hunting and in defense against hostile Indians. Many Russian muskets and rifles reached Hawaii.

Alexander Baranov could have known of the existence of the Hawaiian Islands before leaving Russia, but if he did not, it is likely he learned of them from Captain Hugh Moore in 1792. Moore was in command of the East Indiaman, *Phoenix,* which limped into Prince William Sound for repairs. Baranov came into the Sound in search of belligerent Indians, and during the course of conversation with Moore the Hawaiian Islands could have been mentioned. It is not known if Moore had stopped at the Islands, but it seems likely, since he had a number of Hawaiians among his crew. Moore may have given Baranov the first real description of the Hawaiian Islands the Russian ever heard.

The first Russian ships to visit Hawaii came in 1804. From the island of Hawaii Captain A. J. Krusenstern sailed directly to Japan, while Lieutenant Urey Lisiansky went to Waimea, Kauai. It was from Lisiansky that Kaumualii learned that an epidemic had all but destroyed Kamehameha's army.

Through English or American merchant-captains, Baranov and Kamehameha were made aware of each other's existence and needs. In 1805 or 1806 Kamehameha sent a message to Baranov, saying he would "gladly send a ship every year with swine, salt, batatas [sweet potatoes], and other articles of food if they [the Russians] would in exchange let him have sea-otter skins at a fair price." In 1807 a small Russian vessel, on a voyage from California, obtained supplies and returned to Sitka. Through the captain, Kamehameha sent Baranov a present of a Hawaiian helmet and a feather cape.

The next person of consequence in Russian employ to reach the Islands was Lieutenant L. A. Hagemeister, a German in the Russian Imperial Service, aboard the *Neva*. This captain had been sent by Baranov to secure a shipload of salt, a commodity essential not only for the inhabitants of the Russian colonies themselves, but also for the preserving of furs. In his report to the Russian American Company, Hagemeister wrote that Kamehameha came out in a canoe to meet the ship. The Americans, ever concerned over interference with trade, became suspicious and spread rumors that the Russians wanted to settle in Hawaii.

L. A. Hagemeister reported that enough food could be produced in Hawaii to supply a large part of Asiatic Russia. He listed sugarcane as suitable for making rum, as well as rice, breadfruit, and taro as important products. While Hagemeister got along well with Kamehameha, he wrote that the king himself controlled all trade and that he was not willing to sell his goods at a reasonable price. Hagemeister did not stop at Kauai.

Hagemeister was clearly on a reconnaissance mission. He thought Kamehameha might sell part of an island, and concluded that the Islands could possibly be occupied by friendly methods. If not, then two ships would be sufficient to take the Islands by force. Hagemeister did have reservations about the British. He believed they might object to another nation seizing the Islands or part of them.

Captain Hagemeister probably would have denied his mission to anyone except his superiors, but by chance he had carried with him to Hawaii an unfortunate young English seaman by the name of Archibald Campbell. Campbell had suffered horribly from exposure in an open boat after the ship he served on had been lost. Both feet had suffered frostbite and had been amputated. Baranov sent him to Hawaii aboard the *Neva*. Campbell was nearly illiterate—he had to dictate his journals—and hardly seems capable of giving anything but an honest appraisal of what he saw and heard.

> It would appear that the Russians had determined to form a settlement upon these islands; at least, preparations were made for that purpose; and I was informed by the commandant, that if I choose, I might get a situation as interpreter. The ship had a house in frame on board, and intimation was given that volunteers would be received; none, however, offered; and I never observed that any other steps were taken in this affair.

Meeting a fellow countryman, who lived on Oahu, Campbell also reported their conversation in his journal.

> Amongst other things, I told him that I understood the Russians had some intention of forming a settlement on the Sandwich islands. This reached the captain's ears; and he gave me a severe reprimand, for having, as he expressed it, betrayed their secrets. He desired me to say no more on the subject in future, otherwise I should not be permitted to quit the ship.

Alexander Baranov, like many Russian naval officers of his day, had been trained in the British Navy and spoke fluent English, so there is no question of Campbell misunderstanding through language difficulties.

Little of significance happened between 1809 and 1814. There was undoubtedly some trade and communication between the Russian settlement and the Islands, but Baranov had turned his attention to California as a place where he could grow the foodstuffs he needed and raise animals. Fort Ross, north of what would later become San Francisco, carried his hopes, but the California enterprise developed much too slowly and the Russian general manager thought again of Hawaii.

During the War of 1812 some American captains took the risk of continuing to trade and possibly be captured by the British, others sat out the war in neutral ports, and still others sold their vessels to whoever would purchase them. Alexander Baranov bought two ships in 1814; one was the American ship *Atahualpa*, which was renamed the *Bering*, with James Bennett remaining as captain. She sailed down the Northwest Coast seeking sealskins to be used as partial payment for the vessel, and finally crossed to Hawaii to load the remaining space with food supplies for Sitka.

The *Bering* stopped at Waimea in early October 1814 and at this time Kaumualii apparently dictated a letter to Baranov via Captain Bennett. The letter bears the date 27 December 1814. It is revealing.

> I received from Captn Bennett 50 muskets and 42 rifles but my people not being used to rifles, I would much rather have muskets with a large bore and long; withall I should like to have two hundred muskets and one hundred kegs of Powder and 40 Boxes of musket balls . . . and I should like to have a snug brick (brig) about 90 or 100 tons that was strong built with sails, rigging etc. . . . . I should like to have her coppered . . . .

Kaumualii also asked for twenty cannons and the equipment needed to operate them, for several pieces of cloth, two forges, two anvils, and, among other things, four more stills, but larger than the "last ones." In payment he would give any produce of Kauai except sandalwood. He would, however, pay for the vessel with sandalwood. The letter is proof that Kaumualii already had received arms and supplies from Baranov and was still feverishly trying to equip himself.

Captain Bennett sailed through the Islands obtaining supplies and then returned to anchor at Waimea on 31 January 1815, to seek yet a few more provisions before returning to Sitka. The captain and the Russian supercargo went ashore. A sudden wind came up from the southwest, blowing toward shore. The winds intensified to a gale, and after using all the seamanship possible, the worst had to be faced. At 3:00 in the morning the *Bering* struck broadside on the beach and heeled onto shore. The ship could not be refloated.

The log of the *Bering* reveals that Captain Bennett called on Kaumualii for assistance, which was forthcoming after Bennett agreed the ship would belong to the ruler, although the cargo would still belong to Bennett. Some 200 Kauaians began to unload the wreck. The chests of the seamen were stored in the houses of Kaumualii, who took half of each man's clothes for taking the chests under his care. The crew was given a house to live in on the beach, with food supplied on a day-to-day basis. Bennett wrote that Kaumualii said he would send a canoe to Oahu to bring help, but Bennett claimed this was not done.

About 2,000 Kauaians gathered on the beach to try and pull the wreck of the *Bering* ashore, but without success. The furs were stored in houses near Makaweli, to the south of Waimea. Captain Bennett and his crew at last found passage aboard the passing *Albatross,* which carried them to Sitka where Bennett made an indignant report to Alexander Baranov. Bennett, who seemed unrealistic about his misadventure, wanted to lead an attack on Kauai and regain what he had lost. Baranov knew better. He had few men to spare and, at least initially, chose the road of diplomacy.

Although he wanted to regain the lost property, Baranov also thought this was the right time to pursue that long-considered idea of establishing a colony in the Hawaiian Islands. The stage was set for one of the most dramatic episodes in the history of Kauai. And a man capable of playing the major role in the drama had now come to Sitka.

The man who arrived on the scene was Georg Scheffer, born in Munnerstadt, Germany, in 1779, the son of a miller. In keeping with his exalted views of himself, Scheffer frequently affected the prefix "von" when signing his correspondence. He received a good education and started his working life as an apothecary, passing the examination to practice medicine in 1805. In 1808 he was invited to Russia and served in the army as a staff physician, and at some point he also worked in the Russian police force. In 1812 he was part of an ill-conceived plan to fight Napoleon's invading armies through the use of hot-air balloons. He was cross-grained, quarrelsome, sententious, opinionated, and full of petty conceits, systematically falling out with almost everyone he met.

In 1813 Georg Scheffer signed on with the Russian American Company as a ship's surgeon and sailed for Sitka. His very presence in Sitka was due to a violent disagreement with the captain of the ship, who sailed away without him. But Alexander Baranov had had a falling-out with the ship's captain also, so this was not held against Scheffer.

Baranov was surrounded by a rabble of unlettered men sent to him by the company's directors in St. Petersburg. Scheffer's positive qualities, of which there were several, were sufficient to impress him. As events would show, Scheffer clearly possessed personal charm and credibility. He was a cultured and educated man, and he spoke at least four languages. These were imposing qualifications, so Baranov picked Scheffer for a most delicate mission—indeed, his choice was almost a foregone conclusion. In Hawaii the most common foreign language was English and Baranov could have had only a few men who spoke English. Moreover, Scheffer was a medical doctor, even though there were dark references to unspecified disciplinary problems in his past, which had at one point jeopardized his medical degree.

Scheffer sailed for Hawaii in October 1815 on the American ship *Isabella*. With him were two half-Russian, half-Indian boys; one of them, Antipatr, was Baranov's son. Baranov's instructions were threefold and very specific. First, Scheffer was to present himself initially as a doctor of medical science and a naturalist. While devoting himself to this work he was to win the favor of Kamehameha. When this was accomplished, Scheffer was to inform the king of his commission to obtain the cargo of the *Bering* and the ship's sheathing, bolts, and nails. If payment was necessary it was to be made in sandalwood.

Second, Scheffer should attempt to gain trading privileges from Kamehameha and a monopoly similar to that once granted to William Heath Davis and the brothers Winship. He was also to gain as much information as possible concerning the method of selling sandalwood and the latest prices. Baranov added an interesting instruction. "It is also desirable to pay homage to the wives of the king, because here, as in Europe, they direct the king's wishes according to their own plans and intentions."

Third, Baranov left the scientific role up to Scheffer, but reminded him that he should give credit to the Russian American Company for its participation in any such work. Baranov then warned about the other foreign nationals in Hawaii, who were in competition and jealous of each other. "I shall rely upon your good sense and ability not to miss any opportunity to advance the interests of the Company and the fatherland. You will not let yourself be caught by the clever tricks of such foreigners."

In a letter entrusted to Scheffer, to be given to Kamehameha at a later, appropriate time, the Russian governor was straightforward about what he expected concerning compensation for the *Bering*. He named Georg Scheffer as the man who had the authority to oversee the return of the property or arrange for payment. The final paragraph of the letter is as follows:

> You, the King, know yourself that no Russian ever gave you cause for dissatisfaction in regard to the treatment of the lowest of your islanders and that here your men are always accepted and treated benevolently and kindly. If Kaumualii does not satisfy our just demands, I shall be obliged to take measures myself in order to obtain just satisfaction and, with your permission, I shall treat him as an enemy.

Scheffer the naturalist arrived on the island of Hawaii in early November 1815. The former British seaman, John Young, as one of the chief advisers to Kamehameha, was immediately suspicious, sensing that Scheffer was something more than a scientist. Several Americans who had traveled aboard the *Isabella* felt the same way. It seems in keeping with the character of Scheffer that he could not bear to appear as only a humble naturalist to his fellow passengers during such a voyage. In December 1815 two Americans showed up, John Ebbets and Wilson Hunt. Scheffer and Hunt had met in Sitka, where they had a disagreement, and Hunt's tales added to Kamehameha's concern—and perhaps fears—of this stranger from the Russian colonies.

Then Scheffer's fortunes took a turn for the better. Both Kamehameha and Kaahumanu became ill. In a letter addressed to the Russian American Company in St. Petersburg, Scheffer declared he had "every confidence that I shall recover the valuable cargo, worth about 20,000 piastres. Already I have gained the friendship and confidence of the great King Kamehameha, whom I am treating for heart trouble. I also succeeded in curing his favorite wife, Queen Kaahumanu, of yellow fever." It was in keeping with Scheffer's ambition that the letter was addressed to the headquarters of the company, and so bypassed Baranov.

Georg Scheffer had indeed gained the confidence of the king. A house was ordered built for him in the midst of a breadfruit grove, and Kamehameha agreed to grant land on Oahu where the Russian American Company could establish a factory, or trading settlement. Several other substantial land grants were given him, also on Oahu, together with ten sheep and forty goats. For a brief period Scheffer seemed well along on his plan. He planted tobacco, taro, and several kinds of vegetables.

Although the king was very appreciative, even building a heiau in honor of physicians, he remained fearful because of the constant barrage of stories from John Young and the American traders concerning the real intentions and evil designs of the Russians. In his journal Scheffer wrote that whenever the king saw him he asked, "Will the Russians come to fight? Will they take the island?" No reply Scheffer could give was satisfactory. Kamehameha frequently changed his place of residence.

Scheffer had heard rumors that his life was in danger. His provisions had been cut. He sent a letter to Kamehameha, but received no reply. Becoming more concerned, Scheffer asked permission of the king to go to Oahu. At first the king refused, but at last consent came and the Russian-employed "naturalist" was undoubtedly glad to leave the island of Hawaii.

Before leaving Sitka, Georg Scheffer had understood that Governor Baranov would support his activities in Hawaii with two vessels. The first arrived none too soon. It was the *Otkrytie,* 300 tons, which had been built in Sitka. Its arrival in Honolulu Harbor in the spring of 1816 must have been a great relief to Scheffer; it might even have been his deliverance. One historian believed that the arrival of the *Otkrytie* saved Scheffer's life.

About eight days later, unexpectedly, another Russian ship, the *Ilmena,* struggled into Honolulu Harbor. The ship was in need of repairs and its appearance was a surprise. The *Ilmena* had been purchased from American owners and was under the command of an American captain, William Wadsworth, with a group of Aleuts aboard. After carrying on a brisk poaching business off the California coast, the ship had gotten into trouble with the Spanish authorities. The second promised vessel, the *Kadiak,* a poor, leaky ship arrived in June 1816. The *Ilmena* remained in Honolulu for emergency repairs while Scheffer sailed to Hawaii to get Kamehameha's assistance, or at least blessing, on their planned voyage to Kauai to regain the company's property. Kamehameha seemed perplexed, even frightened. He gave no help.

Sailing northwest, the *Otkrytie* set out for the leeward islands with

Scheffer aboard. The spark for Baranov's deciding to send Scheffer to Hawaii in the first place had been the behavior of Kaumualii in connection with the *Bering,* as reported by Captain James Bennett. It would have been in Scheffer's character to have felt a burning indignation against Kaumualii, an indignation more zealous because he was arriving at Kauai with armed force. Kaumualii, however, had been through many a difficult situation and—through a combination of bluffs, stubbornness, and charm—had survived. Realizing his circumstances, Kaumualii had already shipped some of the cargo of the *Bering* to Sitka, and had promised to ship off or compensate for the rest. In the end the cargo of sealskins brought a 200 percent profit for the investors. Scheffer had expected a hostile reception. Instead he met with a gracious ruler who conceded to his demands. Instead of cannon and musket fire, the two figuratively fell into each other's arms, and immediately each was wondering how the other could serve his purposes.

In the light of what took place, the instructions Alexander Baranov had given in Sitka to Lieutenant I. E. Podushkin, captain of the *Otkrytie,* were completely unnecessary. But as a matter of record it is interesting to note to what length Baranov was prepared to go to bring a final solution to the *Bering* affair. He wrote:

> At first, exhaust all methods which might achieve your ends peacefully. But if he [Kaumualii] fails to respond to peaceful negotiations, then it might be necessary to give him a lesson in the form of military chastisement. . . . Spare, however, as much as possible, human beings and blood, not only for your men, but of the enemies as well, if God will help you to defeat them. In such an event, the whole island Kauai should be taken in the name of our Sovereign Emperor of all the Russias.

Now Kaumualii became ill, as did one of his wives. Scheffer came to their aid and reported that he cured Kaumualii of dropsy and his wife of fever. The ruler was grateful, as had been Kamehameha earlier. Scheffer found conditions on Kauai much more pleasant than on the islands ruled by Kamehameha. Kaumualii, on the other hand, must have carefully appraised the situation. He must have noticed that no representatives of Kamehameha accompanied the Russians. Perhaps this was his opportunity to break his bonds. Kaumualii decided to take the risk.

Georg Scheffer was only too anxious to seize the opportunities he saw. He was the senior man who could make decisions. He would not have wanted to wait the six months it would take to communicate with Baranov and receive new instructions. Perhaps that sentence in his instructions came to mind, "I shall rely upon your good sense and ability not to miss any opportunity to advance the interests of the Company and the fatherland." In the next few days Scheffer became co-monarch of Kauai.

He accepted the allegiance of Kaumualii to the Emperor Alexander I, received what was left of the *Bering*'s cargo, was promised exclusive trade rights on Kauai, and obtained permission to establish factories, or trading posts, anywhere in the king's dominions. In return, Scheffer made the promise of Russian protection of Kauai and of a ship that would be the beginning of a navy for Kauai.

Elaborate compliments were paid, honors traded, and lavish gifts of land were bestowed on Scheffer. Kaumualii was appointed a Russian naval officer, with a silver medal pinned on his uniform. Scheffer accepted the feathered cloak of a Hawaiian chief on behalf of Alexander Baranov. In his journal Scheffer related his own outstanding diplomatic exploits. He had come into the kind of position of authority and honor that he felt was his destiny.

At this point it appears that Scheffer entered into something of a dream world. The ceremonies, the bestowing and receiving of gifts, and the dramatic role of commanding the respect of all about him became ends in themselves. Instead of basking in self-satisfied glory, Scheffer should have been consolidating his position on Kauai. Even Kamehameha might have left him alone. Kamehameha's protectors were the British and they were far away. The Russians, on the other hand, were a reality—in the Islands with guns and ships.

But Scheffer did not have enough. He knew of Kaumualii's hereditary claims to the islands of Oahu, Molokai, Lanai, and Maui. The co-monarchs of Kauai now plotted the conquering of these islands. On 1 July 1816, the two entered into a secret agreement. Expeditions against these islands would be under the complete control of Scheffer. Kaumualii offered Scheffer half of Oahu and all its sandalwood, as well as sections of land on the other islands. Kaumualii would put 500 men into the field and supply them and the Russians with food. Scheffer would supply ammunition and ships, and on every island build a fort that would be under the command of a Russian.

The midsummer treaty of 1816 marked the end of the rise of Georg Scheffer and the beginning of his swift decline. The Russians who were still on Oahu were ordered to begin the construction of a small fort or blockhouse near the shore at Honolulu Harbor. This proved to be a major mistake. At about this time the stalwart *Otkrytie* ran into a storm and sprang two masts. The ship's condition was so serious that Captain Podushkin returned to Sitka for immediate repairs, thus depriving Scheffer of his best ship.

On 12 September 1816 Scheffer began the construction of a substantial lava-rock fort commanding the bay at Waimea. On the same day he sent a ship to Honolulu to see how affairs were progressing there. Ten days later the vessel returned from Honolulu, bringing the men from the factory and a disheartening report. The Russians had apparently raised their flag over their blockhouse, evoking the wrath of John Young, who was backed by a number of Americans. When the people of Oahu saw the flag they informed Kamehameha, who sent a large force and drove the Russians out. Scheffer's warehouse was burned down in the process.

Scheffer was now confined to Kauai. Although he was unrealistic about the collapse taking place around him, he continued to be an industrious person as well as a conceited one. He accepted the suggestion of Kaumualii that Russian names be given to some of the places on Kauai. Scheffer renamed Hanalei Valley Scheferthal. The Hanapepe River became the Don. Several chiefs were given Russian names. When not involved in ceremonial activities Scheffer started a vineyard, grew melons, cotton, and tobacco, and planted a variety of other crops. The only one that did not thrive was wheat. Cotton, he thought, should be the chief product of the island.

The loss of the *Otkrytie* was a serious blow to Scheffer's plans. He decided to make up for this loss by purchasing two vessels owned by Americans, the *Lydia* and the *Avon*. Not being able to pay for them, Georg Scheffer grandly sent the captains off to Sitka with assurances that Governor Baranov would dispense the funds to them. Aboard the *Avon* was Baranov's son, Antipatr, and copies of the agreements with Kaumualii. Scheffer gave the *Lydia* to Kaumualii, and in return the ruler gave Scheffer the valley of Hanalei, together with its thirty families. This transaction took place in the presence of three American sea captains, who undoubtedly were provoked at the ambitious Scheffer but, even more important, were concerned about the possible interruption of trade.

By the end of November 1816 a good portion of the fort at Waimea had been completed. The portions overlooking the ocean and the

Waimea River were finished, and perhaps work had begun on the northern walls. The fort was roughly in the form of a star, a type of construction used in Russia since the seventeenth century. It was named Fort Elizabeth in honor of Emperor Alexander's consort. Fort Elizabeth was impressive. The base of the walls were some 17 feet wide, although they tapered as they rose upward, to 20 feet high in places. Within the fort was a strongly constructed magazine and armory, a barracks, officers' quarters, and, of course, the flagstaff where the Russian flag or the flag of the Russian American Company flew. The single entrance was to the north and here, outside the fort, was a trading house.

At least part of the northern side and the eastern side of the fort were completed after the departure of Scheffer from the Islands. They do not carry out the distinctive star-shaped design to the same degree as that portion built under the Russian American Company official. When the fort was dismantled in 1864 thirty-eight cannon were counted. In Scheffer's time the number was probably less. Scheffer also built two earthenwork forts, near or above the mouth of the Hanalei River. These he named Alexander, after the emperor, and Barclay, after a Russian general.

The situation was disintegrating, but Scheffer apparently did not recognize the series of small happenings that were leading to a sudden and disastrous end. In late September 1816, three American captains at Waimea attempted to haul down the Russian flag but were prevented by a guard placed at the fort by Kaumualii. The distillery at Scheffer-thal caught fire. Then William Wadsworth, the American captain of the *Ilmena,* was arrested at the end of December for speaking badly of the Russians. The only man who could possibly fill his position was the pilot of the vessel, and Scheffer did not like the fact that he too was an American. Through all these misadventures Georg Scheffer kept on with his planting. In the middle of December 1816 he noted in his journal that he had planted 400 grapevines in the garden of the factory at Waimea.

Early in December Scheffer learned that the Russian brig *Rurik,* under the command of Lieutenant Otto von Kotzebue, was at Honolulu. Scheffer had been looking forward to this visit for a long time. He believed he could now receive supplies and reinforcements, and anticipated the ship would arrive on Kauai any day. On the last day of 1816 Scheffer sent the *Ilmena* to Honolulu to deliver a letter to von Kotzebue.

In January 1817 word finally came from Alexander Baranov via the *Cossack*. The letter from Baranov has been lost, but knowing that he was a straightforward disciplinarian, his message would have made interesting reading. He had refused to pay for the *Avon*. He demanded that the *Kadiak* and the *Ilmena* and their crews be returned to Sitka, and that the capital entrusted to Scheffer likewise be returned. Georg Scheffer ignored the letter and instead put his hopes in the expected support of von Kotzebue.

That hope too was quickly dashed. On 7 February 1817, the *Ilmena* returned to Waimea to report that von Kotzebue had departed from the Islands without stopping at Kauai. Otto von Kotzebue had first stopped at the island of Hawaii, where Kamehameha told him about his fears of Scheffer and about the evil things he had done. Von Kotzebue assured the king that Scheffer was not acting on behalf of the emperor of Russia, who had no intentions of injuring or conquering the Islands. Kamehameha, elated by these words from a Russian naval officer, ordered the glasses to be filled and a toast was drunk to the health of the emperor of Russia. Sailing on to Honolulu, the Russian brig was the first ship to fire a salute to the fort the Hawaiians were building over the spot where Scheffer's blockhouse had once stood. It would have been better for Scheffer if von Kotzebue had not shown up at all.

Georg Scheffer spent some time at Hanalei and on 9 March returned to Waimea. He was received warmly, but noticed that the Russian flag was not raised, nor was the usual salute fired in his honor. He also noted that the king had taken more goods from the company warehouse than he should have.

The presence of Georg Scheffer in Hawaii called for a common front among the American traders, because if Scheffer had his way much sandalwood trade would be lost. American captains who came into the Pacific following the American Revolution and during and after the War of 1812 were mostly an aggressive and rapacious group. Nearly all of them were from New England—the term American was synonymous with Bostonian for many years. The memory of the American Revolution and the utter destruction of their merchant marine, followed by the War of 1812 and its disasters, had left New England seaports in desperate poverty. They battled every other nation for trade, and most of the time the American merchant houses battled each other as well. Only when the common good could be served was there a common front.

The Americans probably laughed at Scheffer's vaunted education, the importance he placed on titles, and his love of ceremony. The only thing they could have feared was the armed force he possessed and the possibility that he could call up even greater forces. When Baranov refused to pay for the two vessels Scheffer had bought, and when von Kotzebue disowned the entire adventure, the Americans had nothing to fear.

The Americans' disposal of Scheffer was effected by an ingenious scheme. They spread word on Kauai that there were serious disagreements between Russia and the United States, and that the Russian minister had left America. Scheffer would naturally have been concerned about such rumors. Then on 7 May 1817, while at Hanapepe, he heard that several ships had arrived at Waimea from Oahu. The next day Scheffer went to Waimea, where he found Kaumualii surrounded by 1,000 men and heard the news that Russia and the U.S. were at war. In response Scheffer demanded that his two vessels be loaded. As Scheffer turned to go, he was seized by a Kauaian and six American seamen and told that he and all Russians must leave the island. He was forced to retreat to the leaky ship *Kadiak* without gathering even his personal possessions.

Georg Scheffer remained aboard ship off Waimea for several days, hoping things would change. They did not. The change he did notice was that some mysterious flag was run up the flagpole where once the Russian flag had flown. At last he took the *Kadiak* and *Ilmena* around the island, to Hanalei. He had hoped to make a stand, but the hostility of the Kauaians, who had driven off his cattle and killed two Aleuts, and an order from Waimea to leave left him no choice. The *Ilmena* was sent to Sitka to bear the bad news, and the decrepit *Kadiak* headed for Honolulu with the remaining Russians and forty Aleuts aboard. It took five days to make the trip, with the pumps being manned twenty-four hours a day. The Russian flag was flown upside down as a distress signal, and on arrival off Honolulu a cannon was fired, to bring a pilot aboard. The ship was towed into the inner harbor. At Honolulu Scheffer learned that the story of a Russian-American war was a complete fabrication, designed to get him off Kauai.

Scheffer was not allowed to go ashore. He was told that he could surrender all his arms and that he and his men could go as prisoners to the island of Hawaii. This he refused. On 4 July 1817, the American vessels in the harbor and the Americans ashore held a great celebration in honor of Independence Day. To their annoyance and loud objections, Scheffer continued to run his Russian flag upside down. He was justified in doing so, because if the pumps had not been manned continuously the ship would have sunk in the harbor. The *Kadiak* was taking in two feet of water every hour.

Then good fortune came to the rescue of Georg Scheffer. Into the harbor sailed the *Panther* under Captain Isaiah Lewis. Again Scheffer's medical skills had saved him. A year earlier Lewis had been treated by Scheffer, and the captain now repaid the kindness, taking Scheffer aboard along with one Aleut and one Russian as traveling companions. The *Panther* stopped briefly at Waimea for supplies. Scheffer remained hidden in his cabin, unseen by the Kauaians and Americans who came aboard. The *Kadiak* was beached at Honolulu, and the others who had been aboard finally got passage home, paying their way by poaching off the coast of Southern California.

The rest is postscript. Georg Scheffer traveled to Macao where he stayed with the Swedish consul, Anders Ljungstedt, who later tried to convince the Russian government to annex Hawaii. From Macao Scheffer recrossed the Pacific, sailed to Rio de Janeiro and thence to Russia. He bombarded the Russian American Company directors and the government with memoranda, and they bombarded him with bills. Scheffer then sent bills of his own and more memoranda. By May 1819 the adventure was over. The loss to the company was about 230,000 rubles.

Georg Scheffer emigrated to Brazil and bought a title for himself, surely the fulfillment of a lifelong ambition. He became known as Count von Frankenthal, and his estate was called Frankenthal. He spent much time in Germany seeking colonists for his new home. He wrote a book about Brazil, and died there in 1836.

There were a few aftershocks following Scheffer's departure from the Islands. Anders Ljungstedt made an appeal and so did Peter Dobel, an Irishman who became a Russian citizen and a consul for the czar in China. Dobel visited Hawaii in 1819–1820, and after leaving the Islands he wrote to the Russian minister of foreign affairs about adding the Hawaiian Islands to the Russian Empire. No attention was paid to Dobel's appeal.

Liholiho, the son and heir of Kamehameha I, dictated a letter that Peter Dobel carried with him. It was addressed to the "Emperor of all Russians." Liholiho harkened back to something that could just as well have been forgotten by 25 March 1820, the date on the letter. Liholiho complained about the way the Russian American Company had behaved and then continued:

> The Company also claims to have bought the Island Atoovay [Kauai] from King Tomaree [Kaumualii]. They insist to obtain that island as well as payment for one ship and its cargo, which the Russians themselves wrecked on our coasts. But King Tomaree is our tributary and had no right whatsoever to sell that island. The claim for items sold and for the ship which the Russians themselves wrecked on our shores is equally wrong. . . .
>
> Not knowing French myself, I have asked our Secretary, a French man, Mr. Rives, to write this letter, which I ask your Imperial Majesty to accept as trustworthy as if I had written it myself.
>
> To prove the affection I have for your house, your glory, I have given to your consul general a double canoe made by the natives of my islands.

Some note was taken in American and foreign newspapers of Russian activities in the Hawaiian Islands. New England newspapers carried stories, probably as related to them by returning merchant-captains. The London *Morning Chronicle* for Wednesday, 30 July 1817, in turn printed news gleaned from American newspapers. The story reads:

> The American Papers of which we have received a mass at our Office, further the policy of Russia and its commercial speculations. One of these *The National Advocate* says: "The Russians, whom we have imagined to be a heavy and dull people, without spirit or Enterprise, are giving us daily proofs to the Contrary. They have taken possession of one of the Islands in the Pacific Ocean . . . and have already fortified themselves."

The Russians were gone from Kauai, but memories and some fears remained, as attested by Liholiho's letter. The Russian names on the land were quickly shaken off; the beauty of the name Hanalei replaced Schefferthal, and the Don was once again the Hanapepe River. The rock walls of the Waimea fort eventually fell, but the general shape remained. The earthenworks guarding the Hanalei River were leveled by wind and rain if not by human hands.

And what of that uneasy ruler, Kaumualii? By the standards of Kamehameha I he had rebelled and committed treason. He certainly deserved death for his offenses, but for the moment nothing happened to him. Perhaps Kamehameha was growing too old for revenge, or perhaps the powerful prayer, the Aneekapuahi, which belonged to Kaumualii's mother, was as feared as it had been in the past.

There were other little reminders of the Russians. By 1820 two Protestant missionaries had settled on Kauai. Mercy Whitney, wife of the Reverend Samuel Whitney, lived at Waimea. She loved her garden and was proud of the cuttings she had planted there, taken from the vineyards Scheffer had planted. They did very nicely until a gale blew, such as had driven the *Bering* ashore, and the winds swept salt spray onto the vines.

After Liholiho and his queen died in London, their bodies were returned to Honolulu aboard the British warship *Blonde.* In May 1825 a solemn funeral procession slowly marched through Honolulu, following the two velvet-covered coffins. Among those who marched that day was the botanist James Macrae, from the *Blonde.* In his journal he noted, "Thus we advanced between a line of native soldiers with rusty arms reversed, naked except for the maro [*malo*], save a few that had on Russian military jackets."

Some forty years later Sanford Dole, a growing boy on Kauai, played soldier with his friends. They marched and rode horses and carried Russian muskets. At the Bishop Museum in Honolulu there is a cannon that bears the Russian Imperial emblem and the date 1807.

The events of 1816–1817 should be known as the adventures of Georg Scheffer in Hawaii and not as the work of the Russian government. The Russian government was far away—it took about a year for news to reach St. Petersburg from Hawaii—and the various pronouncements Scheffer made in the name of the emperor were not sanctioned. Events in Hawaii had moved so fast the Russian government could not have effectively passed on instructions even if they had wanted to. The Russians were fully occupied with affairs in Europe and showed only a fleeting interest in Hawaii when Scheffer wrote of his successes. News of his failures closed the affair. After that the Russians only wanted a friendly relationship with the Islands.

The Russian American Company was more directly interested, and they would have welcomed an island or part of an island as a place to grow crops and raise animals. They also would have been pleased to profit from the sandalwood trade. Perhaps Alexander Baranov could have taken the Islands by force, but he could not have received permission from his government to do so. Baranov was no fool. His ill-supplied men had all they could do to keep the Indians from overrunning the company outposts in the Pacific Northwest.

So it was the ambitious Scheffer who was promoting a little empire for himself, hoping by bluff and chance to secure a place where he would rule and receive the honors he so ardently desired. Thanks to the wish of Kaumualii to regain independence, Scheffer's early luck was amazing, but such good fortune could not last and failure was inevitable.

The Kauai adventure of Dr. Georg Scheffer passed like a whirlwind. The physical evidence of its existence is in the remains of the fort at Waimea, and the happenings of those eighteen months stand as an interesting diversion in the history of Kauai and the Islands.

CHAPTER SIX

"I Die With Affection"

By the time the peak season of 1821–1822 had come it was clear what the sandalwood trade had done to Kauai and the other islands. The availability of sandalwood demonstrated the unprincipled greed of merchant-captains who bartered Western goods for wood collected by order of the chiefs. Chiefs, in turn, made unpardonable demands on commoners to collect wood, causing a breach of the age-old trust between the chiefs and their people. The situation continued into the 1830s, and worsened as commoners were ordered to search out the last trees in mountain gullies in an effort to pay for merchandise received by the chiefs years earlier on credit.

Kaumualii held the sandalwood monopoly on the leeward islands and Kamehameha held a monopoly on the windward islands. Kamehameha rigidly controlled the trade until his death in 1819, but his son, Liholiho, under pressure from the chiefs, allowed them to join in the trade. Tempted by the numerous goods enticingly displayed by New Englanders, the chiefs directed the commoners to cut sandalwood as payment. Unaccustomed to this type of labor, the commoners suffered severely. Many died from the cruelties they were forced to endure.

Sir George Simpson visited Hawaii in 1842, at a time when the last sandalwood trees were being hunted down in the recesses of the mountains. His observations and conclusions are direct. He considered the actions of Liholiho and the chiefs:

> That thoughtless and dissipated youth surrendered his father's monopoly to individual chiefs, who knew as little of wisdom as they did of mercy; to hard-hearted oligarchs, in whose eyes satins and velvets, china and plate, wines and sweetmeats, were infinitely more precious commodities than the lives of serfs. Under the new order of things, the men were driven like cattle to the hills, to every clef in the rocks that contained a sampling of the sacred fuel.

Once the chiefs had been tempted by the glittering array of Western goods, however, the welfare of the commoners was important only if it threatened to slow down the flow of sandalwood. After the desire for cloth, rum, and chinaware had been satisfied, other more luxurious items were displayed and sold for sandalwood. Pool tables, top hats, carriages, and dozens of other items were collected by the chiefs. Warehouses became glutted with merchandise, some of which was ruined by neglect, unprotected from the elements. Particularly in the early years, chiefs desired Western sailing ships and New England captains gladly obliged. Ships were often paid for by filling the hull of a vessel with sandalwood, once or twice, depending on the persuasiveness of the captain and the gullibility of the chief. Often ships bought by the chiefs had already begun to rot and their beached skeletons became a familiar sight.

Why were Yankee merchants willing to sail half a world from home, endure hardships at sea, and be extremely polite to a people they could not comprehend and considered to be inferior? The answer was profit. The wars with England had been disastrous to Yankee merchant-captains and there were few places they could trade. Under these conditions all opportunities for trade were ruthlessly pursued and sandalwood was among the best. Vessels sailed from New England around the tip of South America, and on the passage north put in at ports where incidental trade was possible. The important stops were at the Hawaiian Islands and then Canton, China.

John C. Colcord, who was active in the sandalwood trade, reported that goods from New England were marked up 300 to 400 percent in the Islands. Wood was measured by the picul, a unit of weight used in China, equivalent to 133⅓ pounds. The value placed on sandalwood in Hawaii ran between $10 and $15 a picul. In Canton the wood usually sold for only slightly more than what had been paid for it in Hawaii, but more important, sandalwood was one of the few things sought by Chinese merchants. In exchange for wood the merchants took tea, chinaware, silks, furniture, and other items back to New England, where once again a substantial profit was realized. If a merchant could trade a rotting vessel to the Hawaiians for additional sandalwood, his voyage would be a success. A very fortunate voyage meant a captain could retire for life.

Sandalwood was an easy cargo, with the ships' crews required to do very little physical work. The Hawaiians cut the trees, carried the logs from the uplands to the shore, and transported the wood to the ships by canoe. Crews could therefore devote their energies to repairing the vessel and securing supplies. It was an ideal situation for the traders.

Merchant-captains sometimes met with sales resistance from the Hawaiians. John C. Jones, Jr., American trader and consul in Hawaii, met such resistance from Kaumualii, and reported the affair to Marshall & Wildes of Boston, the company he represented. His dispatch sounds similar to a report any traveling salesman might make to his home office.

> I almost dispaired of doing any thing, knowing what I had to contend with. I delivered your letter to the King and offered him the Brig and Cargo he replied that he had bought another Brig and wanted no more; I treated him with every attention and honour, made him handsome presents and gave elegant dinners. After much trouble and difficulty I succeeded in selling the Brig and Cargo including the house for 7700 piculs and wood payable all in one year, the Boat he has given me an obligation to pay when she will be finished, per twice full.

The indiscriminate exploitation of sandalwood, a natural resource difficult to replenish, could not continue for long. The demand continued, but the supply quickly grew thin. Statistics on the subject are incomplete, but such as have been gathered indicate that during the season of 1804–1805 some 900 piculs of wood arrived in Canton on American vessels. Wood imports at Canton then rose continuously for about five seasons, eventually climbing to a peak of 19,036 piculs for 1812–1813. During the years of the War of 1812, trade fell off, but came back to nearly 16,000 piculs in 1817–1818. The all-time high was reached in 1821–1822, when 26,822 piculs were imported into Canton on American vessels. The season of 1828–1829 marked the last substantial year of the trade, when 18,206 piculs arrived in Canton on American ships. From that time on the trade gradually deteriorated and by 1835 had all but expired.

What of the life of the commoners who cut the wood and carried it to the shore? Samuel Kamakau reported that the men sent to fell the trees were often reduced to eating herbs and treeferns. The fields they normally farmed lay in neglect and thus there were times of severe famine, affecting the populations of entire islands. These famines were given the names of the wild plants the people were forced to eat during such times. Often it took these extreme conditions before chiefs would return the commoners to the cultivation of the land.

The Reverend Peter J. Gulick, an early missionary on Kauai, wrote in his journal in April 1830:

> Felt distressed and grieved for the people who collect sandalwood. They are often driven by hunger to eat wild and bitter herbs, moss, &c. And though the weather is so cold on the hills that my winter clothes will scarcely keep me comfortable, I frequently see men with no clothing except the maro [malo]. Were they not remarkably hardy, many of them would certainly perish.

What Gulick did not report was that many did die.

Waimea was practically the sole port of departure for sandalwood vessels stopping at Kauai, and the wood had to be carried there by human beings. The mountains behind Waimea yielded great quantities of wood, but it was a walk of many miles to the seaside village. In Wailua Valley, behind Lihue, and above Koloa there also was sandalwood, which had to be borne around the southern part of Kauai and deposited at Waimea. This was a longer walk, but it was over relatively level land, avoiding the downhill trek from the mountains behind Waimea.

Sandalwood was carried by tying a load of logs to a man's back with rope, which passed over the shoulders and under the arms. One authority said the maximum load was 135 pounds, the approximate weight of a picul. The constant weight on the rope caused calluses on the shoulders that remained to the day of death. The men became known as "callus backs." These human pack animals must have been weakened dreadfully, overcome by hunger, exhaustion, and a sense of futility.

Many visitors to Hawaii commented on aspects of the sandalwood trade, but they were mostly superficial tales of the newly rich chiefs and the profits and hardships of traders. Sir George Simpson looked deeper, to discover what was happening to the commoners, those of the callus backs.

> The procuring of this lucrative medium of exchange caused, in various ways, an enormous waste of life. As the sandal-wood grew chiefly on rugged and almost inaccessible heights, the natives, accustomed, as they were on the coasts, to a temperature approaching more nearly to perfection, both in degree and in steadiness, than perhaps any other in the world, were doomed to endure the chilly air of the mountains without shelter and without clothing, the cold of the night being aggravated by the toil of the

day; and, when they had accomplished their tasks with bodies enfeebled by these constant privations, and not uncommonly also by want of food, they were compelled to transport the whole on naked shoulders to the beach, by paths hardly practicable in many places to an unburdened passenger. As a matter of course, many of the poor wretches died in their harness, while many more of them prematurely sank under the corroding effects of exposure and exhaustion.

The labor of the commoners could not continue without some respite. There had to be some recreation and John Coffin Jones the merchant and American consul in Hawaii, reported with distress one such occasion which took place on Kauai in 1821, "they have not cut a single stick of wood they have done nothing but dance and amuse themselves; however they now seemed determined to make every exertion to pay all their debts."

Kaumualii was among the willing customers of the traders. On 23 June 1820 the king agreed to pay 191 piculs of sandalwood for "sundry merchandise sold the said King Tammorii [Kaumualii] this day." The document also included the sum of 315 piculs of wood still owed from the earlier purchase of the schooner *Bouchard*. The amounts were to be paid off one year later, and if payment were not made a penalty of $6,000 was to be imposed.

On 30 March 1821 Kaumualii bought the brig *Becket* from John Suter for 3,400 piculs of sandalwood. No mention is made in the document as to the date when payment was to be made. In May 1821 Kaumualii bought a brig and cargo, and the cargo of a second vessel. There is a certain desperation in Kaumualii's trading during 1820 and 1821. He went so deeply into debt, there seemed no hope of his ever paying what he owed. John Coffin Jones was concerned about the situation. On 5 October 1821 he wrote "Tomoree [Kaumualii] is fast growing old and I think is not long for this world, should he pop off I tremble for the consequence."

The deaths and the hardships endured during the sandalwood years were disastrous for the Hawaiians, and the resultant corrosion of trust in their chiefs left many confused. The abolition of the kapus in 1819 and the increasing pressure of foreign ways had raised doubts about the sanctity of all ancient values. For generations commoners had looked to their alii for aid and protection and had paid it back with loyalty and service. Now that trust, if not broken, was badly strained. The labor of the commoners had brought no rewards, only the miseries of the

mountains and the specter of famine. There was the realization that
their chiefs had used them badly.

Unfortunately, the sandalwood era did not die when wood became
scarce. So eager were the merchant-captains for the last penny of
profit, they extended credit to the chiefs against promises of future
payments in sandalwood. As the wood resources dwindled, debts
became delinquent and the merchants worried. The American flag, in
the form of two warships, appeared in 1826 to support the men of
commerce. Kamehameha III and the chiefs, faced with this show of
force, acknowledged the debts and hence they became government
obligations. This was the beginning of the national debt of Hawaii. A
tax was imposed on the people and they had to go into the mountains
and find such wood as they could. For the first time the commoners,
as an incentive, were granted the right to cut a portion of wood for
themselves. Each woman also had to pay one Spanish dollar or provide
something of equal value to help erase the debt. Not until 1843 would
all the obligations be cleared.

On 21 July 1821 Liholiho set forth on a voyage from Honolulu to
Waialua, Oahu, where the young successor of Kamehameha I had
gone earlier in the month to inspect the gathering of sandalwood. He
sailed in a small open vessel with several chiefs and about thirty servants. But the little vessel never reached Waialua, because Liholiho
ordered a change of course, into the Kauai channel. The order to sail
to Kauai could hardly have been a decision of the moment.

The others in the open craft protested, saying they were not prepared to sail across the rough sixty-mile channel in a boat overcrowded
with people and with virtually no supplies. Liholiho demanded they
continue. Those on board continued to plead. If they did not drown in
the channel, Kaumualii might prove hostile and they would be at his
mercy.

Liholiho ignored the pleas of his fellow passengers. Although the
wind was in their favor, it was certain they would be on the rough sea
all night. Waves broke over the gunwales. They had no compass. The
king spread out the thumb and fingers of one hand, and pointing them
in the general direction of where they should sail, he is reported to
have said, "There is your compass—head her by this point!" touching
the finger he thought to indicate the best direction.

The retinue of Liholiho still begged him to return. Twice the boat
nearly swamped, but the king persisted. He ordered them to bail the

water from the boat with wooden calabashes and gourds. If they would not continue, he announced, he would jump overboard and swim to Kauai. Waves continued to break over the vessel and then, just before darkness closed off the horizon, they saw the outline of Kauai and altered their course accordingly. The next morning, before daybreak, they landed on Kauai.

Kaumualii hastened to meet Liholiho and greeted the unexpected guest with kindness. He set aside the best houses for him and his party at Waimea. Soon the all-important subject of the sovereignty of Kauai came up, and Kaumualii spoke first.

> King Liholiho, hear!—while your father Kamehameha, lived, I acknowledged him to be my king. He is now dead: you are his rightful successor, and you are my king! I have abundance of muskets and ammunition, and many subjects at my command; these with the vessels I have bought, with my fort and its guns, and with my islands, are yours. All are yours. Do with them as you please; and make what chief you choose governor here!

In a few moments Liholiho replied, "Kaumualii, I have not come to take from you your island. I wish not to place any one over it: keep it yourself; take care of it as you have done; and do with the vessels and all your possessions as you please!" A shout of approval went up from the people surrounding the two and Kaumualii reportedly left the meeting content. One historian states that "After this scene, Liholiho indulged a debauch. . . ."

As soon as Liholiho had arrived on Kauai, Kaumualii sent a brig and a schooner to Honolulu to inform them the king was safe at Waimea and others could join him there. On 23 July a single canoe arrived from Oahu with five persons, and later the luxurious yacht *Pride of Hawaii* arrived, bringing the five wives of Liholiho. The two kings and the principal chiefs started on a tour around the island to inspect the countryside and enjoy the fruits of the land. The trip lasted forty-two days.

On Sunday, 16 September 1821, Liholiho and Kaumualii each went sailing on their respective brigs, coming to anchor again at Waimea in the evening. Liholiho invited Kaumualii aboard the *Pride of Hawaii*. At about 9:00 P.M. orders were secretly given to raise anchor and up sails and the vessel departed for Oahu. No reason or notice had been given for the unexpected leaving and the next morning the people of the village were greatly confused and troubled by the event. The Reverend

Hiram Bingham, who was at Waimea at the time, wrote that, "Haupu, the head man at Waimea, expressing the feeling of many, exclaimed in his sorrow, 'Farewell to our King—we shall see him no more'."

In this bold move Kaumualii had been kidnapped and made a prisoner of state. The guardianship of Kauai was entrusted to Kahekili Keeaumoku, a brother of Kaahumanu. Kaumualii had been the best friend the missionaries had. His condition called forth their sympathy, but there was little they could do except offer consolation. To those who asked, the dejected Kauai king bravely said that he had come to Oahu to return the visit of Liholiho.

While Liholiho was the perpetrator of the kidnapping it seems obvious that he acted according to the wishes—if not the orders—of Kaahumanu. This daring action might have been triggered by the reception given the American missionaries by Kaumualii, who pleaded with them to stay on Kauai. Kaahumanu and Liholiho, on the other hand, had debated whether the missionaries should be allowed to stay at all, and then granted them permission to remain for only a year. Perhaps Liholiho and Kaahumanu remembered that time, several years earlier, when Kaumualii had allied himself with the Russians, and perhaps they feared that Kaumualii would form an alliance with the American missionaries with the United States looming in the background. The train of thought would have been encouraged by John Young, the former British citizen, who was anxious to keep American influence at a minimum.

Kaumualii had yet another and perhaps greater surprise in store for him. On 9 October 1821, four days after landing at Waianae on Oahu, he became the husband of the imperious Kaahumanu, the widow and favorite queen of Kamehameha I. A short time later Kaahumanu, apparently in an effort to make the bond between the windward islands and the leeward islands secure, made Kealiiahonui, Kaumualii's son by his royal wife, her husband as well. James Jarves wrote some twenty years after the event that Kaahumanu was "thus holding father and son in her chains . . . [which] were not altogether silken."

The captive king of Kauai was handsome, rather tall, and compared with most of the alii, slender. One observer described him as having a "noble Roman face" and although he walked slightly stoop-shouldered, he gave the impression of great nobility. In Honolulu he appeared in a black velvet coat and pantaloons, a woolen waistcoat, and white silk stockings, and carried a gold watch. His appearance was in sharp contrast to Liholiho, who wore the customary Hawaiian *malo.* It is little wonder that Kaahumanu enjoyed showing off her newest trophy as she traveled about the Islands. Courteous and dignified in manner, Kaumualii added quality and prestige to Kaahumanu's entourage.

Many women have played leading roles in the affairs of the Hawaiian Islands, but none have matched Kaahumanu's decisiveness or the degree of power she wielded. Since she played a large role in the affairs of Kauai, it is helpful to note some of the events that brought her to power. Kaahumanu was born in a cave on the ocean side of a cinder cone in Hana, on the island of Maui, in about 1777. Her parents were alii, but not of the highest rank. Her father was Keeaumoku, the most trusted of Kamehameha's warrior-chiefs. Her mother was a half-sister of a onetime king of Maui.

Kaahumanu became a wife of Kamehameha when she was approximately fourteen years old. In 1793 she visited George Vancouver aboard his flagship and the captain described her as "being one of the finest women we had yet seen on any of the islands." Kaahumanu and Kamehameha were both persons of extremely strong will, and because of this they came into conflict. Vancouver acted as peacemaker after one disagreement. At another time Kaahumanu fled to the city of refuge on the Kona coast of Hawaii so she would be protected from Kamehameha. On yet another occasion, deciding to leave him, Kaahumanu reputedly made her way to Kauai alone.

While Kaahumanu remained the favorite wife of Kamehameha, she was not his royal wife because her lineage was not sufficiently high. It might be remembered that when Kaahumanu's father, Keeaumoku, was dying in 1804 he warned the king that the person he must fear as rising against him and taking his kingdom was Keeaumoku's own daughter. Thereafter Kamehameha placed a kapu on the person of Kaahumanu, and when this kapu had been broken by a relative of the king, the young violator was sacrificed.

Upon the death of Kamehameha, Kaahumanu saw her opportunity and seized it. Liholiho had been named successor to his father, but Kaahumanu named herself regent and it was soon obvious she was the real power in the kingdom. She is reportedly the one who pushed the new king to abolish the kapu system. If Kaahumanu was excessively zealous in grasping power, she did hold the restless chiefs under control during a time of considerable unrest. Liholiho, too often inebriated, probably could not have done so.

In December 1821 Kaahumanu fell seriously ill. On one occasion she was not expected to live through the day. Two physicians from a Russian exploring expedition then in Honolulu Harbor attended her, as did the missionaries. The result of the close brush with death apparently caused her to view the missionaries with some degree of kindness.

In 1822 Kaahumanu toured the Islands, showing off her two husbands, Kaumualii and Kealiiahonui. In company with her were chiefs and about 1,000 servants. The following year the regent gave a great feast in commemoration of the death of Kamehameha I. It was a notable occasion. The royal wife of Liholiho was borne aloft in a whaleboat, lined with broadcloth and kapa and carried by seventy men with spears firmly fastened to a platform beneath it. Kaumualii must certainly have been there with Kaahumanu, then long past the days of her early beauty and described by a missionary wife as an "amazon." The regent was of immense bulk and on this occasion enlarged it further by being wrapped in seventy-two yards of scarlet and orange double kerseymere. When the material had been wrapped about her it extended out so far that it supported her arms.

Kaahumanu became converted to Christianity, probably in 1824, and the following year was formally admitted to the church. It was the turning point for the missionaries. The regent's acceptance of the new faith made it almost a state religion and thousands followed her example. She was now called the "new" Kaahumanu, and while most would not have wanted to test her, she was probably less arrogant, although her rule was no less firm. After her conversion Kaahumanu retained only Kaumualii as her husband, releasing Kealiiahonui from the earlier forced marriage.

The regent spent much time establishing Christianity in the Islands. She traveled and exhorted the people to go to church and to learn to read and write. Through her influence three missionaries were sent to other Pacific islands to begin work. She put a kapu on the distilling of rum, and played the leading role in establishing a set of laws for the kingdom. In 1832 Kaahumanu became ill and went to her home in Manoa Valley. Here she was attended by her doctor and the numerous persons who waited on her. She grew weaker by the day and just before she died on 5 June, the Reverend Hiram Bingham arrived with a morocco-bound copy of the New Testament in Hawaiian, which he had rushed through the press. Kaahumanu feebly checked to see if all the books were included and, clutching the volume to her breast, died.

By 1823 Kaahumanu no longer had to share the rule of the kingdom. On 27 November of that year Liholiho, his favorite wife, and a small party of chiefs and servants left the Hawaiian Islands for a trip to England. The trip had long been a desire of Liholiho, and with the death of his royal mother the way seemed clear. The king probably was eager to leave behind the demands of his kingdom, the reprimands of the missionaries, and the strong will of Kaahumanu. The delegation arrived in England about the middle of May 1824.

Kaumualii could hardly have been cheered by the thought of spending the rest of his life with Kaahumanu. We know little of their few years together. One scene was recorded in the journal of the missionary Levi Chamberlain. In Honolulu in March 1824, it was the Sabbath and the

> . . . weekly service . . . was well attended this afternoon. Kaahumanu rode up in great stile [*sic*] in a carriage brought out by Capt. Wildes. The coach was drawn by 10 or a dozen natives by means of a long rope fastened to the tongue of the carriage. She was posted on the driver's seat, Keariiahonui [Kealiiahonui] occupied the place of the footman behind and Taumuraii [Kaumualii] thus royally attended occupied the interior alone. This is the first vehicle of the kind which has moved on the Sandwich Islands.

During the second week of May 1824 Kaumualii fell ill. It was not thought serious at the beginning. His condition worsened, and on 22 May he was carried on a sofa through a crowd of wailing Hawaiians to the newly completed home of Kaahumanu, near the ocean in Honolulu. Kaumualii had become frail, but according to the Reverend Charles S. Stewart, who visited him daily, no one thought he would succumb to the illness. On Monday 24 May he made his will, leaving his possessions to Kaahumanu and to Kalanimoku to act as custodian for the absent Liholiho. They were instructed to pay his debts, most of which were owed to merchant-captains.

Tuesday, at about noon, Kaumualii became unconscious. Early Wednesday morning, 26 May 1824, the Reverend William Ellis and the Reverend Stewart were called for. They rushed to the bedside of

Kaumualii and offered prayers. Kaumualii seemed to have improved a little and Ellis left. A few moments later Kaumualii, without a struggle, breathed his last. Stewart recorded "I had the melancholy satisfaction of smoothing his features, after the hand of death had passed across them."

Kaahumanu ordered the door fastened and the curtains drawn when it was evident that death was imminent. After Kaumualii had died Kaahumanu prepared the body for exhibition to the people. A mantle of green silk, lined with pink satin, was spread on a settee. The body was placed on this, the lower portion wrapped in heavy folds of yellow satin. The chest was bare and on his head was placed a wreath of feathers, which covered his eyes. On the back of the settee, by the head of Kaumualii, was spread his war cloak made of red, yellow, and black feathers. Above his feet was draped a large feather cape of the same colors. By now a growing crowd of people had gathered about the house, sensing the worst, and when the curtains were drawn up so the body could be seen, according to the Reverend Stewart, "an indescribable scene of wailing ensued."

For burial the corpse was clothed in the full dress uniform of a British hussar. On Friday morning, 28 May, funeral services were held in front of Kaahumanu's house. The casket, covered with black velvet, was carried from the house and surrounded by chiefs dressed in mourning. Kaahumanu and Kealiiahonui sat behind the head of the casket. The second floor verandah was filled with foreign residents and missionary families. The Reverend Ellis preached from the words "Be ye also ready." The services were concluded with the singing of a Hawaiian translation of Alexander Pope's "Dying Christian."

Some time earlier Kaumualii had become a fast friend of Keopuolani, the royal wife of Kamehameha I. She was of the highest lineage in the Islands and had been converted to Christianity. Keopuolani had died in 1823 and was buried at Lahaina on Maui. Before she died it was agreed that Kaumualii should be buried next to her, as Ellis explained, "that they might rise together in the morning of the resurrection." Immediately after Kaumualii's service was completed the casket was put aboard a pilot boat, which sailed for Lahaina. The body of Kaumualii, after a second service, was placed next to that of Keopuolani on Sunday, 30 May 1824.

The praise of Kaumualii flowed freely after his death. There appear to have been no dissenters to this praise; indeed, praise of Kaumualii had been generous since before he became king of Kauai. The Reverend Charles Stewart wrote, "My mind had been strongly prepossessed in favor of Kaumualii, king of Kauai, before I left America." Later Stewart continued his praise, "and I can, with the strictest veracity, say of him that which I can hardly do of any other in the nation, that I have never heard from him a word, nor witnessed in him a look or action, unbecoming a prince."

James Jarves wrote, "He was remarkable for his personal beauty and dignified and gentlemanly manners." The Reverend Hiram Bingham, a man who expected high standards, wrote that "he was sedate, dignified, courteous in his manners, honorable in his dealings, respected by foreigners, highly esteemed by the missionaries, and beloved by his people." Samuel Kamakau reported,

> Kaumualii was a handsome man, light in complexion and with a nose and general features like a white man's. He was rather slight in build, but he had a good carriage and dressed well. He was gentle of temper, spoke English well, was kind and simple in his ways. It would be well for the nation if there were more chiefs like him.

A glowing account of Kaumualii had been written by John Turnbull, a part-owner of the *Margaret,* which visited Kauai in about 1803. Turnbull wished that George Vancouver had not been such a strong supporter of Kamehameha because he believed that Kaumualii, "bears a character infinitely superior . . . to that of his more powerful rival Tamahama." Turnbull continued on Kaumualii, "He appeared to be loved almost to adoration, and his authority from influence seemed to be increased almost in the same proportion as his actual power had become diminished."

Subjects of Kaumualii on Kauai had heard of the serious illness of their king and some had rushed to Honolulu, but they arrived only in time to witness the funeral. The Kauaians knew he would not return to rule them after he had been stolen away by Liholiho, but knowing that he was alive had kept his islands in a state of order.

Hiram Bingham happened to be on Kauai when the news came of the worsening condition of Kaumualii. Bingham was at Hanalei where a large group of Kauaians had gathered. Liholiho's beautiful brig, the *Pride of Hawaii,* had gone ashore in the bay. It was, according to Bingham, "through the mismanagement of a drinking captain and crew." The *Pride of Hawaii* had been launched in October 1816 at

Salem, Massachusetts, and was christened *Cleopatra's Barge.* The vessel was 83 feet long at the waterline and boasted a main cabin 19 by 20 feet. Paneling was mahogany inlaid with bird's-eye maple and other woods. There were five staterooms and the forecastle had accommodations for ten men and three boys. Built for the wealthy merchant-captain George Crowninshield, it was such a floating wonder that thousands of people lined up to go aboard and view the vessel during its stay in the United States and during a voyage to Europe and through the Mediterranean.

A year later it was laid up in Salem for repairs before beginning another voyage, when Captain Crowninshield suddenly died. The yacht was sold at auction and resold before setting out for Hawaii. Liholiho inspected the ship and bought it for $90,000, to be paid in sandalwood over a two-year period—a sale that would have warmed the heart of merchant-captain Crowninshield. The selling price was $40,000 more than it had cost to build the vessel.

Now the graceful ship was fast aground and Kauaians gathered in great numbers to attempt to haul the brig ashore so it could be fully salvaged. The islanders collected the bark from hibiscus or hau trees and bushes and wove it into several thousand yards of strong rope. Twelve strands of this rope were intertwined to make one very sturdy line, and three such lines were then fastened to the mainmast of the *Pride of Hawaii.* An old chief, Kiaimakani or "Wind-Watcher," ordered the great number of men to take up the ropes—Bingham called them cables—and remain silent. Hiram Bingham reported on what happened.

> Kiaimakani passed up and down through the different ranks, and from place to place, repeatedly sung out with prolonged notes, and trumpet tongue . . . "be quiet—shut up the voice." To which the people responded . . . "say nothing," as a continuance of the prohibition to which they were ready to assent when they should come to the tug. Between the trumpet notes, the old chieftain, with the natural tones and inflections, instructed them to grasp the ropes firmly, rise together at the signal, and leaning inland, to look and draw straight forward, without looking backwards towards the vessel. They being thus marshalled and instructed, remained quiet for some minutes, upon their hams.

A chanter then encouraged the people with an ancient song, beginning with an address to Lono, which had been used when a tree was drawn from the mountains to the shore. Bingham, however, could bring himself to quote only a small portion of the song, as most of it was of a "gross heathen state, and is unfit to appear in an English dress." At a signal in the song the people rose, and at a given line they began to strain on the ropes. The brig rolled upright on her keel, but a side of the ship came firmly up against underwater rocks. The mainmast snapped, and the *Pride of Hawaii* settled back to her original position. The brig was irretrievably lost.

At about this time news came to Hanalei that Kaumualii was seriously ill. The Kauaians disappeared, some to their homes to await developments and some to hasten to Honolulu to be with their king. Shortly the news was received that Kaumualii was dead. No individual was recognized as the rightful successor to the late king, and some chiefs began to seek alliances with the hope of gaining supremacy. The commoners as well as the chiefs gave way to the ancient, often violent, expressions of grief. Bingham wrote, "they believed it would be no great departure from Hawaiian customs if the wildest ebullition of the vilest passions should burst forth around them in the forms of drunkenness, prostitution, revenge, and bloodshed, as on the death of former kings."

When Deborah Kapule, the favorite wife of Kaumualii, returned to Waimea after attending funeral services for the king, she was met by a great throng of people. The people saluted her, joined noses, and mingled their tears with hers. The press of wailing people became so great that she was borne above the masses to safety. Mourning for the late king began anew. The Reverend Bingham stated that Kaumualii had exerted lordship over his people, but he was also considered a friend and benefactor, as witnessed by the reaction of one Kauaian:

One of his old stewards, . . . put on the rudest mourning, and said, partly in imperfect English, and partly in Hawaiian, "I feel very bad. Make loa i ke aloha. King Kaumualii, he have but one heart, and that was a good one. Some chiefs have two hearts—one good and one bad." The Hawaiian phrase, by which he described his sorrow, is so forcible as to make his English very tame. "I feel very bad: I have got no eat to-day," with all his mournful looks, and tones of grief, were but feeble expressions compared with his native phrase—"Make loa i ke aloha—I die with affection."

The turmoil on Kauai did not subside. The first appointed governor, Keeaumoku, died in March 1824 and was replaced by Kahalaia, a nephew of Kalanimoku. There appears to have been no attempt to put

the Kauaians at rest as to their future condition, particularly regarding
the distribution of land. If this had been done following the death of
Kaumualii, later troubles might have been avoided. But time brought
additional doubts and gave the worried and the ambitious the opportunity to fret and to plot. The windward chiefs were following their
age-old habit. They gave no explanations, but simply imposed their
will.

The Reverend Bingham was still on Kauai in June 1824, and if the
windward rulers would have listened he could have given them an idea
of the unrest beneath the surface. Bingham announced to the Kauaians
that there would be an eclipse of the sun on 26 June at 12:57 P.M. The
Hawaiians considered an eclipse as foreboding an evil event, and
pressed Bingham to tell what was in store for them, as their astrolo-
gers had done in the past. When the clergyman said it meant nothing,
that it simply happened at certain times, his explanation was not considered satisfactory. "The gloom of the moon's shadow on the island
corresponded with the political gloom that then hung over Kauai,"
Bingham wrote. Some Kauaians most feared the windward chiefs,
while others feared fellow Kauaians, since the island was now divided
between those who wished to be loyal to Liholiho and those who
wanted to maintain at least the independence they had in the days of
Kaumualii, and possibly even more.

Prince George P. Kaumualii, a son of the late king, was to become
the focal point, if not the leader in the ensuing events. George, often
known as Humehume, had seen a good deal of the world. Sent away
to school in New England at an early age, the money that had been
entrusted for his education was either poorly invested, insufficient, or
stolen. After a period of schooling, George worked for a carpenter and
then for a farmer, enlisted in the U.S. Navy, and then was employed at
the Boston Navy Yard. Stories of his high adventures were repeated
over the years, but many of these tales were fabrications. Later he
became a student at the Foreign Mission School at Cornwall, Connecticut, but he did not show much evidence of being truly converted.
Anxious to return to Kauai, George left New England with the first
missionary company in 1819. During the long voyage home, George
seems best remembered for his ability to play the bass viol and sing.

The return of George in 1820 brought a great outpouring of happiness from his father and was a major reason for the speedy acceptance
of the missionaries on Kauai. Although he had been treated as a prodigal son returned, George did not remain long in the favor of his father

or the Kauaians. He was indolent and drank to excess. On one occasion he burned down a building in Waimea because a merchant there would not supply him with a bottle of gin. Kaumualii paid for the damages in sandalwood. Soon his father wanted nothing to do with him, and George settled in Wahiawa, about eight miles southeast of Waimea. He lived with his wife, a daughter of Isaac Davis, the man who probably saved Kaumualii's life when the king visited Kamehameha in Honolulu.

After the death of Kaumualii, Bingham went to Wahiawa to advise George against the foolishness of any brash actions against the windward chiefs. He found the son of the late king living in squalor, surrounded by some one-hundred commoners and two or three white men, all settled in one small valley. George was a bitter man. He wanted to resist the ruling powers and take revenge on those who had wronged him. He claimed that Kaumualii had been poisoned and that when he, George, had eaten with Kaahumanu she had given him the same sickness, apparently a form of diarrhea. After talking for two hours Bingham left, "with some fears that he would wholly throw himself away."

The missionaries and many Kauaians were beginning to feel uneasy as they sensed the mounting tension about them. This was somewhat lessened when Kalanimoku arrived off Waimea on 1 August 1824, to look after affairs on the island. George apparently was ready to go forth and greet Kalanimoku, but several rebellious chiefs advised against it. Instead, Deborah Kapule went out to his vessel in her double-hulled canoe and carried the visitor to shore. At a meeting of the chiefs later in the same week, Kalanimoku repeated that the island was under the rule of Liholiho and Kaahumanu and that lands would remain in the hands of those who had possessed them before. Those chiefs who wanted more lands were most displeased. Kiaimakani, the "Wind-Watcher" who had chanted at Hanalei, objected, saying that the land should be thrown together and divided anew. He was sharply reprimanded for his views.

Before dawn on the morning of 8 August the noise of battle was heard from the old Russian fort. The Kauai rebels had joined in a surprise attack on the garrison of the fort. The Reverend Bingham and his family were visiting at Waimea at the time, and the house they were staying in was dangerously close to the action. Bingham wrote that insurgents passed and repassed the door of their dwelling and rifle and musket balls whistled over the roof. They had no escape and looked to the Lord for their defense. Bingham recorded the continuing events:

> Some of the insurgents entering the fort, and hoping for a rush of the neighboring inhabitants to ensure the victory over the garrison, one of them stood on the walls and called aloud to the two divisions of the valley on either side of the river, "Ho Waimea!—Ho Makaweli!—come on—the Hawaiians are beaten—the Kauaians have the fort!" Some of both parties rushed to enter, amid balls and bayonets.

The battle lasted about thirty minutes. Kalanimoku rushed to the scene. He was aware of the danger to the missionary families and called for Bingham and Whitney. Kalanimoku could spare no troops to guard the missionaries, but he did put a kapu on their house. Neither side, however, had any wish to intentionally harm them, and the two clergymen went into the fort to administer to the wounded and bury the dead. Ten rebels had been killed, including one of the leading chiefs. Six of the defenders of the fort were killed, including two Englishmen. George and his followers retreated southeast to Hanapepe Valley.

A few hours after the battle had ceased, a contingent of armed Kauai men and women marched into the fort. They had come to help Kalanimoku. Among the women was Kekauluohi, a widow of Kamehameha and later, a wife of Liholiho. Eventually she became regent of the kingdom. Deborah Kapule came too. The former carried a heavy pistol, and the latter a drawn sword.

Kalanimoku was anxious to get word of the rebellion to Oahu so that reinforcements could come to his rescue as quickly as possible. The next morning his small schooner sailed from Waimea, with the missionaries and their families aboard. Also aboard was a chief who had once lived in the windward islands, but had become a Kauai resident. Some sources say he was a leader of the insurgents, and one reporter wrote that he had come to pay his respects to Kalanimoku and was seized. The chief was put in the hold. The following morning Bingham went to speak with him, but he had disappeared. During the night he had been brought on deck, stabbed, and thrown overboard. The captain said he had orders not to land the prisoner. Jarves wrote that a number of others were treated in the same way.

The Reverend Stewart was in Honolulu and reported the arrival of Kalanimoku's schooner. The vessel anchored outside the reef and soon the news spread through the village. "It is War! It is War!" was repeated through the streets. Forces were immediately marshaled. A thousand troops were to embark for the relief of Kalanimoku at sunrise the next morning. Many of those rushing to Kauai did so because of concern, but Bingham feared that in others, revenge was the major motive, and in still others, avarice. Kalanimoku's vessel hurried on to Lahaina, Maui, where Kaahumanu had remained since Kaumualii's interment. Lahaina was gripped in the same frenzy as Honolulu when the news of the rebellion was shouted through the village. Shortly two schooners, each with a company of soldiers, set sail for Kauai. Kaahumanu thought that Kaumualii had been the source of the problem because he had not taken sufficient measures to bring to submission his son George and the chiefs.

George and his followers remained in the area of Hanapepe and Wahiawa. Any small prospect of throwing the windward intruders off the island vanished as the insurgents sat and waited instead of following up with another attack against the weak garrison at the fort. If the fort had fallen into their hands they would have secured supplies of muskets, ammunition, and about twenty cannons. The Kauaians had little military expertise and few firearms. Once reinforcements had arrived, the rebels should have disbanded and gone home. Many lives would have been saved.

On 20 August 1824 a force under Governor Hoapili of Maui, an experienced warrior who had been a counselor of Kamehameha, set out from Waimea toward Hanapepe and Wahiawa. The insurgents held a position overlooking Hanapepe Valley. Hoapili studied the stars and announced to his troops that if the enemy won the coming battle, they would also overcome all the Islands and there would be no place for the soldiers to go for safety. Such a statement could hardly have been taken seriously by any knowledgeable person, but perhaps it did put more determination into his troops. The following day they ascended the heights on the east side of Hanapepe Valley. The troops were drawn up in battle order. Silence was ordered and a prayer offered.

The soldiers were arrayed in a great semicircle, the right and left flanks advancing in the lead. The idea was to encircle the insurgents and capture as many as possible. George's men were behind a rock wall and had a single, small, brass field piece. This was discharged three times. The rebels thought it was doing the desired damage, but actually the advancing troops fell to the ground at each discharge and rose to advance again. The government troops then opened fire and George and his men could not withstand its intensity. The rebels carried spears and digging sticks, with only a small number armed with muskets. They broke and ran for the woods. Some were captured and others killed. Bingham reported that forty or fifty were slain. James Jarves stated in his history, "In the action and pursuit one hundred and thirty were slaughtered, and the loyalists but one fell."

George, his wife Betty, and their infant daughter fled on horseback to the mountains. Betty and the child were soon captured. Kaahumanu, in a flash of her "old" self, renamed the daughter Wahine-kipa, "rebel woman." Several weeks later George was captured in the mountains. He was in miserable condition, suffering from the cold and wetness. He was also drunk, believing he would be sacrificed when caught and hoping to ease the pain. He and his family were shipped to Oahu where they could not create problems. George died in 1826 at about the age of twenty-nine.

Both Stewart and Bingham wrote about the greater humanity shown at Hanapepe-Wahiawa compared with the gruesome slaughters that had been common in pre-Christian times. Stewart commented, "The principles of Christianity have been most happily exhibited by Karaimoku [Kalanimoku] and his chiefs in the prosecution of the war: it has been conducted with as little as possible of the former sanguinary spirit of their conflicts." Bingham, who had left Kauai before the battle took place, was not willing to put it so strongly. After reading a report, Bingham thought the engagement "showed some advancement from the late barbarism of the country."

Samuel Kamakau did not agree with Stewart or Bingham about the tempering effect of Christianity. Kamakau wrote that the chief Hoapili had declared the kapu called *kānāwai* to save lives once the battle at Hanapepe-Wahiawa had been decided. Certainly no warrior would have broken such a kapu if it were known, since it would result in his own death. A charitable view would be to assume that the army units were so widely scattered that word of the kapu did not catch up with some units until days later. Another possibility is that Hoapili did not order the kapu until much unnecessary slaughter had taken place. It also appears certain that Kahalaia was the actual battle leader, while Hoapili probably was at the rear. Kahalaia was later given credit for the victory. He was also known for his cruelty and was soon removed from the governorship of Kauai.

Kamakau is the most specific of the historians concerning the battle of Hanapepe-Wahiawa:

Among the non-combatants even women were cut down, and little children killed. . . . Those were indeed bloody days. Even four years after the coming of the word of God this thing happened on Kauai while George Humehume, one of the sons of Ka-umu-alii who had come with the missionaries to Kauai, was living with Mr. Bingham at Mr. Whitney's on Kauai. A fight took place in the back country during which few of the fighting men were killed, but many, even women and children, were shot or thrust through with bayonets indiscriminately. This fight was called the "Pig eating" (Aipua'a) because the dead were left lying for the wild hogs to devour.

The barbarity of the troops imported into Kauai was confirmed by the observations of Samuel Whitney who, together with Bingham and their families, had been given passage to Honolulu the morning after the attack on the fort. After seeing his family safely settled, Whitney headed back to Kauai. The vessel passed Wahiawa and Hanapepe, where Whitney saw armed men running about. On arriving at Waimea he learned a battle had been fought that morning and the insurgents soundly defeated.

Samuel Whitney traveled to the scene of the battle on 23 August. It was just three days since the fighting had taken place and Whitney was sickened by what he saw. Undoubtedly he would have liked to have been able to report that this had been a humane war compared with the past, but the facts were in front of him. The home of Samuel Ruggles in Hanapepe Valley had been ransacked. Fortunately, Ruggles had been transferred to Hilo earlier in the year. Books, pamphlets, crockery, and other household goods had been carried away. Two large fishponds were empty. Hogs, goats, ducks, and fowls had been taken and the taro fields destroyed. This damage had reportedly been done by the followers of George. Whitney went on to the scene of the fighting:

We soon came to a dead body, it being one of the rebels was not permitted to be interred but left [as] the food for hogs and dogs! . . . They [the insurgents] were closely pursued and many lost their lives. I went to count them but the sight was too shocking and I returned. I was not a little affected by the barbarity of some soldiers who passing by perforated the dead with their musket balls merely to gratify their wanton brutality.

A columnist for *The Polynesian* wrote, in October 1841, of an incident that had taken place after the defeat of the Kauaians. The writer had come ashore at Koloa landing and was traveling northward along

the ancient trail. En route, probably inland from Lihue, he came to a
hill that overlooks a broad belt of tableland.

> The hill is still held in bitter remembrance, as being one of the many spots,
> where acts of wanton cruelty were perpetuated on the prisoners taken in
> the last rebellion. One of their number was ordered to carry a portly chief
> upon his back to its summit, and if he failed in the attempt, he was to be
> bayonetted. He made the attempt, and success seemed to attend his des-
> perate efforts. He was within a few feet of the boundary, when he
> stumbled and fell—his rider, true to his word, stabbed him, and left him
> to perish of his wound.

Hiram Bingham's suspicion that some of the warriors traveling to
Kauai were motivated by a desire for revenge had been well founded.
Once the victors had grown weary of their pursuit and killing they
turned their thoughts to other kinds of revenge. Specific details of
what happened in the aftermath of the battle are now difficult to find,
because there was nothing the victors could be proud of perpetuating.
James Jarves wrote about it in general terms:

> The disaffected chiefs and their tenants were distributed among the other
> islands where it would be impossible for them to combine in another con-
> spiracy. Their lands were divided among the loyal favorites and chiefs,
> who filled the minor offices with their creatures. The poor serfs were
> looked upon in the contemptuous light of conquered rebels; and for many
> years groaned under the heavy exactions of their new lords.

The victors took such property as they wished. Kaumualii had
received presents of horses and cattle over the years and they had
multiplied. Many of these animals were shipped off to other islands,
together with other unknown kinds and amounts of war booty.
Samuel Kamakau recorded that "the soldiers harried the land killing
men, women, and children" for ten days.

The looting of the island was bad enough, but dispossessing the
chiefs of their lands and deporting them to Oahu, Maui, and Hawaii
was an act that even time could not set right. Only three names of
chiefs deported from Kauai have come down to us. One was the afore-
mentioned George Kaumualii, who lived out his life on Oahu.
Another was Kanenoho, a supposed leader of the revolt. The third was
Kiaimakani, the "Wind-Watcher," who later argued with Kalani-

moku about the division of Kauai lands. Even the Kauai chiefs who were still on Maui, having attended the funeral of their late king, and those who sided with the windward chiefs were dispossessed and deported.

What had brought about such vengeance on the part of the windward chiefs? The list of grievances was long and had accumulated over years. Long before Kamehameha, Kaeo, or Kahekili held power, soldiers from Kauai had fought in battles on the island of Hawaii. Kaumualii had also claimed, by historic right, all the islands of the chain except Hawaii. His father and uncle had controlled Maui and Oahu, and there had also been intermarriage with the highest alii of Oahu. Such claims could not be denied, but the reality of Hawaiian life was that land was taken and held by force of arms. The insult in this claim was that the windward chiefs were newcomers to power. They did not have the lineage of those born to power. For them, perhaps the most humiliating, bitter experience of all was Kamehameha's failure to conquer Kauai by force. Two large-scale invasion attempts had ended in disaster, and Kaumualii did not hesitate to taunt Kamehameha or his followers over these failures.

Kaumualii had an interest in Tahiti, which must have seemed suspicious to the windward chiefs. Early on he had sent a representative to Tahiti to see if there was a Tahitian woman of suitable position for him to take as wife. At the time of his kidnapping, Kaumualii was planning a voyage to Tahiti for the purpose of exploring the possibilities there for trade and missionaries. The Reverend Bingham was ready to depart with the expedition and both Liholiho and Kaahumanu had agreed to the trip, possibly knowing it would never take place. It is hard to guess what Kaumualii himself hoped to gain from such an expedition.

And there were yet other events that galled the rulers to windward. For years Kauai had been a place of refuge for the defeated and the persecuted from the other islands, although only a few such escapes have been recorded. One took place in the time of Kahekili during a rebellion on Oahu. Many men and women of chiefly rank who held the prostrating kapu were killed. One such chiefess escaped, however, carrying with her sands from beaches of Oahu, which she symbolically mixed with the sands of beaches on Kauai. After Kamehameha conquered Oahu some persons escaped to Kauai, including a brother of the Oahu king. There was also the alliance between the Russians and the Kauaians. That event had brought forth the vision of a strong foreign power establishing itself in the Islands, rubbing salt in many existing wounds.

In later days Kaumualii was told to put away Deborah Kapule, his favorite wife. It was feared she held too much influence with her husband, and it was not the kind of influence the windward chiefs deemed friendly. Kaumualii ignored these requests. One of the last indignities came from George, the son of Kaumualii, who had enough temerity to write a letter to Liholiho addressing him as "king of the windward islands."

The defeats and insults of many years had grown like a disease in the hearts of the old warriors of Kamehameha. The news of an uprising on Kauai must have come as welcome news for many of them. Their frustrations finally burst into action and fell on the heads of the people of Kauai.

Land remained the source of power in Hawaii in 1824. With land a chief could accumulate wealth, and with the land he acquired the services of those who dwelt on it. When the land was taken from the Kauai chiefs a great portion of it was given to relatives of Kamehameha, many of whom would hold positions of authority for years to come. They were, of course, absentee landlords. Other lands went to warriors or court favorites as a reward for past services. Kamakau stated that "the loafers and hangers-on of Oahu and Maui obtained the rich lands of Kauai."

There is no record of the names of those who lost the use of lands on Kauai, but some idea of who received the lands can be found in the records of over twenty years later, in the Mahele book. In 1847 the privy council adopted a number of rules that resulted the following year in giving Hawaiians the right to make claims to land and to own it in fee simple. Not all claims were approved, but those that were granted appear in the Mahele book. Most of those who made claims listed as documentation the names of the persons who gave them the right to use the land.

Certain names appear regularly on these claims as either having a valid right to claim land in fee simple, or as having given the right to others to live on certain land, which those persons in turn claimed in fee simple. These names include Kalanimoku, Kaikioewa, and Paul Kanoa, the latter two having served as governors of Kauai after the rebellion. The name of Daniel Oleloa also appears often. Few claimants list the names of those who granted them the right to live on lands before 1824. Apparently they did not know the names, or thought it unimportant or unwise to list such names.

Many persons with blood ties to the Kamehameha line or with high connections in the monarchy made no attempt to prove their claims. They simply applied for parcels of land and were granted fee-simple ownership. Victoria Kamamalu, a granddaughter of Kamehameha, received over 51,000 acres of Kauai land. The Native Register, compiled as documentation during the Mahele, is evidence of the vast amount of land taken from the people of Kauai and given to others.

One of the longer and more carefully documented claims for land on Kauai was sent to the Land Commission by a man named Ahukai. Ahukai stated that when Kaeo was king of Kauai he gave the land division of Makaweli to his sister or to a female cousin. When Kaumualii reigned, he likewise granted the use of Makaweli to either his sister or to a female cousin. After Kaumualii died and the revolt had been put down, Kalanimoku gave the land to Kahalaia, the short-time governor of Kauai, who then gave Makaweli to Ahukai. But at the death of Kahalaia, Kalanimoku and Kaahumanu jointly gave Makaweli to Kinau, a daughter of Kamehameha I. Kinau became regent of the kingdom following the death of Kaahumanu. Before Kinau died she told Kekauluohi or Kamehameha III that Makaweli belonged to Ahukai. The king sent Ahukai back to Kauai and the claimant stayed on the land unopposed until 1846 when Kekuanaoa, the husband of Kinau and father of Victoria Kamamalu, claimed the land. Ahukai closed his claim by stating, "When the day comes to work on it and you direct me to come, I will go, with the proper witnesses."

Ahukai's claim is unusual because it extends back to the days of Kaeo. Ahukai was obviously a resourceful, patient man. It appears that he had been deported to another island, but had been allowed to return to Kauai by no less authority than Kamehameha III. In the end, Ahukai's claim was not granted. His documentation was good, but the competition he faced was much too great. Victoria Kamamalu claimed Makaweli, and her claim was all that was needed. She received nearly 22,000 acres of Makaweli land.

If wishing would make it so, one could wish that Deborah Kapule had kept a diary during her life. The favorite wife of Kaumualii, she was a bright and active woman who participated in many of the events of her time and knew most of those who played the leading roles in the history of Kauai during the first half of the nineteenth century.

Deborah was born in about 1798. It is not certain where she was born, but she first appears at Waimea and it is likely that this was the place of her birth, since she later received property there from her father. He is one of the mysteries surrounding Deborah's early life. Deborah called her father Haupu, but she did not adopt that name herself, preferring the name Haakulou. Not until she was converted to Christianity did she take the name Deborah. In written accounts she is most often referred to as Deborah Kapule.

Obviously Deborah was very attractive to men. Through a life plagued with misfortune she did not lack long for male companionship. By 1815 she apparently had married Kaumualii, because at that time the king approved the sharing of her favors with a chief of Waimea. When Samuel Whitney and Samuel Ruggles reunited George Kaumualii with his father, Kaumualii and "his foreign queen, Kapule" gave gifts of food, calabashes, spears, shells, mats, and kapa cloth to the missionaries to take with them to Honolulu.

When the Whitneys and Ruggles settled on Kauai, Deborah was attentive and kind to them. She gave them presents of useful items to make life a little easier, and she was one of the first to study reading and writing. After Kaumualii was carried off to Honolulu, Deborah lived with Kealiiahonui, a son of Kaumualii by his royal wife. Shortly Deborah lost Kealiiahonui when Kaahumanu decided she wanted that handsome man as a husband also.

James Jarves wrote that Deborah was a beautiful woman when she was young. In the years to come she would need not only her charm, but all the diplomatic nerve and wit she could muster. She continued on close terms with the missionaries and, although ill on occasion, she established and maintained a school of some fifty students under the direction of two boys. She had great influence with the people of Kauai, as demonstrated by the crowds who met her when she returned from attending Kaumualii's funeral.

Perhaps the influence of Kapule was most strongly shown during the uprising of 1824. She marched into the old Russian fort together with others to give valuable support to the windward forces. Jarves evaluated her assistance:

> Had the widow of Kaumualii, the repudiated Kapuli, who was greatly
> beloved, joined the rebels, the consequences would have been much more

serious. Her loyalty and firmness preserved many true to the will of their late king, and her exertions, though poorly repaid, were considered as highly serviceable.

Deborah was married again, this time to Simeon Kaiu, a devout Christian who sometimes acted as a judge on Kauai. The marriage appears to have been a happy one, and Deborah bore a son who was named Josiah Kaumualii. Simeon Kaiu went off to the Marquesas Islands with a delegation to determine the possibilities for missionary expansion there, and Kapule would have gladly gone too if it were not for their infant son. By 1835 Simeon had returned, and together with sixteen members of the Waimea church they moved to Wailua. A school was established, and it was hoped a church would soon be erected. Then tragedy, by now familiar to Deborah if no less painful, struck again. Simeon Kaiu died suddenly.

Deborah had done all she could to support the monarchy, which was under the control of Kaahumanu. In December 1825 she had traveled to Honolulu to be received as a member of the church. Others who were received on that Sunday were Kaahumanu and Kalanimoku. Deborah had apparently been given the use of property in Wailua by Kaahumanu, and she continued to live on this land most of the time. After the death of Kaahumanu in 1832 Deborah underwent new hardships. Revenues that she had customarily received from her Wailua lands were denied her.

Deborah's interest in the church withered; she was suspended sometime after her husband's death. Bingham reported that she "gave up her professions, and has, by her worldliness, greatly disappointed and grieved her Christian friends, who had regarded her both as pious and useful. . . . May she yet return to her duty, and find mercy." Perhaps it was during these years that Kapule had difficulties with Governor Kaikioewa of Kauai, resulting in her being sent to Honolulu. Most members of the government were zealous Christians who would not look with kindness on a backslider.

Adding to her troubles at this time, she became involved with a Wailua resident by the name of Oliver Chapin. In 1821 Mercy Whitney had written in praise of the young Chapin: "a large boy . . . an interesting and lovely youth, one of the most favorite scholars in our school." Chapin was a married man whose wife Nahinu, a cripple, was a daughter of Kaumualii by one of the late king's several wives. In November 1839 Mercy Whitney wrote about Deborah's church problems and indicated that the affair between the one-time queen and Chapin was common knowledge.

> At length her conduct became such, that her pastor suspended her from church fellowship, and about a year ago she was excommunicated. Her conduct ever since she left this church has been such as to grieve our hearts. . . . Perhaps she is a Christian now, but I have nearly given her over as apostate, for if she were one, it appears to me that she wants not to be left to continue in so gross & flagrant a sin, as that of living year after year, in concubinage with the husband of another woman.

Deborah Kapule's house was strategically located near the mouth of the Wailua River, and it became a natural stopping-place for travelers going or returning from the north coast. For many it was an overnight stay. Maria Chamberlain, wife of Levi Chamberlain of the second missionary company, stayed there, as did the future historian William Alexander who came as a boy of sixteen, and Father Walsh, the first Catholic priest on Kauai. All were greeted kindly and given food and shelter for the night. One of Deborah's canoes would ferry the visitors across the Wailua River while their horses swam behind.

In late October 1840 Kapule had rather unusual visitors, members of the United States Exploring Expedition, in the Islands under the command of Lieutenant Charles Wilkes. Wilkes did not travel to Kauai, but six of his trained men made a cursory survey of the flora, fauna, and geological aspects of the island. Landing at Koloa, Scientists Titian Ramsay Peale and William Rich rode to Lihue and then proceeded northward over pastures toward Wailua. Wilkes related the experiences of these two men:

> . . . they reached Wailua, the residence of Deborah, a chief woman of the islands, readily known as such from her enormous size, and the cast of her countenance. She has a person living with her called Olivia [Oliver] Chapin, who speaks English, and has learned how to extort money. Deborah has about forty men in her district; but they were absent, being employed in the mountains cutting timber to pay the tax to the king.
>
> Near Deborah's residence are extensive fish-ponds belonging to her, which have been made with great labour: they are of different degrees of saltiness. The fish are taken from the sea when they are young and put into the saltest pond; as they grow larger, they are removed into one less salt, and are finally fattened in fresh water. While our gentlemen were there, Deborah received young fish in payment of the poll-tax, which were immediately transferred to her ponds.

Deborah provided the two men with a canoe so they could explore the Wailua River and record the plants and birds they found. The visitors spent the night, entertained in "white style" at a table set with knives and forks and enjoying tea with sugar. The bed they slept on was about 12 feet square, covered with mats, and with kapa as a covering instead of linens. Peale and Rich continued on to Hanalei, where they met the other four members of their party and returned by schooner directly to Oahu.

It was probably in September 1841 when the correspondent for *The Polynesian*—the same man who had recounted the story of the hilltop bayoneting of a Kauai captive after the rebellion—arrived at Wailua. In a continuation of his column the writer described Deborah:

> She had always been a friend to foreigners, and entertained them with much hospitality in the days of her prosperity; though of late in accordance with the spirit of the age, she expects a handsome remuneration for a bowl of milk, and a mat bed, well lined with fleas, whose nimbleness is sure to relieve the traveller from any fear of stiff limbs by morning. However, Deborah's lot has been a checkered one. A petted queen whose will was law, then humbled and degraded. A warm friend both of the missionaries and strangers, kind and hospitable, yet excommunicated from the church for the same transgression which stole from her arms a fond and royal husband. She was spoiled of her possessions, and tyrannized upon by a government, which stands indebted to her for the preservation of the island. For to her exertions and influence it was owing that during the rebellion, the inhabitants generally remained faithful to the powers at Oahu.

The journalist went on to say that Governor Kaikioewa of Kauai, jealous of her influence, had confiscated Deborah's property, seized her, and sent her to Honolulu a few years earlier. She remained in Honolulu for some time in poverty and disgrace. Through the assistance of the Reverend William Richards, who gained the help of the king, the sentence was reversed and she was given back what remained of her holdings. In closing the writer remarked, "She is now a buxom widow of forty years of age, fat and ugly to gaze upon."

In 1847 Chester Lyman reported spending the night at Wailua.

> Early in the morning Deborah took the arm of Mr. A[lexander] & myself & conducted us to a house near by to see her aged father, who is one of the oldest men on the Island & best acquainted with their ancient customs.

We found the grey headed old man feeble with disease. He had been married some years when Capt. Cook first visited the Islands, & remembers him with perfect distinctness.

On 17 October 1849 Deborah Kapule arrived at Waimea to visit with her close friend of years past, Mercy Whitney. Deborah and the women who accompanied her spent most of a week with Mercy, but the widow of the pioneer missionary was ill part of the time. Mercy reported that she did enjoy the visit. Before Deborah returned to Wailua, she decided to help raise funds for a new meeting house in Koloa where she was now a church member, apparently again in the good graces of the church.

In the early 1850s Deborah's only child, her son by Simeon Kaiu, died. It must have been another severe shock for her, perhaps more than she could bear. *The Polynesian* for 10 September 1855 carried the notice of her death. Under the heading, "Died," were the final three sentences.

At Waimea, Kauai, Aug. 26, of affection of the liver, Deborah Kapule, widow of King Kaumualii, formerly the Sovereign of that island. Deborah had for many years been an active and consistent church member, and her loss is deeply felt by her people, among whom her influence for good was very great. Her age was about 55.

And so passed from the scene the last of the leading participants in the frenzied affairs of Kauai that had unfolded during the first half of the nineteenth century. Deborah Kapule shared some of the admirable qualities of her husband, Kaumualii. During their lifetimes they had struggled against overwhelming numbers, and accepting this fact, had survived through a remarkable resourcefulness. In times of danger they reacted with courage. During years of virtual captivity they demonstrated a royal dignity. They had earned a place with those chosen alii who had served their people honestly and well, and who received the love of their people in return.

CHAPTER SEVEN

"Fruitful Fields . . . and Schools and Churches"

On the afternoon of 23 October 1819, a group of missionaries stood on a wharf in Boston Harbor waiting to be rowed to the *Thaddeus,* which lay a short distance from shore. Their journey's end was to be Hawaii and seldom in history has such a small group of people been destined to bring about so many drastic and lasting changes in their adopted home.

The setting forth of this New England missionary company was the result of a religious revival that had flowered in England in the late 1700s. The London Missionary Society had set an example by establishing missions in the South Pacific. The desire to carry Christianity to the heathen spread from England to New England, and the American Board of Commissioners for Foreign Missions was organized in 1810. The Biblical command "Go ye forth into all the world, and preach the Gospel to every creature" had taken on new significance.

Mission stations were established at Bombay and Ceylon, among several American Indian tribes, and in Palestine. Although there had been much discussion about the Sandwich Islands, ever since New England sailors had brought back tales of the benighted Hawaiians, it took some special motivation to begin the mission. That motivation appeared in the person of Henry Opukahaia (known as Obookiah in the United States). This young man had signed aboard a sailing vessel in 1809 to escape the wars raging back and forth across his native island of Hawaii. Eventually he ended up in Boston.

Henry Opukahaia proved to be a sensitive, earnest man. He came under the care of the church in New England and they found him anxious to learn and to become a devout Christian. Opukahaia was considered a shining example of how a heathen youth could truly learn the ways and meaning of Christianity. He lived with various religious families in New England, including a time in the home of President

Dwight of Yale. Opukahaia would be the ideal young man to return to his native Islands bearing the banner of Christianity. The thought raised the enthusiasm of the missionary-minded.

But it was not to be. In Februrary 1818 Opukahaia died of typhus while a student at the Foreign Mission School in Cornwall, Connecticut. His death created a great upswelling of emotion. Sermons were preached relating the difficulties of Opukahaia, and soon a small book was published telling of his unfulfilled life. At long last the American Board had the momentum necessary to make the Sandwich Islands mission a reality.

Volunteers for the mission were requested and those chosen included Hiram Bingham and Asa Thurston, both ordained ministers. Daniel Chamberlain, a farmer, brought his five children. Elisha Loomis was a printer and Thomas Holman, a physician. Three young Hawaiian men, Thomas Hopu, William Kanui, and John Honolii, who had all attended the Foreign Mission School, were sent to assist the ministers. George Kaumualii also was included. George was not a converted Christian, but he wished to return to his father, the ruler of Kauai.

It was the opinion of the American Board that all the men of the mission should be married before leaving. Three marriages were performed in the five weeks before sailing and the other volunteers, except for Daniel Chamberlain, had recently been married. On 29 September 1819 Thurston and Bingham, who had been classmates at Andover Theological Seminary and who had graduated earlier that month, were ordained. The service was held at Goshen, Connecticut, and a large group of persons gathered.

The Reverend Heman Humphrey preached the sermon. While he believed in the ultimate victory of their calling, Humphrey did not minimize the difficulties the mission company might encounter.

> Satan is not yet bound, and he will not yield the empire of the Sandwich Islands without a struggle. He will instigate his emissaries to oppose all your benevolent plans and efforts; —and how far he may be permitted to prevail for a season we know not.
>
> "Lo I am with you always," does not of course exempt you from disappointments and sufferings. You may be persecuted even unto death. —you will be opposed by the powers of darkness. Prepare yourselves therefore, for whatever may await you. "Endure hardness as good soldiers of Jesus Christ. Fight the good fight of faith, lay hold on eternal life."

In a prayer to solemnize the marriage of Hiram and Sybil Bingham, on 11 October 1819 in Hartford, Connecticut, the Reverend Thomas

Gallaudet concluded with the words, "from thousands of hearts will intercessions for you ascend daily to the throne of grace. Be faithful unto death. And may the mantle of Obookiah descend and rest upon you—FAREWELL!"

On 15 October the group was organized into a congregation in the vestry of the Park Street Church. Eight days later they stood on a wharf in Boston Harbor, where they joined in singing the hymn "When Shall We All Meet Again?" A prayer was offered by the secretary of the American Board, then the missionary company boarded a fourteen-oar barge offered by the USS *Independence* and were rowed out to the *Thaddeus.* None of the missionaries expected to see their native shores again.

The departure was heavy with services and prayers, reminders of the serious task that lay before them. Taking leave was not made easier by the debate over whether or not women should be subjected to such barbarous conditions, and whether the frame for a house should go aboard the *Thaddeus* so the women would not have to live in grass-thatched houses. And the inevitable discussions arose about the cost, when so much church work needed to be done at home. There was considerable feeling among many New Englanders that the whole plan of sending out missionaries was, at best, foolish and probably fanatical. Very likely the most difficult part for the departing missionaries was that nearly all their relatives and friends urged them not to go.

It took 164 days between leaving Boston Harbor and sighting the Hawaiian Islands, time spent in terribly cramped quarters. Seasickness was commonplace. Services, prayers, and contemplation occupied a great amount of time. But there was little complaining because their Divine Calling gave them an overwhelming determination.

The sight of land, Kohala on the north shore of the island of Hawaii, brought relief for the missionaries. Soon they would be on dry land beginning their work. The crew of the *Thaddeus* was cautious, because they did not know the current political situation in the Islands. They strung boarding nets and brought cannon up from the hold in case of hostile action. It soon became apparent that these precautions were not necessary. A landing party returned with the news that Kamehameha I was dead and the joyful tidings that the ancient religious ways had been overthrown. To the missionaries it was a wonderful sign that God had prepared a way for them.

By 4 April 1820 the *Thaddeus* had reached Kailua, on the west coast of the island of Hawaii, and the missionaries presented themselves to King Liholiho. Their request to establish stations in the Islands did not bring immediate approval. The king had been warned by his respected adviser, John Young, that the English might look with disfavor on the presence of so many Americans. After four days of deliberation it was decided that the missionaries could stay for a year. Since Kailua was the residence of the king, the Reverend and Mrs. Thurston and Dr. and Mrs. Holman were assigned there.

The rest of the contingent went on to Honolulu, which became the headquarters of the mission since it was the leading trading port. There the Reverend Bingham, the leader of the company, established the mother church. The young Hawaiian chief, George, requested he be returned to Kauai as soon as possible and asked that Whitney and Ruggles travel with him. George's request was agreed to and on 2 May 1820, the *Thaddeus* set sail. The two missionary wives remained in Honolulu.

At daylight on 3 May Kauai was sighted and as they sailed along the coast toward Waimea, Samuel Ruggles watched the shoreline pass before him. In his journal he wrote, "beautiful plains and fruitful valleys present themselves to view . . . while large groves of cocoanuts and bananas wave their tops, as if in welcoming us to their shores. Can this, thought I, while passing these pleasant fields, be one of the dark places of the earth, which is filled with the habitations of cruelty?"

Anchoring at Waimea the *Thaddeus* fired a twenty-one-gun salute, which was answered from the old Russian fort. Ruggles and Whitney went ashore with George and were met by such a crowd that the Hawaiian escort had to clear a path for them with clubs. King Kaumualii did not know his son had returned until he appeared before him. Samuel Ruggles described the scene: "As soon as George entered the door, his father arose, clasped him in his arms, and pressed his nose to his son's after the manner of the country; both were unable to speak for some time. The scene was truly affecting, and I know not when I have wept more freely." When George explained that Whitney and Ruggles had come with him all the way from America, "The old gentleman then embraced us in the same manner as he had done his son, frequently putting his nose to ours." Apparently that evening George told his father of the many things the missionaries had done for him. The following morning Kaumualii questioned Ruggles about these things, and when he found they were true, he told the missionary, "you my son, I you father, my wife you mother."

In a walk up Waimea Valley Ruggles and Whitney found the countryside "rich and promising." There were a variety of fruits, including an abundance of oranges, lemons, and a few grapevines, the survivors of Russian plantings. The abundance of good soil and water impressed the missionaries, who undoubtedly were considering how they could best sustain themselves if they were permanently stationed there.

There was no doubt as to the wish of Kaumualii. Ruggles wrote, "Today he told me he would support all the mission family if they would come to Attooi—that he would build as many school-houses as we wished, and a large meeting-house, and have a sabbath day and have prayers and singing." It was difficult to ignore the enthusiasm of Kaumualii, especially in contrast to the cool reception given by Liholiho. Ruggles noted the overwhelming desire of the king and queen to learn to read. The two missionaries had apparently given them several books, for "Wherever they go they carry their books with them. I have seen them bathing in the water, stand with their books in their hands, repeating their lessons." Kauai could not be ignored.

On 19 July 1820 Ruggles and Whitney returned to Honolulu. The brethren quickly agreed a station must be established on Kauai and on 24 July the two missionaries and their wives were at Waimea. Several days later a service was held at the missionary residence. The royal family seated themselves and listened, but according to Nancy Ruggles the commoners crowded outside the yard and pulled away the grass of which the fence was made, "anxious to see & know what new thing the white people were performing."

In October 1820 the missionary families at Waimea had visitors, Dr. Thomas Holman and his wife Lucia, who had originally been assigned to Kailua on Hawaii. The dryness, heat, and lack of privacy had made life miserable and the Holmans moved to Lahaina without the consent of the mission. A month later they appeared in Honolulu to attend the sick crew of a ship that had arrived from Manila.

The unwelcome appearance of the Holmans on Oahu had brought charges from Hiram Bingham. The antagonisms went back to the time of departure from Boston, when Lucia Holman was given a farewell gift of fruit and wine. Bingham thought the gift should be added to the common provisions of the company; the Holmans did not agree.

In September 1820 Lucia wrote from Honolulu to a sister: "I believe the females of this Mission have done more, much more towards the prosperity of it thus far, than the men." The wives did possess a patient diplomacy, paramount to mission success and often something their husbands lacked, but to express such an idea in those terms was hardly wise, especially in 1820. Bingham possessed the ultimate weapon. Thomas Holman was excommunicated, and Lucia was suspended from the church.

On 11 October 1820 the Holmans sailed for Waimea. It was a logical place of refuge, since Lucia was a sister of Samuel Ruggles. On 19 October Holman delivered Mercy Whitney's first daughter, the first white child born in Hawaii. In December a daughter was born to Nancy and Samuel Ruggles. In March 1821 Lucia bore a daughter, and in October of the same year the Holmans sailed for Boston by way of the Orient.

Back in New England, Thomas carried on his battle with the Prudential Board of the mission, to no avail. He died in 1826. Lucia is considered the first American woman to have sailed around the world. She lived almost to her ninety-third birthday. Clearly the Holmans did not have the heartfelt dedication required of missionaries. In the end the incident passed into insignificance, and the only damage done the mission was the needless expenditure of a great deal of energy.

In September 1820 Whitney and Ruggles had each been assigned a section of land by the king for their cultivation and also provided with Hawaiian families to work the land. The areas must have been extensive because they produced enough food for the missionaries, for the workers and their families, and for between sixty and seventy children cared for by the mission. The Whitney homestead had twenty goats for milk, taro fields, coconuts, yams, bananas, and sugarcane. Each family was also given the use of two fishponds. In 1820 the missionaries were making sugar and molasses.

Toward the end of April 1821, the Whitneys and Ruggles moved from their first home into a spacious building 54 feet long and 25 feet wide. The home had the luxury of a board floor, and Bingham declared it the "best house on the Sandwich Islands." It had glass windows, five bedrooms, and several large rooms that served as school rooms, for dining, and public worship. The house was on the slope below the fort and above the landing place on the Waimea River. On the mountainside there was a 10 foot-high stone wall, as protection against fire, and beyond was the dwelling house of Kaumualii. The other end of the house overlooked the ocean. Half a mile distant was a well, 20 feet deep, dug by Whitney himself.

In 1821 Kaumualii had been whisked off to Honolulu to become the husband of Kaahumanu. Kaumualii had pledged the missionaries every assistance, and the Kauaians carried out their ruler's wishes. In late 1822 two stone houses were started. One was for the Ruggles at the nearby village of Hanapepe, where it had been decided he should carry on his work. The other, for the Whitney family, was located about a half-mile from the mouth of the Wailua River, situated on a flat some 100 feet from the east bank.

Daniel Chamberlain came from Honolulu to assist and spent about two months at his labors. The house was 26 by 36 feet in size, with a cook and wash room at the rear. A stone cellar extended under the house and Chamberlain wrote, "I never saw but few cellars in America that exceed it."

In March 1824 Whitney wrote, "The rain has fallen in torrents for a day or two past. I sometimes almost tremble for our little mud and stone-wall cottage. It stands on the bank of the river, which has been overflown for some hours past." Two years later the stone house was flooded. Mercy and her three young children escaped in a canoe, which paddled up to the front door of the house.

The Whitneys were away from Kauai during part of 1827, and soon after they returned they moved into a two-story stone house on the west side of the river. The house was conveniently close to the church and about a quarter of a mile from the ocean. In these comfortable quarters the Whitneys spent the rest of their lives.

In the early years of the mission at Waimea services were held at the residence of the missionaries. Soon there is mention of a stone church, which was followed by "a great thatched church." In 1832 Sunday church attendance ran between 1,500 and 2,000 persons. The thatched church burned in 1834 and a stone-and-mud building was erected; it measured 84 by 44 feet and rose 18 feet in height.

In 1848 this church literally fell apart and plans for a new structure, built on the foundations of the old, were undertaken by the Reverend George B. Rowell, who acted as architect and supervisor. These were difficult years financially, and much of the work was done by the parishioners. Deborah Kapule, the widow of Kaumualii, joined in, bringing a pair of oxen from her home at Wailua and urging on the workers. Timbers had to be dragged down the mountains, and large quantities of stone gathered and set in place. Finally, in 1858, the floor and pews were completed. The church still stands in Waimea today.

Whitney and Ruggles were undoubtedly better housed and enjoyed a more plentiful and varied diet than did their brethren on the other islands. Whitney, who enjoyed gardening, developed a vineyard in

Waimea Valley, protected by a fence and locked gate. Some of the wine made from the grapes was used for sacramental purposes in churches throughout the Islands. With these basic concerns at a minimum, the missionaries were free to give their utmost energies to preaching and establishing a school system. And this they did.

Before leaving New England the missionaries had decided preaching and teaching must go hand in hand. Schools were essential, making it possible for the Hawaiians to read and thus enabling them to study the Scriptures for themselves. At first it was thought that the Islanders should be taught English, and with this in mind textbooks had been brought from New England. Progress was painfully slow. It was then decided to attempt to teach the Hawaiians to read in their own language.

There was an obvious, enormous problem. The Hawaiians had no written language. With their usual determination, the missionaries went about the tedious chore of reducing the spoken language to written form. The New Englanders had learned something of the language on the long voyage from Boston, aided by the four Hawaiians aboard the *Thaddeus*. Once in the Islands they quickly grasped an acceptable use of the language. To help them with this immense task they invited the Reverend William Ellis, who had served the London Missionary Society in Tahiti for six years, to come and assist them. Ellis' familiarity with the Tahitian language, so much like the Hawaiian, was of considerable help. Ellis remained for two years and was the first man to preach to the Hawaiians in their own language. It took six years to establish the Hawaiian language in finished form, but the missionaries did not wait for the refinements. A little over a year after arrival, a simple spelling book and a reading book had come off the mission press.

Printing in the Hawaiian language worked some kind of magic. The Islanders were delighted to see their own books and they learned quickly. But there was still an obstacle. For generations Islanders had looked to their chiefs for leadership, and they now awaited their approval. In 1824 approval came with a proclamation by Kaahumanu and the chiefs, encouraging attention to religion and learning. Before 1824 school enrollment had been small, consisting mostly of chiefs, but by the end of that year there were more than 2,000 in the schools, and by 1831 some 52,000 Hawaiians attended 1,100 schools. This was two-fifths of the population of the Islands.

The demand for everything needed in the schools was enormous.

The mission press could not keep up with the clamor for books. Grass-thatched structures to serve as school houses were relatively easy to build, but there was a shortage of everything that went inside. A number of students often used one book. Teachers were a critical problem. As soon as a Hawaiian could read reasonably well, he was sent out as a teacher. On Kauai, at least one school used surfboards as desks. Since paper and slates were at a premium, arithmetic and writing were not emphasized at first. Some students wrote in the sand with their fingers or a stick.

In 1822, before Kaahumanu had issued her proclamation concerning religion and learning, she visited the leeward islands with a retinue of some 800 people. The crowds of Kauaians around the Whitney house were enormous, many of them clamoring for books. Hiram Bingham, who was on Kauai at the time, reported that when Kaahumanu learned what was happening she sent a letter to Honolulu. "This is my communication to you: . . . send some more books down here. Many are the people—few are the books. I want *elua lau* (800) Hawaiian books to be sent hither." Kauai probably responded more quickly to schooling than the other islands, because of the ready cooperation of the people with the mission.

At the public examination of the students at Waimea on 7 January 1829, the Reverend Peter Gulick wrote of the numbers of people then involved in schooling.

> At the examination 850 readers passed in review, they read of various parts of the books which they studied and acquited themselves very much to our satisfaction. One hundred and fifty-two men and forty-two women, most of them neatly dressed in European style, were also examined in the art of writing. They wrote on slates and manifested a very pleasing evidence of improvement. After the examination some 5,000 people gathered at the governor's house.

In a report for Kauai in June 1831 the number of schools on the island was given as 200. The number of students was 9,000, and those able to read numbered 3,500. A large part of the population was going to school. Certainly learning to read was a matter of curiosity, or a fad, for some, but nevertheless the hope of turning Hawaii into a literate nation had been an astounding success.

Literacy did not mean entry into the church, however. The missionaries continued to be very strict about this. A prospective church member had to prove his conversion by his actions over a long period of time. In the year 1830 only seven persons were admitted to membership at Waimea. Among them was Governor Kaikioewa.

Samuel Ruggles, plagued by ill health, did not long remain either on Kauai or in Hawaii. In 1823 he was transferred to Hilo, returning to Kauai for a year in 1825-1826. He and his wife returned to the United States in 1834 and were released by the mission, spending the rest of their lives in Wisconsin. But other missionaries replaced them. In 1823 the Reverend Artemus Bishop and his wife Elizabeth spent a year in Waimea. The Reverend Peter Gulick and his wife Fanny came to Waimea in 1828, staying until 1835 when they started a missionary station at Koloa.

Samuel Whitney spent his entire missionary career on the island of Kauai. As soon as the Waimea station was established he traveled about the island, since there were only the two men to cover the seventy villages on the Kauai circuit. Soon grass-thatched meeting houses appeared here and there, and where there were no buildings, gatherings were held in the open. Whitney did his best to visit each station as often as possible. On occasion the number of people coming to hear him numbered in the thousands.

It will be remembered that Whitney had not completed his theological studies before joining the missionary company, and this meant he could not officially perform certain church functions. But he continued his studies in the Islands and in 1823 received a license to preach. He was officially ordained a minister in late 1825 and from that time he bore the title, the Reverend Samuel Whitney.

Whitney had not been converted to Christianity until he was twenty years of age. From meager information it appears he was a quiet, industrious man, well thought of by Island missionaries, and respected by the mission in Boston. The Reverend Doctor Smith, who served at Koloa, described Whitney as "of rather large stature, of pleasant manners, very companionable, and generous almost to a fault, one of nature's noblemen, and a model missionary." Marcia Smith, a missionary-teacher, described him during a visit to Punahou School in Honolulu, as being "of very commanding presence, a faithful and successful missionary, but most sympathetic and genial."

In addition to his missionary duties Whitney was expected to act as doctor for Kauai. His medical training must have been scant, and he could only have followed common sense. In 1832 he was a member of a missionary group who visited the Marquesas Islands to determine if mission work should begin there. Through the years he also translated several books from English into Hawaiian.

Whitney had great influence with the Kauai chiefs. When William Hooper, the manager of Koloa plantation, could not resolve his problems with the chiefs who supplied him with labor, he called on Whitney to get the problems solved. The pettiness of these problems was exasperating to Hooper, but Samuel Whitney seems to have been able to arrange such matters in a quiet way.

In September 1845 Whitney was taken ill. At first he went to his summer place in the cooler climate above Hanapepe, but no relief came. He sailed for Honolulu, but the vomiting and diarrhea kept occurring. He traveled on to Lahaina, where he spent a night in the home of Sherman Peck, who had once lived on Kauai. The Reverend Whitney moved into a home on Mount Ball, above the mission school of Lahainaluna. He died there on 15 December 1845. Mercy Whitney, his dark-eyed, slim wife, died twenty-seven years later at Waimea, on the day after Christmas, 1872. She is buried there.

Samuel and Mercy Whitney had four children. Their first child was named Maria Kapule, a sign of high regard for Deborah Kapule, and an indication of the warm feelings the Whitneys had for the Kauaians.

On 27 July 1833 three young men arrived in Honolulu aboard the *Hellespont.* They were William Ladd and Peter Allan Brinsmade, both of Hallowell, Maine, and William Hooper of Boston, Massachusetts. All were in their twenties and the two men from Maine were married. Each had invested $2,000 in the formation of the mercantile company soon known as Ladd and Company, and they brought a cargo of goods aboard the *Hellespont* with which they planned to open a general merchandise store.

Two days after arrival they had rented a store and were ready to start business. This kind of industry should have served as notice to other merchants that the newcomers would be serious competitors. Soon Ladd and Company was supplying many whaling ships. It also quickly became evident the partners were sympathetic to the missionary objectives, which gave them influence others did not enjoy. Henry A. Peirce, a rival merchant, labeled the newcomers the "pious Traders."

Ladd and Company was an immediate success and the partners were soon looking for ways to more quickly enhance their fortunes. They settled on the idea of developing a sugar plantation. Making sugar had been tried before, but never on the scale envisioned by Ladd and Company. Sugarcane had been brought to the Islands by Polynesian voyagers, who chewed on pieces of the stalk for sweetness and quick energy. In Hawaii the first attempt to extract juice from cane had been tried on Lanai in 1802 by a Chinese who had arrived aboard a sandalwood vessel. He pressed the cane stalks through stone rollers and then boiled down the juice he recovered. After grinding off a small amount of cane and making it into sugar, he returned to China. The method he used had been common for centuries in China, where sugar was a major industry when Marco Polo visited there in the 1270s.

Samuel Whitney mentioned making sugar and its by-product, molasses, in 1820 at Waimea. In 1825 an English agriculturalist by the name of John Wilkinson, who at one time had been a planter in the West Indies, began growing sugarcane and coffee in Manoa Valley on Oahu. After six months of work, Wilkinson had about seven acres of cane in cultivation. When he died, in 1826, Governor Boki of Oahu took over the operation, and for a time prospects appeared good. Various foreigners became involved and the mill was converted into a distillery for the manufacture of rum. This was viewed with displeasure by Kaahumanu and the missionaries, and the operation came to an end in about 1829. In 1835 William French, a longtime Honolulu merchant, brought a mill and workers from China. French had trouble securing land; eventually he ground cane at Waimea, on Kauai, but the competition of Ladd and Company was too great.

Ladd and Company faced many problems in starting their sugar plantation, among the greatest being land. A large section of fertile land was needed in a location that would provide abundant sun and water. The three partners found the land they wanted in the district of Koloa on Kauai. Perhaps they were most familiar with Kauai because the company apparently had a branch store there at least as early as 1835.

Koloa plantation could never have been founded if the partners of Ladd and Company had not been in harmony with the ideals of the missionaries. Hooper, Ladd, and Brinsmade were devout young men. Peter Brinsmade had attended Andover Theological Seminary and Yale Divinity School. In addition to saving souls, the missionaries were anxious to raise the desperate condition of the mass of Hawaiians and they believed the best way to accomplish this was to induce them to become farmers. The missionaries and the three partners agreed that the establishment of a plantation employing Hawaiians would be a substantial start in the right direction.

In the 1830s, the missionaries had great influence in the running of the Hawaiian Kingdom and they were willing to lend their vital support. It was arranged for Ladd and Company to lease approximately 1,000 acres of land at Koloa, together with the waterfall of Maulili, for a period of fifty years at a lease rent of $300 per year.

The drawing up of this lease was a first in Hawaiian history, marking a revolutionary change in policy concerning the control of land. Prior to this the government had granted the use of small parcels of land to certain foreigners. The use of the land was at the pleasure of the king, and although the terms were usually vague, improvements reverted to the king if the use of the land was withdrawn. In about 1831 William French and a partner had attempted to lease a parcel of land on Oahu to raise cotton and cattle, but the request was turned down. The lease for the Koloa lands was signed on 29 July 1835 by Kauikeaouli (Kamehameha III), Kaikioewa as governor of Kauai, and the three partners of Ladd and Company.

In agreement with the philosophy of the missionaries, the lease stipulated that native laborers be encouraged to work on the land. For this right the company would pay to the king and the governor twenty-five cents per month for each man. And it was further stated that each worker would be paid a satisfactory wage and be exempted from all taxation. This taxation had taken the form of labor performed for the chiefs and such other contributions as the chiefs wished to impose. The contract also stated that no ardent spirits were to be manufactured or consumed on the land.

With the signing of this one document, more far-reaching changes were made than either the missionaries or the Hawaiians could have guessed. Much of the Koloa plantation land, if not all of it, apparently had been granted to Governor Kaikioewa sometime after the uprising of 1824. Unfortunately, not much specific information is available on how Ladd and Company secured their lease. In general terms, it seems obvious that considerable missionary influence was necessary to bring the government around to their point of view. Governor Kaikioewa was under heavy obligation to Kamehameha III, since his position was held at the pleasure of the king, and vast lands on Kauai had been bestowed as a royal favor. Although the lesser chiefs—those who actually lived on the land—strongly opposed granting the use of land to foreigners, Kaikioewa was hardly in a position to do anything but cooperate. Even with this leverage, negotiations to secure the lease were a drawn-out affair.

The employment of Hawaiians had far-reaching ramifications that were to echo through the years. The idea of Hawaiians working for an employer who paid them wages, which could be disposed of as the earner saw fit, suddenly introduced a concept of independence that was not easily understood by the commoners and was feared by the chiefs. Adding to the independence of the commoners was the fact that workers no longer had to pay taxes to the chiefs. It was more than the average Islander could comprehend. There was nothing in their history, no precedent, no legend, that could be used to bridge this gap.

Many difficulties arose. When the Hawaiians thought that they were to be paid their daily wage of twelve and one-half cents by the chiefs, they refused to work; they believed the chiefs would keep the money. When they were paid directly by the plantation, they worked. The laborers could not believe they would not have to pay taxes, and again they refused to work until this idea was repeatedly driven home to them. Realizing they no longer had the control they once had over the commoners, the chiefs tried to upset the new system by refusing to sell poi to William Hooper and by placing a kapu on fishing the waters off Koloa. This would cause problems because the plantation had agreed to supply a meal of fish and poi to the laborers each working day.

On occasion the workers went through the motions of caring for the fields, accomplishing practically nothing. The plantation manager was beside himself. He did not know the Hawaiians still could not comprehend the fact that their wages and the things they bought with them would be their own possessions and could not be appropriated at will by the chiefs.

The man chosen to run Koloa plantation was William Hooper, a small, slender man who was the youngest partner in Ladd and Company. It was a wise choice, because a person of lesser determination would certainly have failed. Hooper immediately ran into difficulties with the chiefs and often had to overcome these problems by appealing to the higher authority of the governor and the king, or to the calm, respected authority of Samuel Whitney. Hooper was neither a farmer nor an engineer, yet he had to grow cane, develop a factory to grind the juice from the stalks, and boil the liquid down to sugar. There was nearly a complete lack of equipment. Fields were spaded with primitive 'ō'ō, digging sticks, and on occasion Hawaiians pulled plows because of a lack of oxen.

William Hooper was able to get twelve acres of sugarcane planted and then went on to coffee, taro, and bananas. But the main business was sugar, and once that was in the ground, attention was turned to building a mill. Hooper had counted on Joel P. Dedman, a carpenter he hired on Kauai, to supply some mechanical knowledge in the construction, but apparently Dedman knew no more than Hooper, so they simply stumbled ahead. In April 1836 work was pushed forward on building a dam and flume at Maulili Pond. Lumber was hard to come by, but a wooden structure with a thatched roof was put up to house the wooden rollers to press the juice from the cane. Try-pots, used aboard whaling ships in rendering oil from blubber, were used to boil the juice.

In July the Ladds were visiting Koloa and Hooper wrote that Mrs. Ladd made some molasses from the cane juice. But the mill did not work well, and it was a matter of constant alteration. In the middle of November Hooper wrote that the mill worked admirably, but a day or a week later he might be frustrated by new difficulties. By the end of 1836 Hooper reported that production for the year amounted to 80 or 100 barrels of molasses. The iron try-pots were ill-suited to boiling juice, and Hooper anxiously awaited the arrival of copper ones from New England.

The wooden rollers very soon showed signs of wear. Three iron rollers arrived in January 1837 and were unloaded at Koloa with the assistance of special gear and a rigger. A new dam was constructed below the old one at Maulili, and then it too had to be rebuilt. By the end of 1837 the iron rollers were in place and the stream of water flowing over the waterwheel caused the rollers to "move with a frightful rapidity." Pans and earthen pots for crystallizing and draining the sugar were imported from China along with several experienced sugar boilers to operate the equipment. The containers for sugar were bags with rawhide handles, woven of rushes by women who were paid three cents per bag.

The iron rollers and other additions were a great help toward getting the plantation functioning. If things worked well the mill could grind enough cane in one day to produce 500 pounds of sugar. But things rarely worked well. Getting the cane to the mill, grinding it, drying the sugar, and arranging for enough water to move the waterwheel and so to supply power, all took a great deal of coordination. Things were constantly going wrong. One morning in December 1837 the thatched roof of one of the boiling-houses caught fire.

William Hooper raced from his bed to fight the flames. Fortunately, the damage was only to the roof. Hooper himself lived in a grass-thatched house, which he called his "barn." Somehow the operation staggered forward.

Coin in sufficient quantity to pay the workers was difficult to come by in Hawaii in the 1830s. William Hooper solved this problem by making his own scrip with which he paid the workers. It was pasteboard currency in denominations of twelve and one-half cents, called *hapawalu,* twenty-five cents, *hapahā,* and fifty cents, *hapalua.* The currency was redeemable at the plantation store in goods. When the Hawaiians made counterfeit currency, Hooper sent to Boston for a set of engravings that were too difficult to duplicate, and eventually Ladd and Company also printed three- and five-dollar bills. Koloa money began to circulate outside the plantation store, its value decreased, and the workers went on strike. When it was known that tax collectors were accepting the money, confidence and buying power returned and the laborers went back to work.

Producing currency became such a satisfactory solution to the shortage of coin that others on Kauai, including Charles Titcomb, paid their workers with scrip that they produced. The Koloa currency remained in use on Kauai until at least 1850. The need to privately print currency was an illustration of the period of transition on Kauai. The age-old barter system was no longer practical.

Some of the missionaries started to grow sugarcane and William Hooper became annoyed with them, particularly with the Reverend Peter Gulick and the Reverend Doctor Lafon, both of Koloa. Gulick also opened a dairy in competition with Hooper. After the American Board of Missions began to withdraw financial support to Hawaii in 1837, these commercial activities increased because the mission in the Hawaiian Islands had to survive as best it could. In exasperation Hooper wrote to his partners, making scathing remarks about missionary commercial activities, but there is no evidence the missionaries learned of his sentiments.

There were other problems—continuing problems of coordinating the supply of cane with grinding, boiling, drying, and shipping. When additional cane was planted, the mill and boiling-house could not handle the load. Soon the chiefs started to plant cane also, and expected the plantation to process it for them, creating yet another problem. The 1837–1838 season brought a yield of 30 tons of sugar and 170 barrels of molasses. In March of 1838 a test acre produced a surprising 5,039 pounds of sugar and 400 gallons of molasses. Koloa was on its way to being a success.

At Koloa Hooper developed a pattern for plantations that was to endure for over 100 years. There was a plantation-owned general store at Koloa where workers and others in the community bought a variety of goods. Housing was provided for the workers, a series of individual thatched homes and stone barrack-type buildings, and space was provided to plant a garden and keep a few animals. The company dairy sold milk to the workers. Medical aid was provided when a missionary-doctor was stationed at Koloa. The supplies the plantation needed were purchased through Ladd and Company, a forerunner of Honolulu's factoring companies. If it was a system that financially benefited the plantation owners, it also helped the Hawaiians make the transition from their ancient system of dependence on the chiefs into a new world of independence. Later, it was an assistance for immigrant workers coming to a strange country. The system continued in operation well into the twentieth century by which time it was considered outdated and paternalistic by the workers.

From his earliest days at Koloa, William Hooper realized he needed agricultural and mechanical help. He corresponded with the Reverend Reuben Tinker at Lahainaluna on Maui, seeking to learn ways to improve the mill, but there were limits on what could be done through letters. For a period of time it was hoped the Reverend Joseph Goodrich, a missionary who was returning to the United States, might serve as manager of the plantation. In April 1836 Hooper wrote his partners, "I beg of you to write to Rev. Goodrich, requesting him to embark immediately. . . . We shall never make this land a profitable one unless we have an experienced farmer with farming utensils."

But Goodrich did not appear. The American Board decided that a former missionary should not enter the secular field in the Islands, and Goodrich stood by the board's decision. Hooper did his best and after a while came to the conclusion that help was more desperately needed at the mill than in the fields.

In December 1837 Hooper asked his partner Peter Brinsmade, then in the United States, to negotiate with Charles Burnham to come to Kauai as manager of the plantation. Burnham, a carpenter, had been in the Islands earlier and had supervised the building of the Bethel Church and a house for the chaplain in Honolulu. Then he had been in charge of building operations at Lahainaluna. His good reputation included the ability to work well with Hawaiians.

Charles Burnham and his wife arrived at Koloa on 27 April 1839 and made an excellent impression on Hooper. On 6 May Burnham took over the operation of Koloa, a tremendous relief for Hooper, who had worked himself to near exhaustion, both physically and emotionally.

Koloa was a nearly viable operation, but the financial drain on Ladd and Company during the development of the plantation had been severe. Instead of retrenching, the company expanded their interests, developing mulberry orchards for the production of silk, as well as kukui and castor beans as sources of oil. Nevertheless, the company did not have the capital to attempt such expansion, especially in view of the shortage of credit brought about by a financial crisis in the United States in 1837.

By 1840 Ladd and Company felt so severely pressed they considered selling out their interests to a person or company having greater resources. When the government and missionaries learned of this they were greatly distressed. They tried to persuade Ladd and Company to change their plans or, at the least, to maintain a controlling position in the company. By way of inducing the partners to remain, the government offered them "the full right and privilege of occupying for the purpose of manufacturing agricultural productions, any now unoccupied and unimproved localities on the several islands of the Sandwich Islands, suitable for the manufacture of sugar, indigo, flour, raw silk, Kukui oil, or any other productions of the country." The government would receive annual rent of fifty cents per acre on all lands used, and ten dollars a year for any mill sites. Leases would run for 100 years.

This agreement was drawn up secretly at Lahaina on 24 November 1841. There was one major condition set on this incredible offer. It was considered unwise to allow the extensive commercial development of the Islands without first receiving the recognition of Hawaii as an independent nation from the United States, England, and France. Such recognition would protect the kingdom from these three major powers and would greatly discourage other nations from interfering in Hawaiian affairs. It was expected Ladd and Company would play a role in securing this recognition.

While Ladd and Company undoubtedly felt they had won a great opportunity, they certainly did not properly value one commodity that was difficult to enter in their account books. That commodity was the high esteem in which the missionaries, the government, and the general population held the company. An example of the company's prestige in the kingdom was the fact that they rightfully took some credit for Hawaii's first constitution in 1840, which, among other things, provided for an elected house of representatives. From the moment it became known that the three partners were considering selling their interests, however, the asset of high esteem began to erode.

Peter Brinsmade went off to the United States looking for financial backers to take advantage of the great possibilities that the contract offered. Not finding the sort of financing he needed in either Boston or New York, Brinsmade set out for Europe. He found little interest in England or France, but had serious discussions with the Belgian Company of Colonization. At this point William Richards, who had been a missionary at Lahaina and had subsequently been named to the important position of instructor to the chiefs, and Timothy Haalilio, secretary to Kamehameha III, arrived in Europe. The two men were seeking recognition of Hawaii as an independent nation by England and France. Brinsmade learned that Richards held the power of attorney for Kamehameha, and he talked Richards into making the king a party to the Belgian negotiations to add prestige to his cause.

While Brinsmade was in Europe, the financial condition of Ladd and Company worsened. The company borrowed funds from the government and from private parties, using their lands as collateral. Hooper and Ladd thought they would have to close down their operation at the end of 1843, but they held on, hoping the Belgian contract would materialize. Brinsmade did all he could, including the drawing up of the many details necessary to complete the arrangements, but consummation always lay just beyond his grasp. William Richards returned from Europe in March 1845 with word that negotiations had failed. Brinsmade also came back, on funds he was forced to borrow from Richards. Ladd and Company was bankrupt. In the angry aftermath the partners claimed that the government had deliberately ruined the company. Arbitration was agreed to, but Ladd and Company withdrew, bringing an end to one of Hawaii's most promising companies.

Eventually the three partners left Hawaii. The demise of Ladd and Company had divided Honolulu into various factions, and the Islands could hardly have been a happy place for those who had lost. Peter Brinsmade went to California in search of new opportunities in the goldfields. His wife lay buried in a cemetery above Koloa plantation. Her headstone bore a Greek inscription, which translated read "the night cometh." William Ladd eventually returned to the East Coast.

William Hooper moved to San Francisco, where he became the first president of the Chamber of Commerce. He died there in 1878.

Koloa plantation survived the demise of Ladd and Company. After more litigation, Dr. Robert W. Wood, the brother-in-law of William Hooper, became its sole owner. Charles Burnham remained as manager for five years. The plantation not only became profitable, but also was long a model for other plantations throughout the Islands.

Traveling on the interisland schooners was an experience few Westerners forgot—or wished to repeat. Sometimes, of course, the passage was a relatively calm overnight crossing, but usually it was a frightful experience aboard an overcrowded, stinking vessel, a voyage that could last up to a week and that tried the endurance of even the strongest-willed. James Jarves first made the trip from Honolulu to Koloa in 1837, and wrote about it with great feeling.

> In voyaging from island to island there is but little choice in the means of conveyance; a canoe, or a miniature vessel of a few tons burden. . . . The captain was a clever fellow, having under his orders a mate and cook. For several years had he commanded this stout schooner, and he knew every wave by sight, and every change of wind and variation of current by instinct. If anyone doubts his seamanship, let him go no farther; as for his face, it was the very picture of inward satisfaction.
>
> Talk about the horrors of the "mid-passage." No slave, pent in his vile hole, ever settled more unwilling account with his brineship than I did in the "mid-channel." Just picture the comfort to be enjoyed in a little-decked vessel, a sort of amphibious craft, not so large as a frigate's launch, whirled and tossed in the froth of the ocean like a mere feather, now under water, now out again, shaking the spray from itself, much like an old water dog.
>
> Being sea sick was bad enough, but possibly even worse was squatting on deck watching a Hawaiian eat poi. Reader, were you ever in such a situation—did your nose ever acquire an extra "turn up" as the reeking odors of poi in all its sweet savor struck upon your nostrils? Have you never envied the graceful nonchalance with which a grinning Hawaiian slips the sticky food down his throat, smacking his lips in the extent of his satisfaction, and with a benevolent smile, offering to share his mess with your forlorn self? Did not the poi smell particularly sour just then?

At Koloa interisland ships anchored in the open roadstead or sailed off-and-on while small boats carried passengers ashore. It was a final trial for passengers who had suffered through the channel voyage. The landing was a rough stone pier, built at the mouth of Koloa Stream, protected by a rocky point.

George Washington Bates visited Kauai in 1853, and when he came ashore at Koloa, he wrote, the Hawaiians on the beach were selling poi, raw fish, bunches of bananas, and sugarcane. They tried to communicate with the foreigners "with detached sentences, composed of Hawaiian and English. . . . Further on is a crowd of sharpers—natives of course, who have learned the art of extorting money—who are very desirous of hiring their miserable horses to a foreigner for $1 to $1.50 per mile, and some foreigners are foolish enough to pay the sum demanded by them."

Along the shore the land was stony and dry, Bates observed. Behind it a rising plain ran gradually upward to a height of a few hundred feet, where it met a range of high hills. Rain fell on these hills and the resulting streams provided ample water for the lowlands. The scene included a variety of distant mountains and hills, plains, and valleys. After the establishment of Koloa plantation a sprinkling of homes, the sugar mill, and Koloa church could be seen from the shore. When Jarves visited the area he found a "flourishing village" with the whole district having a population of about 2,000.

Records of Koloa before the sugar enterprise was begun are scanty. Few Westerners visited there. One known account, written by Samuel Whitney in 1826, mentioned his seeing a Spaniard there, but it is not clear if he was a resident or not. The remains of fishponds and salt pans along the shore, and abandoned fields on higher ground, indicate that Koloa was well populated by the ancient Hawaiians.

With the establishment of the sugar plantation, outsiders began to appear at Koloa. They seem to have been an independent breed of men, most of them former sailors who had decided to come ashore. There were Charles Titcomb and Sherman Peck, who raised mulberry trees to feed silkworms, and George Charman, an Englishman, who took over the small sugar plantation owned by Charles Tobey and Robert Wood. Charman cut and sold wood to sailing vessels and shipped some to Honolulu. He also raised horses and cattle. Fellow residents remember him going about his chores with a clay pipe constantly clenched between his teeth.

John Cook was a carpenter, and Robert Brown a blacksmith. Both were Welshmen. Later they became converted to Mormonism and traveled to Salt Lake City. After Walter Murray Gibson came to

Hawaii, representing himself as a high official of the Mormon church, they followed him to Lanai where he started a colony. Eventually they became disillusioned and returned to Kauai. These men and others supplied some of the mechanical needs of Koloa plantation and its neighbors.

Workers on the plantation spent five days a week at their labors. Saturday was the day for doing personal chores, and one of its pleasures was that it was market day. Jarves wrote that the shops on the plantations were open to redeem paper money and purchase articles that might be brought for sale. Crowds of people came early, "in the rudest attire, or no attire at all." There were vegetables, fish, tapas, mats, and a wide selection of items for Hawaiians and foreigners alike. The Western traders also set out their goods—knives, needles, flints, calicoes—in as tempting a way as possible. James Jarves went on to describe the bartering that followed.

> The rigidity of the facial muscle, which so peculiarly characterizes an American trader, rendering the features stiff and uninviting, forcibly contrast with the varied expression, the shrug of the shoulder, and gesture of the limb, which so strongly imply what words are weak in conveying, and which no Hawaiian fails to use in the greatest profusion, accompanied with certain suspicious grunts.

During the 1840s and 1850s Hawaiians and foreigners patronized the Ladd and Company store and the transient merchants who visited the island. For those adventurous enough to go to Honolulu there were the interisland schooners. Ladd and Company owned a vessel, which plied between Kauai and Honolulu as often as necessary, and later Jules Dudoit sailed his own small ship out of Hanalei. So it was not difficult to get merchandise from Honolulu, where stores stocked a wide variety of goods imported from England, Germany, France, and the United States. The more affluent and patient customer might send to Australia for luxuries.

Koloa was the center of agriculture, and as such it became the center of activity for Kauai. The port of Koloa, while far from ideal, became the most frequented. Most of the whalers seeking supplies stopped there, and sugar was shipped to Honolulu from Koloa. Travelers departed and returned from Koloa, although Nawiliwili Bay was used increasingly because it was closer to Oahu. From the founding of Koloa plantation through the 1850s, the homes of the missionaries—

the Smiths, the Gulicks, the Pogues, and others—became virtual wayside inns for visitors to Koloa. Belatedly, in the mid-1850s, Koloa was named the port of entry for Kauai and a customs officer was stationed there.

Waimea remained the nominal capital and provided a safer anchorage than Koloa. Some whalers stopped there for supplies and interisland vessels put in an appearance, but there was little activity. Samuel Whitney remained at Waimea, but on occasion he apparently was not willing to wait for his mail and he rode to Koloa to pick it up. Governor Kaikioewa kept his main residence at Waimea, although he traveled about the island a good deal.

Hanalei was visited by an occasional whaler and by interisland ships, since there was some cargo to be carried out, but it was a dangerous harbor, especially when winter winds and rain blew down from the north. The ancient capital of Wailua, without any anchorage or landing, was principally known as the residence of Deborah Kapule, whose home served as a hospitable stopping point for numerous travelers on their way to or from Hanalei.

During the years of the mid-nineteenth century, Kauai continued as the most isolated of the major islands. The untamed sea was a buffer against intruders, both physically and psychologically. The island also remained bountiful. Water was plentiful and gardens flourished. Early visitors to Kauai wrote of the abundance and variety of the flora there.

The charge of the Prudential Committee to the missionaries as they sailed from Boston had been eloquent, yet direct.

> Your views are not to be limited to a low or a narrow scale; but you are to open your hearts wide, and set your mark high. You are to aim at nothing short of covering those islands with fruitful fields and pleasant dwellings, and schools and churches; of raising up the whole people to an elevated state of Christian civilization.

Kauai was a fruitful place and Koloa plantation had made it even more so. The missionaries had covered the island with schools and churches. The merchant-farmers of Koloa had combined with the missionaries in an effort to raise up the people to a condition of independence through employment in the sugar fields. Even the austere Prudential Committee would have agreed that attention had been paid to their charge, and that the Almighty had seen fit to grant a degree of success to missionary efforts.

CHAPTER EIGHT

A Conquered Race

On the night of 6 April 1834 a Frenchman by the name of Felix S. V. Geraud was murdered in his store at Waimea. His skull was broken and his neck bore marks of strangulation. Geraud had run a dry-goods store at Waimea and after his murder a good deal of merchandise was missing.

Two Hawaiian men had gone to the store on the pretense of selling sandalwood to Geraud. While one of the men talked with the merchant, the other attacked him from behind. The two then took the things they wanted and left. Part of the stolen goods were soon found in a house nearby and the occupant confessed. A second man, a cousin of the first, was quickly apprehended.

That the victim was Caucasian apparently caused a stir. Otherwise, as Mercy Whitney recorded in her journal, "There has been but little notice of late taken on murder & other crimes . . . [and] in consequence [they] become very bold and daring in iniquity." She continued, "it is distressing to think, that we live in the midst of those, who for the hope of obtaining a little worldly gain do not hesitate to take the lives of their fellow beings." She then recalled two past occasions when her husband had narrowly escaped violence.

While Waimea was in shock over the murder of Geraud, a man and woman were taken into custody on the east side of Kauai and brought to Waimea. Their crime had a different motive. The pair were lovers and together they had murdered the woman's husband. Governor Kaikioewa came to Waimea, and the four persons were tried and pronounced guilty. A gallows was constructed outside Waimea, and the four were hung on 6 May 1834, and buried nearby. For many years the deteriorating gallows remained and the graves became overgrown with weeds. Mercy Whitney supposed it was "a sight probably never before witnessed at the Sandwich Islands."

In his church report for 1834 the Reverend Whitney enlarged on the situation.

> Shocking as it may seem Schools have been taught for two years past for the purpose of acquiring the art of murder. The instrument of death is a small rope with a noose and the art of using it consists in being able to catch the unwary traveller, strangle him and break his bones in an instant. Two of these ropes have been in my possession within the last six months. The owner of one of them confessed that fifteen men had been murdered with his and [with] the other, eight.

Who were these desperate men who had learned the art of murder? It appears these were the people who had been set adrift when the chiefs of Kauai were dispossessed after the rebellion of 1824. They had found no place in the new system of things and deprived of the use of land and leaderless, they existed as best they could.

Samuel Kamakau wrote that "the loafers and hangers-on of Oahu and Maui obtained the rich lands of Kauai." Jarves encountered one of these "loafers" in the 1840s who, years earlier, had been rewarded with the use of land at Anahola. Jarves called the old man a "Prince of Laziness" and said he lived off his "wretched tenants." These newcomers cared nothing for the people who lived on the land and kept only those tenants who were necessary to supply their comforts.

The condition of these people was further described by Jarves. "The Kauaians were, of all others, the most oppressed by their chiefs, being despised and contemned, as a conquered race. Their degradation was beyond account; and when the plantations were first established among them, their stupidity and vicious habits threatened to prove insuperable obstacles to their success."

William Hooper had a difficult time acquiring laborers during his early years at Koloa. He was able to hire some local workers, but their chiefs, afraid of losing their age-old authority over commoners, did everything possible to prevent it. Forced to take whatever laborers he could get, Hooper also employed stragglers, men who roamed the island seeking the necessities of life. Some, both local and transients, proved to be good workers, but others did not: "It was with much difficulty that they [workers] could be obtained; and when procured proved to be off-scourings of the island. Of this number nearly one half were soon discharged for various misdemeanors . . . and punished by the authorities of the place, after a fair and legal trial by jury."

The loss of Kauai's old ruling chiefs had left a void that had to be filled in some way. The windward chiefs, who occupied the lands they had been awarded, were, at best, disinterested in the people who dwelt on them. By neglect they abdicated their roles as chiefs. In time a new group of chiefs emerged on Kauai, people who possessed authority or wealth, and often both. Some of the missionaries provided leadership through authority, through the setting of standards, as well as by demonstrating a concern for individuals. Such ministers as Samuel Whitney, George Rowell, Doctor James Smith, William Alexander, and Daniel Dole were among those who were looked to for guidance.

Deborah Kapule was the most prominent person of rank to remain on Kauai after the rebellion. In an earlier age she would have been deported with the other chiefs, but in 1824 such action would have brought the disapproval of the missionaries, who had already begun to represent a kind of moral judgment. Kapule had also supported the windward chiefs in their time of crisis at the fort at Waimea, an act of great assistance in keeping the rebellion in check. Eventually Governor Kaikioewa became jealous of Kapule's popularity and succeeded in having her deported to Oahu, but with missionary help she was able to return to Kauai. As long as she lived Deborah Kapule remained the most prominent of the alii on Kauai.

The men who ran the plantations and ranches were considered chiefs because of their positions of authority. Not all of them had empathy for the Hawaiians or had gained their respect, but over the years those who had were numbered among the new chiefs of Kauai. Valdemar Knudsen, William Harrison Rice, Duncan McBryde, Godfrey Wundenberg, and Paul Isenberg were among them. As did most of the missionaries, they spoke and wrote Hawaiian. Isenberg, for example, kept the journal of Lihue plantation for a number of years and during his time it was written in Hawaiian.

Among the "new alii" were Mary Sophia Rice and Eliza Sinclair. Rice, who outlived her husband by many years, had a rapport with the Hawaiians that went back to her days at Hana, Maui. Through her long life she influenced many by her example. Sinclair, with her vast land holdings, was certainly considered a chiefess by the people who lived in her domains. She and her descendants employed many Hawaiians on Niihau and at Makaweli.

Some of the sons of these families, who had grown up with the Kauaians, had an even closer attachment and understanding of the Kauaians than their parents. As children, George and Albert Wilcox,

William Hyde Rice, Francis Gay, and Aubrey Robinson had gone to Sunday school with the Hawaiians, and worked with them through their adult lives. William Hyde Rice had a knowledge of the Hawaiian language on its several levels, something very few Hawaiians possessed. He had mastered the inner meaning of the language and said that he thought in Hawaiian, not English. He felt most at ease speaking Hawaiian and preferred that language. Many believe his book *Hawaiian Legends* is the closest written expression of the ancient legends.

Twenty-one years after the Protestant ministers landed at Waimea, a Roman Catholic priest arrived on Kauai. He was Father Arsenius Robert Walsh of the congregation of Sacred Hearts. He had first come to Honolulu in 1836, and like other Roman Catholics, his first years in the Islands were difficult ones. The predominantly Protestant monarchy looked with disfavor on the introduction of a competing religion. The first priests were forbidden to teach their faith and had been expelled in 1831.

Walsh enjoyed an advantage over other priests. Although he belonged to a French order, Walsh had been born in Ireland and was a British citizen. He was among those ordered to leave the Islands at one time, but before this order could be carried out, French, British, and American warships had arrived in succession at Honolulu. They took up the cause of Father Walsh and in the end the Hawaiian monarchy reluctantly allowed him to remain, largely because he was a British citizen and the English occupied a favored status in Hawaii at that time.

On 22 December 1841, at age thirty-seven, Walsh arrived at Koloa and immediately began his labors. On Christmas Day Walsh recorded in his journal, "I have celebrated the first mass that has ever been celebrated to my knowledge on the island of Kauai and founded the mission of St. Raphael the Archangel." This first mass was conducted before a crude altar of stone under a tree, a short distance east of the stone pier at the Koloa landing. The Catholic priest received enough help from the people of Koloa to start him on his missionary efforts. Thomas Pratt, who owned a store and boarding house, brought him a horse, on instructions of William French. John Hobbs, a harnessmaker at Koloa, provided other assistance. Walsh was given shelter at the home of Jacob Pehu.

Father Walsh began proselytizing right away. He began a class of instruction for interested persons and started a school. He then set out for Hanalei, accompanied by Thomas Pratt. At Hanalei James Kellett treated Walsh well, as did Charles Titcomb. On his return to Koloa Walsh stopped at Moloaa where he made a list of thirty-four persons who wanted religious instruction.

Waiting for Walsh at Koloa was Father Barnabe Castan, who had just arrived to serve as an assistant. Castan proved to be a hardworking man, performing many chores for the mission. News of the presence of Castan quickly spread, and a delegation of people came from Moloaa to ask that he be stationed in their village. Walsh hesitated, but the villagers were so determined in their request that he gave in to their wishes. Moloaa became a center of Catholicism during these early days. In the school built there, the girls worked at spinning and recited their lessons at the same time.

At Moloaa the Catholics had their first substantial success and also their first problems with Kauai officialdom. At the time Kekauonohi, a staunch Protestant, was governess. She was a high chiefess of Maui, married to Kealiiahonui, who was a son of Kaumualii and had once been a husband of Kaahumanu. The governess did not personally order trouble for the Catholics, but her attitude was well known and she was slow to rectify the actions of chiefs who felt the presence of Walsh and Castan was an affront to their own beliefs.

The chief at Moloaa, annoyed that some children were attending the new Catholic school, decreed that the parents of these children could not cut wood in the mountains, fish in the sea, or take taro from their own lands. This virtually cut them off from the essentials of life. These restrictions were relaxed by Governess Kekauonohi, but they were typical of the harassment encountered by the followers of Walsh and Castan during the early years.

Father Walsh's years on Kauai were divided between two activities. First, he attempted to convert people to Catholicism—an effort that carried him on a constant round of the villages. Second, he devoted much effort to trying to reverse judgments against Catholics he considered to be the victims of prejudice on the part of the government. The Protestant missionaries remained aloof from the priests, although they spoke of Walsh as a man of low character—he drank on occasion and frequently smoked a pipe. Walsh proclaimed that the textbooks used in Protestant schools were composed of lies.

Arsenius Walsh made his first trip to Niihau in July 1842. He ran into the usual opposition, but in the end preached to a sizable gathering of people. Earlier in the year, in March, Walsh had constructed a small chapel at Koloa and he continued to establish churches and schools at a fast rate. The methods of the Protestants and the Catholics in accepting members into their churches bore a curious contrast and both were criticized. Many believed the Catholics accepted members much too quickly, while others thought the Protestants required candidates for church membership to wait much too long.

A major problem of the Catholic church on Kauai was the continuing number of French and Belgian priests who were sent to the island. Usually they spoke only French on arrival and learned Hawaiian in the course of their stay. Because of this the Catholic church on Kauai was commonly referred to as the French church.

Malcolm Brown, a son of Thomas Brown of Wailua Valley, remembered Walsh from Kauai. On one occasion Walsh had been thrown from his horse near their home and suffered fractured ribs. He was nursed back to health by the Browns. Later, when the Browns and Walsh were living on Oahu, Malcolm and his brother Cecil continued their friendship with the priest. They considered him a down-to-earth, pleasant man.

Arsenius Robert Walsh left Kauai in 1848 to return to Oahu. His assistant, Barnabe Castan, had left four years earlier, and his place on Kauai was taken by Denis Maudet, who stayed on the island until 1879. Churches and schools continued to be built, including a chapel at Hanalei, dedicated 23 October 1864. It was built at the mouth of the Hanalei River on land that had been deeded to John Brosseau by Kamehameha III in 1849. The land subsequently ended up in the hands of Godfrey Rhodes, who donated it to the Catholic church in 1860.

As for Father Walsh, he spent his last years of service to his church at Ahuimanu on Oahu, where he died on 14 October 1869. He was held in high esteem by the Hawaiians and at his funeral a Catholic Hawaiian-language newspaper reported "many were the tears that flowed."

Optimistic reports of progress in cultivating sugarcane at Koloa plantation raised interest in other agricultural crops. The most promising of these new experiments, begun at Koloa, was silk culture, started in 1836 by Sherman Peck and Charles Titcomb. Land was leased from Ladd and Company, and thousands of mulberry slips were planted to grow the leaves on which the silkworms fed. Initial trials exceeded expectations, and Sherman Peck went to the United States in search of more information, machinery, and silkworm eggs. Interest in the project was aroused in the United States. In 1839 a second silk-producing company was started at Koloa.

By 1840, just as it seemed success was about to be realized, a severe drought hit Koloa. Then a species of aphid covered the trees, followed by an invasion of spiders and then unusually strong Kona, or southerly, winds. The leaves and blossoms of the ravaged trees wilted and blew away. By 1841 Peck and Titcomb had no more capital to expend and the silk industry at Koloa succumbed. Sugarcane was planted where the mulberry trees had stood. Sherman Peck went to Lahaina, where he became a successful merchant, and later he became a partner in the Honolulu firm of C. Brewer and Company, Ltd. The undaunted Charles Titcomb still had hopes for the development of a silk industry and tried again at Hanalei.

John Wilkinson, who had planted sugarcane in Manoa Valley on Oahu in 1825, had also planted young coffee trees which he had brought from Rio de Janeiro. When Wilkinson died the following year, the coffee was left to grow wild. Many years later, in 1842, John Bernard and Godfrey Rhodes started a plantation at Hanalei with plants and seeds taken from Manoa. Soon Charles Titcomb, who had finally given up on the silk industry, replaced the mulberry trees at Hanalei with coffee, and also planted coffee on land at Kilauea. In 1846 Thomas Brown established a dairy and laid out coffee fields in Wailua Valley. These were the only systematically organized plantations in the Islands in the mid-1840s.

In the summer of 1845 Gorham Gilman traveled to Kauai from Honolulu, planning to spend two weeks looking after the coffee plantation at Hanalei while Titcomb was in Honolulu. It was more than a vacation. Gilman recruited twelve "boys" in Honolulu who agreed to work on the Hanalei plantation for two years. The recruits sailed with Gilman to Koloa and then proceeded to Hanalei. Gilman rode ahead, and the workers walked, trailing along at their own speed. One night was spent at Wailua, and Gilman recounted the hospitality of Deborah Kapule there. Eventually the group of twelve straggled into Hanalei.

Once at their destination the adventure of travel was at an end, and Gilman began to pay the price for his haphazard method of recruiting laborers. He admitted, "I had picked them up in the streets never having seen them before and being unacquainted with the characters, dispositions & trusting to management to bring them to subjection and regularity."

Gorham Gilman noted that before the first day's work was begun, "the romance of the thing was over." It became apparent "as far as work was concerned they could do as little as any—and for mischief they were ripe." Gilman did not report on how Titcomb reacted to his new employees or what happened to them. After two weeks at Hanalei, Gilman left his recruits behind and was off to visit Niihau before returning to Honolulu.

Coffee-growing on Kauai was a wildly erratic business, affected by a shortage of labor, drought, and diseases, and by fitful swings of supply and demand for coffee in the California goldfields. There were several financially successful early years—just enough to keep farmers optimistic about the future. Export records show that 248 pounds of coffee were shipped from the Islands in 1845. In 1847 over 26,000 pounds were exported, but in the same year two weeks of heavy rains cut streambeds through the fields. Earth, masses of rock, and uprooted trees were strewn through the orchards. Starting in 1848 men were lured to the California goldfields, and labor shortages became even more severe.

Some planters, such as Godfrey F. Wundenberg and John von Pfister, went to California to seek quick fortunes as did Herman A. Widemann. Wundenberg and Widemann both returned safely to Kauai, but von Pfister was murdered in San Francisco.

There were one or two good years after 1850, but competition for the California market, drought, and blight were too much and by about 1857 coffee at Hanalei and on Kauai was a thing of the past. Several years before coffee came to an end at Hanalei the fields of Thomas Brown at Wailua had been abandoned. Saline water, bad seed, and an invasion of caterpillars combined to bring Brown's coffee plantation to an end. Brown's dairy, however, did well. He shipped kegs of butter to Honolulu.

Tobacco seemed to be a possible commercial crop. It was grown in Hanalei beginning in 1851, but cutworms destroyed the plants. During the few years of production, enough tobacco had been grown to ship cigars to Honolulu. In 1853 two plantations were established in the dryer climes of Mana, each about 250 acres. The now familiar pattern unfolded. Initially the plants grew exceptionally well, but insects and disease brought an end to the enterprise by 1856.

Many other crops were grown, mostly on a small scale to be sold locally and to visiting whaling ships. For several years during the gold rush potatoes and oranges were exported to California. Oranges were grown near Hanalei, packed in straw, and shipped directly to California. Limes, figs, and grapes were grown mostly for local consumption.

In 1831 Richard Charlton, the British consul for Hawaii, leased an undefined stretch of land near Hanalei from Governor Kaikioewa. About 100 cattle roamed over this land, but Charlton did not meet his commitment to deliver lumber, to be cut into 560 boards, as the lease rent. After some legal adjustments Jules Dudoit, who had been French consul for Hawaii, took over the ranch in 1848, moving to Hanalei to personally handle the operation. He shipped cattle from Hanalei to Honolulu and packed salt beef for whaling ships. Eventually Dudoit returned to Honolulu.

Joseph Gardner in 1831 "was conducting a small cloth factory at Waioli, Kauai, in which business the Governor was associated with him." Gardner was in charge of the government sheep and was rewarded with the wool for his work. In the small factory there were several spinning wheels and a loom, and woolen and cotton blankets and saddle girthing were made. At Moloaa John Mitchell set up shop as a shoemaker and saddler. Later he moved to Kilauea where he ran a tannery.

Kauai had only the beginnings of a sugar industry and a meager whaling trade as sources of income, but with a handful of craftsmen, a few ranches, and the produce from a scattering of small tracts of land, Kauaians were self-sufficient in many essential respects.

Kaikioewa, a cousin of Kamehameha I, was a warrior-chief who believed in the absolute authority of his rank. Western men and ideas softened his attitudes only insofar as rapidly changing times made it necessary. As governor of Kauai he was the unqualified ruler of the island. Born at Waimea on Kauai in 1765, Kaikioewa spent his early years there, before moving to Hilo on the island of Hawaii. Although he was a cousin of Kamehameha, the young Kaikioewa joined the chiefs of Hilo in opposing the future king.

After the battle of Hilo, Kaikioewa with some local chiefs joined the forces of Kamehameha. Over the years he proved his value to the windward king as a decisive, brave, and loyal warrior. Kaikioewa was with Kamehameha when he conquered Oahu. At an early time Kamehameha had saved Kaikioewa's life after the rash warrior had stolen the wife of another chief. The chief had then captured Kaikioewa and was about to kill him in revenge when Kamehameha came to the rescue. Later Kamehameha gave a sister of his to his faithful follower, as a wife. When Kaumualii came to Honolulu in 1810, Kaikioewa was among those who had knowledge of the plot to kill the leeward king. In 1819 Kaikioewa was wounded helping to put down the rebellion that followed the announcement that the old kapu system had been abolished.

Kaikioewa became even more closely entwined with the monarchy at the birth of Kauikeaouli, who would become Kamehameha III. The infant's mother had promised him to Kuakini, but that high chief heard that the child had been born dead and refused the offer. Hearing of this, a prophet retained by Kaikioewa quickly came and announced that the child was not dead. The prophet fanned the child and said prayers, and soon the infant stirred and cried. Because of this Kaikioewa became the guardian of the child, taking him to Kekaha on Kauai where the boy remained for five or six years.

With Kamehameha's wars over and the kingdom secured, Kaikioewa joined many other chiefs in a life of ease and dissipation. He is reported to have stayed at Lahaina for a period of time taking great pleasure in drinking. His friends were foreign traders and liquor merchants.

Christianity apparently was not of deep concern for Kaikioewa at first, although he was considerate of the missionaries long before he became a church member. In 1824, before sailing for Kauai to put down the rebellion, he asked the advice of the Reverend Hiram Bingham as to how he should conduct himself toward the enemy. Later he helped missionaries on Kauai by sending men into the mountains to cut trees for church construction, and on occasion he transported missionaries from Waimea to Hanalei in his double canoe.

Eventually Kaikioewa's curiosity about Christianity led to study and he worked diligently learning to read and write. The process was difficult for him, according to Samuel Whitney, but once he had made up his mind to become a Christian he spent long hours reading the Bible. He was admitted to the church at Waimea in 1830, at the age of sixty-five. From then until his death he was an aggressive supporter of the church.

When news reached Kaahumanu in 1824 that an uprising had occurred on Kauai, she wanted to help the besieged Kalanimoku, but was not certain whether a high chief should be sent. At a gathering Kaikioewa showed his customary decisiveness by stepping forward and announcing that he had played with Kalanimoku as a child, and that they had fought together for many years. Now that they were both old, he would not desert Kalanimoku, but would go to his rescue and so would his men.

Governor Kaikioewa seems to have had little interest in administrative work. When decisions had to be made, however, he made them with dispatch. No one on Kauai doubted that his word was absolute law. As governor of a conquered people his orders and demands were severe, although he does not appear to have been unduly harsh compared with other chiefs. Kaikioewa traveled about the island a good deal, accompanied by as many as 200 people. This was a hardship on the Kauaians, who were expected to feed the sizable crowd as they moved from place to place. Kaikioewa usually preceded the others, riding a white mule, followed by his guard, then by officials, and lastly, a collection of followers. During his years as governor Kaikioewa was known as an easy target for foreign merchants, from whom he bought a great variety of things whether they were of practical value or not. This put a heavy burden on the commoners who cut the sandalwood needed to pay the bills.

In 1835 the Honolulu merchant William French, hoping to go into the sugar business, brought some experienced workers from China. He searched about for a place to set up his crude stone mill and to gather sugarcane to process. He did not meet success until about two years later, when he worked out an arrangement with Kaikioewa. The governor would order the cane cut and carried to the mill, and French would grind it and produce the sugar and molasses. Each party would receive 50 percent of the profits. The mill was located at Waimea and wild cane was cut in the vicinity.

For some reason the final papers for the enterprise, which required the signature of the king, were never signed. Kaikioewa, unexplainably, stopped supplying French with cane. The project came to an end in 1838 when French took his men and equipment back to Honolulu. At this same time Ladd and Company was struggling to establish its sugar business, and it is possible that the three partners in that company, who had considerable political influence, were able to prevent French from getting permission to become a sugar producer as well. Whatever the reason for the failure of the Waimea project, it seems likely that Kaikioewa developed enough of an interest in the sugar business to want to pursue it further.

Through the years the governor had felt economic pressures and these were probably intense in the 1830s. The sandalwood forests were nearly depleted, and Kaikioewa could have earned very little from the trade of whaling ships, which then came only infrequently to Kauai. Perhaps sugar was a means of staying ahead of the New England merchant-captains, who were determined to collect their debts.

At about the time William French left Kauai the name Lihue first appeared in reports. In 1839 Dr. Thomas Lafon made his home in what became known as the Lihue district. The church he was in charge of there had been built by order of Kaikioewa. There must have been considerable activity in the Lihue area to cause Lafon to move there from Koloa. James Jarves, who passed through the area in 1840, reported that in addition to the church there was a "straw palace," built for Keaweamahi, the wife of Kaikioewa.

Little is known about Kaikioewa's plans for Lihue. It can be surmised it was intended to be a place of considerable importance, since the governor had built a residence and church there. Jarves mentioned in his description that Kaikioewa had selected Hanamaulu Bay as his harbor, "entirely overlooking the fact that it opened directly to the windward." Much later the Ahukini landing in Hanamaulu Bay would be used as a hauling point for sugar from Kauai.

Governor Kaikioewa died in 1839 and Lihue reverted to its quiet state for several years. Jarves, who was there in the year following the governor's death, wrote:

> There is a fine tract of land which the late governor selected as a site for a plantation, many acres of which he caused to be planted with cane, and also built a large church, and a house for himself. But death soon terminated his scheme, and his city, that was to be, still retains its original diminutiveness, while all the improvements, like his own body, are wasting away to mother earth again.

In October 1840 some members of the United States Exploring Expedition came through "Lihui." They noted that the Lafons were very industrious and their large school attracted children from five miles away. But the chroniclers of the expedition noted the same trend as did Jarves. "As yet there is little appearance of increase in industry, or improvement in the dwellings of the natives."

It would be several years before Henry A. Peirce would arrive at Nawiliwili Bay and visualize sugarcane covering the hillsides. Peirce's efforts would carry on the plan of Kaikioewa, who, as his last great effort, established a village that eventually would become the county seat of Kauai and its largest town.

There is no explanation for the choice of the name Lihue. It would be assumed it was the choice of Kaikioewa. Elsewhere in the Islands the name is found only near Wahiawa on Oahu, where it seems to have been of little significance. The name can be interpreted as meaning "cold chill," although it might well have had another meaning in ancient times.

On Kaikioewa's death his wife Keaweamahi, often known by her Christian name of Amelia, became interim governess of Kauai. She had been early opposed to foreigners and their ways, but came to be a faithful church member. After the death of her husband Keaweamahi remarried and lived in Waimea.

The new ruler of Kauai was the chiefess Kekauonohi of Maui, a granddaughter of Kamehameha I, who became governess in 1840. Kekauonohi had been a wife of Kamehameha II and had been on Kauai in 1824, the year of the rebellion. She later married Hoapili, the governor of Maui. Later yet she married Kealiiahonui, a son of Kaumualii, and he was presumably of valuable assistance to her in the role of governess. Kealiiahonui had the qualifications necessary to be governor, but through his life he was kept in the background because of the continuing jealousy of the windward chiefs. Kekauonohi remained governess until 1845, and died in 1851.

In 1846 Paul Kanoa was appointed governor of Kauai by Kamehameha III. Kanoa had been born in South Kona on the island of Hawaii and during his early life had been considerably influenced by the missionaries. As a young man he had spent some time in the home of Dr. Gerrit Judd. On at least two occasions Kanoa accompanied Hiram Bingham to Kauai to assist the missionary in his work.

Kanoa ruled Kauai in much the same fashion as had Kaikioewa. Each man practiced the concept of one-man government and each carried out his duties with dispatch. There was, however, an important difference between Kaikioewa and Kanoa. Kaikioewa was aloof from the people of Kauai and his attitude was one of condescension, the relationship of the conqueror to the defeated. Kanoa was no less firm in his decision-making than his predecessor, and during the early years of his rule, his arbitrary ways brought about complaints. Nevertheless, over the years he developed many close friendships with the new chiefs of Kauai.

After being named governor of Kauai, Kanoa had a home built near the beach on Nawiliwili Bay and later a more formal home on a nearby hill. He had received extensive and valuable lands on Kauai, extending from Koloa to Hanamaulu. These lands had been granted to Kanoa through Kekuanaoa, the governor of Oahu and husband of a daughter of Kamehameha I.

During the thirty-one years Paul Kanoa remained as governor of Kauai the sugar industry developed from small beginnings to a sizable and profitable enterprise. One of the leaders in sugar was Paul Isenberg, who became a close friend of Kanoa. William Hyde Rice was also a close friend. Kanoa had an understanding of the history and legends of the Islands and over the years the two had long talks, of assistance in Rice's writing of *Hawaiian Legends.*

On one occasion the governor was sailing to Honolulu on the schooner *Excel* when the captain lost his bearings. After several days of sailing aimlessly about and with provisions running low, the captain asked for advice. Kanoa suggested they turn back, attempt to reach Kauai, and then start over again. The captain took the governor's advice and with the aid of directions from a passing ship, again sighted Kauai. When the captain had gotten his bearings anew he headed for Oahu. The whole voyage was a thirteen-day adventure.

Paul Kanoa remained as governor of Kauai until 1877. He had served through numerous legislative sessions and in 1882 was appointed minister of finance by King Kalakaua. In November 1885, apparently suffering from poor eyesight and old age, Kanoa fell from the second floor of his home in Honolulu and died. He was about eighty-two years of age.

In the summer of 1855 the Reverend Daniel Dole and his family moved from Honolulu to Koloa. The family consisted of Daniel, his wife Charlotte, and their two sons, George and Sanford. Daniel Dole had been principal of Punahou School for fourteen years, and his sons were born there. His first wife, Emily Ballard, had died after the birth of their second son, Sanford. Dole married Charlotte Knapp, the widow of the Reverend Horton Knapp, in 1846.

There had been differences between Dole and some of the trustees of Punahou. Although he was urged to stay by some in the mission community, Dole thought it was time to seek other surroundings. There was a problem, however, in finding a new station for Daniel Dole. He had not learned Hawaiian sufficiently to preach in the language. This nearly eliminated the possibilities of his securing a congregation of his own.

There was a need for a school on Kauai, as mission families found it expensive to send their children to Punahou. They were also hesitant to send such young children off the island. It was for this reason that Dole came to Koloa. A house was built consisting of two rooms and a garret. The cook house was separate. The two Dole boys occupied one end of the garret and Maria Rice, the first student, occupied the other part. In addition to tending to the school, Daniel Dole found his preaching in English to be in demand and he alternated on Sundays between Lihue and Koloa.

In coming to Kauai the Doles were in the company of many friends. William Harrison Rice and his wife had worked with the Doles at Punahou. Charlotte Knapp Dole had spent some time on the island with her first husband, and the Doles had made friends on the island during earlier visits.

The first schoolhouse was a single room, a clapboard building with bare timbers inside and a thatched roof. To this school came children from the missionary families as well as part-Hawaiian children. The two Dole boys, of course, attended. Mary Burbank and her brother attended. Their father was manager of Koloa plantation. Five Smith children attended. Henry and William Charman were there, as were Sophia and Henry Heywood, whose father was a stone mason in Koloa, and also Hattie Fredenburg, whose father cultivated cane on contract.

More room was needed, because other parents wanted to enroll children who lived too far from the school to travel back and forth each day. So the house was enlarged and boarding students were admitted. Four Rowell children came from Waimea, and Emily and William Rice joined their sister, Maria. From the north shore of Kauai came Edward Wilcox, Henry Bertelmann, and George and Charles Titcomb. Aubrey Robinson and Francis Gay came from Niihau.

The Reverend Elias Bond, at Kohala on the island of Hawaii, sent his three oldest children to the Koloa school, and Alfred Wight, also from Kohala, attended. Three Pogue children came from Maui, as did George and Mary Richardson and James Robertson. The Dole home had become a boarding house.

Sanford Dole, who would later play a prominent role in Island affairs, was eleven when the family moved to Kauai and his brother George was thirteen. It was an exciting outdoor life, particularly for Sanford, who loved to explore the valleys and climb the mountains. He hunted and sailed, and when he became a little older worked at such jobs as he could get. During the evenings Sanford had long discussions with his father and he later remembered how valuable these had been to him.

By 1862 the American Civil War had aroused patriotic zeal throughout the Islands. The ardor reached Kauai and a group called the Koloa Volunteers, many of them old Koloa students, drilled and held target practice. By 1863 a cavalry troop had been formed with Sanford Dole as captain. There were fifteen in the troop, armed with eight ancient muskets with bayonets and one sword, sent over from the old Russian fort at Waimea by Valdemar Knudsen.

In 1863 Sanford's parents felt they had saved enough money to send him to Punahou for a full year. Back on Kauai after the school year Sanford worked for Duncan McBryde in the sugar fields, plowing and planting, saving his money to continue his education on the mainland. His goal was to save $100, which would allow him to attend Williams College for one year. With his money earned, and with the encouragement and help of his parents, Sanford spent the school year of 1866–1867 at Williams.

From Williams College Dole moved to Boston where he studied law by following cases in Boston courts, a not-uncommon method of studying law at the time. He was admitted to the bar in Massachusetts in 1868 and returned to the Hawaiian Islands the same year to practice law in Honolulu. Before him lay not only a successful career, but also a prominent place in Hawaii's history.

Many of the parents who sent children to Dole's school were members of a magazine club and a book club on Kauai. The arrival of new books, magazines, and newspapers in the 1850s and 1860s was a happy occasion because it was the major link to outside news and the world of new ideas. The magazine club was made up of persons who shared the cost of subscriptions to a variety of magazines. A list of the members was pasted on the back cover of each magazine, with space to write in the date it was received and the date it was sent on to the next family. After a magazine had made the rounds, a family was designated to keep it.

Among the publications received were *Harper's Monthly, Littell's Living Age, The Eclectic, The Edinburgh Review, Blackwood's,* and the *North American Review.* The names on the subscription list were the Johnson, Wilcox, and Rhodes families at Hanalei, the McBrydes at Wailua, the Bond, Hardy, Reynolds, Rice, and Widemann families at Lihue, the Burbank, Dole, Smith, and McGregor families at Koloa, and the Knudsen and Rowell families at Waimea.

Doctor Smith mentions attending meetings of the book club, and William Harrison Rice was a member. The members apparently met periodically to discuss books that had made the rounds. One of the dedicated young readers on Kauai was serious Hannah Maria Rice. The letters she wrote and received frequently mention books she was reading or which had been recommended to her. She owned a complete set of Sir Walter Scott, and her reading ranged from biography and history to novels such as *Adam Bede* by George Eliot and *The Newcomes* by William Thackeray.

The Hawaiian Islands faced a crisis that threatened its existence during the years of the mid-nineteenth century. It was the crisis of an ever-decreasing Hawaiian population headed toward extinction. The seriousness of the situation was plain as soon as the population was counted. The news came as no surprise to those who had been searching for plantation field-workers.

The downward spiral was much bemoaned in the newspapers, which reported the plight of both the planters and the government. For the planters it was a critical matter. William Hooper had faced an acute shortage of workers at Koloa and Charles Titcomb had the same problem at Hanalei. Such field-workers as were available sometimes demanded wages beyond the ability of the planters to pay. Without an adequate population there would be no commercial life. The government feared that if the small population decreased further, the kingdom would be so insignificant other nations would not bother to acknowledge its existence at all.

Diseases from the Western world were the major causes for the population decline. More deaths than births became the tragic yearly pattern. Year after year tuberculosis was the consistent big killer. Venereal diseases were another scourge. Periodic epidemics dramatically speeded the decline. In 1839 mumps carried away "great numbers." In 1848–1849 measles, whooping cough, and influenza killed some 10,000, and four years later smallpox decreased the Hawaiian population throughout the Islands by 5,000 to 6,000.

Causes other than disease also helped reduce the Hawaiian population. The California gold rush lured Hawaiians away, and for decades young Islanders had signed aboard ships as sailors. Some never returned and many young men were gone for years, during the time of life when they would normally be fathering children. On Kauai the population dropped from an estimated 12,000 in 1831–1832 to 7,800 in 1853. During the same period the estimated population of all the Islands decreased from 129,800 to 73,100. This decline continued, reaching its low in 1872, when the estimated population of Kauai was 5,200 and the total population of the Islands 56,900.

A major reason for the founding of the Royal Hawaiian Agricultural Society in 1850 was to seek workers, and through the society's efforts a group of 280 Chinese was brought to Hawaii in 1852. Charles Titcomb took on some Chinese at his coffee plantation at Hanalei and wrote enthusiastically about them as workers. Apparently both Koloa and Lihue plantations also received some Chinese from this first group.

More Chinese came, but in small numbers. By 1866 the census showed there were only 1,306 Chinese in the Islands. It was not until 1875 that the Chinese came in appreciable numbers. Laborers in the sugar fields remained dominantly Hawaiian, even though the number of plantations increased, particularly after the American Civil War.

The Hawaiian kingdom could do little to give protection to the Islanders who went away as sailors, and their plight was generally a sad one. In 1846 the government did pass an act relating to the shipping of Hawaiians on whalers. Captains were then obligated to file shipping articles for each seaman who enlisted and to post a $100 bond toward his safe return.

In 1850 an act was passed, For the Government of Masters and Servants, detailing the rights and responsibilities of employers and employees. The law of 1850 provided a basis for the drawing up of legal contracts for bringing workers to Island sugar fields. The laws of 1846 and 1850 had their basis in early American apprentice and shipping laws. Signing shipping articles for a voyage had similarities to signing a contract to work on a plantation for a specified number of years. These laws provided a primitive kind of protection for both sailors and field-workers and for their employers. For many years workers who came under contract to the sugar plantations were referred to as having "shipped."

The need for laborers would continue to be a leading worry for planters for decades. To the end of the century the search would continue, always an aggravating problem, overcome somehow, but never to anyone's satisfaction. In the meantime other problems had to be solved if the plantations were going to survive. It was necessary to find ways to do just about everything on the plantations better, and to secure the capital required to do it. Ever so slowly things did improve.

In about 1850 William L. Lee came back from Louisiana with the news that sugarcane was planted in rows there, not in clumps as was apparently being done in the Islands. And there were improvements in boiling, the advent of irrigation, and the invention of the centrifugal separator.

If the sugar planters needed support in forging ahead they found it in the columns of *The Polynesian.* The way to success lay in scientific advancement. This was the text the newpaper used repeatedly in its morale-supporting articles. In March 1853 an article stated:

> There has been no period since the commencement of the world, in which so many important discoveries tending to the benefit of mankind, were made [as] in the last century. . . . Some of the grandest conceptions of genius have been perfected. It is remarkable how the mind of the world has run into scientific investigation, and what achievements it has effected in that short period.

Hopeful as they were for scientific advances, the planters, however, were much more concerned with current problems. In 1850 Dr. Robert W. Wood stated a somber fact at a meeting of the Royal Hawaiian Agricultural Society. "Most of the mills now in operation in the different Islands, yield but about one half, and the best two thirds, the quantity which mills . . . yield in old sugar growing countries."

At the society meeting in 1853 Richard Armstrong graphically described some of the problems faced daily in the fields. Ordinary plows were unsatisfactory. On Kauai a mammoth plow had been built of wood and iron. It required eight to twelve oxen to draw and turned the soil 15 to 20 inches deep. It was necessary to plant this deep because sugarcane has shallow roots and easily suffers from drought. Like the original plows, the carts that were imported were too fragile. They either had to be made on the plantations or rebuilt if bought elsewhere.

The Polynesian kept pointing toward the future. On 12 February 1853 the newspaper gave extensive space to an article that had appeared in the *London Morning Chronicle,* headlined "New Mode of Manufacturing Sugar." The article outlined four remarkable improvements in the production or processing of cane. It was an age when there was a mystical belief in the achievements of machines. In the end *The Polynesian* was right. The sugar industry survived, then prospered. For many years it was nearly Hawaii's sole source of income, and every other business rose or declined with the fortunes of sugar.

CHAPTER NINE

Profits Yet To Be Made

The Hawaiian Islands escaped becoming just another backwater string of Pacific islands by being fortunate enough to have a new source of income appear just as the old source was beginning to fade. Provisioning the China traders had been the first small, unreliable source of income. Then followed the sandalwood trade which, destructive as it was to both the forests and people, nevertheless provided a means of economic subsistence. The China traders had come because of Hawaii's geographic location. The sandalwood trade flourished because Hawaii had a natural resource that was hard to find elsewhere.

In 1819 the *Balena* and *Equator,* whaling vessels from New England, dropped anchor at Kealakekua Bay on the island of Hawaii. The ships were searching for new grounds not yet exploited by whalers from New England and Europe. A whale was taken off Kealakekua Bay by the two ships and the voyage was so encouraging that by 1824 the number of whalers touching the Hawaiian Islands reached 104.

In the early days of whaling, the popular regions in the North Pacific were the Japan grounds, about thirty days' sailing time westward from Hawaii. The strategic location of the Islands gave the whalers a valuable stopping place for supplies, repairs, and rest, allowing ships to stay on the whaling grounds for long periods of time. Hawaii became a necessary stop for whalers sailing north of the equator. Once again the location of the Hawaiian Islands came to her economic rescue.

Honolulu was the most frequented port, offering marine repair services and the safety of an enclosed harbor where a vessel could tie up at a wharf. Lahaina, on Maui, became just as popular as Honolulu, although vessels had to lay at anchor offshore in Lahaina road. The island of Hawaii was visited by a far smaller number of ships.

Ever since the time of James Cook, Waimea on Kauai was considered the port for the island, if only because that was where Cook had dropped anchor. Waimea was the official port of entry for Kauai until about 1855 when Koloa belatedly received that designation. On occasion whalers also showed up in the rough seas off Hanalei, but that was considered a risky anchorage. Ships at Koloa did not always anchor, but lay off-and-on while whaleboats rowed to the stone pier to bargain for provisions. This was inconvenient, but for thrifty Yankee captains there were compensations. Prices were lower than in Honolulu, and Koloa became known for the quality and variety of goods sold.

George Charman was sought after by Koloa merchants to bargain for them with the Yankee captains. Charman, who appears to have been an outgoing and gregarious man, was involved with many enterprises in Koloa, including his own provisioning business. He ran an advertisement in the *Honolulu Advertiser* on 28 January 1858, listing his prices. "Wood of superior quality can be had at Koloa at $5 per cord; fresh beef at 4 cents per lb; sheep at $3 per head and goats at $1.50 a head."

If Honolulu and Lahaina were more comfortable ports, Kauai benefited by shipping supplies to Honolulu where they were sold by local merchants. From Wailua Valley went kegs of butter and barrels of salt beef. From Hanalei, oranges and coffee, and from Koloa came a whole variety of produce, including Irish and sweet potatoes, melons, kegs of molasses, and wood to stoke the fires under try-pots when blubber was rendered into oil at sea.

By the mid-1830s the whaling grounds of the Bering, Arctic, and Okhotsk Seas were attracting more ships. Before this, ships had usually headed directly for the Japan grounds from Honolulu or Lahaina. But the northern grounds abounded with whales and more ships stopped at Kauai, since it was en route to and from their destination.

Coral reefs added to the hazards of whaling in the Pacific, and in June 1842 the reefs at Waimea claimed the *Jefferson* as a victim. Mercy Whitney reported in her journal that Captain Cash had come ashore for supplies. He had instructed his mate to stay well off the land, but the ship eased in closer and closer. The Hawaiians at last ran to the shore and shouted of the danger. It was too late: "In a few moments more she struck on the coral reef. Every effort was made during the day to get him off, but in vain, she stood fast."

Stephen Reynolds, a Honolulu merchant, made an entry in his jour-

nal on 28 June. "Reported the loss of the ship Jefferson—Capt. Cash
—at Wymea on Thursday night last 23 by getting on the lee Reef at
ten p.m. was lost . . ." On 8 July Reynolds added more information.
"Sch Victoria arrived from Kauai Jefferson had split open about 1200
bbl. & some said 1900 bbl—!! too much—." The official count of the
barrels aboard was 2,480 of sperm oil and 80 of whale oil, an even
greater fortune than reported to Reynolds. In 1842 sperm oil brought
a conservative ninety cents a gallon at Nantucket and the *Jefferson* carried nearly 77,000 gallons of sperm oil. The oil aboard the *Jefferson* was
of far greater value than the ship itself.

On 23 June William Ladd and Dr. Robert W. Wood were about to
sail for Honolulu from Koloa when they heard of the disaster at
Waimea. Ladd was an American consular agent and as such he took
charge of the wreck. During the next three weeks the officers of the
Jefferson and William Ladd took their meals at the Whitney house. By
13 July merchants had come from Honolulu and the salvaged cargo of
the *Jefferson* was auctioned off. The crew of the wreck probably signed
aboard other ships, although two men, an Abeel and a Marcus, were
employed by Koloa plantation at the end of 1842.

Another kind of peril nearly destroyed the ship *William Thompson*
on 18 April 1847. The vessel was some forty-five miles northwest of
Kauai when a fire broke out aboard ship. Fire was the dread of every
sailor, particularly aboard whalers, which carried barrels of inflamma-
ble oil and whose decks were saturated with oil every time a whale was
tryed-out aboard ship. This fire was despicable because it was set deliberately by crewmen. The fire was discovered at 10:30 P.M. in the forehold. Captain A. G. Ellis ordered the hatches battened down and
made for Kauai. The outlook was grim, and as they grew closer to
Kauai Captain Ellis ordered two boats to pull for shore with the ship's
papers. On 19 April the *William Thompson* reached Waimea.

Putting the fire out was no easy matter. Holes were bored in the
deck and water poured down, but this did no good. The sails were
spread over the deck and kept wet. By 21 April the fire had subsided
enough for the crew to ascertain the damage. The decks were nearly
burned through from the forehold to the main hatch on the starboard
side. Beams were destroyed and the sides of the ship charred.

The *William Thompson* returned to Honolulu for repairs. It was the
third time crew members had tried to fire the ship. The first time this
occurred two men were sent to the United States to be tried. The second time no one was apprehended, and after the Kauai attempt three

men were locked in the fort in Honolulu as suspects. In spite of these adversities the whaler safely returned to its home port and reported a financially successful voyage.

It took desperate men to set a ship afire at sea, and the story of the *William Thompson* can only make us wonder what conditions aboard the ship were like. There is little information about the *William Thompson,* but generally life aboard a whaling vessel was a brutalizing experience. Captains and mates were harsh, sometimes sadistic, with a constant eye toward economy on the voyage, at the expense of the crew. By the 1850s and 1860s crews often consisted of the dregs of a dozen nations, sullen malcontents, mixed with naive lads on their first voyage who knew little of the ways of seasoned sailors or the bizarre methods of officers. The only advantage of the green hands was that they were in the majority, since few men who could do anything else signed aboard a whaler twice.

When a seaman sailed he was provided with an outfit, which included the clothing he would need at sea. The outfit was commonly of inferior quality and the merchants who sold them made, on the average, a 100 percent profit. The outfit was charged against the sailor's wages. At sea, needed supplies were sold from the "slop chest," again at the usual 100 percent markup over cost. The purchases were deducted from wages at the end of the voyage, with interest charged on the amount borrowed.

Home at sea for the crew was the forecastle, a cramped, low, dark compartment that followed the contour of the ship to the bow. Bunks were in tiers along the sides of the compartment, and the only ventilation was through the hatch that led to the deck. If the weather did not allow the men to eat on deck, the cook brought the food to the forecastle in a common bucket and each ladled out whatever he could get. Fare at sea consisted mainly of salt beef or pork together with hardtack. There was molasses for the hardtack and coffee or tea to drink. The longer a ship was at sea the worse was the stench of the meat and more numerous the weevils in the biscuits. The dank forecastle reeked of sweat, tobacco, whale oil, mildew, and food. According to the mood of the officers, the crew was driven to chores with curses, kicks, and sometimes worse. For an infraction of a serious kind, flogging was not uncommon, although it was illegal aboard American ships starting in 1850.

In March 1852 the *Hillman,* from New Bedford, stopped at the island of Hawaii for supplies. While there, two or three men—it is not clear from the ship's log—deserted in a whaleboat, carrying stolen clothing with them. After a chase the first mate captured the deserters. The men were placed in irons and the *Hillman* sailed on to Kauai, where water and hogs were taken aboard on 18 and 19 March. On 20 March 1852 the ship departed Waimea and on the same day the prisoners were taken "out of irons and put . . . in the rigging and punished . . . by [being] given 12 lashes."

Desertion was bad enough, but stealing a whaleboat in the process was a very serious matter. In flogging the men the captain was committing an illegal act. It is possible Captain Christopher Cook of the *Hillman* bypassed Lahaina and Honolulu to avoid the possibility that knowledge of the deserters would reach the United States consuls there, since consular agents were supposed to look after the welfare of seamen. But there was no representative on Kauai, and once at sea the captain would not have to worry about interference. The captain was the only law that existed and there was no appeal.

Another instance of flogging took place in 1853. The whaler *Helen Augusta* was sailing from Honolulu to Koloa before going on to the northern seas. Two men taken aboard at Honolulu refused to do their chores. After a warning from the captain they were allowed a few minutes to reconsider their decision, and then were tied to the rigging and given a dozen lashes each.

Not all captains were demonic aboard ship and suspicious of those ashore. Some made contributions to worthy causes and others donated supplies that added to the comfort of the missionaries. Mercy Whitney recorded in her journal on 16 March 1821 that a captain had given them, among other things, "a considerable quantity of tea, several hams, a pot of pickles, a large pitcher of cranberry preserves, a bottle of pepper & some mustard seed." Three months later a Captain Masters gave them other provisions and, "in addition to this, he has given us a box of elegant china & four dozen stone china plates, soup dishes etc." And there were even a few pious captains. Dr. James W. Smith was invited on occasion to preach aboard whaling vessels off Koloa.

A whaler was not a pretty vessel. It sat high in the water, looking rectangular and heavy. In part this was because six whaleboats were usually hung in heavy wooden davits so they could readily be put in the water. Appearance was the last thing captains were interested in. A whaler was really a floating storehouse where provisions for long voyages could be stored and where bone and barrels of whale oil could be secured. It was also a factory for boiling-out oil from blubber. The sails of a whaler were streaked black from the boiling process and a ship could be spotted at a distance as a whaler for this reason if for no other.

Whaling vessels primarily sought oil from the sperm whale, prized as fuel for lamps. Oil from other whales was also taken, although it was smelly, sticky, and did not burn as brightly as sperm oil. In addition, whalers sought whalebone, more technically called baleen, the long flexible strips in a whale's mouth that serve to sift the animal's food out of the water. Each bowhead whale had several hundred such bones, ranging up to 15 feet in length. When heated the bone could be bent and would hold a shape. It was used for stays in women's clothing, for ribs in parasols and umbrellas, and as the framework for luggage. As time went on, baleen sold for as much as $1.10 per pound and made up an important part of the profit on every voyage.

When a whale was killed it was secured to the starboard side of the ship and the cutting-in process was begun by crewmen working on scaffolding, stripping the blubber from the mammal as it was rolled over and over in the water. Strips of blubber were cut to size and put into the try-pots located behind the foremast. Housings of brick were built to hold the try-pots and to protect the deck from the fires lit beneath them. The process continued day and night until it was completed. It was an eerie sight to see a whaler thus illuminated at night. Boiling-out was dangerous too, because of the hazard of fire and the risk of handling boiling oil on a rolling deck. Once a fire was kindled with wood beneath the try-pots it was fed with oil-soaked remnants fished from the pots.

After months of brutality, danger, and privation at sea, it was little wonder that sailors on leave did not act like saints. Still compensating for the toss of the deck, the men swarmed into the streets of Honolulu and Lahaina looking for grog shops and prostitutes. After finding these necessities—and there was an ample number of "landsharks" available to lead the way—events took their own turn. For these times ashore sailors were advanced funds against their "lay," which was a percentage of the profit of a voyage.

Violence was often the outcome of drinking sprees. Policemen were tolerant because they were usually outnumbered by the sailors, and the sailors left a lot of money in port. It was not too difficult for a policeman to walk around a fistfight in the middle of the street, but on occasion violence took on larger and uglier forms. In November 1852 Honolulu Harbor was so crowded with ships that only a narrow passage remained for vessels wanting to put to sea. Some 3,000 sailors spilled from their ships into the streets. Quickly things got out of hand. The police made arrests, which inflamed the sailors. When a sailor, imprisoned in the fort, was killed by a club-wielding policeman, the control of Honolulu passed into the hands of sailors shouting for revenge. Ignoring the pleas of officials who tried to calm them, the sailors burned the police offices in a three-story building near the waterfront. When the fire department arrived sailors cut the hoses and kept the firemen away from the blaze. Several nearby shops also burned, and it was fortunate that the prevailing winds that day were inland and not toward the sea. If the fire had reached the whaling ships the conflagration would have roared through the tightly packed fleet. Eventually the effects of alcohol and exhaustion quieted the town.

Koloa avoided such serious troubles. The number of ships visiting the port was far smaller and a ship laying off-and-on needed much of its crew aboard. But Koloa was not immune from some of the less violent practices followed at the two more-frequented ports. G. W. Bates described going ashore at Koloa in 1853. A Hawaiian seaman off the *Helen Augusta* was approached by two Hawaiians who lived in the neighborhood. They described to the sailor the hard life that awaited him at sea, and how wonderful life ashore could be, particularly with their "fine sister." The sailor agreed and was hidden away awaiting the arrival of the "sister," while the two Hawaiians went to the captain of his ship and said they had located a deserter and would take the captain to him for a sum of ten dollars. The captain went ashore and was led to his wayward man, who was duly escorted back to the ship. In this instance the ploy of the two landsmen was discovered, but more often it was an easy way to make money at the expense of a sailor.

John Cook, a one-time English sailor who worked as a carpenter on Kauai, recalled the boatloads of women who sailed for Honolulu where they became prostitutes. Cook tried to explain to them the sad end that would result. "Many's the time one would see a fine, healthy, strapping young girl, with fresh, clear complexion, leave Kauai and return in six months or so with her face all blotched and sodden, an utter physical wreck, who would help to further spread disease like wildfire through the countryside."

Young Hawaiian men were regularly recruited by whaling captains, who discovered Islanders were adept at nearly every chore on water. A captain could man his ship sufficiently to reach Hawaii, then dispose of the least desirable crew members and take on Islanders. Once the season was over they could be discharged in Hawaii and such hands as needed signed on to reach home port.

Koloa felt some of the aftershock that turned Honolulu and Lahaina into places of decadence, but it was no overhwelming problem on Kauai. Dr. James W. Smith noted in his journal in April 1865, "Three whaleships here at anchor & bad proceedings are expected on shore." But if "bad proceedings" took place they could not have been too glaring, since Smith made no mention of them in later entries.

In later years Samuel W. Wilcox, who attended the Reverend Dole's school in Koloa as a boy, remembered the provisioning of the ships rather than the rowdiness of the crews. Wilcox recalled "the whaling vessels lying at the Koloa anchorage strung with crook-necked squashes all about the stern and even up into the rigging, when ready to set sail in the spring of the year. Besides barrels of salt beef, pigs, and cattle were shipped on the hoof, to be slaughtered later, as the vessel approached northern latitudes, and hung up in the rigging to freeze."

In about 1844 the *Citizen* came to Koloa to buy pigs. The number of pigs and the price was agreed upon. The rest was up to the sailors of the ship, who chased the pigs across the sand dunes along the beach, tied them, and took them aboard ship. The *Citizen* was the only whaling ship to be lost in the Arctic during the season of 1852.

Sometimes captains brought their wives and even children along on voyages. In January 1857 Dr. Smith noted, "Capt Cox & his wife and daughter came on shore from the Magnolia and stopped with us." And again, "Capt. Perse . . . had his wife and two daughters aboard." Another entry states "Mrs. Jones & child was with him [Captain Jones] & spent several days with us." In return for their kindness the Smiths were often given several gallons of whale oil for their lamps.

The *Scotland* was a familiar sight off Koloa during her years of Pacific cruising. A 388-ton vessel out of New Bedford, she voyaged into the northern Pacific and regularly brought a good return on investment for her owners. On 22 June 1851 the *Scotland* left New Bedford to begin her second voyage into the Pacific. She crossed the Atlantic and sailed through the Indian Ocean and south of Tasmania into the Pacific. George A. Smith was her captain.

The 1853 season must have been a good one, because in October of that year the vessel was in Honolulu, where whalebone was bundled and shipped to her home port. The crew was given liberty and the ship was painted before moving on to Kauai. The journal of the voyage records that on 21 November 1853 the ship was off "Atooi." Provisions had been taken on at Honolulu, but Captain Smith was in need of more. The ship's journal continues for the same day, "one Boats crew on shore at 11 P.M. crews on board with some Bananas and water Melons."

On 22 November the ship took on wood and traded "Two Barrels of oil for potatoes." The next day "4 cords of wood, 26 bbls. of potatoes, 1200 Oranges, and few other things" were taken aboard before the *Scotland* set her course for the Arctic seas. On 25 April 1854 the whaler was once again at her home port of New Bedford.

The third voyage of the *Scotland* into the Pacific began in mid-August 1854. The whaler rounded the Horn and stopped at Talcahuano, Chile, for supplies, then cruised for whales on her way north. On 1 April 1856 the whaler was at Koloa, where the port account book shows the ship bought "4 bullocks—$40.00, 40 bbls. sweet potatoes—$50.00, 4 hogs—$16.00, 2 doz. fowls—$6.00." Also, the usual $2.00 fee for entry and clearance was paid. Dr. Smith recorded in his journal for 1 April 1856, "Whaleship Scotland Capt. Smith off this port. Sold the Capt. two small beeves [beef cattle] for one barrel of Flour." The captain was taking on provisions for his northern trip. On 14 October the *Scotland* was back at Koloa. Dr. Smith wrote, "Capt. S generously made me a present of 5 gals of Oil—the 2^{d} can full I have received from him the same way—He is homeward bound."

It was a very profitable voyage for the *Scotland*. The ship returned to New Bedford with 162 barrels of sperm oil, 2,945 barrels of other whale oil, and 15,500 pounds of whalebone. At 1857 prices, the value of this cargo amounted to approximately $72,000. Ship repairs and other costs might have reduced this figure by $15,000, leaving a profit for the voyage of $57,000 before wages.

George Smith's lay was one-sixteenth of the profits, so his income for two years and nine months of work came to approximately $3,600. In addition, he received an undetermined commission for sales from the "slop chest" and from possible trade privileges. But figuring simply on the basis of his lay, Captain Smith's annual income for this period amounted to $1,308. In comparison, William Harrison Rice, manager of Lihue plantation, started work in 1845 at $400 a year, although he earned a top salary of $1,500 in 1861, the year before his death.

A seaman would receive between one two-hundredth and one one-hundred-sixtieth as his lay. Thus, at home after the third voyage, sailors aboard the *Scotland* would have been due between $285 and $356 for two years and nine months of work. But this was before charges, advances, and interest were deducted, usually reducing wages by $50 to $100. Subtracting the minimum $50, a sailor would end up with an annual wage of between $85 and $111. If the voyage had been unsuccessful, a seaman would be in debt to the ship. During this same era a Hawaiian field worker earned approximately $64 per year.

After all expenses were paid, the owners of the vessel would divide the profits. A vessel was seldom owned by a single person—usually the risks and profits were spread among six or as many as twenty individuals. And risks there were, since the loss of a ship could come to as much as $35,000. Less dramatic but more frequent risks were depressed oil and bone prices, or a ship that returned with a small cargo. In the case of the third voyage of the *Scotland,* the profit for the owners amounted to an incredible $43,000. Half the sum would have been a respectable return.

Whaling was most profitable for Kauai from the mid-1830s until about 1861. The trade filled a desperate economic need. Sandalwood was depleted and sugar was going through a trial-and-error time, struggling with the problems of growing, processing, and marketing. While Honolulu and Lahaina, as the busiest ports, gained the most from whaling profit-wise, they also suffered most from its harsh and demoralizing effects. Kauai received fewer benefits in trade but, comparatively speaking, escaped the bad effects of whaling.

Then, beginning in 1861 four events followed one after another, which in ten years would mean the near demise of the industry. The first event took place early during the American Civil War, when the Union devised a plan to decrease the number of blockade runners that helped supply the South. It was decided to sink ships loaded with boulders at the entrances to certain Southern harbors, adding another risk for blockade runners. One of these ports was Charleston Harbor and forty-five vessels, mostly whalers, were bought by the Union for this purpose. Only some of these ships, laden with New England granite, were sunk at the entrance to Charleston Harbor, but eventually they all became casualties of the war. Of the forty-five ships, which became known as the Great Stone Fleet, at least a quarter were familiar names at Koloa, and others were known at Honolulu and Lahaina.

The second event was the appearance of a Confederate privateer in the Pacific. Near the war's end the *Shenandoah* made a destructive sweep around the perimeter of the Pacific. Entering the Pacific through the Indian Ocean, the *Shenandoah* sank four ships at Ponape on 1 April 1865, one of which was of Hawaiian registry, and sank another in the Okhotsk Sea. Entering the Bering Straits, the privateer sank twenty-four whalers between 22 and 28 June 1865. Among the ships sunk was the *William Thompson,* which fourteen years earlier had nearly perished by fire off Kauai. Four vessels were captured and used as transports, loaded with the crews of destroyed ships. It was needless destruction, since Robert E. Lee had surrendered on 9 April 1865. The captain of the *Shenandoah* refused to believe the news of the fall of the Confederacy when told by the crews of captured ships.

The distress brought on by the destructive work of the *Shenandoah* was felt on Kauai. In August 1865 the sheriff of Kauai wrote of two men who were affected. "Krull has been jubilant over his anticipated season's work of 500 Bbls.--That game is blocked and I'm sorry for him." Krull owned a dairy and probably sold kegs of butter to the whaling vessels. Of Charman, who sold potatoes, the sheriff wrote, "Charman can now cultivate his cane & let his potatoes rot."

The fleets would have been rebuilt, except for a third set of events that made whaling economically obsolete. This was the discovery of shale in Canada and of petroleum in Pennsylvania. Starting in about 1860 kerosene, derived from these two natural resources, was found to be superior to whale oil for lamps. Petroleum products also proved to be better lubricants than whale oil. Whale-hunting was thus made uneconomical, and even though there was still some demand for whalebone, the industry soon dwindled to insignificance.

The fourth and final blow fell on the remnants of the whaling fleet in September 1871, when thirty-three of forty whalers were caught by ice floes and an early freeze in the Arctic. Starting in June, the ships had pushed on toward the Arctic Sea as the ice opened. The vessels passed through the Bering Straits between 18 and 30 June. Whaling prospects were good, but heavy ice floes were frequent and fog made visibility poor. On 2 September the brig *Comet* was crushed by the ice. On 7 September the *Roman* was caught by an ice floe while cutting-in a whale. A second floe appeared, over two miles in length, crushing the timbers of the *Roman* against the first floe.

A sudden freeze now firmly gripped the ships in ice. Most of the vessels were within short distances of each other and the captains conferred on their plight. On 12 September they jointly signed a document stating that the situation was not the fault of anyone, and two days later they abandoned their ships, dragging whaleboats and such supplies as they could manage across the ice. To the south they were picked up by the seven surviving whale ships. In all 1,219 persons were saved, including the wives and children of some captains. Not a single human life was lost in the retreat from the ice, although crew members had earlier been lost in the hunt for whales.

These survivors were carried to Honolulu, where the gloom was heavy over the disaster of the Arctic. The first news of the tragedy was carried to the United States by survivors who traveled on to San Francisco. Again the casualty list included the names of many vessels familiar on Kauai. The *Victoria* was one of them, owned by Hoffschlaeger and Company, the same firm that leased land in Wailua Valley and had sold kegs of butter and salt beef to the whaling fleets. The *Julian, Monticello,* and *Arctic,* all completely or partially owned in Hawaii, were also lost.

Henry Augustus Peirce is a name that enters, fades, and reenters Hawaiian history for half a century. He was from a Boston merchant family, went to sea at age eighteen, settled in Honolulu in 1828, and eventually became a partner with James Hunnewell and later with Charles Brewer in the firm known as C. Brewer and Company, Ltd. In 1843 he returned to Boston. But in 1849 the California gold rush stirred thoughts of profits yet to be made, and Peirce set out with a cargo of trade goods to be sold to the gold seekers.

Disposing of his wares in San Francisco, Peirce sailed to Honolulu, where his ship took on a cargo of oil and whalebone for transshipment to New Bedford. Peirce remained in Honolulu and chartered another ship to sail for Canton, where he planned to purchase a cargo of miscellaneous goods to be sold in Hawaii. The ship paused at Kauai briefly before crossing the Pacific, and it was during these days that Peirce noticed the lands above Nawiliwili, around the village of Lihue, and became enthusiastic about their potential as a sugar plantation. Peirce interested two longtime, prominent Honolulu friends in joining him in this venture. One was William L. Lee, Chief Justice of the Supreme Court of Hawaii, and the other, Charles R. Bishop, who later founded Hawaii's first permanent bank. The firm was called H. A. Peirce & Co. Total capital was $16,000, with Peirce putting up half. The first manager was James Fowle Baldwin Marshall, also a successful Honolulu businessman.

Marshall had performed an important service for the kingdom in 1843, when he secretly carried dispatches to Washington and London concerning the annexation of Hawaii by the English naval captain, Lord George Paulet. Marshall had traveled ostensibly on business for Ladd and Company, but his real purpose was to acquaint the United States and England with the feelings of the monarchy concerning the arbitrary action of Paulet. In due course the independence of the Islands had been restored.

Part of the reason for Marshall's selection as manager of the new plantation might have been related to the fact that the kingdom was in his debt for services rendered; to obtain land for the new plantation, special access was needed to the government. At any rate, whatever the reason for selecting Marshall, the new company was able to obtain between 2,000 and 3,000 acres in the desired location. The land was purchased from the estate of Oahu Governor Kekuanaoa. As manager Marshall was paid the unusually high salary of $1,000 a year.

In 1849 few illusions remained concerning the difficulties that had to be endured in order to make a sugar plantation a success. Koloa had shown that the greatest amount of determination and innovation were the essential beginnings. At Lihue much of the land was wooded and had to be cleared. The first seed cane used came from gullies where enough water flowed to allow the cane to sustain life. In 1851 a mill was started in Lihue where a dam could be built to supply the water power necessary.

Hawaiians made up the labor force. They built their homes on the land surrounding the mill. Workers were very scarce, however, and more Hawaiians were imported from the neighbor islands, including prison laborers from Lahaina. Planting was begun in 1850 and the first crop, amounting to a little over 100 tons of sugarcane, was ground in 1853. In January 1854 a wild storm hit Lihue. William Lee reported to the Royal Hawaiian Agricultural Society for that year that the rain was "accompanied with terrible thunder and lightning, and blasted our smiling fields as with the breath of fire." The cane turned brown, rotted, and died. The expected yield for 1854 was about 400 tons of sugarcane. Instead, Lihue plantation brought in 50 tons of sugarcane from the fields.

The cane was hauled to the mill in carts, each drawn by three pairs of oxen. The rollers in the mill were of granite, brought from China in 1852. They were bound with iron and turned by water power. Only about 50 percent of the juice could be extracted from the cane until better rollers were finally installed. Boiling the syrup extracted from the cane was another hazard. The temperature had to be carefully watched if the sugar was to granulate properly on the bottom of the boiling pans. If the temperature was too high, the batch was ruined and was fed to pigs. After successful boiling, the pans had to sit for weeks to separate the sugar from the molasses. The sugar was shipped to Honolulu in wooden kegs that had been assembled by a plantation cooper.

Shipping presented yet other problems. Service to Honolulu was uncertain and it often took a week beating against the wind to make Oahu. In Honolulu the sugar might be sold to a second party and then shipped to various markets, such as California, Mexico, South America, or Australia. The price at which sugar would be sold at those markets was unknown when ships left the Hawaiian Islands. From field to final sale, the business of sugar was a long and precarious trail.

The odds had to change for the better. The solutions for some problems came from two men, each of whom made a most timely appearance in the Islands. Victor Prevost was the first on the scene. He had come from the Isle of Bourbon, had long experience as a sugar boiler, and appeared at Lihue plantation in about 1854. A Frenchman, Prevost greatly helped the struggling enterprise. His skill as a boiler saved a considerable amount of syrup that otherwise would have been burned and useless. He was probably the same man who had worked at Koloa in 1842–1843 and whose name was spelled Provost, also a sugar boiler.

Prevost and his wife felt like exiles in a foreign land. Their home was as French as they could make it. They were not unfriendly, yet invited no one to their home and were little interested in the world about them. Each year, after the sugarcane had been harvested and ground, Mary Sophia Rice gave a great *lū'au* for all the people on the plantation. Even to this important and festive event the Prevosts would not come. But Victor Prevost was a valuable man, who held the art of sugar-boiling as a secret and was responsible for the high quality of sugar produced at Lihue. He became a substantial owner in the plantation, most of which he eventually sold to Paul Isenberg. In the end he taught Carl Isenberg, Paul's brother, with the understanding that Carl would pass the skill of sugar-boiling on to no one else as long as Prevost had an interest in the company. Victor Prevost finally saved enough money to retire to his beloved France.

David M. Weston solved another crucial problem in sugar production. Weston had been sent to Hawaii by Peirce to set up the mill at Lihue. In 1850 or 1851 Hawaiian planters read reports about the use of a centrifugal machine in the manufacture of sugar. Using these reports, Weston built a centrifugal separator, which was tested in late 1851. The center of the machine was a fine mesh into which raw sugar was placed. When this basket whirled around at a high speed it spun the molasses from the sugar. The centrifugal was a revolution for Hawaii's sugar industry. Now, in a matter of minutes, sugar could be separated from molasses, whereas earlier it had taken weeks. In addition to saving valuable time, a higher-quality sugar was produced, which meant a higher sales price. David Weston founded Honolulu Iron Works Company, which built heavy machinery for sugar plantations around the world for a century.

The hardships of organizing a plantation bore heavily on Marshall, just as they had on William Hooper earlier at Koloa. The storm of January 1854 and a subsequent drought particularly depressed him and he wanted to leave. In searching about for a suitable man to take his place, Judge William Lee came upon William Harrison Rice.

Rice had come to Hawaii in 1841, a member of the ninth missionary company. William Harrison and his wife Mary Sophia, both born and educated in New York State, had been married on 28 September 1840 by Mary's father, the Reverend Jabez B. Hyde. Rice was under appointment as a teacher by the American Board of Commissioners for Foreign Missions, but he did not know where he would be sent. Before they sailed aboard the *Gloucester* in mid-November 1840 from Boston, he was informed he was going to Oregon. But his destination was changed when he reached Honolulu, because of troubles in Oregon with Indians, and the Rices were assigned to Hana, on Maui.

The Rices' first child, Hannah Maria was born at Hana. But the dampness of the place was too much to be endured. Mary Sophia wrote, "The sea at Hana almost surrounded the house, which was so close to the beach that the windows were always covered with spray in a storm." The Reverend Daniel Conde, the minister stationed there, left and soon afterward the Rices departed as well. It was a dreaded journey for Mary Sophia, who was pregnant with her second child. They traveled along the Hana Coast toward Wailuku in an outrigger canoe, but came ashore well short of their destination. They struggled across the deep-cut valleys behind the rocky shore, and finally reached Wailuku. The Rices retreated to the warmth of Lahaina and remained there until their second daughter was born.

At the general meeting in Honolulu in the summer of 1844 the Rices were assigned to Punahou School, which had been started only three years earlier for the children of missionary families. William Rice was in charge of financial matters and out-of-door work and Mary Sophia was expected to act as mother to ten or twelve boys. She mended clothes, looked after their rooms, and prepared meals in a fireplace and brick oven. In addition she taught. William supervised the boys in the cultivation of the school garden, work that began at dawn, was put aside during classroom hours, and was resumed from dusk to dark.

Punahou was without flowers or trees, according to Mary Sophia Rice, but "we had the priceless spring." Water from the Punahou spring was so prized it was carried across the treeless plain to Honolulu, some three miles distant. It was a hard life, but not without satisfaction. There was milk from a cow that Rice pastured on a piece of land he purchased in Manoa Valley, and the school menu was as good as the Punahou garden could produce. In addition the Rices had the devoted help of Opunui and his wife, Kaniho, who had attached themselves to the Rices at Hana and stayed with them through their lives.

During the first years in Hawaii the missionaries received the necessities of life from "common stock." A missionary would send a list of his needs to Levi Chamberlain, the secular agent in Honolulu, and the supplies were shipped to the family. It was an unsatisfactory system, and later it was made more flexible by allotting each adult and child in missionary households a certain sum of money to purchase the things they needed.

At the annual meeting of the missionaries in 1852, discussions concerning the Hawaiian mission becoming a home mission took on substance. This meant the missionaries would eventually have to become self-supporting. King Kamehameha III, concerned that many of the missionaries might leave as a result, provided an incentive for them to remain in the Islands. He offered each family, at a low price, a piece of land as a partial means of support. Many took advantage of this offer, including Rice, who bought his Manoa pastureland at about this time.

The decision to change the status of the Hawaiian mission emanated from Boston and, even though it evolved over many years, the consequences were much more complex than the American Board could have guessed. In the end the decision was a critical mistake in light of the purpose of the mission, because it diluted the energies of the missionaries between church work and making money. Congregations were poor and few could support a minister. Perhaps the most pressing

The sugar factory of Wyllie's plantation can be seen on the right side of the Hanalei River. The factory was built at great expense and contributed to the financial downfall of the plantation. The white buildings along the river banks are the homes of plantation management.

Anahola Valley was typical of many valleys on Kauai during the years when rice growing was profitable. Taro lands were easily converted to rice culture. A constant

Leong Pah On (left) became one of Hawaii's most successful rice planters. Coming to the Islands as a young man, Pah On developed rice fields and owned a milling factory at Waimea. For many years he grew rice in the swamplands at Mana.

Jean Sinclair married Thomas Gay, a whaling captain with his base at Pigeon Bay in New Zealand who had bought land near the Sinclair family. Gay captained the *Bessie* to Hawaii, and after the Sinclair family was settled on Niihau he returned to sell the vessel in Australia. He died there of pneumonia in 1865. Jean raised a stepson together with four children of her own and died in 1916 at the age of eighty-seven. (Canterbury Museum, New Zealand, photos.)

supply of fresh water was necessary for both crops. (Bernice P. Bishop Museum photo.)

Paul Isenberg was an emigrant German who became one of the most successful sugar planters in the Hawaiian Islands. He was influential as a legislator and in Hackfeld and Company, predecessor of Amfac. He married Hannah Maria Rice. She was a serious, studious girl who grew up on Kauai. She died in 1867 of tuberculosis at the age of twenty-five.

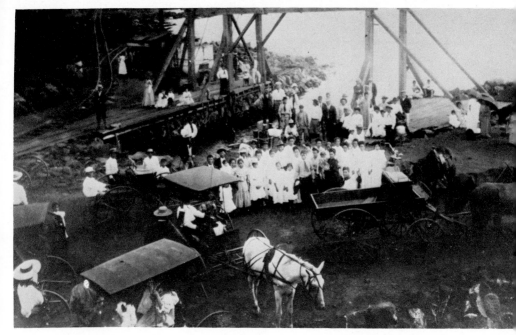

In the late nineteenth-century people dressed in their best and gathered at the stone pier at Koloa on boat day to see friends off, greet visitors, or just to watch. The superstructure above the pier was used to load and unload heavy equipment and supplies.

The Makaweli House built by Eliza Sinclair overlooks the ocean and the distant island of Niihau. The home was the center of activities for Eliza and her children.

Portable, narrow gauge railroad tracks were laid through the fields to make hauling cane to factory easier. A pile of tracks at Kilauea plantation can be seen in the foreground of this photo. Stretching to the left, workers stand atop flatbed cars loaded with cane. (Hawaii State Archives photo.)

Colonel Zephaniah Spalding, one of Kauai's most successful sugar planters, stands before Valley House, his home near Kapaa. Here Spalding entertained lavishly and surrounded his family with refinements imported from around the world.

George N. Wilcox turned Grove Farm plantation into a success and his various enterprises made him one of the wealthiest men in the Islands. Wilcox headed the Queen's cabinet, which survived only briefly, just before the overthrow of Liliuokalani.

Christian Bertelmann is buried on a hill near Kilauea on the north shore of Kauai. Bertelmann had gone to Japan where he unsuccessfully sought a cure for leprosy. The wording on the headstone reads, "Christian Bertelmann, March 24, 1838–Feb. 15, 1895."

Mary Waterhouse Rice had a deep concern for the welfare of the people of Kauai and was affectionately known as "Mother Rice." Her husband, William Hyde Rice, was a rancher and legislator. He was fluent in Hawaiian and was the author of *Legends of Hawaii*. Rice served as the last governor of Kauai and is shown here in the uniform he wore in that capacity.

This interisland steamer is at anchor in Nawiliwili Bay. Vessels could come no closer to shore than shown here and passengers and freight were rowed to and from the ship in open boats. Eventually Nawiliwili became Kauai's major port.

Before bridges crossed Kauai's rivers, scows and barges carried passengers, freight, and animals across. This scow served people crossing the Kalihiwai River.

The *Likelike,* an interisland steamer, stands off the small wharf that was located behind a short breakwater at Ahukini. Unsatisfactory as it was, the small facility remained the best on Kauai for many years. The photograph was taken shortly after the turn of the century. (Hawaii State Archives photo.)

This is a view of the sugar factory at Kealia at the turn of the century. The juice from sugarcane grown on Zephaniah Spalding's plantation was crushed from the stalks and converted into raw sugar at this factory. (Hawaii State Archives photo.)

concerns for the missionaries were funds for the education of their children and sufficient income during their old age. Their work, of necessity, was now divided between the spiritual and commercial. William Rice was a good example. He knew he was not well—he already was suffering from the effects of tuberculosis—and he worried that his family would be wretchedly poor if he did not provide for them.

The concern of Rice coincided with the desire of James Marshall to leave Lihue plantation. Rice was essentially an agriculturalist and when William L. Lee offered him the job as manager of Lihue, Rice accepted, figuring that with hard work and good fortune he could put aside money for his family's security. The starting pay was low, $400 per year, plus a house and space for a garden, but the position was an opportunity and in 1854 the Rice family moved to Kauai.

For the first time in their marriage the Rices could settle into a home where they could expect to stay. It was a home the family remembered with great fondness all their lives. It was situated on a hill overlooking the pond, which was dammed up to provide water power for the mill, and nearby was the company store. The house was long and low-gabled with interior teakwood paneling, probably brought from China by Henry Peirce. The house was shaded by koa trees from which it took its name—Koamalu, shade of a koa tree. In two years an existing nearby orchard was producing figs, muskmelons, peaches, breadfruit, oranges, limes, bananas, grapes, watermelons, and pineapples. William Rice built furniture for the home, and those who visited them remembered the red geraniums that surrounded the house.

One of the chief worries of Marshall had been inadequate rainfall, and this became one of the earliest concerns of Rice. The future of Lihue depended on whether or not clouds would drop their moisture in the right places at the right time. Rice pondered the problem and came up with a solution that sounds simple in retrospect. He would build an irrigation ditch from the mountains, where the Hanamaulu Stream supplied ample water, to the fields of Lihue. It was a tedious job, but appeared to be the only answer. In March 1857 *The Friend* took notice of the undertaking:

> One enterprise in the island is especially worthy of notice. We refer to an effort of introducing a stream of water from the mountains to flow over the Lihue plantation. A trench ten miles long (about two-and-a-half feet wide and the same deep) has been dug. It has been an immense work; and

whether it answers the purpose or not, it shows what labor will accomplish. This summer will test the experiment, and most confidently we hope the enterprise may succeed.

The enterprise succeeded very well. Through a series of ditches, tunnels, and flumes, water saved the fields of cane during times of drought. Later in 1857, when the project had proven a success, *The Polynesian* commented, "Almost as far as the eye can reach, the difference in color and condition of the fields of cane subjected to irrigation and that beyond is perceptible. Let us rejoice with the owners of Lihue Plantation."

The Rices were energetic people, well liked around Kauai and by their friends in Honolulu. Dr. Smith of Koloa was a frequent visitor. As the only doctor on Kauai, he was called day and night to various parts of the island to aid the sick and injured. It would seem that Smith seldom passed Lihue without stopping at the Rices, unannounced, and remaining for a meal before going to or from his duties. Smith wrote on one occasion "It is a great blessing to have such a family in the field—a family that cordially sympathises with me and is always ready to lend a helping hand."

The condition of Lihue plantation improved, but the health of William Rice did not. He labored long hours in the fields and worried about his financial situation, including the paying of debts he had incurred for buying shares in the plantation. In 1861 he traveled to California for his health, and while the trip raised his spirits, it did little for his body. On 27 May 1862 William Harrison Rice, not yet forty-nine years of age, died of tuberculosis at Lihue. As might be expected, Rice left his earthly affairs in good order. He had succeeded in providing adequately for his family and they prospered as Lihue prospered.

Victor Prevost followed Rice as manager of Lihue for a short time, and then young Paul Isenberg became manager. Isenberg, a physically large, alert youth, trained in agriculture, had arrived from Germany in October 1858 to work for Hoffschlaeger and Company, which operated a dairy and ranch in Wailua Valley. On the long voyage from Germany Isenberg had studied English, and once in the Islands he set his mind to learn Hawaiian. For some reason, Florens Stapenhorst, a partner in Hoffschlaeger and Company, did not approve of Isenberg, so young Paul went to work at Lihue plantation. When Duncan McBryde left the managership of Wailua in 1860 Isenberg was asked to fill the job.

In November 1860 Paul Isenberg and Hannah Maria Rice announced their intention to marry. Isenberg had failed to ask the permission of Stapenhorst first, and this so angered him that any hope of a successful relationship between the two was lost. The health of Rice was failing and help was needed. Isenberg was offered a job at Lihue again, and he made the move in the summer of 1861. Hannah Maria and Paul were married in October 1861. Mary Sophia Rice had considered returning to the United States in the event of her husband's death, but she now felt secure in staying at Lihue where Paul Isenberg looked after her well-being.

The ebb and flow of the bloody American Civil War was anxiously followed by Kauai's transplanted Americans. War news gleaned from letters and newspapers was quickly passed on to others. Since nearly all the Americans came from northern states, with many having relatives in the armed forces, sympathy lay heavily with the Union.

Several former Kauai residents gained prominence during the war. William Reynolds first visited Hawaii with the Wilkes Exploring Expedition and later was partially disabled during an Antarctic cruise. He settled on Kauai in 1852 and leased a hundred acres of land at Malumalu, where he grew corn. Later he became U.S. naval storekeeper in Honolulu. In 1861 he rejoined the Union navy. After the war, in 1867, Reynolds was ordered to Hawaii in command of the *Lackawanna*. On one occasion he brought his ship to Hanalei, entertained the residents on board, put on a target practice demonstration, and carried the missionaries to Honolulu for their annual meeting.

During the year and a half the *Lackawanna* was in Hawaiian waters, a reciprocity treaty between Hawaii and the United States was being hotly debated. The long stay of the *Lackawanna* was viewed as a form of pressure by the Hawaiian monarchy and the government protested the presence of Reynolds and his ship in Hawaiian waters. Reynolds was loudly in favor of annexation, not reciprocity, and his feelings were well known. He remained in the navy, eventually becoming a rear admiral, and for a few months served as acting secretary of the navy.

Another one-time Kauai resident, James F. B. Marshall, had been the first manager of Lihue plantation. He had returned to Massachusetts to live and at the outbreak of war was put in charge of recruiting for the state. He became paymaster general for Massachusetts troops and was later assigned to the Sanitary Commission, which included the hospital corps. Marshall's biggest job was to care for the large number of wounded from Grant's Army of the Potomac. He retired a brigadier general.

A man with a near-fanatical anti-slavery feeling had come to Kauai in 1837 and departed long before the war began. He was Dr. Thomas Lafon, the first missionary-doctor on Kauai. Originally assigned to Koloa, Lafon started a church and school at Nawiliwili. He resigned from the American Board for Foreign Missions in 1841, the year he left Hawaii, because they accepted contributions from slaveholders. Lafon had been born in Virginia, had owned slaves, and had bought and sold them. After his conversion he came to the conclusion that slavery was against the teachings of the Bible. He emancipated his slaves and offered his services to the American Board. After leaving Hawaii Lafon lectured on the evils of slavery, comparing it with the conditions of the commoners in Hawaii under the domination of the chiefs.

Many Southern sympathizers in Hawaii were found among the English-born population. There were a few on Kauai. Robert C. Wyllie, who was foreign minister of the kingdom and a Scotsman, owned a sugar plantation at Hanalei which he frequently visited. Wyllie felt the South had the right to secede, but because of his position in the government he did not express his personal feelings publicly.

When Josephine Wundenberg, a daughter of Godfrey Wundenberg, made a small Southern flag and flew it from the bow of a boat that plied the Hanalei River, Wyllie thought it could lead to a wrong impression. Wundenberg, a Southern sympathizer, was manager of Wyllie's plantation at the time and it appears that he found it difficult to take seriously Wyllie's request to remove the flag.

Herman A. Widemann, a German by birth, well known and respected on Kauai over the years, loudly proclaimed the Southern cause. Widemann had grown coffee at Hanalei, been active in the sugar business, and held many public offices on Kauai, including that of tax collector, sheriff, and judge. His intense feelings appear to have made him a voice unto himself. Widemann was a monarchist, although he believed that the annexation of Hawaii by the United States was inevitable. When Queen Liliuokalani was deposed he acted as one of her lawyers when she was brought to trial for treason.

Robert Crichton Wyllie, of the minor aristocracy of Scotland, had a partial medical education from Glasgow University and had gathered a small fortune as a merchant in Mexico and South America. He had served as surgeon aboard British ships, practiced medicine in Chile, been a merchant in London, and traveled to Australia, India, and the United States before continuing as a merchant in Mexico. In 1844 Wyllie came to Hawaii with General William Miller, newly appointed British consul.

Wyllie displayed a combination of curious traits. Socially pretentious, he was a lifelong bachelor who had a great interest in nearly everything he saw. He was held by a sense of chivalry that was centuries out of date if, indeed, it had ever existed at all. In 1845 Robert Crichton Wyllie was offered the position of minister of foreign affairs, and he served the Hawaiian kingdom in that capacity for twenty years.

It was important to Wyllie that the highest officials in the kingdom make a dignified impression. He wrote detailed instructions describing the liveries to be worn by their retainers, and the etiquette to be followed when the king and queen left Iolani Palace. He wrote endlessly to foreign governments, taxed the capacity of the government printing press in producing documents, then investigated and wrote more. He sought and received recognition of Hawaii as an independent nation by countries—both powerful and powerless—around the world. Wyllie gave a dress ball for the king and queen, at which he wore his Scottish kilt "in the national color of buff turned up with red." He criticized the American missionaries for interfering in government affairs, fostered ties with England, and encouraged Queen Emma to invite the Episcopal Church in England to Hawaii. Through it all, no one seriously questioned his devotion to the stability and independence of Hawaii.

In Honolulu Wyllie lived at Rosebank, his comfortable estate in Nuuanu Valley. But he had dreams of spending the last years of his life on a romantic estate where he would indeed be the laird. He found the place for this estate. It was Hanalei, and in March 1853 he bought the lease on Godfrey Rhodes' coffee lands. Later in the same year he bought out Rhodes' business interests. Godfrey Frederick Wundenberg, returned from Honolulu to manage the estate.

Wundenberg had come to Hawaii in 1843 from Hildensheim in Hanover, Germany, where he and Herman Widemann had been friends. For a short time Wundenberg worked for Wyllie as secretary. Then he grew coffee and potatoes at Hanalei, and in 1845 he married Ann Moorea Henry, who was visiting Hanalei and was the daughter of the Reverend William Henry, a missionary who had gone to Tahiti from England in 1796. The marriage was performed by George Rowell. In 1848 Wundenberg spent a short time in California with Charles Titcomb and Widemann. He returned to farm in Hanalei, later moved to Honolulu, but came back to manage Princeville for a time.

During the years 1861–1862 Wyllie constructed his great sugar mill at the eastern end of Hanalei Valley, next to the river. Much of the machinery was brought from Glasgow, Scotland. A brick chimney rose 110 feet high. As would be expected of Wyllie, his factory set the standard of excellence for sugar factories in Hawaii. Sugarcane was brought down the Hanalei River in a fleet of eleven scows and unloaded onto a conveyor belt to be carried into the factory. After the juice had been extracted from the cane, the bagasse was carried out by conveyor belt. Reputed to have cost $40,000, the factory was more than the most complete in the Islands. It was a reflection of Wyllie—a display to be admired.

In 1860 Kamehameha IV, Queen Emma, and their son visited Hanalei. Wyllie could not be present and Mr. and Mrs. Wundenberg entertained the royal guests for over two weeks. From this time the estate was known as Princeville, after the young prince of Hawaii. In fact, Wyllie renamed his schooner, which plied between Hanalei and Honolulu, *The Prince of Hawaii*. He even suggested the heir bear the title, "Baron de Princeville." Sadly, the young prince died in 1862, at the age of four.

Wyllie continued to buy land. In 1863, for $29,000, he bought some 750 acres from Charles Titcomb, who earlier had led the way by converting his lands from coffee to sugar. As Wyllie sat overlooking Hanalei Valley, he thought that the lands acquired from Titcomb should appropriately be named for Queen Emma. He sent the queen a letter stating that this portion of the estate would henceforth be known as Emmaville. In 1863 the first sugar crop was harvested, after which manager Wundenberg returned to Honolulu.

Robert Wyllie's life was busy, full of important people and affairs of state. If these chores turned into a kind of monotony for Wyllie, it was broken by the visit of Lady Jane Franklin. Lady Franklin was the widow of the explorer Sir John Franklin, who had disappeared on his fourth expedition into the Arctic. Ships were sent in search of him, and finally in 1859 records and a few remnants of Franklin's expedition confirmed his death a dozen years earlier. Lady Franklin, herself, helped to finance five ships to search for him between 1850 and 1857. Through these efforts and her strong personality she became an internationally known figure in her own right.

Lady Franklin turned her energies to travel and arrived off Honolulu on 20 April 1861 aboard the clipper ship *Yankee*. Wyllie sent the queen's carriage to bring her and Sophia Cracroft, her traveling companion and husband's niece, to Rosebank in Nuuanu Valley. At one end of his home was a tower with a spacious apartment in which the English lady stayed. To the sixty-three-year-old Wyllie the sixty-nine-year-old Jane Franklin was a delight. She was small in stature, a gray-haired, gray-eyed, aristocratic lady, set firm in the belief that English aristocracy and manners were superior to all others. She was intelligent, energetic, adventurous, and most willing to prejudice the Hawaiian monarchy in favor of England. Lady Franklin awakened dreams in Wyllie's heart.

Several years before Jane Franklin's visit to Hawaii, Wyllie had written, "but for what are called fine and fashionable Ladies, I have always liked them better as Partners for a Waltz, than as Partners under the same roof for life." But what Wyllie wrote at an earlier time was perhaps not quite his sentiment in 1861. After Jane and Sophia had visited the island of Hawaii, Wyllie was determined they should visit Princeville with him. Lady Franklin agreed.

Robert Wyllie planned on building a fashionable home at Princeville, but in the meantime he rented a house called Kikiula on a hill overlooking Hanalei Valley. The house faced toward the west, commanding a sweeping view of the valley, its winding river, green cane fields, and the steep mountains to the left, often with a dozen long, white waterfalls vivid against the dark green of the foliage. On the north a hill sloped down toward the mouth of the Hanalei River, and over this was a glimpse of the ocean.

Godfrey Wundenberg came to meet Wyllie and Franklin in a longboat in Hanalei Bay on the afternoon of 30 May 1861. The visitors came up the river to the landing place under the weeping willow trees below Kikiula. Kikiula had been built by Captain Charles Kellett, longtime resident and port pilot of Hanalei. There were terraces leading downward to the valley floor, and the whitewashed, red-roofed homes occupied by plantation management stretched away below the house. Around the residence was a broad lawn and there were orange trees and flowers that perfumed the idyllic setting. A mound of earth, not far from the house, must have come to Lady Franklin's attention. It was marked with an iron tablet, "Sacred to the Memory of WM. LUXFORD, Late Quartermaster of H.B.M. Ship *Enterprise*." Luxford had died at Hanalei in December 1850 while the *Enterprise* was wintering at Hanalei, having returned from the Arctic after searching for Sir John Franklin.

Twelve days were spent at Kikiula in rest and doing such things as

Jane and Sophia wished. They read, drew, and sewed, uninterrupted by cares. They never tired of the changing beauty of the valley world in which they were immersed. On Sunday they went to church, part of the way by boat on the river and the remainder on horseback. Jane could pick out only the words Britannia and Victoria from the sermon, preached in Hawaiian. After church they took tea at the home of the Reverend Johnson, the minister. Jane could find nothing of merit in Americans or American missionaries in particular.

The Wundenbergs had seven children and life at Hanalei was not easy. Lady Franklin did not set their minds at ease. She urged Ann Moorea to let her take one of the Wundenberg girls away from primitive Hanalei to England for a proper upbringing.

Lady Jane Franklin and Sophia Cracroft sailed away from Hawaii, but not out of Wyllie's thoughts. At the end of 1861 discussions were under way concerning a treaty with Japan. Wyllie wrote to the king suggesting that Jane be appointed ambassador to Japan, with the authority to negotiate a treaty with Hawaii. Lady Franklin might have done a good job, but nothing came of the idea.

Before leaving Hanalei Wyllie offered to deed a piece of land above Kikiula to Jane. It was a spot she enjoyed, with sweeping views of the sea and the mountains. The deed was never drawn, for later, when Jane wished to give the land to the Episcopal Church, no legal basis of her ownership could be found.

In his correspondence, Wyllie on one occasion referred to the two ladies and described how he felt: "Of all the ladies that I have ever met with, they are just the ladies that suit me. They are of high mettle and breeding—not Prudes, humdrum and Pernickatenackate." He wrote concerning his plans for their return to Princeville and wanted Lady Jane to send a portrait of herself. In 1863, in a letter to Queen Emma, Wyllie referred to gossip that he and Lady Franklin were to be married. He assured the queen that it was only a rumor, without foundation, and that it had started as a joke that some had taken seriously.

Robert Crichton Wyllie was not destined to retire to his estate on Kauai. In 1864 he entered into correspondence with the Reverend Rufus Anderson concerning his evaluation of missionary work in Hawaii and mentioned his poor health. He wrote that he suffered from dysentery, "which is very depressing and often dangerous." He wished to move to Hanalei. On 12 September 1865, he wrote to Kamehameha V for the last time. He mentioned a fever, which he was nearly rid of, and an "open blister on my stomach." In unusually large handwriting Wyllie continued "Therefore I am laying down in Native fashion propt up by a cushion in my large drawing room unable to rise or lay down without a servant on each side."

On 19 October 1865 at 10:55 A.M., Wyllie died. Flags flew at half-mast and government offices were closed. With courtly honors Wyllie was buried in the Royal Mausoleum. Four days before he died he had ordered his papers and diary destroyed.

Several months before his death Robert Wyllie had decided he wanted to leave his estate to a relative. He invited a nephew, Robert Crichton Cockrane, to come to the Islands from Waltham, Illinois, and become his heir. There was one condition—that the young man change his name to Wyllie. This the nephew agreed to do.

The young Robert Wyllie lived at Hanalei. Little is known of him, although Abner Wilcox, then a teacher at Hanalei, thought he was about twenty-five years of age. Sometime after his arrival he met Ida von Pfister in Honolulu, and they became engaged. Her father, John von Pfister, had grown coffee at Hanalei and was murdered in San Francisco during the gold rush.

Reports of the time state that Wyllie examined the books of his uncle's plantation and became terribly depressed. In retrospect it is obvious that the sugar factory was an extravagance, built more for show than as a practical business investment. Charles Titcomb, by contrast, had produced sugar in a primitive factory that no one bothered to praise, but which got the job done. The Princeville factory could easily have been enough to break the plantation financially. In addition, by 1866 it might have been suspected that Hanalei Valley was too wet a place to get adequate yields of sugarcane, although attempts continued for another twenty-five years.

Mary Sophia Rice wrote of Princeville, "The property was encumbered with so many mortgages and prohibitions of selling that the inheritance was like coming in possession of a drove of elephants." Whatever the details of the problems, they overwhelmed young Wyllie. On Sunday evening, 4 February 1866, a group of men gathered at the home of John Low, the plantation manager, to enjoy the musical performance of some local residents.

According to John Cook, who was present that evening, Low went to get some lime to make more limeade and young Wyllie went to get a jug of water. Low returned, but Wyllie did not. After waiting some time, Low said, "Where's Wyllie, we must find him. He's been off his head for some weeks."

Cook continued, "We searched the house and at last, on opening the door of a large privy situated outside, Wyllie fell forward into the arms of Low, the blood gushing from a wound in his throat, which he had cut with a razor." It was about 9:00 P.M.

Young Wyllie was still alive. He was carried into the house on a mattress and attempts were made to sew up the wound and stop the flow of blood. Abner Wilcox estimated the wound was big enough to insert four fingers and a thumb. At last Wyllie recovered consciousness. A whaleboat was sent to Honolulu for Dr. Robert McKibbin, and a rider headed toward Koloa for Dr. Smith, still the only doctor on Kauai.

According to John Cook, Wyllie "became perfectly sensible." On a piece of paper he wrote, "Oh! my poor mother, don't tell mother. Fix it up so she won't know." John Low suggested that Wyllie might want to make a will. Wyllie agreed. At first Wyllie wrote the word "Mother." Low suggested he might want to leave something to Ida von Pfister, and Wyllie took the paper back and wrote, "Ida." Asked if they should share alike in his property, Wyllie nodded.

The words were put down: "I Robert Crichton Wyllie do hereby bequeath all my property personal Real to my Mother and, Miss Ida von Pfister jointly and equally." And underneath, "Princeville February 4, 1866." Beneath this, Wyllie wrote his signature in large letters, obviously with great effort. With growing weakness the letters of his signature became smaller as they trailed off and downward. The signing took place about 11:00 P.M., Sunday. There are blood stains on the paper.

Wyllie did not want to die. On a piece of paper he wrote several short sentences, including "I will live." He also asked for the Reverend Johnson, pastor of the Waioli Church, who was summoned and duly arrived.

The messenger who had gone for Dr. Smith arrived in Koloa about sunrise Monday morning. Smith recorded in his journal, "I left home about ¼ before 8 o'clock. . . . Changed horses at Wailua & reached Princeville at ¼ past 12 only 4½ hours from Koloa." The distance was 45 miles. It was a remarkable ride, considering the terrain and the number of rivers he had to cross.

Smith continued in his journal, "The cut was made with a heavy razor was very deep—the cut ends of the trachea or rather larynx were widely separated—and I was unable to bring them together—The loss of blood was great & on my arrival there was no pulse in his arm—

during the afternoon & a part of the time next day there was percept-
able a slight thread like pulse at the most."

It was an impossible situation. Smith could not connect the two
ends of the trachea and nothing could be gotten into Wyllie's stomach.
The loss of blood was so great that Smith thought it impossible for
him to bleed further and survive. On Monday evening Wyllie became
delirious. On Tuesday he became rational, but was delirious all night.
Young Wyllie finally died at 6:05 on Wednesday evening. Dr. Smith
entered in his journal, "I pray I may never see another [such] case."

Robert Wyllie was buried in the Waioli churchyard in an unmarked
grave surrounded by an iron fence. The press hardly took notice of his
demise. In a terse notice the *Hawaiian Gazette* mentioned that he died
"suddenly." The friends of Wyllie in Waltham, Illinois, were not willing to believe the young man had committed suicide. In a card published in *The Friend* three men who knew him well stated they would
"appreciate every effort put forth to unravel the deep dark mystery of
his death."

In September 1867 Princeville was auctioned off. Debts included
two mortgages plus interest, which came to $38,150. The plantation
sold for $40,050. Princeville had cost Wyllie at least $200,000. Rosebank, the Nuuanu estate, was sold and Wyllie's books were disposed
of at auction. The Wyllie fortune was gone, and the Wyllie name was
not perpetuated on Kauai or in Hawaii.

CHAPTER TEN

An Island All Their Own

The northeast trade winds that blow ponderous clouds laden with moisture onto Kauai have a difficult time finding Niihau. The rains fall over the mountains and envelop the north, east, and south coasts of Kauai. Precipitous Na Pali, Kilauea, Wailua, Lihue, and Koloa receive ample attention. But the supply of moisture is not enough to cover the circumference of Kauai. The western coastal plains of Mana and Waimea are touched by only a trace of rain. Seventeen miles of channel lies between these dry coastal plains and the island of Niihau. Niihau is an arid place, and when the once-heavy rain clouds reach the small island they are no more than elongated streaks in the sky.

The highest peak on Niihau rises only 1,281 feet. Called Paniau, it is on the eastern side of the island, a point near the edge of a stark cliff that drops away into the sea. From this high point the heavily eroded island slopes quickly downward to the north, west, and south. The higher land on the island is limestone, which gives way to sand dunes at lower levels. Most of the island is low and flat, rising only 50 to 100 feet above sea level. On the western edge of the 18-mile-long, 6-mile-wide island, rainfall is less than an inch a year. *Kiawe* trees, scrub brush, and a few grasses dominate the vegetation.

Toward the southwest, near sea level, are three lakes. One is called Halalii, and its size of 840.7 acres makes it the largest natural lake in the Hawaiian Islands. The lakes are called "intermittent," because they are usually dried reddish flats with small saline ponds in the middle. After a rain they become reddish mud-flats. On the fringes of these intermittent lakes grows the sedge from which the famous *makaloa* mats were woven.

Makaloa mats are as flexible and soft as cloth and were long prized by kings and high chiefs on all the Islands. When Kauai became a tributary part of Kamehameha's kingdom, makaloa mats were a part of the yearly tribute. A visitor who received such a mat as a gift had been truly honored.

Captain James Cook sent two boats and twenty men ashore on Niihau for supplies. His men were unable to come back through the high surf for two nights and a day. When the boats did start their return to the ship they lost most of their supply of yams in the high surf. Niihau became known as Yam Island to subsequent sea captains who visited the Islands.

Other early captains rediscovered what Cook had found. The anchorages were risky, the currents contrary, and the surf unpredictable. And they found the landscape inhospitable. In 1826 Captain F. W. Beechey simply noted, "The soil is too dry to produce tar." In 1845 Gorham Gilman found the island held "very little of the beautiful." Gilman noticed "a number of wells dug through the thin strata of coral or sand stone and in which was a small quantity of water green and brackish." Mercy Whitney returned from a visit to Niihau in 1848 and remembered the island as a place of coarse grass and some small shrubs, but with no large trees or timber.

On 17 September 1863 the barque *Bessie* entered Honolulu Harbor. The arrival of yet another vessel was no reason for notice, but this one was different. Aboard was the Sinclair family and that made the coming of the 300-ton *Bessie* an uncommon occurrence. The newly arrived Sinclairs and the isolated island of Niihau were destined to have a long and deep effect on each other.

The person in charge of the ship's company was a slight, five-foot-tall, blue-eyed, sixty-three-year-old woman named Elizabeth McHutchison Sinclair. The captain of the *Bessie* was Thomas Gay, her son-in-law. In all there were thirteen persons aboard, all related, who bore the names of Sinclair, Robinson, or Gay. The ship on which they reached Honolulu had been their only home for five months.

The Reverend Samuel Damon, who was seamen's chaplain in Honolulu, went down to the dock to look at the ship and his observations were recorded by Isabella Bird. "On going down to the wharf he was surprised to find the trim barque with its large family party on board, with a beautiful old lady at its head, books, pictures, work, even a piano, and all that could add refinement to a floating home, with cattle and sheep of valuable breeds in pens on the deck."

The Sinclairs were warmly received in Honolulu. The newcomers were well-educated people, religious, and of financial substance. They rented a house on King Street, on the road to Manoa, from George Luce, a prominent Honoluluan who was a sailing captain and harbor pilot. Many of the city's leading citizens were anxious to have the Sinclairs remain in Hawaii.

Where did this remarkable family come from? The road that eventually led them to Hawaii had its beginnings in Scotland. Elizabeth McHutchison was born in Glasgow on 26 April 1800. At the age of eighteen Eliza, as she was known, accompanied her father on a business trip and met Captain Francis Sinclair, formerly of the Royal Navy. He was tall and curly haired, and to Eliza he was very handsome.

After the battle of Waterloo Captain Sinclair was returning the Duke of Wellington to England aboard his ship when a storm threatened to drive them onto shoreline rocks. Sinclair personally took the tiller and brought the ship safely to harbor. The Duke of Wellington presented Sinclair a folding desk with a silver plate on which was engraved "To Captain Francis Sinclair, in token of his splendid seamanship."

In 1819 Eliza and Francis were married. Francis continued to be absorbed in government and private business. By 1839 the family included three sons and three daughters. In spite of the large family there was a spirit of adventure in the Sinclairs and they decided to emigrate to New Zealand, which was then being opened to English colonists. They arrived in 1841 and while searching for suitable land Captain Sinclair traded along the coast in a vessel he had built. In 1843 the Sinclairs settled on the central coast of the South Island, on a tract of land on Pigeon Bay, which is located on the north shore of Banks Peninsula. The place became known as Sinclair Bay, later being renamed Holmes Bay. The closest town was Akaroa, which lay over the hills fifteen miles away.

It was a pioneer life. At first the Sinclairs shared a tent and then a grass-thatched house with another family. Francis Sinclair raised sheep and cattle, built a small vessel for transportation, and planted and harvested. In May 1846 Sinclair sailed for Wellington carrying with him all the family cash and the year's produce. His mission was to buy additional property and the variety of supplies needed for the coming year. With Francis Sinclair were his oldest son George and two other men. The ship never reached Wellington, nor was a trace of it ever found. Eliza Sinclair was left destitute, forced to supervise the affairs of the family.

For a while Eliza and her family lived in Wellington and then Akaroa, returning to Pigeon Bay in 1849. She managed wisely and the family prospered. In 1848 the oldest daughter, Jean, married Captain Thomas Gay, a widower who had a five-year-old son. Gay was a whaling captain who had brought his ship into Pigeon Bay and who later bought land adjoining the Sinclairs. Two years later Helen, the second daughter, married Charles B. Robinson, a prominent and prosperous man who lived in Akaroa. Robinson had played an important role in securing the South Island for England at a time when France was also attempting colonization, and he became the first magistrate of Akaroa. Two years after the marriage Helen walked to Sinclair Bay from Akaroa carrying her only son, Aubrey. She announced she was home to stay and offered no explanation for leaving her husband.

The years brought prosperity but not contentment. In about 1862 son Francis and daughter Helen became restless and wanted the family to move to British Columbia or California where larger tracts of land were readily available. After much family debate the decision was made to leave. The New Zealand land was sold at a good price because its forests were valued as timber. The *Bessie,* owned by Thomas Gay, was loaded with possessions and supplies, and in April 1863 the Sinclair family set forth on yet another adventure. It was an event reminiscent of the Swiss Family Robinson story.

Aboard the ship were Eliza Sinclair, Captain Gay, his son by his first marriage, his wife Jean and their four children, Mrs. Robinson and her son, and the three unmarried Sinclairs. There were also several servants, in addition to the ship's crew. The first port of call was Tahiti and then they sailed northward, where the ship passed within sight of Mauna Loa and Mauna Kea on the island of Hawaii.

In June the clan arrived in British Columbia where they liked the town of Victoria, on Vancouver Island, and the people. But the dense forests, the Canadian Indians, and the clouds of mosquitoes were discouraging. In Victoria Henry Rhodes, a brother of Godfrey Rhodes of Honolulu, advised them to go to Hawaii. California, Rhodes thought, would not be a good place to visit since winter rains there would make travel into the interior difficult. So the decision was made to steer for Honolulu, where the ship arrived on 17 September 1863.

The Sinclairs were anxious to find land on which to settle and they were offered several large tracts on Oahu. Robert Wyllie, minister of foreign affairs, arranged for them to be offered Kahuku, and Dr. Seth Porter Ford offered to sell them Ford Island in Pearl Harbor as well as

lands in Ewa. Apparently they were also offered land between Honolulu and Diamond Head. None of these offers appealed to the Sinclairs
and they tentatively decided to sail for California. The king heard of
their planned departure and offered to sell them the island of Niihau.

Francis and James Sinclair went off to Niihau to inspect the island.
Some 300 Hawaiians lived there at the time. The Sinclair brothers
returned from their inspection, enthusiastic about its prospects as a
place to live. The Sinclairs offered $6,000 for the island. The govern-
ment countered. The island could be leased for $750 a year or bought
outright for $10,000. The Sinclairs bought Niihau at the govern-
ment's price.

It is difficult to understand how Francis and James could have been
so impressed with Niihau. It might have been in part because the
thought of an island all their own was a pleasant, romantic prospect.
A descendant of the Gays remembered a family story relating that
Niihau had exceptionally heavy rains before the visit of the two
brothers and appeared a greener and more hospitable place than usual.

The Sinclairs and their possessions moved to Niihau. Three pre-cut
houses were carried ashore and assembled at Nonopapa on a long dune
facing the great western expanse of the Pacific. The three houses were
built adjoining one another, connected by broad lanais. The building
was painted white and there was a white picket fence in front. As time
passed a number of other buildings, for stables and servants' quarters,
were constructed behind the house.

When everything had been set ashore, Captain Gay steered the *Bessie* to Australia and sold her in Sydney. Gay was never to return to
Hawaii. He died of pneumonia on 9 February 1865, and was buried in
the Presbyterian cemetery in Newcastle, Australia.

In April 1865 Luther H. Gulick wrote to Rufus Anderson of the
American Board, concerning Niihau. "The whole island is now
owned by a Presbyterian family of Scotch origin, who received me
very kindly, & who will assist our work there very materially & very
heartily. The native population now remaining there is about 250 in
number."

Anne Sinclair, who was called Annie, was the youngest of the Sinclair girls. She was an active, gregarious person and Niihau offered little company. Annie had many suitors in New Zealand. Even while she
was living on isolated Niihau, suitors continued to seek her company.
Among them was Valdemar Knudsen, who lived across the channel at
Waiawa, between Kekaha and Mana, on Kauai.

Knudsen had come to Kauai in 1854 and had taken over the Mana leases of Gruber and Archer, who had failed in their efforts to grow tobacco there. Knudsen planted an orchard and raised cattle and horses. He was a welcome visitor on Niihau where he often came to visit Annie. Valdemar hesitated to ask Annie to marry him because he was twenty years older, but he finally summoned up the courage and Annie accepted his proposal. The two were married in the church on Niihau on 12 February 1867 by the Hawaiian minister, in the Hawaiian language. The next morning the couple crossed the channel in the Niihau whaleboat to their home at Waiawa.

Eliza Sinclair remained the assertive leader of the clan. She was not content with owning only the island of Niihau. Perhaps she realized very soon that the island lacked the water needed to make it anything more than marginal. Wanting to provide an inheritance for her two elder daughters and their children, Eliza Sinclair purchased the *ahupua'a* of Makaweli on Kauai.

Makaweli had come into the possession of the descendants of Kamehameha I following the crushing of the revolt on Kauai in 1824, when so many chiefs were dispossessed. At the time of the Mahele, or division of lands, in 1848 it was recorded that Makaweli was the property of Victoria Kamamalu, a granddaughter of the first Kamehameha.

On 29 June 1865 Eliza Sinclair purchased all the Makaweli lands of Victoria Kamamalu, as recorded in the Mahele book, through her trustee Charles C. Harris for $15,000. Eliza paid $10,000 in cash, with $5,000 due in sixty days. She then discounted the $5,000 for $4,900, payable on the same date. The *ahupua'a* of Makaweli contains 21,844 acres of land, and in the years to come the Sinclair family continued to buy land in Makaweli and the adjoining district of Hanapepe. These lands were the basis of their successful sugar and ranching operations.

In the early 1870s most of the Sinclair clan moved to a spacious new home on the upper slopes of Makaweli. Among the problems of life on Niihau had been the education of the children. A collection of tutors taught the children on Niihau, and in 1868 the Robinson and Gay boys were boarding students at the Reverend Daniel Dole's academy at Koloa.

After the clan moved to Makaweli a talented tutor came to live with the family. His name was Waldemar Muller, a former Prussian army officer who had volunteered to serve Maximilian in his attempt to become emperor of Mexico. Muller had been wounded several times and during the final battle at Queretaro he was again wounded. He was released by the triumphant Mexicans with a bullet in his arm and another in his side. In the U.S. Muller recuperated from his wounds and learned English.

Waldemar Muller sailed to Hawaii and during the voyage read the Bible for the first time, becoming intensely religious as a result. He arrived in Honolulu from San Francisco aboard the *Queen Emma* on 4 October 1871. The *Hawaiian Gazette* wrote on 11 October that he came "highly recommended [and] has established himself in this city as a teacher of piano, vocal music, and languages, as will be seen by his card elsewhere. Those employing Mr. Muller will find him a teacher of rare ability."

The "card" referred to was a small advertisement. In it Muller declared that he had decided to remain in the Islands permanently, and in addition to teaching was available "to play for concerts, parties, etc., made on reasonable terms; also pianos tuned and repaired." During the school year of 1871–1872 he taught several languages and music at Punahou School.

Isabella Bird, who stayed at Makaweli in 1873, reported that Muller taught Greek, German, mathematics, music, and English. Classes started at 6:30 A.M. and lasted until 8:30 A.M. Study continued until noon. The tutor was not only a teacher who inspired enthusiasm, but he became an important part of the household. He was an artist and a poet. He played the Erhard piano with great skill. Isabella Bird wrote that "His prayers are wonderful and everything he says is so beautiful." On occasion Muller conducted services for the family.

While Isabella Bird was impressed by the accomplished tutor, she was disturbed by the intensity of his Christian zeal. He had given up all reading for his own pleasure, except for the Bible. He had also given up fern-collecting and the enjoyment of nature in general, because it was under the curse of God. Isabella Bird admired Muller's brilliance in so many things, but there was something about his ideas that depressed her.

It appears that Muller stayed with the Sinclair family only for about a year because in 1874 he was teaching in a manual training school for Hawaiians. The school was not a success, and Muller moved to Koloa, where he established a business growing *pia,* arrowroot. This lasted for several years and by 1882 Muller had moved to the island of Hawaii, where he married and made a living by teaching school and later growing coffee.

Eliza Sinclair was the ruler-matriarch of the Sinclair-Robinson-Gay clan. Makaweli was the headquarters, and Niihau became the colony of her domain. She had lost her husband and a son by drowning, a son-in-law had died in Australia, and another daughter had left a second son-in-law in New Zealand. In 1873 Eliza's clan included two remaining sons, Francis and James, with Francis managing affairs on Niihau, daughter Helen Robinson and her son, and the widowed daughter Jean Gay with her stepson, three young sons, and two daughters. The third daughter, Annie, was married to Valdemar Knudsen.

At the age of seventy-three Eliza was an active, physically fit woman, the center of a loving, religious, and cultured family. She spoke English with a refined, slightly Scottish accent, and habitually wore a bonnet. In the morning she was up at 5:00 A.M. and radiated enthusiasm and humor wherever she went. She was an excellent horsewoman and regularly rode long distances.

The spacious Makaweli house was at 1,800 feet elevation on the mountainside. During winter it was cool enough to keep a fire going in the fireplace most of the day. Outside were flowers and trees, and on the surrounding plains were some 150 broken saddle horses and 500 wild horses. In 1873 the young men were beginning to raise cattle.

Francis Sinclair was the master of affairs on Niihau. His generosity as well as his simple and strict rules are reflected in the church reports that were prepared for several years. Each Sunday there were services morning and evening. Each Tuesday the Bible was read and explained. On Wednesdays the people were exhorted through Bible lessons. In his report for 1871 A. Kaukau wrote:

> The Hawaiians are very grateful for their haole chief in several ways. . . . F. Sinclair gave graciously an eighth of the whole island of Niihau as an open country where the horses of the people may run.
>
> He gave freely lands for planting sweet potatoes—two planting places . . . perhaps 100 or more acres. . . .
>
> To eat; people are to gather fish surrounding Niihau; there is no disputing about fish, like the days of the Konohiki. . . .
>
> He will punish the persons indulging in sexual gratification and drinking liquor. The Government will punish persons outside of their house lots. He will punish the persons who drink liquor inside of all the houses, if discovered. . . .
>
> He and his family go regularly to the church service. . . . He marks the children that do not go to Sunday School and punishes them if they always stay home. Therefore his Sunday School is full throughout the year.

In the 1872 report Kaukau wrote that Francis Sinclair had told the
people

> . . . not to go in large numbers to Honolulu to "waste time" . . . and he
> has instructed the Hawaiians to go to church and that it is not well to go
> to sleep.
>   He is like a father and acts rightly and helps the sincere people and is
> provoked at those who act mischievously. The Hawaiians produce true
> love for him.

Francis Sinclair, always the lover of literature, became a Hawaiian
citizen in 1874 and remained on Niihau or Kauai during the years
when the Robinson and Gay boys were growing up. He had returned
to New Zealand to marry his cousin, Isabella McHutchison, in 1865.
Isabella was an accomplished artist who painted the flowers for *The
Indigenous Flowers of the Hawaiian Islands,* a classic book in its field,
published in London in 1885. Eventually Francis and Isabella moved to
England, where Francis wrote several books, including one of verse.
In one of his poems he referred to himself as the "prodigal returned."
He regretted ever leaving his homeland.

> Higher far I hold my birthright, and the name my father bore,
> Than all magic dreams of beauty from earth's furthest shore to
> shore.

After the death of Isabella, Francis married her sister, Ina McHutchison. He had no children by either marriage. Francis died on the Isle of
Jersey in 1916.
    James Sinclair had died in 1873. A tree had fallen on him while he
was still in New Zealand, and he continued to suffer from the injuries.
He had never married. On 16 October 1892 the matriarch Eliza Sinclair died at Makaweli. She was ninety-three years of age.

Among the things Annie Sinclair and Valdemar Knudsen had in
common was a love for plants and birds. Many specimens of plants
were pressed and kept. Valdemar, particularly, enjoyed seeking unknown species and because of his interest botanists sought him out.
One of these men was William Brigham, who came to Hawaii with
Horace Mann, the young botanist son of Horace Mann the educator,
in 1864. Knudsen's hospitality toward Brigham cooled when he

learned he was also a suitor of Annie Sinclair. In 1865 Horace Mann returned to Harvard College and published some of his findings, but he died of tuberculosis at the age of twenty-four. William Brigham published some of Mann's remaining findings. Among the genera Brigham named for Mann is one called "Evening of Mann." William Brigham later became the first director of the Bishop Museum in Honolulu.

Another botanist, Heinrich Wawra, came to Waiawa in late December 1869. Wawra was the ship's surgeon aboard the Austrian steam frigate *Donau,* which was on government business. The ship had sailed from Yokohama and had encountered a cyclone and then western gales that lasted ten days. The ship lost its rudder and twenty-six sails; it took thirty-six days to reach Honolulu.

While the *Donau* was being repaired, Wawra went to Kauai where he stayed at the Paul Isenberg house. Knudsen took the botanist to see various trees and bushes, including a tree that Knudsen had discovered, as yet unnamed. Wawra took Knudsen's specimens and later named the tree after himself. Annie and Valdemar were very angry.

Before Wawra left Kauai, George N. Wilcox guided him to the top of Mount Waialeale. Wilcox chose the dangerous Wailua side of the mountain to climb. No known white man had scaled that face of the mountain before and the overgrown path was seldom if ever used by the Hawaiians by that time. The first night was spent at the base of the mountain and they started the ascent the next morning. With them were four Hawaiian men and one woman. They pulled themselves up the steep and slippery trail. The night was spent on a rounded mound of ground looking down on the plain and valley of Wailua.

The next morning Heinrich Wawra announced he wanted to head down again, since the time for him to return to Honolulu to catch the *Donau* was close at hand. Wilcox convinced the botanist that the peak —the "bud in the summit of Waialeale"—was close at hand and they continued to the top. Once on the plateau at the summit they saw the platform where the ancient Hawaiians had annually come to pay homage to the god Kane. The moss-filled ditch also remained, guiding a stream of water from the pool to feed the Wailua River, just as it fed the Wainiha River. The little ditch had been dug ages before by Hawaiians as a symbol. Waialeale was the source of water, and it was proper that it flow down all sides of the island as it brought life to all of Kauai.

The climbers descended, half-sliding down parts of the wet mountain trail in their rush. The base of the mountain was reached by dark and the waiting horses carried them to Lihue by ten o'clock that night. Later Wawra published his Hawaiian findings in book form and sent King Kalakaua an elaborately bound copy.

Jules Remy might have been the first visiting botanist Knudsen met in the Islands. Remy had held the chair of natural history at Rollins College in Paris and arrived in Hawaii in November 1851. In addition to collecting botanical specimens he became interested in Hawaiian history, remaining in Hawaii until 1855. Anne Knudsen wrote of the help her husband had given Remy in his search for botanical specimens. This must have occurred shortly after Knudsen arrived on Kauai, since Remy left the Islands about a year after Knudsen came. The botanical collection of Jules Remy ended up at Harvard University.

There was a place of rest and escape for the Knudsen family, high up the mountain behind their Waiawa home, in the coolness of the slopes that lead toward Waialeale. The little valley was called Halemanu, place of birds, a place where the ancient Hawaiians came to collect the colorful feathers for the cloaks and helmets of the chiefs. Surrounded by koa and lehua trees, it was a refuge from the dryness and heat of Waiawa during the summer. It was a fifteen-mile trail upward from the flatlands by the ocean. The boards for the house had been brought part way by wagon and carried the rest of the way to a small clearing, where trees were cut back to let the sun shine in. Wild cattle pushed through the brush and there were Hawaiian birds, ferns of numerous variety, and a nearby stream, always cold to the touch.

Valdemar Knudsen was an adventurous Norwegian, who had come to Kauai by way of New York and California. In New York he was on his way to a promising career with a publishing company, and in gold rush California he had been a successful merchant and a delegate to the constitutional convention under which California became a state. In 1852 Knudsen returned to Norway for a visit and on his way back to California he contracted malaria as he crossed the Isthmus of Panama. Left to die in a small village, he was nursed back to health by an old woman over several months of time. He finally made his way back to California.

But Knudsen was not well and he was advised by a doctor to seek a warmer climate. He boarded a ship for Mexico, but the wife of the captain proved to be a noisy, swearing woman, and Knudsen left the ship before it sailed rather than endure a voyage with her. On the waterfront he found a ship displaying a sign, "Sailing for Hilo." Instead of heading for Mexico, Knudsen was on his way to the Hawaiian Islands.

The ship ended up at Koloa, not Hilo. For a time Knudsen managed Grove Farm, when it was owned by Herman Widemann. But he sought a dryer, warmer place and bought the leases to Kekaha and Mana on the western side of Kauai.

Ranching in the Islands had its beginnings with the coming of the earliest Western explorers. James Cook brought sheep, goats, and a new breed of pig. George Vancouver brought the first cattle as a gift to Kamehameha. The cattle were sent to the uplands of Waimea, on the island of Hawaii, and a kapu was placed on the animals for ten years, allowing them to multiply. And multiply they did. The wild, long-horned animals became a menace to humans and invaded cultivated fields. Richard Cleveland and William Shaler brought the first horses in 1803. Cleveland thought Kamehameha did not appreciate his gift as much as he should have. Kamehameha believed the horses would eat too much, and indeed, all of these introduced animals did enormous damage to the indigenous plant life of the Islands.

Kamehameha was not about to share his cattle and horses with his enemy Kaumualii, but they became numerous on Kauai because other captains supplied the Kauai king with these treasures. After the brief rebellion of 1824 the windward conquerors reportedly carried away to the other islands large numbers of horses and cattle as plunder. In 1831 Richard Charlton, the irksome British consul in the Islands, reached an agreement with Governor Kaikioewa to run cattle on an unspecified area of land between Kilauea and Hanalei for twenty years. Kaikioewa agreed to transport the cattle from Oahu to Kauai, and Charlton's only payment was to supply boards to be used in building a home for Kamehameha III. Little came of the effort. Members of Wilkes' expedition reported in 1840 seeing an estimated 100 head of cattle in the vicinity.

In the 1830s hides and tallow from both Hawaii and California were sold on the East Coast. Cattle, often wild, were killed for this purpose and the meat was left to rot. In 1831 John C. Jones, U.S. consul in Hawaii, returned from a trip to California with horses tethered on deck and hides stored below. Horses could be bought for $5.00 a head in Monterey, California, and sold at a good profit in the Islands, where they were scarce at that time. The hides Jones brought to Hawaii were transshipped to New England, and while the sale could hardly qualify as substantial business, the income loomed large at a time when money was scarce and exports few. Twenty years after John C. Jones had made trips to California, C. Brewer and Company Ltd., a Honolulu trading firm, was still shipping hides to Boston to serve as partial payment for merchandise sent to the Islands.

Thomas Brown, whose coffee plantation at Wailua had been devastated, had been successful with his dairy. His herd included some 700 milch cows. By the time Elard Hoffschlaeger and Florens Stapenhorst took over Wailua the whaling industry was demanding large quantities of salt beef. In the 1850s the ranch at Wailua sent as many as 3,000 barrels of beef to Honolulu each season. Christian Bertelmann, who had his own ranch near Kilauea, was called in to assist with the slaughter and cutting up of cattle during times of greatest demand. Outside of salting and drying there was no way to preserve the meat. In Lihue in 1850, when a bullock was slaughtered it was difficult to find enough people to buy the meat, which sold for two cents a pound. Meat was either in oversupply or unavailable.

Robert Wyllie estimated in 1846 there were at least 25,000 wild cattle in the Islands and 10,000 tame ones. Six years later Charles Bishop estimated there were a total of at least 40,700 head of cattle. Wyllie considered the situation "ruineous." On Kauai the Reverend Samuel Whitney could attest to the danger of wild cattle. On more than one occasion he had close calls with wild bullocks while making his pastoral rounds. In 1857 Duncan McBryde, then manager of Wailua ranch, was given the right to catch and brand unmarked wild cattle roaming the uplands of Wailua. He was required to render an account every six months to the government and paid $1.75 for each head he branded with his own mark.

By 1851 the government had decided to go out of the livestock business on Kauai. In that year the privy council voted to sell its horses on Kauai to Dr. Gerrit P. Judd for $3,000. Judd then sold them at a profit. In the same year 450 government sheep on Kauai were sold to Jules Dudoit, who had taken over the land Charlton had once leased.

By the middle 1850s horses as well as cattle had become a problem. A good horse could easily be bought at Lihue for between $10 and $15. For the economy-minded, a horse could be purchased at the government pound for twenty-five cents. In 1854 a Royal Hawaiian Agricultural Society report called attention to the

. . . lamentable increase of the miserable creatures to be seen every day on the streets of Honolulu and in all the horse breeding districts on the islands. Horses are evidently fast becoming a curse and nuisance. . . . About one-half of all the horses . . . are never used for any purpose but multiplication—are never bitted or backed—are born, live and die without being of any advantage at all.

Valdemar Knudsen raised Longhorn cattle as well as horses at Waiawa, improving his herds by adding Durham and Holstein blood as he could. Not many years after his coming, the demand for beef dropped with the decline in whaling, and Knudsen was pressed to meet the $1,500 he paid in leases each year. He supplemented the income from his ranch by serving as road supervisor for Waimea and Niihau.

William Hyde Rice, a son of missionary-planter William Harrison Rice, raised cattle and horses on lands at Kipu, between Lihue and Koloa. Rice managed the ranch belonging to Lihue plantation from 1867 to 1869. He started his own ranching endeavors in 1872, a time when the sugar plantations were taking up lands used for pasture. The loss of so much land caused men like Rice to become more efficient by improving the quality of their herds to produce better beef. Rice and George N. Wilcox both imported Herefords from Australia, and Rice brought Ayrshires from New Zealand prior to 1879. Rice also shipped Herefords to California—the first introduced there. He imported Dexter cattle from Ireland as did Joseph B. Rowell, who reportedly had a herd of about 100 such animals at Waimea. The Sinclairs probably brought Shorthorn cattle aboard the *Bessie* on their arrival in 1863 and imported more later.

William Hyde Rice, a dedicated horseman, imported thoroughbred horses from England by way of Australia in the early 1880s. Several years later Rice shipped some horses to Japan, including a stallion for the emperor. In 1884 Aubrey Robinson imported Arabian horses from Arabia and India. George Charman had a pair of well-trained Clydesdale horses, which he used for teaming.

Joseph Gardner, who wove cloth on a single loom, had been placed in charge of all government sheep on Kauai in 1845. These were the sheep sold in 1851 to Jules Dudoit. The Sinclairs had brought Merino sheep from New Zealand, but they did not wait for these to multiply before importing more. Several months after settling on Niihau they received permission to transport 3,000 sheep from Molokai to Niihau on board the *Bessie*. These sheep probably came from the flocks of Kamehameha V.

In the 1871 church report for Niihau, A. Kaukau mentioned "April is the regular month for sheep-shearing. That is the time when 3,000 or more sheep are slaughtered; to eat the mutton and throw (the entrails) into the sea for sharks." Tallow was rendered from the carcasses, with each person on the island receiving one or two barrels. After 1870 most of the wool was sold on the Atlantic Coast and some was sold in Germany. Wild dogs were the greatest enemy of sheep everywhere. The problem was solved on Niihau with the elimination of all dogs from the island by 1874.

Princeville plantation had 700 head of sheep in 1877, kept mainly for manuring the fields after the cane had been cut. Two years later the manager of Princeville gave up on the idea and attempted to sell the sheep, which were dying-off fast. By 1880 sheep raising on Kauai all but came to an end, except for the Sinclair flocks on Niihau. The profitability of shipping wool to the West Coast became marginal as sheep ranches there became able to supply the demands. The demand in Hawaii for wool, mutton, and tallow was negligible.

Ranching on Kauai was primitive. Horses and cattle ran wild, crossing property lines as they roamed. It took years to build stone walls and fences. By about 1848, brands were registered on Kauai, giving ranchers a way to identify their animals. Some semblance of organization occurred when plantations began running their own ranches and dairies to supply workers and surrounding communities with meat, milk, and butter. There continued to be an oversupply of cattle and horses on Kauai until the 1880s. By that time grazing lands had diminished, and animals had decreased in number but improved in quality. In 1900 Kauai could do no more than meet its own demands for beef.

Sugar plantations had been considered sound investments ever since the American Civil War had driven prices up. Then the reciprocity treaty of 1876 seemed a virtual guarantee that money could be made in the business. King Kalakaua was among those anxious to benefit.

David Kalakaua urged Hawaiians to clear land and plant, and on 14 February 1877 he wrote an urgent letter to Valdemar Knudsen requesting the sublease of some of his lands at once. Knudsen either would not or could not comply with the king's request, and Kalakaua joined with several others in forming the Makee Sugar Company on

28 April 1877. The king had a one-quarter interest in the plantation, which was located behind Kapaa on eastern Kauai.

In 1877 Kalakaua also promoted the Hui Kawaihau, a group made up of thirty-two of his retainers and friends, whose intention it was to grow cane near the Makee plantation. The cane would be ground at the Makee mill on shares. Some twenty sugar-growers sailed on the *Kilauea* and went ashore at Wailua beach with their baggage and equipment. These amateur sugar-growers, used to city and court life, were greeted with amusement by the farmers of Kapaa.

Houses were constructed and an octagonal building was raised for meetings and social events. In the building in 1878 a luau, attended by King Kalakaua, marked the entry of the *hui* into the life of Kauai. In the same building, unfortunately, heated meetings took place that broke the group into factions.

The first sugar crop to be taken off brought good profits for the Hui Kawaihau. But from then on matters deteriorated. Succeeding crops were not as good. James Makee died in 1878 and his son-in-law, Zephaniah S. Spalding, did not have the patience or understanding to deal with the newcomers. Bickering became the most important activity, and by 1881 the hui was through. The octagonal building was dismantled and moved to Kapaa flats with the help of ox teams loaned by William Rice and George Charman. The farm lands became a part of Makee Sugar Company.

Queen Emma returned to Kauai in late 1870. She had been disconsolate after the deaths of her only son in 1862 and her husband the following year. Emma's friends were concerned about the effect of these tragedies and were pleased when she agreed in 1865 to travel to Europe, where she was received by Queen Victoria in England. In the United States she met with President Andrew Johnson at the White House and also visited Canada, arriving back in Hawaii toward the end of 1866.

By 1870 Emma had regained some of her former spirit of adventure and was at Lawai, not far from Koloa, on the south shore of Kauai. Lawai at that time was a barren place, with only a few trees around the frame houses. The queen certainly was familiar with the stories and legends of Waialeale and the Alakai Swamp, and she now decided to see the area for herself. The difficulty was to locate someone who could still find the old trail through the Alakai. Valdemar Knudsen suggested Kaluahi, an elderly Hawaiian, as the man to lead the way. It had been years since Kaluahi had walked the trail, but he reluctantly agreed.

What Kaluahi thought would be a small party grew into a sizable group. There were perhaps a hundred people—men, women, and children, dancers, musicians, and retainers. The procession, mostly on horseback, wound its way upward from Waimea. They were a happy crowd as they followed the narrow trail in single file. The early going was the easy part of the trip.

Eventually they came to the edge of a deep valley called Kauaikanana, where the trail stopped. From this point it was impossible to go on by horse. The animals were left behind, and proceeding a short distance, Queen Emma paused to admire the view toward the Alakai. The setting so entranced the queen that she called forward her dancers and musicians, bidding them to perform. Kaluahi was thinking of the need to push on, but Queen Emma would not be rushed. Only after one performance had followed another was she satisfied and willing to descend the pali and continue toward the Alakai.

The journey across the swamp was tedious and haunting. There had been a rude trail through the Alakai in earlier times, across the swamp and then down the hazardous cliffs to Wainiha Valley on the north shore. The trail had been used by the ancient Hawaiians and occasionally by early missionaries—and it was restored for Queen Emma. It was a "corduroy road" made of tree-fern logs dropped one next to another over the bogs. Beside the road were clumps of grass and sedge. Between the clumps was black mud composed of rotted vegetation, where a person could sink knee-deep into ooze. There were towering ferns, dwarfed gray ohia trees, and makaloa grass, the same as used by Niihauans to weave their mats. There were violets that grew into virtual trees, four of five feet high. Mosses, brown, orange, and near-white, circled the bog pools. It was a world from an early day of creation.

Before the party could reach the Wainiha lookout, night descended and they made the best of the strange world in which they were caught. Passing the night on a small platform of ohia branches collected for her by her retainers, Queen Emma chanted meles and sang modern songs to hearten her soaked and chilled companions.

The cliffs above Wainiha were only a short distance away and from this great height spread the valleys of Hanalei, Lumahai, and Wainiha. The streams and rivers below meandered through the valleys toward the beaches and into the northern sea. This spectacular sight was the reason Emma had made the journey, and once she had absorbed the scene she turned to begin the trek back across the swamp and downward toward the sea.

At Waimea a luau was held in honor of Emma on the evening of 29 January 1871. A lanai was constructed before a house that had been built years earlier by Governor Kaikioewa. The village of Waimea was in attendance, and meles were recited in honor of the queen's trip. Emma returned to Lawai, which was renamed Mauna Kilohana, Mountain Lookout, in honor of the queen.

During the 1850s the supplying of whaling vessels continued as the foundation of Hawaii's economy. The sugar industry, so long in developing, was about to assume dominance, but no one could know how quickly that day would come. There were other smaller sources of income such as coffee, hides, wool, and tallow. A few persons thought rice could be added to this list.

The reason for the interest in rice was the arrival in 1852 of about 290 Chinese contract laborers to work on the sugar plantations. Eight years later their number had grown to 816. California had a population of nearly 35,000 Chinese by 1860, most attracted by the feverish growth brought on by the gold rush. The food staple of the Chinese was rice, with an estimated consumption of two pounds per person a day. With California and Hawaii as potential markets, rice-growing was viewed as a new source of income.

In 1853 an estimated $10,000 to $12,000 was sent out of the Islands to import rice. Minor attention was given rice planting in 1858 when a former taro patch was planted with seed rice from the East Indies. The Royal Hawaiian Agricultural Society undertook planting in Nuuanu Valley, but it was not a success. There was no rice mill in the kingdom then and the grain was hulled at the flour mill in Honolulu. The grains were so small and dark that the rice was considered unmarketable. More experiments were attempted, but results were no better. Enthusiasm waned.

The whaling season of 1859 was the most successful ever, with 549 ships visiting the Islands. The American Civil War quickly changed this. In 1860 the number of whalers dropped to 325, and in 1862 only 73 whalers stopped in the Islands. The business of supplying whaling ships, so firm for over thirty years, was in a state of distress.

The depressed condition in which the merchants of Honolulu found themselves gave new impetus to sugar and revived interest in rice culture. In August 1860 the Royal Hawaiian Agricultural Society received a small supply of South Carolina seed rice. It was planted under two breadfruit trees in Nuuanu. Securing South Carolina rice was important because the earlier East Indian strain had not been to the liking of the Chinese.

From a pound and a half of South Carolina rice, forty-four pounds of seed rice were produced. Dr. Seth Ford obtained four pounds, planted it on about one-fifth of an acre, and in March 1861 harvested 1,163 pounds of full-grained unhusked rice. It was enough of a success to excite many people. Thomas G. Thrum later wrote of that time, "rice swept over the islands like wildfire, or like an epidemic."

Oahu and Kauai were the most suitable places to grow rice because of the abundance of water. The marshlands beyond Honolulu, toward Waikiki, became prime land. On Kauai the banks along streams were turned into rice fields. Taro fields were the most desirable. The taro could be uprooted quickly, and the fields usually carried water rights. The eventual result of this conversion was a shortage of poi. Along the dry strip of land at Mana, a large oblong swamp covered over 1,800 acres of land. Rice was planted on the edges of this swamp and for years continued as a profitable venture.

In 1866 there were 1,306 Chinese in the Islands, and having completed their sugar plantation contracts, many began growing rice. Leong Pah On came to Hawaii in 1864, an orphan lad of sixteen. Pah On saved some money and before long moved to Kauai, where he began growing rice in the upper Waimea Valley. Valdemar Knudsen befriended the young man by allowing him to plant some swampland at Mana. Pah On leased more land, dug ditches to let out stagnant water, increased his herd of water buffalo, bought horses, and eventually rented railroad cars to carry rice to the wharf at Waimea.

By 1870 Hawaii exported 152,068 pounds of rice and 535,453 pounds of unhusked rice—most of it destined for California. In that year there were nearly 44,000 Chinese in California. In addition, a substantial amount of rice was consumed locally. By 1878 the number of Chinese living in Hawaii had risen to 6,045, slightly more than 10 percent of the total population.

To work the rice fields Pah On and other planters sought laborers from China. This was done through the awarding of contracts by the government to Chinese firms in Hawaii. The main importer of laborers for the rice fields was the Honolulu firm of Chulan and Company, which was paid $25 per laborer by the government in 1876.

Through representatives in China the company brought workers to the Islands as contract laborers or as free workers, who sought jobs after their arrival. Chulan and Company was involved in nearly every phase of rice-growing, including the financing of planters. The company operated its own large rice plantation at Hanalei, with 300 acres of the land leased from Princeville plantation. In other business ventures Chulan and Company held the license to sell 'awa, the traditional Polynesian narcotic drink, in the district of Hanalei and expressed an interest in obtaining a license to sell opium.

Birds that feasted on the ripening green rice were the constant enemy of the planters. To deter them, tin cans were tied to strings stretched across the fields, but soon their clatter was anything but threatening. The worst predator was a gray-brown bird about four inches long. Introduced from Malaysia in 1865, it was commonly called the rice bird and was so voracious the legislature appropriated funds for its destruction. The legislative assembly was informed in 1876 that an estimated 13,000 birds had been destroyed on Kauai. The birds were usually killed with shotguns, for a bounty of one cent per bird plus an allowance of one-half cent per shell.

The need for labor was constant, especially during planting and harvesting, and a feud arose between Pah On and Ah Hoy, a neighboring rice planter. Each accused the other of stealing laborers, and high feelings ran to violence when they dynamited each other's artesian wells.

In 1875 the Norwegian ship *Krik* brought 114 Chinese to the Islands. The contingent was typical of the time. The Chinese were free laborers who sought work in the rice fields and there were only five women in the group. The hope of the workers was to save enough money in Hawaii to be able to return to China and start businesses of their own. The monarchy, however, wanted to encourage the Chinese to become permanent residents, and the plantations hoped for a more stable work force. It was agreed that married men were more likely to remain on the plantations. Girls, many from orphanages, were brought from China as wives. Sometimes gunny sacks were put over their heads and the men chose their wives sight unseen. Such girls were called "gunny sack wives."

The reciprocity treaty of 1876 between the United States and Hawaii had as its goal the entry of Hawaiian sugar into the U.S. duty-free. Rice from Hawaii was also included as a tax-free import under the treaty, and together with a protective tariff passed by Hawaii's legislature, the competitive position of Island rice was greatly strengthened. While rice production increased dramatically, the number of Orientals also increased, resulting in high local consumption. As the Chinese population became larger, planters switched to Chinese seed and later, when Japanese immigrants arrived in large numbers, their taste was accommodated with strains imported from Japan. The high point of the rice industry was reached in 1890 when 10,597,000 pounds of rice were produced in the kingdom.

The Chinese were generally considered good workers, but they remained such a closed group that others looked upon them with suspicion. It was reported they fought a great deal, but it was agreed it was mostly among themselves. The Chinese gambled—a vice that was deplored—and they organized themselves into secret societies considered as devious, dangerous groups capable of any evil. Most of the Chinese had no intention of remaining in Hawaii, and they were criticized in the community because their savings were sent to China and did nothing to finance Hawaii's economy.

One fear that proved a reality was the introduction of opium into the Islands. It followed on the heels of the first workers. On occasion the government declared opium illegal, but smuggling made it easily available. In an attempt to exercise some control and to gain money for the treasury, the government then sold monopoly rights for the importation and sale of opium in the kingdom. This brought embarrassment to the government, particularly on one occasion when the monopoly was promised to two different bidders.

Leong Pah On prospered through both the real and suspected problems. In 1889 he bought an abandoned rice mill at Waimea, near the wharf. The mill was restored and Pah On was able to compete with the Honolulu mills, where his rice had previously been milled. Pah On had come a long distance, from an orphaned immigrant boy to a wealthy, respected rice planter.

Rice-growing at Mana continued under Pah On's direction until 1922. In that year Hans P. Faye, then manager of Kekaha plantation, suggested that Pah On not bid on the government lease for the lands he farmed. After receiving the lease the plantation would sublease the lands to Pah On. It was agreed. But when Kekaha did receive the new lease the controlling plantation authorities in Honolulu refused to honor the agreement. Pah On was out of business.

By the time Pah On lost his lease the rice industry was already in a decline, and ten years later it was virtually finished. For years the tedious business of growing rice had attracted fewer and fewer workers.

The serious blow, however, came from farmers in California, who improved methods of growing and who could afford to use expensive labor-saving machinery on vast tracts of land.

The unpredictable channel between Kauai and Oahu, which had destroyed an invasion fleet of Kamehameha, had lost none of its anger. The trials of sailing to and from Kauai had been borne because there was no alternative. For years small coastal schooners had struggled across the channel, then made their way along the coastline, leaving supplies and carrying away a varied cargo. Each voyage was a gamble. It might take a day, or four days. A vessel might be lost to westward or blown back to its port of origin.

The first steamer-sailing vessel to come to Hawaii was HMS *Cormorant*. She visited in 1846 and certainly made an impression on everyone involved in interisland travel. A steamer could overcome many of the elements, making way against winds and currents to the port of choice.

Again it was the indefatigable writer, Robert C. Wyllie, who pointed out the advantages of steam transportation between the Islands in his "Notes." Wyllie published his comments in 1844, but financing a steamer was a big undertaking and no one made the attempt until 1852. A San Francisco company brought the 530-ton steamer *Constitution* to the Islands in that year. She made one interisland trip and then returned to the West Coast.

In August 1853 the privy council allowed another San Francisco firm to establish interisland service, and the side-wheeler SB *Wheeler* was brought from the Bay City. She made a satisfactory run between Lahaina and Honolulu. By December the new company was granted a charter to operate between the Islands. To make the venture financially feasible, the government granted the company a monopoly on interisland steamer service and other advantages for a period of ten years.

The ship was renamed *Akamai*. She was a small steamer, just 106 feet long and 114 tons. On her first regular trip the vessel sailed from Honolulu to Kauai. She stopped at Nawiliwili and Hanalei and returned to Honolulu with a number of passengers and considerable freight, including 14,000 pounds of coffee from the Rhodes & Co. plantation at Hanalei. The *Akamai* had left Honolulu on 28 November and returned on 2 December. It was a good start. *The Friend* commented on the occasion, "We regard the presence of this steamer as marking a new era in the prosperity of the Islands."

Unfortunately it was not as profitable to travel to the leeward islands as it was to sail southeast, where the islands of Maui and Hawaii could both be visited on one voyage. But the real problem was the size of the *Akamai.* She was too small for traveling the rough waters between islands. Her last voyage took place the end of August 1854 when she left Honolulu in a seriously overloaded condition, bound for Lahaina. She was struck by a squall and encountered heavy seas. The *Akamai* sprang a leak and was lucky to be able to come about and make Honolulu Harbor. The water was ankle-deep in her cabin. Soon after, the vessel was declared unseaworthy and used as a tug at Honolulu for a time before being broken up for firewood.

This interruption of interisland steamer service was short, since two other side-wheelers were on their way to the Islands soon after the *Akamai* made its last voyage. The two vessels arrived in October 1854. The *West Point,* renamed *Kalama,* at first served the Kauai-Honolulu run, but the ship did not long survive. In the early morning hours of 5 January 1856 the *Kalama* dropped anchor at Koloa and immediately began to take on freight. Between 10:00 and 11:00 in the morning the wind shifted from northeast to southwest. This meant the wind came off the ocean—the beginning of a Kona storm. There were squalls and the wind rose. At 1:00 P.M. the captain decided to leave the remaining freight behind. The engine was started, the anchor pulled up, but the winds and currents were stronger than the power of the engine. The *Kalama* turned broadside and "in a few moments she struck heavily fore and aft on the point and immediately bilged and in a few hours was a total wreck." Later the shaft was cut from the *Kalama* and sent to Honolulu, where parts of it were used in repairing the rollers from the Lihue plantation mill at Honolulu Iron Works.

The Islands were again without a steamer, since the second vessel had returned to San Francisco seven months earlier. The government searched for another group of people to run a steamship service. In 1859 the legislature voted to grant two Honolulu men the right to run an interisland service, and on 28 June 1860 the 400-ton *Kilauea* arrived in Honolulu. It had been built to specifications in Boston, with two masts that allowed the use of sails to supplement the two engines. At first the *Kilauea* served Hawaii, Maui, and Kauai, but as had happened earlier, the Kauai trip was the least profitable.

The *Kilauea* was a favorite with passengers, but interisland freight often went by schooner. For years individuals and companies who owned plantations had run their own sailing vessels to Kauai. Ladd and Company, Robert C. Wyllie, and Jules Dudoit each operated their own ships. Hoffschlaeger and Stapenhorst had three whaling vessels of their own to carry salt beef to Honolulu. Much freight was controlled by the men who owned the small sailing ships, and they naturally chose to use their own vessels.

With the *Kilauea* hardly a factor in Kauai transportation, an eighty-ton steamer, actually an altered coasting schooner with an engine constructed at Honolulu Iron Works, served the leeward island until 1866. The small steamer was the *Annie Laurie* and she had been built with the Kauai run in mind. In late September 1865 the vessel was damaged when she scraped bottom entering Honolulu Harbor. Her engine was then removed, but she remained in service as a sailing schooner.

Back on the Kauai run, the *Annie Laurie* arrived at Koloa on the morning of 5 February 1866. Passengers were being transferred to small boats to take them ashore. There was a heavy swell and not enough room for the ship to maneuver. The anchor was dropped, but at 7:30 A.M. the *Annie Laurie* went on the rocks. She was a total wreck. Two weeks later what little could be salvaged was sold at auction. Obviously interisland travel continued to be a hazard. As the *Annie Laurie* lay broken on the rocks at Koloa, the *Kilauea* was also in serious trouble, stranded on a reef at Kawaihae on the island of Hawaii.

The battle to gain steamer service for Kauai was a continuing fight. The *Kilauea* had frequent repair problems—she had a tendency to run on reefs—and she had constant financial problems as well. In 1870 the legislature voted a subsidy for the operation of the ship with an additional $5,000 if she were put back on the Kauai run. With the aid of young William Hyde Rice, who was serving his first term as a representative in the legislature, the run to Kauai was resumed. The *Kilauea* maintained a haphazard schedule. In 1876 cabin class from Honolulu to Kauai was $8.00. Deck space, with food, was available to Hawaiians only for $3.00. Many cabin-class passengers moved on deck, preferring the wind and spray to the stuffiness of the cabin.

The *Kilauea* survived until 1877, when the *Likelike* arrived in Honolulu to continue interisland service. The *Likelike* was built in San Francisco and was 592 tons, larger than any of her predecessors. Her first voyage was to Nawiliwili on 17 August 1877. The government, which had ordered the ship built, quickly sold her for $96,000 to Samuel G. Wilder of Honolulu, who had arranged for the construction of the vessel. At the same time Wilder bought the worn-out *Kilauea* for $5,000.

The year 1877 was a time of new prosperity because of the passage of the reciprocity treaty. Plantations were begun or enlarged, and bulky machinery had to be brought in and tons of sugar transported out. The arrival of the *Likelike* was perfectly timed. Other steamships were added to interisland service over the next several years, and competing companies were formed. At last the volume of freight created enough interest to provide frequent service with Honolulu. Still needed was a reasonably good harbor on Kauai.

The problem of maintaining interisland schedules was complicated when a ship was pulled from regular runs and pressed into government service. The day after Christmas, 1870, saw such an occasion. The emergency had its beginnings on the night of 29 October, far to the northwest at Kure, the most distant island in the Hawaiian chain. That night the USS *Saginaw* ran onto the reef. By morning the ship had broken in half.

The mission of the *Saginaw* had been to carry a construction crew to Midway Island, where they were to dredge a channel through the reef. The Pacific Mail Steamship Company wanted to use Midway as a coaling station on voyages to and from the Orient. A construction crew had been left on Midway on 24 March, and during the following months the *Saginaw* made trips to Honolulu to collect supplies for the workers. The $50,000 appropriation for the job was exhausted, and even though the dredging was not finished the *Saginaw* sailed from Midway with the construction crew aboard on the afternoon of 29 October. The captain planned to circle Kure before sailing to San Francisco, and that night the *Saginaw* lay ripped open on Kure's coral reef.

The crew of the *Saginaw* was fortunate enough to make their way to the sand island within the reef. Seals and birds on the atoll along with salvaged supplies allowed the men to exist. Through more good fortune the gig of the *Saginaw* was recovered. The gig was decked-over, fitted, and provisioned for a long ocean voyage. Five men volunteered to crew the little vessel on its trip for help. Leaving Kure on 18 November the gig sailed north, then east until they caught the trade winds, which carried them south. The little boat was battered by storms, the oars were lost, and seawater ruined most of the provisions. Lieutenant John G. Talbot, in command of the vessel, suffered from dysentery. The rest of the crew was exhausted.

During the night of 19 December 1870 the gig lay helpless off

Hanalei Bay. About 2:30 A.M. she was caught in the breakers and rolled over. Two of the five men aboard were drowned. Lieutenant Talbot clung to the bottom of the gig, but was struck on the head in the turbulence and lost hold.

The boat drifted onto the beach at Kalihiwai before dawn. William Halford was able to struggle ashore, where he was met by Hawaiians. The fifth crewman, incoherent, collapsed and died on the beach. On 20 December Halford told his story to Sheriff Samuel W. Wilcox at Hanalei, and that same evening accepted the offer of Jules Dudoit to sail on his ship for Oahu. It took four days to reach Honolulu, where Halford told the U.S. consul the tale of the *Saginaw* and showed him the dispatches that had been entrusted to Lieutenant Talbot.

Not all the people at Kalihiwai were thinking of giving aid to the men cast ashore. One man tried to negotiate with Sheriff Samuel Wilcox. He would help if he were given the gig. Wilcox refused. The bodies of two of the men, including the man who died on the beach at Kalihiwai, had been stripped of their clothing. One man was sentenced to two years in prison for his part in the thievery. The body of one sailor who had drowned at Hanalei was never recovered.

On 26 December the *Kilauea,* on orders from King Kalakaua, was pulled from its interisland runs and sent northwest from Honolulu. On 3 January 1871 the men of Kure sighted a thin line of smoke on the horizon. To their great relief it was the *Kilauea,* which had arrived to carry the castaways to Honolulu.

CHAPTER ELEVEN

Kauai Could Excel at
This Enterprise

The vast heart of Kauai, the center of the island, is made up of steep mountains and deep valleys. The mountain heights are the origin of Kauai's natural resources and in these high reaches rivers form that water the lowlands. But the mountains are inhospitable to man and it is along the plains that lie between the sea and the mountains that people lived. These plains enfold the island, except for Na Pali on the north, where mountains plunge perpendicular into the sea, and one place in the south where a range of hills cuts across the plain. This range diminishes as it goes south, turns abruptly eastward above Koloa, and at last ends as the southern mountain wall of Nawiliwili Bay.

There is one way through this thin mountain ridge, a place where the barrier briefly parts. This lapse in the ridge is the way between east and west Kauai. It is called the Gap and travelers have used it since the beginning.

The Gap is on the way from Lihue, beyond Puhi and before the road turns to Koloa, at a place where there is a depression and at the bottom is a dense growth of hau trees. Here, among these nearly impenetrable trees, robbers hid long ago, waiting to surround the traveler. But robbers, no matter how desperate they might be, were human. The greater fear was of the *akua* who dwelt here, supernatural spirits more frightening and unpredictable than humans.

Tales of the Gap come from ancient days, but they seemed no less real in later times. During the years when Dr. James Smith served all Kauai, many a horseman riding to Koloa to seek the doctor's help at night approached the Gap with foreboding and, passing through, felt danger had been left behind.

The Gap is the place that divides the Kauai of ample rain from the Kauai of little rain. The change is not an abrupt one, as clouds drift westward over the Gap and drop their mist on Lawai, Kalaheo, and

Wahiawa. Westward at Hanapepe, Makaweli, and Waimea it is dryer and the grass is often brown. At Kekaha and Mana the earth can become ash-dry. South of the Gap are the rich lands of Koloa. On the east are the lands of ample rain, Kipu, the plains of Lihue, and, northward, the lands of Hanamaulu, Wailua, Kapaa, and Kealia. Reaching along the north shore is Kilauea and then Hanalei.

These are the coastal plains of Kauai, mostly level enough for plowing and sought after by the men who wanted to grow sugarcane. There was the warmth of the sun by day, a slight coolness at night, water from the mountains above—the things sugarcane needs to flourish.

Some early leaders viewed these coastal plains idyllically, visualizing the green fields of one independent farmer adjoining those of another. Many details from the early years remain unclear, but it was here that the industry developed that became the basis of the economy of Kauai. In the fields at Koloa and Lihue and then expanding to other places, the sugar farmers refined their skills in the years between the American Civil War and the first reciprocity treaty with the United States. When the reciprocity treaty was signed in 1876 expansion was immediate and extensive. Never before had Kauai seen such activity—so many new people and amazing machinery.

The excitement and change continued through a second reciprocity treaty and to the end of the century. During these years some basic facts were looming clear. It was evident the potential for growing sugarcane was enormous, that Kauai could excel at this enterprise to a degree that excited the imagination, holding economic promise leading to an unknown affluence.

It was also clear Kauai was not going to become an island of small independent farmers as some ardently hoped. The length of the growing season for cane and the heavy investments necessary were prohibitive for the small farmer. It took eighteen to twenty-four months from planting to harvesting. This meant long-term financing, and the risks of a bad season made it difficult for a small farmer to qualify for loans. There was also the matter of milling the cane. A milling factory was far too expensive to be owned by a small farmer who could utilize it for only a fraction of the year. So an independent farmer had to depend on the mill of a neighboring plantation to grind his cane, paying for the milling work with a percentage of his crop. This came to be known as grinding on shares. The danger with this arrangement was that small planters were at the mercy of mill owners. Although in the end George N. Wilcox did very well, during his first years at Grove Farm he paid half of his crop to Paul Isenberg for grinding his cane at the Lihue factory.

Before the introduction of heavy equipment, small farmers had been able to survive and sometimes prosper, but the new costly equipment made them obsolete. Hauling cane to the factory was an example. An ox-drawn cart loaded with cane traveled at the rate of one mile per hour. Additional time was required for loading and unloading the wagons. Planting cane three miles from a mill was considered marginal because of travel time, thus increasing the number of carts and oxen needed to keep the mill continuously supplied with cane and running. When Kilauea plantation introduced the narrow-gauge railroad to Kauai in 1881, it ushered in a new era. The portable tracks, twenty-four inches wide, were laid in the field and greater amounts of cane could be hauled to the mill from greater distances in less time. After one field was harvested the rails were taken up and laid in another field.

There was the incredibly difficult job of plowing fields with the giant, cumbersome plows, drawn by teams of as many as eighteen oxen. If things went well a good ox team could plow a single furrow, two miles long, in an hour. When Grove Farm introduced two steam plows in 1888, working as a team they could plow five miles in an hour, cutting three furrows at a time instead of one. It may have been exasperating to keep steam plows in repair and to prevent cane-hauling railroad cars from tipping over in uneven fields, but it was better than looking after the herds of oxen that a plantation would otherwise require. Kilauea had 400 oxen in 1880. With the introduction of the new machinery the chore of keeping these animals was a thing of the past. Mechanics suddenly replaced herdsmen.

There was the matter of water for irrigation. It took engineers time to build ditches. At Kekaha artesian wells were sunk with success, the first such wells in the Hawaiian Islands, but the amount of water was insufficient to irrigate the acreage available for farming. Other sources were sought in the mountains above the plantation, but it took eight years and sixteen miles of ditches to bring Kekaha its first substantial water supply. Fortunately the resources of Paul Isenberg and George Wilcox were behind Kekaha, a partnership having been formed in 1880. The investment was made by Isenberg and Wilcox because, in each case, they wanted to offer their brothers opportunities to prosper from the sugar business. More funds for Kekaha's development were made available upon its incorporation in 1898 with an initial capitalization of $600,000.

Before 1893 two irrigation systems in the Islands stood out from the rest because of their complexity. One was the project that brought water to the central plain of Maui, and the other was the irrigation system at the Hawaiian Sugar Company, which later became known as Olokele Sugar Company. The Hawaiian Sugar irrigation system was completed in April 1891 and was a marvel of engineering. By flumes, ditching, piping, and tunneling, water was carried thirteen and one-half miles from the Hanapepe River to the fields. About two miles of this was cut from solid rock.

McBryde plantation had its special problems. Water had to be pumped to higher elevations in some places and this meant high electrical costs, which put McBryde deeply in debt during its early years. At last power lines carried electricity from the northern side of the island, where a subsidiary company generated electricity from the Wainiha Stream. Water for McBryde came from the Wahiawa Stream and the Hanapepe River.

The water systems, the mills, the steam plows, the railroads—all meant great outlays of capital. Except in rare instances sugar plantations cost more than one person could afford. Kilauea Sugar Company was incorporated 30 January 1880. The corporation was authorized to initially offer 300 shares of stock at $1,000 per share. The money allowed the plantation to do the things necessary for success. On Kamehameha Day 1881 Kilauea held a celebration when a large stone reservoir, a flume, and a ditch were completed. The people of the village, led by a band, marched along the flume and ditch to the reservoir, which had been built across Kilauea Stream. A hymn was sung and the national anthems of Great Britain, the United States, Germany, and Sweden were played. The Chinese shot off firecrackers. A prayer was said and the sluice gates of the reservoir were opened.

There was another celebration on 24 September 1881 with the arrival of the railroad engine, twenty-four cars to carry cane, and three miles of portable track. The princess, who would later become Queen Liliuokalani, had landed at Hanalei the day before, and she was asked to drive in the first spike. The future queen was met at the Kong Lung store by plantation manager Robert A. Macfie, Jr., who gave a short talk, as did Governor Paul P. Kanoa, a nephew of the earlier Governor Kanoa. The princess drove the spike home with two blows and the railroad was in operation.

At Kekaha extensive work had started with the partnership in 1880, and when James A. Tuthill arrived in late November 1898 the plantation was well established and the railroad, mill, and steam plows were in operation. Tuthill was an engineer from Honolulu who went to Kekaha to assist in surveying land in the mountains behind the plantation, through which irrigation ditches were to be built. When he arrived at Waimea by steamer Tuthill was advised to take the railroad to Kekaha.

> The railroad is a cute affair, only 30 inch gauge—cars mostly flat for hauling cane and sugar in bags—a few are box cars made of corrugated sheet iron and no wood. All cars are no more than 4 feet wide. Engines come from Germany and are regular toys—they weigh about eight tons. . . . Their floors are only two feet from ground. . . . [We] bowled over the four miles of toy railroad to the headquarters of the Plantation. . . . They have engineer *only*—no fireman—no breakman. No *breaks* on cars. Roads are dead level.

Tuthill also reported on the mill at Kekaha. It was well mechanized for its time, with the cane being dumped from the cars onto a conveyor belt, which carried it to rollers that crushed the juice from the cane. The juice was boiled to evaporate the water, then cooled and placed in centrifugal separators, which spun the molasses from the sugar. The sugar was packed in 100-pound sacks, which were carried on the railroad cars to Waimea to be shipped to Honolulu.

James Tuthill also described the way in which steam plows were used.

> They consist of two stationary engines placed at either side of a big field. A horizontal drum on engine winds up a $1/2$ mile long wire cable and pulls plow across field—latter runs on wheels—. Engine at opposite side pulls plow back and so on. Plow has three shares—i.e., turns three great, deep furrows at once. There are really six shares—three work at a time, as one set of three is elevated and runs backward while others are working.

A milling factory was the largest single expense for a plantation. A basic mill cost $25,000 to $30,000, and few planters could find their way clear to make such an expenditure. In 1872 there were four on Kauai. At Hanalei stood the elaborate mill built for an estimated $40,000 by Robert C. Wyllie. The mill at Kilauea was certainly small and improvised, built by the industrious Charles Titcomb, who was ranching and growing sugarcane at that time. There was the mill at Lihue plantation, which was still new, having been installed in 1869. The factory at Koloa was the oldest on the island.

George Charman had his cane ground at Koloa, and Governor Paul P. Kanoa's cane was ground at Lihue. Donald F. Nicholson and Charles Grant grew cane on shares near Kilauea. Dr. James W. Smith and the Reverend Peter Gulick, missionaries who had planted cane to supplement their own livelihoods as well as to aid their congregations, had cane ground at Koloa. Duncan McBryde grew some cane at Kalaheo and carted it to Koloa to be ground, but the trip was too long and McBryde gave it up. Dozens of such individuals faded in and out of the sugar scene on Kauai.

Efficient mills required complicated equipment built by companies that specialized in its construction. Several companies were represented by agents in Hawaii, the most successful being Miriless, Tait & Watson of Glasgow, Scotland. Sir William Renny Watson, a partner in the company, was a familiar figure in Hawaii. He was not only interested in selling sugar mills; in 1889 he obtained a lease from Gay and Robinson, and this was the beginning of Hawaiian Sugar Company. Watson had hoped to control the plantation together with his English friends, but he lost out in a few years to men of American descent, including Charles Bishop, the banker and part-owner of Lihue plantation, and Henry P. Baldwin of Maui.

Failure to control Hawaiian Sugar was one of the few reverses Sir William Watson suffered. He sold mills to August Dreier at Eleele, and to Kilauea, Kekaha, and Hanamaulu plantations. There was heated rivalry between British and American interests in the islands— the British were not willing to concede Hawaii to United States dominance either economically or politically. Americans thought more orders for mill equipment should be going to American companies. Watson's success was well known, and Charles Bishop, with annoyance and admiration, explained the situation in a letter to his friend Elisha H. Allen.

A large part of our machinery for the new plantations has come from Scotland, because Mr. Watson, who knows all about such works, came right out to the spot where the machinery was to be used; told the planter (what the would be planter did not know himself) just what he wanted, just what he would deliver it for with a time stated, duty paid, in Honolulu, and offered him *long credit* for a large part of the cost; and *low interest*

—thus enabling parties to have machinery, and such as was suitable who otherwise could not have had any at all. No body from the U.S. came to compete with Miriless, Tait & *Watson*.

Eventually, however, American companies did become the major suppliers of heavy equipment for the plantations, along with the Honolulu Iron Works.

Kilauea was another example of the battle between Americans and British for plantation control. Charles Titcomb sold most of his lands to John Ross and Edward P. Adams in 1877. Two years later Robert A. Macfie, Jr., bought out John Ross and became manager. Robert W. T. Purvis, who served as head luna and bookkeeper when Macfie was manager, remembered Macfie had been shipped off to Hawaii by his father, who considered him the black sheep of the family. The elder Macfie was a successful sugar refiner with substantial financial interests in Liverpool, England, and he was actually the majority owner of the plantation.

Young Macfie's career at Kilauea lasted until the end of August 1890, when his father decided his son was too extravagant and wrote him about the ever-increasing indebtedness "the magnitude of which appals me." Macfie, Jr. moved to Honolulu, where he remained for a short time before returning to England. Continuing to be concerned about the growing influence of the U.S., including its exclusive right to use Pearl Harbor, Macfie wrote to the British foreign office that he believed the Hawaiian monarchy would be receptive to granting the use of Hilo Harbor as a coaling station for British ships. This possibility was not pursued by the British.

At Kilauea Macfie had surrounded himself with Scotsmen and Englishmen in an attempt to keep the plantation British. He brought Alexander Lindsay, together with his wife and seven children, from Scotland. Robert Purvis had come from England. In 1890 George R. Ewart, from Newcastle-upon-Tyne, followed Macfie as manager. The plantation engineer and the two schoolteachers were also British.

At Hawaiian Sugar William Watson had brought Robert Catton with him from Scotland as his right-hand man. In 1892 the manager and the two engineers were British subjects. At Gay and Robinson plantation, where family ties were historically British, the manager was British, as was the doctor. Even their Honolulu agent, John T. Waterhouse, was a British subject. When McBryde incorporated in 1899 their agent was the British-owned, Honolulu-based company of Theo. H. Davies.

Much of the investment at Kilauea remained British for many years. In 1883 it was reported the Kilauea mill was half-owned by British and half by American interests. Hawaiian Sugar passed from the dominance of Watson and others at an early date, but British influence lingered in plantation management. August Dreier's Eleele plantation, which was not incorporated, was listed in 1891 as being half German- and half English-owned.

Mechanical equipment and irrigation systems made it possible for plantations to expand the acreage they cultivated by acquiring the land of small independent growers or securing previously unused land. Lihue plantation expanded more successfully than others. In 1863 Paul Isenberg leased the *ahupua'a* of Hanamaulu and in 1870, on the death of Princess Victoria Kamamalu, he bought the 17,000 acres at auction for $7,250 for Lihue plantation. Wailua lands were leased in 1887 for thirty years. In 1916 Hans Isenberg, as his last major business transaction, arranged for the purchase of the plantation started by James Makee and owned for many years by his son-in-law Zephaniah S. Spalding. This brought the lands of Kealia and Kapaa under Lihue control and extended Lihue plantation along nearly the entire length of the east coast of Kauai.

George N. Wilcox bought the embryo Grove Farm plantation in 1870 from Herman Widemann for $12,000, three-quarters of which was borrowed. Four years later he had 200 acres under cultivation. In 1881 Wilcox bought 10,500 acres of land at Haiku from Princess Ruth. This increased the acreage of Grove Farm tenfold and made the plantation economically feasible. With machines, irrigation ditches, and Wilcox's ability, it became a very profitable enterprise.

When Kekaha plantation was incorporated in 1898 it combined the sugar lands of William Meier and Emil Kruse, located at Mana, as well as the lands subleased from Valdemar Knudsen, and lands leased from Hans Peter Faye. At McBryde Sugar Company Elizabeth McBryde, with the early assistance of Herman Widemann, combined the Wahiawa and Kalaheo lands, which she inherited from her husband, with the lands of Dr. Jared K. Smith of Koloa. Extensive Lawai lands had been acquired from the estate of Queen Emma. The August Dreier plantation became a part of McBryde through B. F. Dillingham of Honolulu, who was the organizer, promoter, and a heavy investor in the new plantation.

Before the end of the century the style and structure of Kauai's economy could be understood by looking at how its sugar plantations were organized. The plantations were large, the investments were great, and field and milling operations were increasingly mechanized. In some cases the Honolulu-based agencies, which handled so many of the affairs of the plantations, controlled the companies, although there continued to be minority shareholders. It had taken years to sift the various ingredients that had gone into forming the sugar business and use only those essential to its success.

The development of machines and irrigation systems was a great accomplishment, but there was always the human resource—the labor necessary to make everything function—particularly in the fields. From the beginning of the industry, planters always considered the labor force inadequate. For years the Hawaiian population had been dwindling, and they could no longer be counted on to carry the labor burden in the expanding industry. Chinese had been imported to supplement the Hawaiians and between 1876 and 1882 nearly 15,000 arrived. They were considered good workers, although they were a mystery to the rest of the population, remaining a tight, closed society. Perhaps to a greater degree than any other racial group who came to the Islands, the Chinese were determined to work out their plantation contracts and save enough money to start businesses on their return to China. Many did return, and others eventually moved to settle on the West Coast of Canada and the United States.

The fear of a large Chinese population raised visions of a heavy Oriental influence and this was considered undesirable, even frightening. Most wanted were Western and Polynesian settlers. The former would help maintain the Islands as a Western civilization, while Polynesians would bolster the declining Hawaiian population. Westerners had to be sought in Europe, since there was practically no interest in the United States. The difficulties were substantial and the search for a supply of laborers took Island people to many parts of the world.

Dr. William Hillebrand, most distinguished for his work as a botanist during his years in Hawaii, was residing on the island of Madeira in 1876. Hillebrand had been active in affairs of immigration during his time in Hawaii and he called the attention of the planters and the government to the qualities that would make Madeira Portuguese welcome immigrants. The doctor noted the similarity of climate and pointed out that farming was vital in the Portuguese islands also.

Hillebrand wrote, "In my opinion your islands could not possibly get a more desirable class of Immigrants than the population of the Madeira and Azore Islands. Sober, honest, industrious and peaceable, they combine all the qualities of a good settler."

Prior to 1876 some Portuguese had found their way to the Islands and remained. It was estimated there were about 450 by the time Hillebrand was engaged in his correspondence, and so the planters could evaluate for themselves what they could likely expect from potential immigrants. What the planters saw they liked. Some Portuguese worked on plantations, some had their own farms, and others were in the dairy business. They were good citizens who tended to be permanent residents. What was more, they would reinforce Western culture in the Islands.

On 29 September 1878 the bark *Priscilla* arrived in Honolulu with 120 Portuguese from Madeira. They were well received on the plantations and it was quickly decided to bring more. In 1882 a sufficient number of Portuguese had come for a full-time consul to be stationed in Honolulu. By 1888 over 11,000 Portuguese had arrived from Madeira and the Azores islands. In that same year immigration came to a virtual halt because of the high cost of transportation.

As workers and residents the Portuguese were just what the government and the planters wanted. The only problem was the distance the workers had to be transported, and since many workers were married they brought wives and children, which added to the expense. In 1887 an analysis showed that of the fourteen shiploads of immigrants to date, 30 percent were men, 22 percent were women and 48 percent were children. Bringing families made for solid citizens, but it meant high costs to a government constantly looking for ways to pay its bills. In addition to transportation costs, Portuguese demanded higher wages from the plantations than did Orientals.

In 1886 there were 309 Portuguese working in the fields of Kauai, of which 44 were women and 3 were children. In that year there was a total of 1,988 workers on all the plantations of Kauai. By 1888 the number of Portuguese workers increased to 480, with 151 being women and children.

In the same year as the arrival of the first Portuguese, Captain Henry W. Mist brought 86 men and women to Hawaii from Rotuma, an island north of Fiji, and from the Gilbert Islands. The arrival of these South Pacific islanders was hailed first as a means of rebuilding the plantation work force. Over a period of six years some 2,500 persons came to Hawaii from the South Pacific. Of this number, about 2,000 were from the Gilberts.

Gilbert Islanders and others from the South Pacific proved unsatisfactory either as workers or as a means to reinforce the Hawaiian race. They did not like either the climate or plantation work. A large proportion of the Gilbertese immigrants ended up on Kauai, where they were assigned to various plantations. The largest group went to Lihue, at a camp that became known as Kilipaki—Hawaiian for Gilbertese—located in the shadow of the plantation mill.

The number of Gilbertese on Kauai varied greatly from year to year. They came on three-year contracts and departed as soon as their time was up. The Reverend Joel H. Mahoe, a patient and dedicated Hawaiian minister who had served as a missionary in the Gilberts, tried his best to preserve the souls and bodies of the unhappy Gilbertese. He was stationed at Kilauea, although he tried to assist all the Gilbertese on the island since he was able to speak their language and was familiar with their customs. In his report to the Hawaiian Evangelical Association for 1880, Mahoe stated there were 391 South Pacific islanders on Kauai, with 113 at Kilauea. During the year consumption, pneumonia, and dysentery had killed 34. The Reverend Mahoe worried about the damage being done by liquor, opium, and gambling, as well as the inroads made by the Mormons. In January 1892 there were only 51 South Pacific islanders on Kauai. Once their contracts had expired many of them moved to Lahaina, Maui, while awaiting transportation home. The warm, dry climate there better suited them.

Hackfeld & Company was responsible for bringing the contingents of German workers to Hawaii. The company had been founded 1 October 1849 in Honolulu by Heinrich Hackfeld, a German merchant-captain. Four years after he started business Hackfeld was named agent for Koloa plantation. The Koloa connection led to other associations on Kauai, the most important being with Paul Isenberg. Hackfeld & Company supplied services for many of the enterprises on Kauai with which Isenberg was involved, and Paul Isenberg and his brothers played important roles in the growth of the Hackfeld enterprises.

In 1878 Paul Isenberg returned to Germany, making his permanent residence in Bremen, although for years he remained one of Hawaii's powerful men, returning to the Islands every two years to direct his extensive business interests and to continue as an active member of the legislature. In 1881 Paul Isenberg became a partner in Hackfeld & Company, and in 1898 was named president. Eventually the company would evolve into the international giant corporation called Amfac Inc.

While the government financed the transportation of most of the German workers, the idea of bringing them in the first place, the selection of immigrants, their transportation on Hackfeld-owned ships, and their placement on plantations in Hawaii, were nearly all in the hands of Hackfeld & Company.

German workers were sought in the vicinity of Bremen and were processed through the Bremen office of Hackfeld & Company. Isenberg gave his personal attention to the project. The Germans were better screened than most other laborers and results on the plantations showed the wisdom of this. A few tradesmen were recruited, but most were farmers from the countryside who had hopes of eventually owning a farm. The *Ceder* brought the first load, arriving 18 July 1881. It carried 71 men, 19 women, and 34 children. All were sent to Lihue plantation.

The following year the *Iolani* brought 182 Germans, most of whom went to Kilauea plantation. In 1883 the largest group of all arrived aboard the *Ehrenfels*. There were 806 immigrants, accounting for over 60 percent of all the German contract laborers to come. En route an epidemic of measles had killed 43 children and 3 adults. Burials became a near-part of the daily routine at sea.

Most of the immigrants came to Hawaii on four-year work contracts. Louis Depken of Bremen was among them, a single man who arrived aboard the *Ehrenfels*. His contract with Kekaha Sugar Company was printed in both German and English. Depken's pay was sixteen dollars gold per month for the first year, seventeen dollars the second year, and eighteen dollars a month for the third and fourth years.

Louis Depken was provided free lodging and free medical attention. A work month consisted of twenty-six days, ten hours a day in the field, or eleven hours if he worked in the sugar house. On irrigation days, which would not be more than twice a week, a twelve-hour day was required. If Depken wished, he had the privilege of purchasing from the plantation a weekly ration of twelve pounds of wheat flour, ten pounds of beef or mutton, two pounds of raw sugar, and one-half pound of tea or coffee. These items cost $1.50 per week, which would be deducted from his pay.

The cost of Louis Depken's passage from Bremen was to be paid by the plantation if he remained four years. Depken could terminate his contract, however, any time after two years had passed by paying the plantation the amount of his passage proportionate to the time remaining on his contract. Such cost would not exceed seventy dollars, and six months notice was required of Depken. On arrival at Kekaha he was to receive an advance of twenty dollars which was to be repaid, deducted from his wages at one dollar per month, without interest.

The contract was signed by Louis Depken and Hackfeld & Company, as agents, 8 February 1883.

Depken decided to leave Kekaha plantation before his four years expired. A handwritten notation at the end of his contract states that Louis Depken "has paid his passagemoney" and the contract was cancelled. The date of cancellation was 30 April, but no year is given. The notation was signed by Otto Isenberg, a brother of Paul, who was manager of Kekaha, and by Louis Depken.

Of the approximately 1,200 German immigrants to come to the Islands by 1897, all but about 290 went to Kauai. Of those on Kauai more than half ended up at Lihue plantation and this group was better able to preserve familiar customs because of numbers. The work the Germans did at Lihue was no less difficult than that done by others. The difference lay in their supervisors, who were often German, and the attitude of the plantation, which was sympathetic. Plantation management, for example, contributed toward the building of a Lutheran church and school in Lihue and plantation carpenters helped in the construction.

Nearly all the newcomers were of the Lutheran faith. It was a spiritual and social bond that was comforting and unifying. Friedrich Richter, a young theological student who had come from Germany as a tutor for the H. F. Glade family in Honolulu, was hired as the first teacher. Richter had completed most of his theological studies, but he could not be officially ordained until he took a final examination in Germany. The Lihue congregation nonetheless voted to make him pastor of the church.

In 1885, during Friedrich Richter's time, a church and school were built and dedicated. The place of worship was designed in the fashion of a German village church. For some reason the floor of the church was constructed to slope downward from the center like the deck of a ship. An area next to the church was designated as a cemetery. Substantial contributions toward the buildings were made by the Isenberg, Rice, and Wilcox families, as well as by individuals and companies in Honolulu. On Kauai the little complex of homes and church became known as German Hill.

Richter returned to Germany in 1887 to complete his theological work. At the time of his departure Hans Isenberg, the youngest brother of Paul, was visiting Kauai. An ordained minister, Isenberg was married to his niece, Mary Dorothea Rice Isenberg, known as Dora, who was the first child of Paul Isenberg and Maria Rice. Dora had moved to Germany in 1878 with her father and stepmother, and she married Hans in 1883. Hans Isenberg not only stayed to become the minister of the Lutheran church in Lihue, he was active in the business affairs of Hackfeld & Company and Lihue plantation. A determined, aristocratic man, Isenberg ran his church and business affairs with authority. He died in January 1918 and is buried by the Lutheran church in Lihue.

With a school where German and English were taught, a church where sermons were preached in German, and with plantation supervisors who often spoke German, there was little incentive for the immigrants to learn English or Hawaiian. Some of the Germans at Lihue lived out their lives with only a minimal knowledge of a second language.

For German workers at Kilauea and Koloa there were differences between what had been promised them and what was delivered. In April 1883 some of the newly arrived workers at Kilauea went on strike and were put in jail. They claimed the housing promised them was not available and that they were not given the use of plots of land that had also been promised. They carried the matter to court in Honolulu, and some of the laborers were released from their contracts as a result. At Koloa, later in the same year, there was a strike over working conditions. The newcomers claimed justice was impossible at Koloa because the plantation controlled the courts. Eventually matters were settled, but hard feelings persisted.

By and large the Germans were considered good workers, but like other immigrants most left the plantations once their contracts were completed. The hope of owning a farm seemed out of reach in Hawaii, and some moved to the West Coast where land was less expensive. Many Germans left Hawaii during World War I, when an anti-German hysteria engulfed the Islands. During those years some plantation workers, regardless of position, were fired because they had German names. Hackfeld & Company passed into American hands on orders from the United States Alien Property Custodian. Even the German school at Lihue was forced to close.

The Portuguese, South Sea islanders, and Germans combined did not begin to solve the labor shortage. In 1886, for example, there were 246 German workers on Kauai's plantations, of which 62 were women. It was not a sizable number among the 1,988 laborers on the island. By 1888 the number of German workers had dropped to 121. The plantations were continually seeking a large number of workers who could be imported at a low cost. Well before the last Germans came, such laborers were again being sought from China, but they were considered a temporary solution. The long-term hope was for workers from Japan.

The people who made it possible for the German contract workers to maintain their cultural identity had come to Kauai long before the *Ceder* arrived. Hoffschlaeger & Company, which farmed Wailua Valley, had been an early importer of Germans. They obviously recruited capable men, but could not hold them as employees. The company brought to Kauai such trained men as August Conradt, who became a manager of Princeville, August Dreier, who developed an exemplary small plantation at Eleele, and Paul Isenberg, who turned so many ventures into success. Others who came to Kauai independently included E. Lindemann, who planted hundreds of trees in Wailua Valley, including the coconut grove at Wailua Kai. There was Krull, who ran a model dairy at Kealia. Charles Newman was valued as much as a musician as he was as a cooper. The list is long and impressive.

There were many Germans in the supervisory ranks on Kauai's plantations. It was difficult to find fault with their dedication or effectiveness. A few of these, however, like W. E. Anton Cropp, who became manager of Koloa in 1882, were hard men. Cropp was a reserve officer in the German army and ran his plantation the way he would an army unit. Each morning his supervisors, all of whom were German, assembled in the kitchen of his home at 5:00 A.M. for coffee and pilot biscuits while Cropp issued each man his orders for the day.

Anton Cropp was aloof from others in the sugar business, choosing not to attend the annual meetings of the Hawaiian Sugar Planters. He was outspoken, fearless, and honest. No one at Koloa would have described the manager as likable, and Cropp himself probably would not have considered it a compliment. The account books at Koloa were proof of his success, but they did not reflect the hard way in which this prosperity was achieved.

Hackfeld & Company had an office in Bremen and the accomplishments of Germans in the Hawaiian Islands were common knowledge and the subject of conversation in the commercial world there. Captain Heinrich Hackfeld and Paul Isenberg must have been heroes to many. Stories of Germans who had emigrated to Hawaii and achieved success spurred yet others.

Some of the Germans who came were recruited because of their professional training or experience. Many others were well educated, coming from backgrounds of achievement and expecting success themselves. Most were determined people who firmly believed that hard work brought material gain. They came to Kauai at the right time and their skills and beliefs were rewarded.

What made Kauai different, however, was the presence of Paul Isenberg. While he was not the first prominent man of German ancestry on Kauai, his achievements and influence went far beyond that gained by any other. Some Germans came to Kauai because Paul Isenberg invited them and helped them. Others were attracted by what he had accomplished and wanted to follow their careers in the atmosphere of success he had created.

On the night of 15 July 1886, the *Dunnotter Castle* was sailing before steady winds, all sails set, far north of Kauai. She was a 1,700-ton British vessel bound from Sydney to San Pedro, California, with a load of coal. At about midnight the *Dunnotter Castle* crashed onto Kure atoll. Fortunately the vessel did not run head-on into a coral reef, but hit the island at about the point where there is something of a natural entrance into the lagoon, and so the shock of impact was softened.

No one was lost in the tragedy and the crew got safely ashore on the sand islands within the lagoon. On the reef could be seen the skeletal ruins of an earlier wreck, very likely that of the *Saginaw*. For the next five days Captain H. A. Martin worked his crew at jettisoning the cargo of coal in hopes the ship could be floated. It did not help. The vessel was firmly stuck.

The crew of the *Dunnotter Castle* went through many of the same experiences as had the crew of the *Saginaw*. They set up such shelter as they could and rationed provisions. On 24 July a boat was ready to set out and seek help. In command was first officer Henry L. Norman, with supplies for twenty-eight days and a crew of five men and a boy.

The crew and boat enjoyed better luck than had the men from the *Saginaw*. On 12 September the little boat reached Kalihiwai on the north shore of Kauai. It had been a trying trip, the boat's crew was on half-rations, but one last bit of good fortune was yet to shine on them. As they lay beyond the reef they were spotted by Hawaiians on shore who came out to bring the boat safely through the reef. Near this same stretch of beach the boat from the *Saginaw* had finally and cruelly been thrown ashore in 1870.

The crew was rushed from Kauai to Honolulu on the *James Makee*. In Honolulu efforts to send a rescue ship were started immediately.

The *Waialeale* was pulled from its scheduled runs and steamed northwest. To the Honolulu newspapers the loss of the *Dunnotter Castle* was reminiscent of the *Saginaw,* and as much space was given to recounting the former tragedy as the current one.

The government decided that other vessels might go aground on Kure, and aboard the *Waialeale* went lumber to build a house, corrugated iron for a roof, and a tank to catch rainwater. Coconut palms and algaroba trees were sent to be planted on the sand islands. In the end the voyage of the *Waialeale* proved unnecessary. After thirty-three days on Kure, the castaways had been rescued by a passing vessel which carried them to Valparaiso, Chile.

Earlier in 1886 another vessel had been lost off Niihau. She was a small steamer named the *Planter.* At 10:30 on the evening of 27 January she pulled away from Waimea. At about 1:00 in the early morning she was approaching Kii on the eastern end of Niihau when she came heavily against a boulder. The passengers and crew took to a boat, but the captain delayed leaving his vessel for a moment and was washed overboard. He was pulled from the water by the men in the boat and no lives were lost. The sea rushed into the empty hold of the *Planter* and she sank.

News of the loss of another ship was hardly surprising, even if it was difficult to accept. The people of Kauai lived in sight and sound of the sea and they had witnessed often enough what an angry ocean could do. They depended on the sea that surrounded them for so much, and the sea took such tribute as it wished.

King Lunalilo died on the evening of 3 February 1874. He had no heirs and had not chosen a successor to the throne, so the choice of Hawaii's next ruler was in the hands of the legislature. The day after Lunalilo's death David Kalakaua and Dowager Queen Emma announced their candidacies. For the next ten days a bitter battle for votes was fought by the two.

In the early afternoon of 12 February the legislature gathered in Honolulu and voted Kalakaua as the new king of Hawaii. During the morning supporters of Queen Emma began gathering around the courthouse, where the legislature was meeting. When word of Kalakaua's election was made known the supporters of Emma became a mob, invading the courthouse, breaking windows, and destroying everything at hand. One legislator was killed and over a dozen were beaten. The police had little interest in controlling the mob. Some, in fact, joined the rioters. With the permission of the king-elect and the governor of Oahu, troops were landed from three warships, two American and one British, which were anchored in the harbor. For days Honolulu was in a state of tension. Rumors of coming violence persisted.

A month later, on 17 March, King Kalakaua felt safe enough to leave Honolulu. He sailed aboard the *Kilauea* and arrived at Hanalei, undoubtedly glad to leave the turmoil of the capital and to be among subjects who gave every indication of great affection for their new king.

The steamer entered Hanalei Harbor at about 11:00 on a Tuesday morning. There was a royal salute of twenty-one guns from shore as the *Kilauea* came to anchor. "Not precisely guns," the reporter from the *Advertiser* noted, "but big ohia logs which the people of Hanalei had placed in line on the bluff overlooking the landing place, bored and charged with powder, . . . these improvised cannon were fired by a train, going off with great regularity, each one bursting and splitting into firewood." Over the "battery" was a banner with the words Hookahi Puuwai, One Heart.

The people were out en masse to greet the king. It was a holiday for everyone. Kalakaua was rowed ashore and stepped onto the wharf beneath an arch that proclaimed "God Save the King." The words were formed with fern leaves against a background of white. The path the king followed was strewn with rushes and lined on each side with red and yellow flowering branches of lehua. The people loudly cheered and the band, which had come ashore earlier, played the national anthem. The *Advertiser* reporter noted a flag far up the mountain, only a white speck against the green vegetation, which was the means of signaling from point to point the progress of the *Kilauea* and the king.

D. Kaukaha, a legislative representative from Kauai, led the way through a grove of lehua branches to an area thatched with ferns and maile. Girls and children scattered flowers in Kalakaua's path. Here the king sat for a great luau. In the afternoon some of the royal party were rowed up the Hanalei River while others rode horseback.

During Kalakaua's stay at Hanalei the residents of the valley practiced the ancient custom of *ho'okupu,* gift-giving. They brought the traditional things—pigs, fowls, fish, fruits, and vegetables. The personable king shook hands with each person who approached him. The night was spent at the home of Representative Kaukaha.

The next morning was dark, drizzling, and windy, yet a large number of people stood on the beach to bid the king farewell. The *Kilauea* proceeded in the rain along Na Pali to Waimea, where a small group of people met the ship. Isaac K. Hart, once a representative from Kauai, was on the beach to welcome the king. The people brought the king gifts, although there was less enthusiasm than at Hanalei. The lack of a warmer welcome was due to the large number of Emma's supporters at Waimea and also to poor economic times, with rice as almost the only commercial crop in the district.

The next day it was on to Koloa, where the king was hailed by a crowd when he landed in the early afternoon. A group of young people, all dressed in white, formed two lines, and as Kalakaua walked between them flowers were scattered before him. Hundreds of people in carriages, ox-drawn carts, on horseback, and afoot accompanied the king through the rain to the home of Judge Edward Lilikalani. People came from the whole district to bring gifts and greet the king. Lilikalani's house was decorated with evergreens for the occasion.

On the following day the people gathered at the church. The Reverend Doctor Smith offered prayers, Judge Lilikalani publicly welcomed the king, and other speakers followed. Then it was on to Lihue, along the road that led through the Gap, with the king and many others on horseback. Some 500 persons traveled along, a procession of people excited and pleased to be with their king. A luau was given at the home of Judge Kolomona at Nawiliwili. Before long the king boarded the *Kilauea* and the royal progress of Kauai was over.

Kalakaua's journeys on Kauai and the other neighbor islands were among the few relaxed times he enjoyed during his years as ruler. During the first few years of his reign there was cautious approval by the business community. At this time he went to Washington, D.C., to promote the reciprocity treaty. After that Kalakaua's reign became a time of financial turmoil, racism, and nearly constant tension.

Kalakaua had dreams of grandeur, and he spent money on his dreams rather than establishing an efficient government and improving public facilities. He was encouraged in his dreams by Walter Murray Gibson, his ambitious foreign minister, and by Claus Spreckels, who loaned money to the king and in return was granted favors that helped his attempt to monopolize Hawaii's sugar industry in particular, and the economy of the Islands in general.

By late 1880 the case against Kalakaua was building in the minds of many in the non-Hawaiian community. At the end of that year he made a trip to Kauai to bid farewell before departing on a world tour in 1881. A new Iolani Palace was completed in 1883, and an elaborate coronation followed, considered by many an expensive embarrassment. These things could not be paid for through regular sources of income and there was a constant search for places where money could be borrowed. A stream of noisy criticism followed these events, but it brought no response.

Two new and unpleasant events were about to unfold, leading to a showdown. The first occurred toward the end of 1886, when King Kalakaua accepted a "present" of $71,000 from Tong Kee, known as T. Aki, who understood he was to receive a monopoly on the importation and sale of opium into the Islands. Then another man came forward and made a larger "present." Aki wanted his money back, but it was not forthcoming and he went to the *Hawaiian Gazette* with documentation of his story. The story became public in May 1887.

Granting a monopoly for the sale of opium had been made legal by the legislature, but accepting a bribe for securing the monopoly was not. The public demand that Aki be given back his money was met with murmurs on the part of the king, but no money was forthcoming. Indignation in the business community rose to an even higher level.

A second event, which began to evolve during these same months of 1886, brought matters to a climax. For some time Kalakaua and Gibson had been enamored with visions of a Polynesian Confederation. Among the islands that would fit into this scheme was Samoa. At that time there was unrest in Samoa, aided by Germany's wish to make it a colony. England and the United States were concerned observers. Into this unsettled situation Kalakaua sent John E. Bush, whose mission was to bring Samoa into a confederation that would be headed by Kalakaua. Bush, who had been governor of Kauai from 1877 to 1880, was officially appointed Hawaiian ambassador to Samoa and Tonga and departed in late 1886.

To impress the people of Samoa Kalakaua purchased a small steamer and converted her into a training ship. She was crewed partially by boys from a reform school and commanded by an alcoholic captain. The ship was called the *Kaimiloa,* The Far-Seeker. Two days before the ship was to sail from Honolulu a drunken brawl took place aboard and three officers were dismissed.

On 18 May 1887 the *Kaimiloa* sailed from Honolulu and tolerance by the business community for the government's actions was at an end. When the vessel reached Samoa matters soon deteriorated. Discipline collapsed aboard the *Kaimiloa,* which eventually limped back to Hawaii. The whole adventure ended up an expensive mistake that made the Hawaiian monarchy look foolish. Costly foolishness was something Hawaii's businessmen would not accept.

On 13 June Sanford Dole wrote to his brother George, manager of the Kapaa plantation of Z. S. Spalding. "When he [Kalakaua] drives out to Waikiki he has a squad of mounted armed police around him." Kalakaua obviously knew of the feelings of part of the community, yet he did nothing to calm their concerns. By early 1887 an organization called the Hawaiian League had been formed by the business community, through which they could express their displeasure with the policies of the monarchy. The Hawaiian League was supported by a military unit called the Honolulu Rifles, which was also an official unit of the monarchy.

On 29 June in Honolulu posters appeared in English, Hawaiian, and Portuguese announcing a mass meeting to be held the next day at 2:00 P.M. at the armory. Iolani Palace was about a block away, and any commotion at the armory could easily be heard at the palace. The following day business houses closed at 1:00 P.M. and something in excess of 2,000 persons filled the armory or gathered outside. Members of the Honolulu Rifles were on hand in uniform while others, on official request, stood guard duty at public buildings in the town.

One speaker followed another to the platform, receiving loud applause—loud enough to reach Iolani Palace. The assembly was of one mind. There had to be a change in the government and the only question was how it should be done. It was agreed the present cabinet had to be dismissed and a new constitution written. Paul Isenberg, speaking to the crowd, said the legislature should draw up the new constitution, not members of the Hawaiian League. He was the most conservative voice to be heard and his views drew no support.

William Hyde Rice, by now a veteran legislator, addressed the assembly in Hawaiian, as several other speakers had done. "Hawaiian citizens from Hawaii to Niihau, . . . the roads are wasting and groaning from one end to another of the land. Where is the money for the roads? Sent on an exploration with the Kaimiloa. . . . It has been well said that the ship of this movement has been launched, . . . now let us take the helm and steer."

A committee of thirteen was appointed to make the demands known to Kalakaua. Paul Isenberg headed the committee and William Rice was a member. Kalakaua was willing to give the committee an immediate answer granting all their demands, but the committee insisted he take twenty-four hours to consider. The cabinet was dismissed and when a new constitution was drawn up the king signed it. The end result was that Kalakaua was shorn of most of his power and Hawaii became a constitutional monarchy.

Of all the diseases that afflicted the Hawaiians the most dreaded was leprosy. The disease was probably introduced to the Islands in about 1840 from China, where it was common. Not until 1863 did the board of health take notice of leprosy. Three years later Kalaupapa, an isolated, flat projection of land cut off from the rest of Molokai by sheer cliffs on one side and the ocean on another, was designated as the place where all persons diagnosed as having leprosy were to be sent.

Leprosy was hideous and there was no arresting it, no cure. It usually attacked the extremities first, deadening feeling, eventually decaying ears, fingers, or toes until they fell away. Once the disease was contracted it became a matter of watching it progress. It was simply a question of how long it would take before the horrible end came. The conditions at the leprosy colony on Molokai soon gained a grim reputation. Housing was bad, if available at all. Food was scarce, the strong stealing from the weak. Medical attention hardly existed. Some of those who contracted the disease did what they could to avoid going to Molokai and to escape the degradation of living out their lives under those dreadful conditions.

Hawaiians sometimes hid their friends or relatives without thought of becoming leprous themselves. Others sought isolated places where they could live, free at least from the horrors of Kalaupapa. Kalalau Valley on Kauai's northern coast became such a gathering place. Steep cliffs overshadow Kalalau on three sides and the ocean dashes against the open north shore. The way in and out of Kalalau is by boat or by two or three trails, steep, narrow, and tedious.

Little was heard of the afflicted persons living in Kalalau. They were probably glad to live unobtrusive lives without attracting attention. Judge J. Kauai became their leader. The judge had been a longtime resident, first of Hanapepe, and then of Waimea. Neither Judge Kauai nor his wife Kaenaku had been born on Kauai. Kaenaku's father had been a faithful warrior of Kamehameha, and after the revolt of 1824 he was among those who shared the spoils by receiving land on Kauai. His land grant, which later went to his daughter, was in upper Hanapepe Valley. Kauai's activities were centered in Waimea and so he traded his Hanapepe land to the Sinclairs for land in Waimea.

J. Kauai was a respected man. He was active in the Waimea church and his opinions were sought in important matters. He served as a judge at Waimea and was elected to the house of representatives several times. At some point J. Kauai contracted leprosy, and rather than go to Molokai he took refuge in Kalalau Valley.

There had been serious troubles with those declared leprous, mostly at Waimea, for a long time. On one occasion, in April 1888, Constable S. Aukai went up Waimea Valley to arrest several leprous persons. When he approached the house where they were staying he was met by two leprous men who pointed rifles at him and threatened to shoot if he came closer. There were fifteen or sixteen leprosy victims armed with rifles living in the area. Friends kept them supplied with food. Two months later, when a leprous person was arrested, two of his companions opened fire on police. By June of 1888 three of the five constables at Waimea had resigned and it was difficult to find replacements. Sheriff Samuel Wilcox reported, "The public sentiment in Waimea is against the removal of the lepers. . . . Some of the foreigners back them [the lepers] and assist them."

By the end of March 1889 it was estimated that twenty-five to thirty-five leprous people were living in Kalalau. In addition there was the longtime, even larger non-leprous colony in the valley. There were more instances of violence on the west side of Kauai, and nearly every report of the sheriff mentioned leprous men and women being sent to Honolulu. In May 1893 Deputy Sheriff Louis Stolz of Waimea resigned, but agreed to stay on until Sheriff Wilcox returned to Kauai. Stolz wrote to Edward G. Hitchcock, marshal of the republic, saying he would be in Honolulu in June to discuss the matter.

Among those who went to the valley was Koolau, a cowboy at Kekaha, who was known as a fine saddlemaker and an expert shot. Koolau had been declared leprous and he agreed to go to Kalaupapa on Molokai if his wife Piilani would be allowed to go with him. In earlier times it had been common for a spouse to accompany an infected person to Molokai, but the rules had been changed, and special arrangements had to be made for Piilani. At the last minute, however, it was announced that she would not be allowed to go, and this so angered Koolau that he fled to Kalalau Valley with his wife and young son. He vowed he would never be taken alive. Koolau became a symbol of resistance to the way those with leprosy were treated.

In early June 1893 Louis Stolz was in Honolulu, discussing with Edward Hitchcock the leprosy problem and his reasons for resigning as deputy sheriff. Stolz felt he had to round up the leprous persons during the summer when landing on the beach of the valley was possible.

Hitchcock said he would assist Stolz if he would delay his Kalalau trip for a short time.

Soon after returning to Waimea, Louis Stolz decided to go to Kalalau alone. Late in June he landed on the beach, Winchester rifle in hand, and asked where he could find Koolau. While looking for Koolau, Stolz came across Paoa, a leprous resident, and ordered him to come along. They walked up the valley toward the height where Koolau was hiding.

When Stolz got to the open narrow ridge leading to the hiding place, Koolau called out. Later some said Koolau simply fired on Stolz, and others said he warned him to stop and when he kept coming, shot him. It is certain that Koolau fired and hit the deputy sheriff in the stomach. Koolau called to Paoa, asking if Stolz was dead. Paoa said he was not and Koolau fired again, hitting Stolz in the chest.

The death of Louis Stolz caused excitement and anger in Honolulu. Plans were organized to send troops to the valley. On 30 June 1893 the steamer *Waialeale* was on her way to Kauai carrying twelve special police and fourteen soldiers. Their equipment included a Krupp field howitzer. Among those aboard was Luther Wilcox, a brother of Sam and George Wilcox, who went along to act as interpreter. Sanford Dole, president of the Republic of Hawaii, declared martial law in the districts of Hanalei and Waimea. At Hanalei the ship paused briefly and Samuel W. Wilcox, sheriff of Kauai, joined the group. On 2 July the troops had landed and established a base near the beach, which they called Camp Dole. They started rounding up the leprous persons and working their way up the valley.

From his secure hiding place above a waterfall, Koolau had a clear view of anyone who attempted to approach him. Koolau's sister was brought from Kekaha in an effort to talk him into surrendering or betraying his hiding place. The attempt brought no results. An army dispatch stated that when troops tried to approach the hiding place by the exposed ridge trail, Koolau shot and killed two of them. A third soldier was killed when he accidentally shot himself in the head.

The death of three men pretty well ended any serious attempt to capture Koolau. The howitzer was brought up and nineteen rounds were fired in the direction of Koolau's hideout. The shells caused a great racket, echoing back and forth in the quiet valley. By 4 July all the leprous persons in the valley had been accounted for except Koolau, Piilani, and their young son. Then the soldiers boarded the *Waialeale* for the return to Honolulu.

Fourteen of the afflicted persons were brought to Honolulu.

Among them was Judge Kauai, who was then about sixty-eight years of age. He had to be carried ashore in Honolulu by four men. One foot was bandaged and both hands were nearly useless. Another leprous man aboard was Kapahee, also in his sixties, who had once been a famous swimmer. His face was badly swollen. The disease did not spare children. A nine-year-old girl was in the worst condition of all those brought to Honolulu, and another victim was a one-year-old child. The afflicted ones were sent on to Molokai.

Koolau continued to live in the valley and surrounding mountains with his wife and son. The family received supplies from friends who considered the onetime cowboy a hero. Koolau's son, who had contracted leprosy, died in 1896 and Koolau died several months later. Both were buried in the mountains. Two rifles were placed next to Koolau in his grave. Piilani returned to Waimea and eventually married again.

Koolau was the most celebrated person with leprosy, but he was not the only one to turn to violence. Dr. Jared K. Smith, a son of Dr. James Smith, was the government physician at Koloa. As such he had to determine who had leprosy. On the night of 27 September 1897 Smith was writing a letter to his future bride when there was a knock at the door. When he opened the door he was shot in the heart and died instantly. The man who shot Smith did so to prevent him from signing an order sending to Honolulu a young girl who was suspected of having leprosy.

Leprosy most often affected Hawaiians and part-Hawaiians, but Christian Bertelmann, born in Germany, was an exception. His leprosy could not have become apparent until after 1888, because he represented Kauai that year in the legislature. Christian Bertelmann's leprosy was one of the best-kept secrets on Kauai.

The story goes that Christian Bertelmann was smuggled off Kauai, disguised as a woman, and put aboard a ship for Japan after his affliction was established. There were stories of leprosy cures in Japan, but they did Bertelmann no good and he was smuggled back to Kauai, where he returned to his old home near Kilauea. The family kept him hidden in a secret room that had been built into the center of the house.

Before his affliction Bertelmann had been a member of the George Ewart family musical group. The Ewarts lived nearby and they would often gather for an evening of music. During these gatherings Christian played the flute.

Once he had contracted the disease he did not go out during the day, but at night saddled his horse and rode across the pasturelands. There was a stream near the Ewart home, and here Christian Bertelmann would stop and listen to the family play. He took his flute with him and would sit on the ground and join in the music.

One night the Ewarts heard ghostly music accompanying them from outside. It was Christian Bertelmann playing the flute. When they went to find the flute player all they discovered was the place where Bertelmann had tethered his horse. When Bertelmann died he was quietly buried near his home.

In Favor of Maintaining the Monarchy

The patience and money spent in bringing Portuguese and Germans to the plantations had not been good investments. Negotiations took too long, the travel distance was great, and workers were too few in number. The importation of South Sea islanders had been a disappointment in every way. The need for labor became more critical and, as much as Europeans were desired, the fact remained that Chinese workers were easily available. Negotiations were not necessary and there was no waiting in securing Chinese, even though there was never a treaty or agreement between Hawaii and the government of China. The Chinese were anxious to come, they would accept lower wages than others, and they were generally considered good workers.

The old objections to the Chinese, however, would not disappear. The Chinese fulfilled their contracts on the plantations and then many started businesses of their own. They represented competition for shopkeepers and tradesmen, who bitterly resented the fact that Chinese only rarely had families to support and were willing to accept a standard of living that others would not tolerate. Very few women came with the Chinese workers, which increased the imbalance between males and females in the Islands.

In a four-month period, from December 1880 to April 1881, more than 4,400 Chinese were landed at Honolulu. This influx and earlier ones alarmed Island authorities. Because of the lack of regulations, the Chinese who came were poorly screened for possible health problems. In 1880–1881, when so many Chinese arrived, smallpox was brought to the Islands aboard one of the immigrant ships. The epidemic raged over Oahu and was discovered in the district of Kawaihau on the northeast coast of Kauai. There were a total of 797 cases of smallpox with 287 deaths throughout the Islands. Five of the deaths occurred on Kauai. As usual, the Hawaiian population suffered most from this epidemic. The episode heightened resentment of the Chinese.

Sheriff Samuel Wilcox had hoped to keep smallpox off Kauai by inspecting persons arriving on the island, but his efforts failed. A Hawaiian medical kahuna brought a heavily veiled old woman to Kauai aboard the *James Makee* on 3 February 1881. The kahuna had promised the woman he could cure her and she was not discovered until 11 February, when she was already gravely ill. Eleven days later, ten cases of smallpox were reported on Kauai. Wilcox quarantined the villages of Pilaa and Moloaa, and guards were placed at the Kawaihau district borders.

Wilcox ordered rice, salmon, hard bread, and kerosene to provide for the sick and quarantined. An old schoolhouse near Moloaa was turned into a quarantine station. A nearby church became a hospital. The greatest worry was over a lack of vaccine. At last it came from Honolulu and by 11 March over 800 persons had been vaccinated. There was a total of twenty cases of smallpox on Kauai. Wilcox proposed charging the kahuna with manslaughter.

In March 1882 plantation owners formed the Planters' Labor and Supply Company in a united effort to organize and speed up the importing of laborers. A program was adopted that included as an essential point the bringing of Japanese to the Islands. In fact, Japanese immigrants became the hoped-for solution to the Chinese problem. They were looked to both as laborers and as a permanent addition to the population.

In spite of the proclaimed wish of the Hawaiian government and the planters that Chinese stop coming to Hawaii, Chinese immigrants kept arriving. In the spring of 1883 some 3,400 Chinese males arrived at Honolulu, causing an angry Hawaiian government to send an official protest. The Chinese government replied that the matter was out of their hands, because the Chinese came from the British colony of Hong Kong. Finally the British in Hong Kong took action. Still, by one means or another, Chinese kept arriving. They came because the steamship companies could make money bringing them, and their chances of staying were good because laborers were needed. After 1 April 1886 the Hawaiian government required all Chinese entering Hawaii to have passports.

When Chinese could no longer come easily to Hawaii directly from Hong Kong, some still managed to arrive and stay through a technical loophole. They first sailed to San Francisco from Hong Kong and then claimed they had reached Hawaii not from Hong Kong, but from their last port, which was in the United States. Chinese coming from the United States could not be refused entry into Hawaii.

The only way to really cut down on Chinese arrivals was to push Japanese immigration. In 1880 Robert W. Irwin, an American businessman long resident in Japan, was enlisted to give assistance. Irwin was married to the daughter of a prominent Japanese family and had won the respect and confidence of the Japanese. In 1883 he was named special commissioner of immigration for Japan.

The first Japanese, about 150 of them, had come to Hawaii in 1868. A number had returned to Japan, but those who remained were well considered. Unfortunately these Japanese had left their homeland during a time of political turmoil and their departure had not been approved by the Japanese government. Feelings against any further emigration remained strong for many years.

Japan was wary of all foreign nations and it was a complicated, delicate process to work things out with the Japanese government. A treaty had to be agreed upon before anything could be done. In Hawaii, friction between the government and the planters delayed matters. When Kalakaua visited Japan in March 1881 he eased matters by making a good impression. The Hawaiian king's enthusiasm for the Japanese was swayed by his belief that the Japanese were racially connected with the Polynesians. At least two envoys, John M. Kapena and later, Curtis P. Iaukea, traveled to Japan and built on the goodwill Kalakaua had started. In 1883 a minister of the Japanese Imperial Household was commissioned as envoy to Hawaii and came on a trip of observation.

At last arrangements were reached, speeded forward by a severe economic depression in Japan, which particularly affected agricultural workers. With the way cleared, the first group of immigrants arrived at Honolulu on 8 February 1885. There were a total of 943, about two-thirds of them men. In mid-June 1885 a second group of immigrants totaling 978 arrived. The ever-conscientious Robert Irwin accompanied both the first and second groups to Hawaii. From the second group 106 men and two women were sent to five Kauai plantations. Makee was allocated 40 workers, the largest number of any Kauai plantation.

It was hoped 6,000 laborers would come to the Islands from Japan during 1885, but that hope was optimistic. By the end of 1885 about 1,950 immigrants had arrived. Newspapers gave Kalakaua and the government high praise for successfully beginning what was generally considered an important milestone in the history of the Islands. Even skeptical planters joined in praising the accomplishment.

With the first group of Japanese immigrants came G. O. Nakayama, who was appointed inspector of Japanese immigrants. His duties were to act as interpreter and liaison between laborers and employers. Nakayama did much to smooth the way in numerous disputes. His staff eventually included fourteen deputy-inspectors and five doctors. At least two of these doctors spent considerable time on Kauai.

In 1886 there were 223 Japanese workers on Kauai's plantations, 24 of them women, as well as 563 Chinese workers and 409 Hawaiians. Four years after the Planters' Labor and Supply Company was organized, their intention of replacing Chinese with Japanese was showing results.

Each year more Japanese arrived. In 1890, 3,087 came to the Islands, and only 360 Chinese arrived in the same year. And while fewer Chinese were arriving, more were departing. From 1886 through 1896, 14,896 Chinese arrived in the Islands while 13,994 left. During the same period 32,056 Japanese came and 8,969 departed.

Efforts to control Chinese immigration through a variety of laws had been attempted for several years, but in 1892 an act became law that firmly kept Chinese out of the trades and effectively discouraged them from becoming permanent residents of the Islands. Chinese would only be admitted to the Islands to work in "domestic service, or agricultural labor in the field, or in rice or sugar mills." Conditional work permits were issued to Chinese for three-year periods and each month money from the workers' wages was deposited with the government to go toward payment of their return passage to China.

On Kauai there were 2,828 Japanese working on plantations in 1896, and by June 1901 there were 5,921. The Japanese constituted 58 percent of Kauai's plantation work force in 1896 and in mid-1901, 71 percent of Kauai's workers were Japanese. The objective of replacing Chinese with Japanese had been successful.

This deluge of new people brought about a disruption of life on Kauai. In the period from 1890 to 1900 the total population of Kauai increased from 11,859 to 20,734, nearly a 75 percent increase. Of the total population in 1900 nearly 15,000 were Japanese and Chinese.

For those who had lived on Kauai before 1890, the new conditions on the island must have seemed unsettled and terribly crowded, particularly in the camps around the sugar mills. The new population was constantly in motion, with most of those who had completed their three-year contracts departing and being replaced by new workers. Free laborers might stay even shorter periods of time. And, of course, these newcomers spoke strange languages, followed strange religions, and even preferred rice to poi.

If old-timers watched with uncertainty, the immigrants were usually bewildered. They were in a foreign place, far from familiar customs. Most could neither read nor write. Although the Japanese had Japanese nationals to help them, some of the deputy-inspectors swindled their trusting countrymen, taking money for services for which there should have been no charge. Most workers knew or saw little of the island on which they lived. Life was restricted to the fields and camp. Many workers had only a hazy idea of where they were. Their hope was to save money and return to the familiar surroundings from which they had come.

In the fields and mills frustrations were intensified by language barriers and, on a few plantations, management viewed workers as being similar to a piece of equipment, of having a work-expectancy equal to the length of their contracts. Laborers sometimes ran away from plantations and sometimes a group would go on strike. Runaways were sought by the police, and when a worker was returned, the plantation customarily paid a reward, usually about ten dollars, although police sometimes demanded twice that amount.

Those who went on strike were arrested by Kauai police and fined. There were no general strikes. The pattern was for a relatively small number of workers of the same race and with a common grievance to join together and refuse to work. If strikers seemed dangerous or particularly determined, or if jails were crowded, prisoners were sent to Honolulu. Strikes rarely received public notice.

Men would stop working for a variety of reasons, which often were not clear. In January 1881 a group of Portuguese at Kilauea refused to work for Robert A. Macfie, the manager. Eleven were sent to Honolulu and Sheriff Samuel W. Wilcox reported to the marshal of the kingdom that "none of the road supervisors want them as they are an ugly crowd." Wilcox wrote he expected to arrest eleven more shortly.

Christian Bertelmann was willing to take a chance on some of the imprisoned workers and, being a road supervisor, he put a gang to work. The *Hawaiian Gazette* reported that the eleven men sent to Honolulu had struck because the salt beef provided by the plantation did not agree with them. The newspaper added caustically,

Perhaps in future when making contracts plantations will arrange to give their laborers champagne and truffles. . . .

Joking apart, such fellows deserve severe punishment. They are white men who no doubt are desirous of breaking their contracts. . . . We sincerely trust that the owners of the plantation will be very firm with them.

On 9 February the newspaper wrote that the strikers had been working on a bridge and were marched back to jail each night.

In September 1881 a case came to trial titled R. A. Macfie vs. Jacintho Moniz et al. The defendants had refused to work at Kilauea. They charged they had been sent to the wrong plantation and had been forced to work where they did not belong. It is hard to know if the strike of January and February and the court case of September were connected. Such confusion over causes of strikes was not unusual. The court ordered each worker fined $5.00 with an added $3.50 for court costs.

Another type of disturbance had taken place at Princeville plantation much earlier, in November 1865, when men from two provinces of China battled each other, a continuation of animosities carried from their homeland. One man was killed in the fighting and the manager of the plantation, John Low, moved the Chinese of one province across the Hanalei River to separate them from the second faction. There were 30 men in one group and about 80 in the other. No specific reason for the violence was given, but for the next several years there was concern over a general uprising at Hanalei.

In January 1889 manager Anton Cropp had trouble at Koloa. On 29 January Sheriff Wilcox had 63 Japanese from Koloa in jail for refusing to work, and he expected 20 more would be arrested in a day or two. Wilcox's total prison population was 121 men: "The prison is over crowded the cells are full also the hall and cook house."

By early February 1889 Keigoro Katsura, a deputy inspector of Japanese immigration, had made his report, and Lorrin A. Thurston, minister of immigration, wrote a letter to H. Hackfeld & Company, the agent for Koloa plantation. The source of the trouble, Thurston wrote, was the prosecution of two men who did not work as well as the plantation thought they might. The problems arose because the men were being prosecuted as deserters. There had been nine prosecutions, apparently of the same sort, in a three-week period. In his letter Thurston recalled the advice of Robert W. Irwin and the board of immigration, which had cautioned,

Rough measures and harsh treatment are the worst possible means of handling Japanese. But the history of Koloa seems to show that this advice is not heeded. . . . The whole situation shows a lack of tact and consideration of the feelings of the laborers.

One of the examples Thurston mentioned in his letter concerned the death of a Chinese worker. Fellow laborers were selected to dig the grave and only four of his countrymen were allowed to stay away from work to attend the funeral. The reason for this cruel act, Thurston continued, was that "one man could bury the corpse in one half a day! . . . The manager's conduct is to say the least urgently and exceedingly exasperating to the men." Thurston warned action would be taken if conditions did not improve.

Police and plantation managers were often feuding. Opium possession was a reason for police searches and since this was principally a Chinese problem, the barracks of Chinese workers were the targets. The plantation management was not informed of such raids in advance and were greatly annoyed by the troubles the invasions caused. Some managers encouraged workers to resist searches and the violence that followed was another source of anger.

When the Japanese arrived in large numbers the police raided their quarters also, usually in search of gambling activity. Apparently any racial group might be involved in the illegal importation or sale of liquor, which brought on yet other raids.

In late December 1889 police raided the barracks of Chinese workers at Kilauea. They arrested two men for possession of opium and were leaving with their prisoners when they were attacked by a mob of Chinese who had gathered outside. The Chinese threw rocks and bottles, badly injuring one of the policemen in the face. The police fired their pistols in the air, the Chinese retreated, and the two prisoners were taken away.

Manager Macfie was upset enough by the incident to write to John Soper, who was the marshal of the kingdom. He complained about the police coming at night, firing pistols, and causing panic among the workers. Macfie thought the invasion was inexcusable.

Sheriff Wilcox defended the actions of his police. He wrote that the police only fired their pistols after they were attacked. He went on to say Kilauea was a center of opium traffic and claimed that Robert Macfie encouraged his workers to resist the police. The two prisoners were convicted. Three months later Kilauea was again raided. There was more violence, and this time a Chinese was shot in the shoulder by a policeman.

If the actions of the police often seemed harsh, the workers they were dealing with were often less than ideal citizens. At one time there was a rumor that some Chinese on Kauai had once been pirates along the China coast. Whether the story had any foundation is unknown. Some workers, usually among those who came from the cities, had left their native lands because going to Hawaii was a convenient way to escape the trouble they were in at home. Other laborers knew only of a life of endless, dulling toil. Years passed with a comprehension of only a minimum of Hawaiian and English words. And there was the constant problem of communicating with management, of translating from one language to another the worries and complaints of workers.

The jails of Kauai were busy places during the 1880s and 1890s. There were usually four jails on the island, located at Wailua, Hanalei, Waimea, and Nawiliwili. There was also a jail for women at Koloa and another at Anahola. Most of the constables were employed part-time or were simply on call when their help was needed. Deputy sheriffs usually had other employment on the side.

Plantations also had their own police to enforce plantation rules. Plantation police resented the intrusion of government police on their territory, believing they could best handle matters on their own. The workers were more aware of plantation police because they were the men who enforced curfews, kept peace between hostile factions, and generally tried to keep laborers regularly in the fields. When serious troubles arose, help was sought from the sheriff.

The police force of Kauai was untrained and the men had only a general idea of what was expected of them. The increasing population of the island made their jobs more difficult. Little attention was paid to the niceties of law, and many illegal things were probably done through ignorance in the pursuit of their duty. They also had their own internal problems—some had criminal records, there was fighting and drunkenness, and there was a constant turnover in the constabulary.

For some kinds of offenses police received a part of the fine imposed by the judge on the convicted. This ill-conceived practice led police to search out persons involved in the crimes that brought them the greatest rewards. For example, a policeman who had arrested a person who was then convicted of possession of opium received half of the fine imposed by the judge. With such an incentive, police were out to catch opium smugglers and this led to abuses of entrapment. Disputes sometimes arose when judges were accused of cheating policemen out of their portions of fines.

Those who were convicted were not allowed to sit idly around in prison. They were put to work at any chore that could be found for them. The most common employment was road work, and the roads of Kauai were in constant need of repair. Individuals also hired prisoners to do various jobs. Money received from the labor might go toward paying a prisoner's fine. If a prisoner had money he could pay his jailors a sum and go free for the day. When not working, inmates milled about the jail area with little thought given to security.

The growth of the sugar industry could be added up in all sorts of ways—in tonnage per acre, in the percent of juice extracted from cane —but there were other kinds of totals as well. There were displaced persons in the new economy, there was additional crime, and there were irritations brought on by disillusionment. There was no simple way to cope with any of these problems.

For years visitors to Kauai had to find lodging as best they could. In the 1820s and the 1830s this often meant finding shelter and board in the thatched house of a hospitable Hawaiian. Into the 1840s Deborah Kapule offered board and lodging to numerous visitors who passed through Wailua. She even had lodgers ferried across the Wailua River, and on occasion her canoes provided transportation up the winding waterway. Many early travelers wrote with appreciation of her hospitality.

The homes of the Smiths, Doles, and Gulicks, as well as the succeeding managers of Koloa plantation, served as a place of lodging for people arriving and departing from Koloa. At Lihue the Rice family had a constant stream of people stopping for a meal and often for the night. At Waimea the Whitneys and Rowells sheltered many, as did the Alexander, Wilcox, and Kellett families at Hanalei.

In the early days of Koloa plantation Tom Pratt opened a boarding house to accommodate single men, many of whom held supervisory jobs on the plantation. The house built by Thomas Brown in Wailua Valley, which was taken over by Hoffschlaeger & Company, served as a boarding house there in the 1850s. Duncan McBryde was the manager for a time and advertisements for the Wailua House were run in *The Polynesian,* describing it as a respectable and convenient place to stay. For those who wished to check further, several prominent persons were listed in the ad as references.

When Liliuokalani toured Kauai in 1891 she stopped at Kealia as the guest of Makee plantation. Her visit was brief—she spent only several hours there before going on to Hanalei—but during that short time she was given the use of the plantation hotel, decorated with flowers and ferns for the queen's visit.

With increased plantation activity on Kauai, accommodations were necessary. A variety of engineers, surveyors, and equipment salesmen came to the plantations and they needed a place to stay. Before the hectic days of the 1890s these persons would stay with the manager or a supervisor, but when visitors became too numerous, hotels were built.

In the late 1880s or early 1890s the plantations at Kilauea and Kekaha had accommodations similar to those at Kealia. The management at Kilauea became involved in an argument with the government over whether their hotel needed a liquor license. The plantation believed the hotel was for their own use and did not need a license, while the government thought the hotel was used by others and must have a general license.

By 1890 Charles W. Spitz was operating the Fairview Hotel and Restaurant in Lihue. Spitz was engaged in a number of business activities on Kauai, and by 1894 William H. Rice, Jr., a son of the rancher-legislator, was listed as the manager. The hotel was advertised as having a new building, well-furnished, with a seaside annex for sea-bathing. The Fairview, later renamed the Lihue Hotel, was probably the first establishment that could qualify as a full-fledged hotel.

The Fairview Hotel took a burden off the families who had extended hospitality to visitors for so long. In 1893 Juliette Smith reported that Dr. Hutchinson was stopping at the hotel. She went there to have a tooth filled. A few years earlier Kauaians had to travel to Honolulu to have dental work done. In 1896 Frederick W. Carter, Kauai's new sheriff, was staying at the hotel with his wife until permanent accommodations could be found. It was a sign of how new needs were changing Kauai in small ways.

By 1890 there were villages and hotels where once there had been no inhabitants at all, a reflection of how the centers of population were shifting. The places that had offered the most to Hawaiians—the sea to fish in, a stream to provide water for taro—these things became less important as the new commercial world took increasing control. Although some Hawaiians preferred the old life-style, many moved close to the plantation mill with the nearby company store, and their generally thinning numbers reduced old villages to fragments of what they had once been.

Places like Anahola Valley, Moloaa, Kalihiwai, and Waipouli had previously been centers of population. Valleys along Na Pali coast once had extensive terraces for growing taro. Among them was Kalalau Valley, one of the most intensively cultivated places in all the Islands. On the dry western lands, at Kekaha and Mana, where Hawaiians had been scattered through the district, the population was drawn closer to the center of things, which was again the mill at Kekaha. Hawaiians who lived along the Waimea River found their taro lands in demand by Chinese and later Japanese rice farmers, and they often sold or leased them.

At Koloa, where the Hawaiian population had once been more dispersed, there was a tendency to gather closer to the mill at Koloa village or about the stone pier where cargo was shipped and passengers arrived and departed. Hawaiian workers had begun to build their homes by the mill in 1836. Later, stone barracks were constructed to house Chinese laborers. Mahaulepu, once a populated place, became isolated and unimportant.

At both Hanapepe and Wailua, the choice taro lands running far up the valleys had been replaced by rice. On the nearby flatlands sugarcane was grown. In these valleys as elsewhere, Hawaiians were beginning to feel the pressure of Chinese who wanted to put new crops on old lands. At Haena, taro had been grown at the foot of the mountains. Wainiha had a sizable amount of desirable lands. At Lumahai Valley, Liliuokalani leased ninety-four acres of her land in 1890 to the rice-growing company of Chulan & Company, for ten years at $800 per year.

When a new mill was built at Kilauea and when McBryde built one at Wahiawa, new communities appeared where there had been none before. The Makee plantation was responsible for the village at Kealia. Lihue came into existence as a plantation community. Nawiliwili grew with the importance of its harbor, but earlier nearby Niumalu was of much greater importance.

All of this was disruptive. Changes were sudden and severe. There was a shifting population, a new government, amazing machines. Even the police on Kauai were changing. By October 1895 they were wearing uniforms for the first time—blue jackets with gold buttons, although for a while such buttons were in short supply. There were also new diversions. Bicycles were introduced to Waimea in about January 1898. They aroused much interest and police were asked to stop the races that took place on Sundays.

While Kauaians were attempting to solve the problems that beset them, events taking place on the windward islands were brought to Kauai by the visit of Queen Liliuokalani in the summer of 1891. On the death of her brother in January 1891, Liliuokalani became Hawaii's queen. When she ascended the throne there was much joy among the Hawaiians and guarded hope in the business community. Liliuokalani, who was fifty-two when she succeeded Kalakaua, was a familiar person throughout the Islands. In 1862 she had married John Dominis, son of Captain John Dominis, an early Honolulu merchant-captain. The young Dominis was prominent in monarchy affairs, serving for many years as governor of Oahu.

As queen, Liliuokalani followed her brother's example and made a tour of the major islands, arriving off Kauai before dawn on 8 July 1891. The ship came to anchor before Nawiliwili Bay and the queen was greeted by beacon lights on the surrounding hills and mountains. But the surf was running high, and boats could not safely reach the landing until 5:30 A.M. A crowd of Kauaians had waited patiently to welcome her. Once ashore she was driven by carriage under arches of welcome to the home of William Hyde Rice.

Hale Nani, the Rice home, was decorated with flowers, ferns, vines, and palms, and "Welcome to Hale Nani" was over the stairway within. At noon 300 to 400 children passed before the queen. The royal band played and school children greeted Liliuokalani with songs. There was a luau, followed by *hoʻokupu,* gift-giving. The queen spoke to the crowd, expressing her appreciation and asking for their support in her efforts to maintain good government. That evening the lanais of the house were hung with Japanese lanterns as the prominent members of the community were presented to Queen Liliuokalani. The royal band, conducted by Henry Berger, performed on the lawn before the house.

The next morning Queen Liliuokalani visited the industrial school at Malumalu, near Lihue. It had been started in 1889 through contributions from friends on the mainland, from Island planters, and from Liliuokalani. Thirty acres of land had been bought for $1,500. A three-story building had been constructed and there were plans for another building to be used as a dormitory and for classes.

The goal was to have about seventy-five students. The girls were taught homemaking and the boys were taught to be printers, carpenters, blacksmiths, and farmers. The supporters of the school had high hopes for its success. When Liliuokalani visited, two women teachers had just been hired from Hampton Institute. Although the cost was low, only $40 a year for boys and $50 for girls, the school closed in about 1898 because of a lack of interest.

From Malumalu the party set forth for Wailua Falls. It was a time of high spirits and laughter. Some went swimming in the river. There was again a luau in the late afternoon, presided over by the queen who reclined under a bower at the head of the guests. Paul Isenberg, son of the sugar pioneer, sang a solo in Hawaiian. After the luau there was a grand procession to Hale Nani, the queen at the head.

The following day the royal party returned north, beyond Wailua to Kealia where they were entertained by the management of Makee plantation. The band came by ship to Kapaa and then by train to Kealia. In the afternoon it was by carriage to Hanalei, where there were yet more receptions. Two days later the queen embarked aboard the *James Makee,* but the seas were rough and the vessel spent the night in the lee of the cliffs near Lumahai. The ship dropped anchor off Niihau the next day, and Liliuokalani was entertained ashore. Then it was on to Waimea, where the arrival of the queen was welcomed by a salute fired from the fort.

The progress continued by carriage to Koloa for another reception and more speeches. Finally at Kalapaki, the Rice residence on Nawili-wili Bay, a great farewell luau was given for some 2,000 persons gathered to honor the queen. Mindful of ancient legend and to honor Liliuokalani, William Rice sent to Kipukai for drinking water from a special sacred spring.

Accompanying the queen on her tour of Kauai was Prince Jonah Kuhio Kalanianaole. Kuhio, as he was known, and his brother David Kawananakoa were nephews of Queen Kapiolani, who had adopted them. At the time of the coronation of Kalakaua and Kapiolani in February 1883, the two boys were named princes of the kingdom. Kuhio was then twelve years old.

Both Prince David and Prince Kuhio were great grandsons of King Kaumualii. They had been born in the district of Koloa on Kauai, and when they were named princes they dropped their surname of Piikoi. When Liliuokalani came to the throne she named Kaiulani, her only niece, as heir apparent. David and Kuhio were named heirs presumptive.

During the counter-revolution of 1895 Prince Kuhio took an active part in the attempt to restore the monarchy and as a result was imprisoned. He was released together with others and, under territorial status, was elected as Hawaii's delegate to Congress, a position he occupied for twenty years. When he died in January 1922 he was the last royally designated heir to the Hawaiian throne.

The period of goodwill that marked Liliuokalani's tour of Kauai was short-lived. Three months after she returned to Honolulu, her husband died. John Dominis had been a modifying influence on the queen and without his presence she appears to have quickly turned her thoughts toward establishing a constitution that would restore the power of the monarchy. The two years of Liliuokalani's rule were reminiscent of the years leading up to the ultimatum given to Kalakaua and the resulting constitution of 1887. Controversial measures before the legislature included a lottery bill, an opium licensing bill, and bills affecting the monetary system of the country. Cabinets were formed and promptly voted out of existence by the legislature. Little work was accomplished, and the affairs of the kingdom deteriorated to near-chaos.

In October 1892 George Wilcox was asked to form a cabinet and to hold the position of minister of the interior. Wilcox had first been elected to the legislature in 1880 and his quiet, straightforward manner earned him the respect of people of diverse opinions in the community. Reluctantly Wilcox accepted the chore of organizing a cabinet. The names of his cabinet members were submitted to the queen, who felt pressured at the time into accepting them.

Chances for George Wilcox's success initially seemed good. E. C. Macfarlane, a legislator and one-time minister of finance, who was a royalist and known as anti-American, stated "I think he [Wilcox] would be not only satisfactory to this legislature but to the whole country." These were words of high praise by the opposition during a time of stress.

On 8 November the cabinet was in operation. All the old issues again arose, but the cabinet was endangered not so much by the issues as by the battle for power between the supporters of the queen and those who wished to restrict her authority. At last the queen exerted her influence in the legislature in opposition to Wilcox, and on 12 January 1893, the cabinet was ousted. The vote of no confidence was exactly the two-thirds majority necessary for dismissal. The following morning the queen named a new cabinet.

Affairs were skidding toward an unpleasant conclusion. Queen

Liliuokalani pursued her wish for a new constitution with single-mindedness. On 14 January she prorogued the legislature. That afternoon the queen announced she would proclaim a new constitution the same day. Liliuokalani then called her new cabinet together and requested that they sign her constitution. The cabinet members were startled and alarmed. They said they could not do so, and asked for time to study the constitution. Liliuokalani became very angry at the cabinet's refusal to grant her request. The crowd that had assembled waited doggedly to hear her announcement. At last the queen appeared and said she would proclaim a new constitution within a short time.

When the news reached Honolulu's business leaders that the queen was planning on proclaiming a new constitution, they hastily assembled to decide what action to take. As a precaution they formed a Committee of Safety to lay plans and guard their interests. Albert Wilcox, a brother of George Wilcox and also a legislative representative from Kauai, was for a brief time one of the thirteen members of the committee. Lorrin A. Thurston, a leader among those who wanted the monarchy overthrown and the Islands annexed by the United States, said the action of the queen was an act of revolution and the monarchy must be brought to an end. On Sunday the Committee of Safety called for a mass meeting to be held the next day at 2:00 P.M.

Realizing their desperate situation, four of the new cabinet members sought the advice of businessmen who were considered loyal to the queen, and jointly they drafted a statement that they hoped would appease the opposition. The statement said the matter of a new constitution was at an end. Any changes in the fundamental law of the land would be sought by constitutional means. This proclamation was signed by the queen, who must have at last realized her actions had placed the monarchy in danger of its very existence. The statement was issued on Monday morning, 16 January. But it was too late for proclamations. The life of the monarchy could be measured in hours.

On Sunday a group of royalist supporters had met to decide what could be done in addition to issuing a proclamation. Some wanted to declare martial law and arrest the Committee of Safety. It was decided this might bring violence, something the group very much wanted to avoid. It was agreed a mass meeting of royalist supporters should also be held on Monday.

The Monday meeting that had been called by the Committee of Safety was attended by between 1,260 and 1,500 people and was characterized by emotional speeches calling for the overthrow of the mon-archy. The mass meeting of the royalist supporters attracted a shifting crowd of between 500 and 1,000. The royalists had little to cheer about, since the queen had publicly withdrawn her demand for the establishment of a new constitution. At about 5:00 P.M. Monday, a 162-man armed force was landed from the USS *Boston* on the request of John L. Stevens, U.S. minister.

The next day brought an end to the monarchy. Albert Wilcox went to see if Aliiolani Hale, the government building, was held by royalist troops. He reported back that it was not. Sanford Dole, who just that morning had accepted the offer to head the new government, walked to Aliiolani Hale with a small group of men. A proclamation was read announcing the demise of the monarchy and the establishment of a provisional government. It was about 2:00 in the afternoon. Accom-panying Dole was the Committee of Safety, and soon armed sup-porters of the new government began to arrive to supply protection should it be needed. Later the same evening Queen Liliuokalani sur-rendered her kingdom, under protest, not to the provisional govern-ment, but "to the superior force of the United States of America." Liliuokalani was referring to the 162 men landed from the U.S. war-ship *Boston*.

The controversy would continue for years over whether U.S. troops had been landed to intimidate royalist forces or were ashore simply to protect American property and lives. In the end the controversy altered nothing. A great change had taken place in Hawaii and it was done with a surprising lack of violence or commotion.

The men who caused the monarchy to fall were united in one thing. They believed the authoritarian ways of Liliuokalani had to be elimi-nated. What would take their place was much debated. On the one extreme was Lorrin Thurston, who wanted immediate annexation to the United States. Sanford Dole had argued the evening before the overthrow that Princess Kaiulani should occupy the throne under a regency. George Wilcox reluctantly agreed with the annexationists. Herman Widemann, the longtime Kauai resident, remained a royalist, although he realized changes were needed.

Paul Isenberg was in Germany when these events took place. As powerful and persuasive as he was, it is nevertheless unlikely that his presence would have made a difference in the events of January 1893. When he heard about the end of the monarchy Isenberg expressed his opinions to William R. Castle in a direct way, writing that "the actions of the leaders of the mass meeting were too rash." He thought the idea of seeking annexation by the United States was a humiliating one for the Islands.

Paul Isenberg went on to say, "I am surprised that you and your friends could deny the Hawaiians the right of a vote on the question of independence." The statement by Isenberg was not to be taken as an endorsement of democracy, but rather as reflecting his belief that by denying this vote, the constitution of Hawaii had been violated. Isenberg made himself very clear on his concept of governing by popular vote: "I consider universal suffrage the great mistake of the nineteenth century."

Annexation would mean Hawaii would have to abide by U.S. laws governing immigration of laborers, and this could be difficult for the planters. Isenberg thought the dethroning of Liliuokalani had been the right thing to do but he believed the monarchy should have been maintained with Princess Kaiulani on the throne and the nation ruled by a regent with the assistance of able advisers. Finally, he believed the United States did not need to annex Hawaii, because the American government had all the advantages it wanted without any of the expenses of maintaining the Islands.

Annexation was very much an American concept. The residents of English and European descent agreed with the Americans that Liliuokalani had to be removed, but they were against annexation because that meant the Islands would be dominated by Americans. Theo H. Davies, who had earlier retired to England, was moved enough by events to set forth on a crusade to Washington, D.C., to get Princess Kaiulani placed on the throne. Davies was eloquent in his efforts, but they were of no avail. The Americans and the Hawaiian citizens of American descent had their way; they had a plan of action, and they were willing to follow a few leaders who wanted annexation. The annexationists were clearly the most aggressive, if not dominant in numbers.

And so the monarchy came to an end. The leaders from Kauai who were in Honolulu were there only because they were taking part in the legislative session. Once Honolulu's business community felt they had the backing of those who attended their mass meeting, they proceeded, decisions being made by a handful of men. The overturn of the monarchy was a Honolulu-managed affair.

The number of people deeply involved in the overthrow was small. Perhaps a total of 2,500 persons on both sides had enough interest to attend one of the two rallies on Monday afternoon. Certainly many of those in attendance were there out of curiosity. Perhaps 100 men, led by about six intense leaders, made the revolution happen.

From Kauai, George N. Wilcox, who had headed a cabinet for a time and therefore was deeply involved in the final days of the monarchy, was not part of the actual overthrow. His brother, Albert, remained in Honolulu long enough to see the government change hands, and then he returned to Kauai. Paul P. Kanoa, the one-time governor of Kauai, August Dreier, and the Reverend Joseph A. Akina were in the legislature. William O. Smith was also elected from Kauai, although his law office was in Honolulu. Smith's office served as headquarters for the Committee of Safety, and he was one of the most influential men in the planning of the overthrow of the monarchy. William Hyde Rice had been appointed governor of Kauai in 1891 and was not in the legislature or in Honolulu when the critical events of 1893 took place.

If others from Kauai were in Honolulu there is no record of their involvement. Even if some had wanted to be on hand for the momentous event it would have been impossible, for by the time Kauai knew of the crisis it was over. A number of men born on Kauai, or longtime former residents, were in the center of things with one side or the other. Sanford Dole, Cecil Brown, Fredrick Wundenburg, and Herman Widemann were among them, all residents of Oahu at the time.

Not only was the overturn of the monarchy a Honolulu affair, but even more decidedly the idea of annexation had its strongest supporters in Honolulu. If a vote had been taken among Kauai's leaders, it certainly would have been in favor of deposing Liliuokalani, but also of maintaining the monarchy. George N. Wilcox, well disposed to the United States as he was, went along with the idea of annexation reluctantly.

The many people of German and English ancestry on Kauai found a monarchy a more familiar kind of government. In addition, a monarchy would have kept the Americans from gaining additional authority. Generally, their philosophy would have been similar to that expressed by Paul Isenberg, to maintain a monarchy much like that of Great Britain, where the ruler had only symbolic power.

Newspapers had long reflected the mistrust of the monarchy by the business community as well as the frustrations of the monarchy over the restrictions imposed on it. Many considered a confrontation inevitable. Then, in a moment, that confrontation flared forth and was over. The close advisers of the queen later expressed little surprise at the decisive step that had been taken, although Liliuokalani continued through the years to claim dismay about the actions of her adversaries.

On Kauai the news created little excitement. No reports of celebrations or disturbances were made by the sheriff. Juliette Smith, a sister of William O. Smith, noted in her journal on 1 February 1893 that she had heard that her brother and other leaders of the new government were in danger in Honolulu, but there were no further entries on the matter. At Kilauea the pro-British manager, George P. Ewart, was angry enough to at first deny the republic a post office station in his plantation town, although there had been one there previously. Sheriff Wilcox thought it was because Ewart disliked the new government. It was one way the manager could vent his frustrations at the turn of events.

After the feeble attempt at counter-revolution took place in January 1895, a Citizens' Guard was formed on Kauai, as on the other islands. The Citizens' Guard was part-police, part-military. The marshal of the republic issued forms for commissions, and the sheriff on Kauai filled in the names. The Kauai guard was divided into two sections. The Lihue, or east side, was under Edward Broadbent, who later became manager of Grove Farm plantation, and the west side was under T. H. Gibson, a schoolteacher at Makaweli.

The Kauai units of the Citizens' Guard were small in number, although they took their duties seriously. At first they used rifles supplied by the government, and when these were shipped back to Honolulu the guardsmen used their own rifles. They were supplied with ammunition by the republic and continued target practice and held shooting matches for several years.

The change of government was considered less than ideal or perhaps even deplorable to some people on Kauai. For the large number of immigrant workers on the plantations the establishment of a new government was probably of little interest. The Hawaiians, generally, would have preferred a continuation of the monarchy. For the men who ran the plantations the revolution hopefully meant a release from the frustrations of the Kalakaua and Liliuokalani regimes. The Republic of Hawaii promised to provide a firm government that would be financially conservative and would push public improvements. The question of becoming a territory was being debated, and by far the strongest point in its favor was security, both politically and economically.

George Dole was among those who thought Hawaii should not become a territory. Dole, the longtime manager of the sugar plantation at Kapaa on Kauai, had moved to Riverside, California, and he corresponded frequently with his brother Sanford. In January 1896 George wrote to Sanford, "A commercial treaty of general reciprocity with the United States, and self government will be infinitely more satisfactory to you than annexation can ever be."

George Dole felt the push for annexation had gone too far for it to be withdrawn, so he suggested that Hawaii demand so much from the United States that the Islands would be refused. Dole believed the size of the federal government in faraway Washington would make it difficult to have wrongs righted. There were others, of English and German ancestry, who thought there must be a solution other than annexation, but no one came forth with a practical suggestion, and the Islands moved along the path toward union with the United States.

The end of the monarchy marked the close of an era. The years of the provisional government and the republic served as an interlude. With the coming of the territory, a new era began for Kauai and for all Hawaii.

Epilogue

The news that Hawaii had been annexed by the United States reached the Islands on 14 July 1898. From that time on the American flag flew in Hawaii, but for some two additional years the government in the Islands continued to function as it had before. Hawaii would officially become a territory only when the laws of the Islands had been revised to conform with the laws of the United States. The constitution of the republic had been drawn up in anticipation of Hawaii eventually being annexed, but much remained to be done. A Congressional Law Commission performed this tedious chore, formulating the Organic Act, which became the basic law of the territory. Congress approved the Organic Act on 30 April 1900 and in the Islands territorial status was celebrated as an accomplishment on 12 August 1900.

By the time the republic became a territory, Kauai had long ceased to be a separate kingdom. The term leeward islands was no longer applied to Kauai and Niihau, but now meant the small islands that stretched away to the northwest. Old injuries became ever more dim in the minds of successive generations, better transportation reduced the strain and time of travel between Kauai and Oahu, and common hopes for economic well-being through a successful sugar industry further erased distinctions between what had been known as the windward and the leeward islands. And in Washington, D.C., Hawaii was viewed as a single entity, not as a collection of islands with individual distinctions.

To achieve territorial status the men who ran the republic had to make two difficult concessions. The first concerned labor. For decades Hawaii had imported workers under the contract system, a means by which immigrants were brought to the Islands, agreeing to remain on a plantation for a specified length of time, usually three years. The contract system had been opposed by certain leaders in Hawaii for years, but it had been maintained because it filled a need. Newspapers across the United States called the contract labor system "slavery." Finally, the contract system was brought to an end with the Organic Act. After that, workers came as free laborers, able to leave plantations at any time they wished.

Another point of disagreement between the power structure of the republic and the government of the United States was the matter of voting. The leaders of the republic did not believe the mass of people in the Islands were qualified to vote—an idea unacceptable to Congress. In the end, all citizens of the republic would automatically become citizens of the Territory of Hawaii. All males over twenty-one years of age who had been residents of Hawaii for the required length of time were given the right to vote.

If the leaders of Hawaii had to give up the contract labor system and allow broader suffrage than they wanted, they also received welcomed protection. With the great influx of Japanese workers a common question became, "Shall Hawaii become Japanese or Western?" Japan was taking a keen, somewhat aggressive interest in Hawaii. In 1897 Japan had protested to the United States about the possible annexation of Hawaii, and had sent a warship to Honolulu in a show of force. After annexation the rulers of Hawaii felt safely under the protection of the United States, assured that Western influences in the Islands would remain dominant and secure.

Businessmen on the mainland reacted quickly to territorial status. United States control meant security, and the Islands were now viewed as a safe place for investments. The result was a leap in real estate values and in the value of personal property. Total collected real estate taxes for Kauai and Niihau in 1898 were $27,341, and collected taxes on personal property were $37,571. In 1900, when Hawaii was securely in United States hands, collected taxes on real estate on Kauai and Niihau had reached $52,472, and collected taxes on personal property had leaped to $69,432.

There were numerous signs of change, some coming quickly, others coming slowly and inevitably, as the distant United States bureaucracy awakened to its new responsibilities. One of the quicker changes was in the postal system. In 1901 Frank Crawford arrived in Lihue as the first United States postmaster. He came from Indiana and the new Hawaiian names he encountered bewildered him, to the amusement of the Kauaians.

Among the things that came slowly were federal funds for roads, bridges, and port improvements. Expensive and time-consuming, these improvements could never have been afforded by the kingdom or the republic. Before annexation, in 1898, for example, a survey indicated that Kauai had eleven landings with wharfs. At none of these locations was the ocean deep enough or the sea calm enough to allow an interisland steamer to tie up at a pier. As had happened for decades, ships anchored offshore and cargo and passengers were carried to and from the piers in rowboats. Of the eleven wharfs, two were owned by the government and the others were privately owned. The most the government could afford was buoys to mark the passage to a safe anchorage. Likewise, bridges and scows, which took travelers and goods across Kauai's rivers, were often built and maintained by private companies, sometimes with government assistance.

When the port survey of 1898 was made, the small facility at Ahukini in Hanamaulu Bay was only in the planning stage. Ahukini was dredged, and a wharf and a short breakwater were built by Lihue plantation after the territory granted a fifty-year lease on the land around the harbor. Although small and exposed, Ahukini played an important role for years, eventually closing in 1951.

Port Allen on the west side of Kauai, named after Samuel C. Allen, a Honolulu businessman who financed much of its development, was in use from the early 1900s. The harbor remained privately owned by the Kauai Railway Company until the 1930s. Federal help was early recommended for Port Allen, but this aid did not come until the 1940s.

A study of Kauai's ports was authorized by Congress in 1909. The report was made by the Army Corps of Engineers in 1911, recommending that Nawiliwili be the place where major harbor construction be undertaken. A long battle ensued between Ahukini, Port Allen, and Nawiliwili, with the promoters of each location lobbying for territorial and federal support. Nawiliwili eventually won the battle. Ever so slowly the bureaucracy in Washington, D.C. provided funds for construction of a breakwater, for harbor dredging, and for a seawall. The Territory of Hawaii also helped in the effort, constructing a 500-foot concrete pier and a storage warehouse. Work on Nawiliwili Harbor began in 1921 and the harbor was opened in 1930.

At long last Kauai had an adequate, safe harbor. It was a luxury for Kauaians to step from dock to ship and to cross the channel to Honolulu on schedule and in safety. Nothing could have been more symbolic of the change taking place in Hawaii than the establishment of a permanent harbor on Kauai.

The enthusiasm that came with the prospects of a harbor spread to other situations as well. Available capital made it possible to finance enlarged factories, build railroads, and buy heavy field equipment. Mechanical advances meant increased sugar acreage for Hawaii's farmers, and this brought the industry to the point where a new kind of expansion was practical. The expansion took the form of a sugar cooperative, started in 1906 with the purchase of a large refining factory in Crockett, California. The refinery was located on San Pablo Bay, north of Oakland, where ships carrying raw sugar from Hawaii docked at the piers next to the refinery.

The cooperative, named the California and Hawaiian Sugar Refining Corporation, not only processed an increasing amount of Hawaii's raw sugar as the years passed, but also marketed the sugar under the C and H label. The cooperative had been spurred on by Hawaii's increased sugar production and in reaction to Claus Spreckels, who attempted to monopolize West Coast sugar refining and control the price paid to Island planters for raw sugar. With C and H in operation, sugar growing, grinding, refining, and marketing were all controlled by the Hawaii plantations or their agencies. The cooperative was a unifying and stabilizing force for Hawaii's sugar industry.

Most of the changes that marked the turn of the century were in their formative stage when Sanford Dole, pencil in hand, sat down to write his thoughts on yellow, legal-sized sheets of paper. Much had happened since those earlier days when Dole had played soldier at Koloa with antique Russian weapons. Dole had served as president of the republic and was the first appointed governor of the territory. He was well qualified to report on the worries and attitudes of Hawaii's people. At the top of the first sheet of paper he wrote the words, "Hawaii Under Annexation." There followed pages of observations on the situation in the Islands. Dole was candid in his remarks.

> The majority of native Hawaiians have opposed annexation, some from political reasons, based upon the hope of an eventual restoration of the monarchy; others from traditional familiarity with nominal native rule, involving their feelings and prejudices; others from an undefined anxiety lest the annexation of Hawaii to the United States would injure them through loss of civil rights, political privileges, social standing or in some

other way which they could not forecast on many or all of these grounds, with all of which race sentiment was an element of more or less force.

Dole echoed the feelings of many of those who were in power. "The average Hawaiian feels more than he thinks. He has never been able to analyse the political situation very thoroughly, or to carry out any line of thought relating to Hawaiian affairs very far; and he is unable now to think out the question of annexation and how he is to be affected by it." Some Hawaiians, Dole thought, had lost confidence in the monarchy, but would rather have seen the republic remain than have annexation come.

The Portuguese had been in favor of annexation. The Chinese favored maintaining the republic and had many anxieties concerning the possibility of territorial status. The Japanese were not pleased with the extension of American sovereignty in Hawaii, but they accepted it with good grace. Dole thought the number of Japanese as well as Chinese would diminish because many would return to their homelands.

Annexation had brought a "rise in land values of real estate and sugar stock and a general upward tendency in all kinds of business." Land speculators were not happy with the existing land system, wanting to get their hands on government lands. There was some discontent among those who had been involved with the civil service under the republic. They found the spoils system had been disrupted, but hoped it would reappear under the territory.

It was very important, Dole believed, that there had been an intermediate period between the time of the monarchy and the territory.

It is most important that the political development of Hawaii shall be a growth from former conditions rather than that the present political plant should be uprooted and another started in its place. It is fortunate there was no sudden change of the civil system upon the transfer of sovereignty. That in itself was shock enough for the time being.

The time of transition had been slow. It "had a quieting effect upon the political situation, with its enthusiastic annexationists, its enthusiastic anti-annexationists, its royalists and its great mass of puzzled and anxious people without definite views."

Sanford Dole had a dream that he shared with other leaders of the territory, a dream that Hawaii should become a land of small farmers: "[If] they are, as a rule, men with families, content to make their permanent homes on their holdings and looking to the cultivation of the soil instead of speculation for a living, the political and social future of the country will be secure." Dole's dream never materialized. Even as he wrote of his hopes, the number of sugar farmers was decreasing while plantations were growing in size.

Dole recalled that Hawaii as a civilized community was older than any part of the United States west of the Rocky Mountains. "I do not know that anywhere there is a civilized community whose social life is more natural and unconventional without loss of refinement than that existing in the Hawaiian Islands. . . . A charm of Hawaiian society is its cosmopolitan quality. Every large social gathering has representatives from the great world races—Polynesian, Anglo-Saxon, Celt, Scandinavian, Franks, Mongolians."

Dole noted the increase in population that territorial status had brought, and he was concerned that people would come so fast that Hawaii would lose some of its good qualities. "What will be the result when the American comes as he is coming now, and faster? Will the Hawaiian community still continue to dominate the situation and assimilate the arrivals as fast as they come or will the newcomers, before they become Hawaiian assert themselves and be a law unto themselves and the old society, making their social sentiment and indifference toward the native Hawaiian to be the paramount unwritten code?"

In his final paragraphs Sanford Dole was optimistic, but he was also cautious.

> Without doubt the union of little Hawaii with great America lifts the curtain before a future full of great possibilities to Hawaii. . . .
>
> We shall undoubtedly have our disappointments. There will be some bad mixed with the good. But there will be growth beyond all our precedents. Our local world will be larger and we shall be in touch with the great communities of the rest of the world. We are Americans now, for better or worse.

Notes

The brief references in the notes are keyed to the Bibliography. The following abbreviations are used. Fuller information is given in the bibliography which is listed in alphabetical order.

ABCFM   American Board of Commissioners for Foreign Missions
AH   State Archives of Hawaii
BPBM   Bernice P. Bishop Museum
F.O. & Ex.   Foreign Office and Executive
HEA   Hawaiian Evangelical Association
HHS   Hawaiian Historical Society
HMCS   Hawaiian Mission Children's Society
Int. Dept.   Interior Department
KHS   Kauai Historical Society
KM   Kauai Museum
PMB   Pacific Manuscripts Bureau
RHAS   Royal Hawaiian Agricultural Society
UH   University of Hawaii, Hamilton Library

CHAPTER ONE   *A Rippling on the Water*

Waialeale: Wilcox; George Dole; Eric Knudsen, "Waialeale."

The Hawaiians were sensitive to the world about them: Luomala, "Creative Processes"; Kamakau, *The Works of the People of Old*, 3–19.

"Beautiful is Kauai": Plews, 188.

Flora and fauna: Hillebrand, XV-XXIV; Rock, 76–78; Berger generally; Neal generally.

Wailua Valley: Dickey; Walter Smith; Salisbury; Lydgate, "Wailua."

Heiaus of Wailua: Bennett, 125–128; Damon, *The Heiau at Wailua;* Thrum, "Tales from the Temples," 39–41.

The story of Maui: Dickey, 16–18.

Holoholoku: Stauder, "A Study of Two Sites at Wailua."

"The child of a chief": Damon, *The Heiau at Wailua.*

The Crest of the Bird: A conversation with Juliet Rice Wichman, 20 July 1975.

The story of Moikeha: *Fornander Collection* vol. 4, 118–124; Emerson, "The Long Voyages of the Ancient Hawaiians," 14–24.

Geology: Macdonald and Abbott, 381–401; Stearns, 82–93.

"The density of the population": Handy, *The Native Culture in the Marquesas,* 9.

Origins of the Hawaiians: Buck, 239–258; Joesting, 7–11; Oliver, 1121–1122; Golson generally; Lewis, 302–305; Sinoto, "The Marquesas"; Bellwood, 97–109.

Indonesian-Polynesian connections with the Republic of Malagasy: Thompson and Adloff, 3; Mervyn Brown, 10–15.

Canoes of the Marquesas and Tahiti: Haddon and Hornell, vol. 1, 32, 79–81.

The story of Paao: Emerson, "The Long Voyages of the Ancient Hawaiians," 5–13; Stokes, "Whence Paao?"

CHAPTER TWO   *There Were a People Called Menehune*

Poi pounders: Buck, *Arts and Crafts of Hawaii,* 27–33; Bennett, 65–71; A conversation with Yoshihiko Sinoto, 7 September 1976.

A discovery of significance in the Marquesas: Sinoto, "An Archaeologically Based Assessment," 116.

Heiaus: Bennett, 50–53; Emory, *Archaeology of Nihoa and Necker Islands,* 108.

Language: Rev. Ellis, 13; Fornander, *An Account of the Polynesian Race,* vol. 2, 59; Kuykendall, vol. 1, 104.

Menehune: Oliver, 765–769; Handy, *History and Culture in the Society Islands,* 7–8; Luomala, *The Menehune of Polynesia;* William Hyde Rice, 3–46; A conversation with Kenneth Emory, 1 December 1977.

"Go to the Mountains": Handy, *History and Culture in the Society Islands,* 8.

Menehune in Wainiha Valley: Lydgate, "The Affairs of the Wainiha Hui," 125–126.

"It is a matter of observation": Emerson, *Unwritten Literature of Hawaii,* 119.

Social organization: Kamakau, *Ka Poe Kahiko,* 3–9; Malo, 52–76.

Kapus: Kamakau, *Ka Poe Kahiko,* 9–17.

Kukona: Kamakau, *Ruling Chiefs,* 194.

Death: Malo, 96–99; Kamakau, *Ka Poe Kahiko,* 33–44.

Pele legend: William Hyde Rice, *Hawaiian Legends,* 7–17; Emerson, *Pele and Hiiaka.*

Ke'e: Pukui, "The Hula"; Bennett, 136–138; Emory, "Ruins at Kee," 88–93; Kelly.

"In the forests": Emerson, *Unwritten Literature of Hawaii,* 18.

"Laka dwells in a beautiful forest": Interview with Mary Kawena Pukui, 19 September 1977.

CHAPTER THREE   *"Their Hospitality and Generosity Were Unbounded"*

Chapter title: Portlock, 193.

Cook expedition: Cook and King, vol. 2, 190–252; vol. 3, 88–99; Beaglehole,

Journals, vol. 3, part 1, 263–288, 574–582, 585–591; Kamakau, *Ruling Chiefs,* 92–104.

Clerke "Obviously . . . must make for Kauai": Beaglehole, *The Life of Captain James Cook,* 677.

Cook expedition contact with the Russians: Cook and King, vol. 2, 495–524; vol. 3, 184–234; Beaglehole, *Journals,* vol. 3, part 1, 449–458, 646–654, 659–676; Hotimsky.

Portlock and Dixon: Portlock, 81–90, 169–194, 302–312; Dixon, 54–56, 108–117, 256–261.

"They received us with joy": Meares, xxxix.

Early traders: Ingraham; Delano, 387–403; Bradley, 15–27; William D. Alexander, "Early Visitors to the Hawaiian Islands"; Bernice Judd, *Voyages to Hawaii Before 1860.*

The sandalwood tree: C. S. Judd, "The Parasitic Habit of the Sandalwood Tree"; Degener, 261–267.

The sandalwood trade: Lydgate, "Sandalwood Days"; Bradley, 53–120; Kuykendall, vol. 1, 85–88.

"Sandal wood &c from Canton": quoted in Bradley, 29.

Vancouver: Vancouver, vol. 1, 167–190; vol. 2, 213–233; vol. 3, 72–79; Bradley, 42–45; Kuykendall, vol. 1, 39–44.

"Previously to the departure": Vancouver, vol. 1, 188.

Broughton: Broughton, 44–47, 72–80.

CHAPTER FOUR *"Is It Face Up or Face Down?"*

Chapter title: Kamakau, *Ruling Chiefs,* 195, on meeting of Kaumualii and Kamehameha.

Political situation in Hawaii: Kuykendall, vol. 1, 29–31.

"The island was suffering": Jarves, *History of the Hawaiian or Sandwich Islands,* 182.

After the conquest of Oahu: Charles Bishop, 134, 142–144.

"Young seem'd to wish": Boit, 7–8.

"He told me he meant": Charles Bishop, 146.

Age of Kaumualii: Stokes, "New Bases for Hawaiian Chronology," 32–33.

Lineage of Kaumualii: Kamakau, *Ruling Chiefs,* 165; Kuykendall, vol. 1, 30.

"short and lusty": Surgeon Ellis, vol. II, 134.

First invasion attempt of Kauai: Kamakau, *Ruling Chiefs,* 172–173; Charles Bishop, 143–144.

Second invasion attempt of Kauai: Shaler, 100–109; Turnbull, vol. 2, 13–45; Lydgate, "Kaumualii," 21–43; Kamakau, *Ruling Chiefs,* 187–189; Jarves, *History of the Hawaiian or Sandwich Islands,* 191–192; Kuykendall, vol. 1, 48–49.

"Do not go": Kamakau, *Ruling Chiefs,* 188.

"Let us go": Kamakau, *Ruling Chiefs,* 187.

"It was a very virulent pestilence": Kamakau, *Ruling Chiefs,* 189.

News of the epidemic reaches Kauai: Lisiansky, 112.

Early Western traders: Bradley, 1–52; Morison; Kuykendall, vol. 1, 20–28.

"A youth who had rendered": Charles Bishop, 141, 306–307.

Meeting of Kaumualii and Kamehameha: *Kuokoa,* 10 August 1867, Article No. 36, Kuykendall Collection; Kamakau, *Ruling Chiefs,* 195–196.

CHAPTER FIVE *An Interesting Diversion*

Early explorers in Alaska: Gruening, on Bering, 3–8, and on Steller, 9–16; Golder, *Bering's Voyages,* vol. 2, on Bering and Steller; Stejneger on Steller.

The Russian American Company and Baranov: Chevigny generally; Khlebnikov generally.

Hugh Moore: Joesting, 58; Khlebnikov, 8.

"gladly send a ship": Pierce, 2, quotes George Heinrich Langsdorff.

Russian trade with Hawaii: Kuykendall, vol. 1, 55–56; Langsdorff, 165; Bradley, 51.

Campbell: Campbell, 83, 88.

The *Bering:* Howay.

"I received from Captn Bennett": Pierce, 40.

Scheffer: Pierce generally; Arthaud.

"It is also desirable": Pierce, 43.

"I shall rely": Pierce, 44.

"You, the King": Pierce, 46.

"every confidence": Pierce, 60.

Arrival of the *Otkrytie:* Mazour.

"At first": Pierce, 49.

Scheffer and Kaumualii agreement: Pierce, 12, 72–73; Khlebnikov, 93–94.

Fort Elizabeth: McCoy.

Scheffer and Americans: Khlebnikov, 93; William D. Alexander, "The Proceedings of the Russians on Kauai," 10–11; Pierce, 20.

Departure of Scheffer: Daws, *Shoal of Time,* 52–53.

"The Company also claims": Dobel, 334–335.

"The American papers": Pierce, 122.

The Whitney vineyard: Gilman, "Journey of a Canoe Voyage," 8.

"Thus we advanced": Macrae, 21.

CHAPTER SIX *"I Die With Affection"*

Chapter title: Bingham, 224, quoting one of Kaumualii's stewards.

"That thoughtless": Simpson, vol. 2, 14.

Sandalwood and Yankees: Morison, 15–23; Colcord, 1–2; Bradley, 26–32.

"I almost dispaired": Morison quotes letter to Marshall & Wildes from John C. Jones, 6 July 1821, 32.

Sandalwood statistics: Schmitt, 368.

"Felt distressed": *Missionary Herald,* XXVII(December 1831), 382.

Carrying sandalwood: Lydgate, "Sandalwood Days," 52.

"The procuring": Simpson, vol. 2, 13.

"they have not cut": Morison quotes letter to Marshall & Wildes from John C. Jones, 6 July 1821, 33.

"sundry merchandise": F.O. & Ex. 1820.

Kaumualii buys the *Becket:* Morison quotes letter to Marshall & Wildes from John C. Jones, 6 July 1821, 32.

"Tomoree is fast growing old": Morison quotes letter to Marshall & Wildes from John C. Jones, 5 October 1821, 36.

Bad effects of sandalwood trade: Bradley, 69–71; Kuykendall, vol. 1, 434–436.

Liholiho travels to Kauai: The story of Liholiho's trip was reported in the *Missionary Herald,* XVIII(August 1822), 242–244, by Stewart, 83–84, and by Bingham, 138–139. The accounts agree in major aspects.

"King Liholiho, hear!": Jarves, *History of the Hawaiian or Sandwich Islands,* 228; also Kamakau, *Ruling Chiefs,* 252.

"Haupu, the head man": Bingham, 146.

Kaumualii and Kaahumanu: Stewart, 229.

"thus holding father and son": Jarves, *History of the Hawaiian or Sandwich Islands,* 229.

Kaahumanu: Carter.

"weekly service": Levi Chamberlain, 31 March 1824.

Kaumualii's death: Stewart, 289–290.

"that they might rise together": note by Rev. Ellis in Stewart, 293.

Praise of Kaumualii: Stewart, 291–292; Jarves, *History of the Hawaiian or Sandwich Islands,* 244; Bingham, 224; Kamakau, *Ruling Chiefs,* 254; Turnbull, vol. 2, 33–34.

Pride of Hawaii: William D. Alexander, "The Story of Cleopatra's Barge."

"Kiaimakani": Bingham, 221–223.

"One of his old stewards": Bingham, 224.

On George P. Kaumualii: Spoehr; Stauder, "George, Prince of Hawaii."

"Some of the insurgents": Bingham, 234.

Battle at the Russian fort: Stewart received his information secondhand, 312–313; Jarves, *History of the Hawaiian or Sandwich Islands,* 244–245, wrote about fifteen years later. Bingham was an eyewitness, 233–235.

Battle at Wahiawa: Bingham, Jarves, *History of the Hawaiian or Sandwich Islands,* Kamakau, *Ruling Chiefs,* and Stewart all wrote about the battle, but were not there. Samuel Whitney walked across the battlefield three days after the fighting, journal, 23 August 1824; Kamakau, 268, and Jarves, 246, essentially agree with Whitney. The columnist from *The Polynesian,* "Drippings From My Journal," 3 October 1841, was probably Jarves.

Dispossession of the Kauai chiefs: Jarves, *History of the Hawaiian or Sandwich Islands,* 245–246, and Kamakau, *Ruling Chiefs,* 269, give forthright accounts.

Lands received on Kauai by Victoria Kamamalu: Indices of Awards, 160–164.

Makaweli lands granted to Kamamalu: Indices of Awards, 164.

Claim of Ahukai: Native Register, vol. 9, number 6508, 186B. The refusal of his claim is in Land Commission Awards, number 6508, 318.

Deborah Kapule: Bingham, 98, 220–221, 477.

"Had the widow of Kaumualii": Jarves, *History of the Hawaiian or Sandwich Islands,* 246.

Chapin: Mercy Whitney journal, 13 August 1821.

"At length her conduct": Mercy Whitney journal, 14 November 1839.

"they reached Wailua": Wilkes, vol. 4, 68.
"She has always": "Drippings From My Journal," *The Polynesian,* 3 October 1841.
"Early in the morning": Lyman, 171.
Obituary of Deborah Kapule: *The Polynesian,* 10 September 1855.

CHAPTER SEVEN   *"Fruitful Fields . . . and Schools and Churches"*

Chapter title: *Instructions of the Prudential Committee,* 27.
Departure of missionaries from New England: Bingham gives a good account of this, 60–64.
Opukahaia: Dwight.
"Satan is not yet bound": *Missionary Herald* XV(November 1819), 504.
"from thousands of hearts": Gallaudet, 15.
Difficult departure for missionaries: Bingham, 62.
"beautiful plains": From the journal of Samuel and Nancy Ruggles in the *Boston Recorder,* 21 April 1821.
"As soon as George": *Boston Recorder,* 21 April 1821.
"anxious to see": *Boston Recorder,* 28 April 1821.
"I believe the females": Holman, 38; also see Halford, 12–22.
"best house": Mercy Whitney journal, 24 April 1821.
"I never saw": Daniel Chamberlain to American Board, 11 November 1822. ABCFM.
Preaching and teaching: *Instructions of the Prudential Committee,* 19–33.
Reducing Hawaiian to a written language: Bingham, 152–156; Spaulding.
"This is my communication": Bingham, 172.
"At the examination": Gulick, 124–125.
Statistics on church and schools: These can be found in the Mission Station Reports, HMCS.
Description of Samuel Whitney: *The Friend,* 15 April 1846; Damon, *Koamalu,* 146.
William French's attempt to grow sugarcane: *Sandwich Island Mirror,* 15 April 1840.
Ladd and Company store on Kauai: Hooper Diaries, 19 February 1835.
Lease of Ladd and Company: Jackson, Appendix B, 126–129.
French's attempt to lease land: Levi Chamberlain journal, 3 February 1832.
Problems and development at Koloa: Hooper Diaries; also see Jackson, and Arthur Alexander.
Koloa money: Medcalf and Russell, 5.
"I beg of you": Hooper Diaries, 29 April 1836.
"the full right": *Report of the Proceedings,* Appendix B, 30.
Ladd and Company held in high esteem: *Report of the Proceedings,* 66–72; *The Polynesian,* 19 June, 17 July 1841.
Interisland travel: Jarves, *Scenes and Scenery,* 88–94.
"with detached sentences": Bates, 157.
Koloa before Ladd and Company: Journal letter of Samuel Whitney, vol. 2, 395, Missionary Letters; Bernice Judd, "Koloa."

Outsiders at Koloa: W. O. Smith, 6 April 1915, *Garden Island;* John Cook, 23–24.

"The rigidity": Jarves, *Scenes and Scenery,* 104–105.

"Your views are not to be limited": *Instructions of the Prudential Committee,* 27.

CHAPTER EIGHT   *A Conquered Race*

"There has been": Mercy Whitney journal, 12 April 1834.

Kaikioewa orders culprits hung: Reynolds journal, 26 May 1834; *The Friend,* June 1896.

"a sight probably": Mercy Whitney journal, 5 May 1834.

"Shocking as it may seem": Mission Station Report, Kauai, 1834.

"the loafers": Kamakau, *Ruling Chiefs,* 269; Jarves, *Scenes and Scenery,* 158–159.

"It was with much difficulty": Jarves, "Sketches of Kauai," 71.

Father Arsenius Walsh: Kuykendall, vol. 1, 144–147; Yzendoorn, 175–178.

"I have celebrated the first mass": Walsh journal, 25 December 1841.

Father Barnabe Castan: Walsh journal, 27 and 29 January 1842; Yzendoorn, 176.

Troubles at Moloaa: Walsh journal, 18 and 19 February 1842.

Brown remembers Walsh: Malcolm Brown, 23.

Death of Walsh: *Hawaiian Gazette,* 20 October 1869; Johnson, 323–325.

Gorham Gilman recruits workers: Gilman, "Rustications on Kauai and Niihau," 4–15.

Coffee: Thrum, "Notes on the History of Coffee Culture"; Kuykendall, vol. 1, 316–317.

"was conducting a small cloth factory": *Hawaiian Annual,* 1903, 169.

Kaikioewa's early life: Kamakau, *Ruling Chiefs,* 350–351.

Kaikioewa and Kauikeaouli: *Hawaiian Annual,* 1914, 195.

Kaikioewa goes to aid of Kalanimoku: Bingham, 237.

William French and Kaikioewa: *Sandwich Island Mirror,* 15 April 1840.

Lihue: Mary Agnes Rice; Damon, *Koamalu,* 401–408; Wright.

"There is a fine tract of land": Jarves, *Scenes and Scenery,* 146.

"Lihui": Wilkes, vol. 4, 67.

Kekauonohi: Kamakau, *Ruling Chiefs,* 280, 397.

Paul Kanoa: Damon, *Koamalu,* 598–600, 738–741.

Excel: Damon, *Koamalu,* 477–478.

Death of Kanoa: *Honolulu Advertiser,* 11 and 13 November 1885.

Daniel Dole: Damon, *Sanford Ballard Dole,* 4–8, 17.

School at Koloa: Damon, *Sanford Ballard Dole,* 32–41; Burbank.

Students at the Koloa School: Various dates during 1858, Daniel Dole journal; Damon, *Sanford Ballard Dole,* 38–39.

Magazine club and book club: Damon, *Koamalu,* 469–470.

Statistics on declining Hawaiian population: Schmitt, 25.

Royal Hawaiian Agricultural Society *Transactions:* The first annual report was issued in 1850.

An Act For the Government of Masters and Servants: *Penal Code of the Hawaiian Islands,* 170–176.

American apprentice and shipping laws: An Act For the Government and Regulation of Seamen in the Merchant Service, 20 July 1790, First Congress Sess. II, Ch. 29, *The Public Statutes at Large of the United States of America*, 131–135; also see Kuykendall, vol. 1, 330; Coman, 491–495; Johannessen, 49.

"Most of the mills": RHAS *Transactions*, 1850, 69.

Mammoth plows: RHAS *Transactions*, 1853, 66–67.

CHAPTER NINE *Profits Yet To Be Made*

Balena and *Equator: Sailor's Magazine and Naval Journal*, VI(August 1834), 357.

"Reported the loss": Reynolds journal, 28 June and 8 July 1842.

Official count of barrels of oil: Starbuck, 366–367.

William Ladd and Robert Wood: Mercy Whitney journal, 24 June 1842.

Abeel and Marcus: Knapp journal, 6 November 1842.

William Thompson: The Friend, May 1847.

Deserters from the *Hillman:* PMB microfilm 858, from 6 March through 20 March 1852.

Helen Augusta: Bates, 150–152.

Whaling vessels and crews: Hohman, 114–182; Joesting, 91–94.

Sailors on shore leave in Honolulu: Davies, 2–3.

Riot in Honolulu: Parke, 35–44.

Ashore at Koloa: Bates, 171.

"Many's the time": John Cook, 6.

"Three whaleships": James W. Smith journal, 8 April 1865.

"the whaling vessels": Damon, *Koamalu*, 201.

Citizen: Bills, 50–51.

Scotland: The arrivals, departures, and catch of the several voyages of the *Scotland* as reported in New Bedford are recorded in Starbuck; the log of the third voyage is on PMB microfilm 726.

"one Boats crew": PMB microfilm 297, 21 November 1853.

"Two Barrels": PMB microfilm 297, 22 November 1853.

"4 bullocks": Waimea and Koloa, Kauai, Account Book, 1 April 1856. Collector General of Customs, Ports of Entry.

Value of cargo of the *Scotland:* The catch of the *Scotland* on its third voyage is listed in Starbuck, 516–517. Morgan, 143, charts the New England price of sperm oil, whale oil, and bone. For calculating purposes 31 gallons of oil were figured per barrel. Expenses of the voyage are based on information in Hohman, 244–271.

Estimated income of George Smith: Captain Smith was entitled to one-sixteenth of the profit of the voyage of the *Scotland* starting 18 August 1854, according to the "Whalemen's Shipping Papers," PMB microfilm 407.

Estimated income of seamen on the *Scotland:* The lays of the crew of the *Scotland* are listed in the "Whalemen's Shipping Papers," PMB microfilm 407.

Estimated income of Hawaiian field workers: Based on the twelve and one-half cents a day paid workers at Koloa plantation.

Great Stone Fleet: Gordon.

Shenandoah: Hunt. For a list of ships sunk in the Pacific, 272–273.

"Krull has been jubilant": Marshal of the Kingdom, from the Sheriff of Kauai, 16 August 1865.

Destruction of whalers in the Arctic: William King; *Honolulu Advertiser,* 28 October 1871.

Founding of Lihue plantation: Damon, *Koamalu,* 408–413; Kuykendall, vol. 1, 324–325.

James F. B. Marshall: Sullivan, 81–84.

"accompanied with terrible thunder": RHAS *Transactions,* 1854, 7.

Victor Prevost: Damon, *Koamalu,* 582–586; RHAS *Transactions,* 1850, 68.

William Harrison Rice: The life story of William Harrison Rice is interspersed through the first 600 pages of *Koamalu* by Ethel Damon.

"The sea at Hana": Krout, 37.

"Common stock": Common stock v. Salaries 1831–1848, Sandwich Islands Mission Collection, HMCS.

Home mission: Anderson, 315–326.

Koamalu: Damon, *Koamalu,* vol. 1 generally.

"It is a great blessing": James W. Smith journal, 14 April 1855.

Paul Isenberg: Damon, *Koamalu,* 533–569; Nellist, 125–129; *Pacific Coast Commercial Record,* 1 May 1892.

Thomas Lafon: Halford, 159–174.

Robert C. Wyllie: Phillips; Hopkins, 497–512; *The Friend,* November 1865.

The dignified impression made by officials: Wyllie (no date) Doc. 74, F.O. & Ex.

"in the national color": *The Polynesian,* 1 December 1860.

Godfrey Wundenberg: Damon, *Koamalu,* 341–342.

Kamehameha IV and Queen Emma at Princeville: Josephine Wundenberg King.

Emmaville: Wyllie to Emma, 2 August 1863, Queen Emma Collection, AH.

Lady Jane Franklin: Korn, *The Victorian Visitors;* Woodward, 305–320.

"but for what": Wyllie to Ricord, 19 October 1857, Foreign File, F.O. & Ex., Misc.

"Sacred to the Memory": *Hawaiian Gazette,* 16 September 1865; Collinson, 103.

"Of all the ladies": Copy of a letter to Kamehameha IV from Robert C. Wyllie, 3 September 1861. Jane Franklin (Lady) Collection.

Gossip concerning Franklin and Wyllie: Wyllie to Emma, 2 August 1863, Queen Emma Collection.

"which is very depressing": Wyllie to Anderson, 26 December 1864, Misc. Foreign, F.O. & Ex.

"open blister": Wyllie to Kamehameha V, 12 September 1865, Local Officials, F.O. & Ex.

"The property was encumbered": Damon quotes from a letter by Mary S. Rice in *Koamalu,* 607.

" 'Where's Wyllie' ": John Cook, 26.

Abner Wilcox on young Wyllie: Estate of R. C. Wyllie Junr., First Circuit Court, Probate 2327.

"became perfectly sensible"; John Cook, 26.

"I Robert Crichton Wyllie": Estate of R. C. Wyllie Junr., First Circuit Court, Probate 2327. With the will are the original papers including the phrases and words written by Wyllie.

"I left home": James W. Smith journal entries from 3 through 7 February 1866.

Obituary of Wyllie: *Hawaiian Gazette,* 17 February 1866.
"appreciate every effort": *The Friend,* July, 1866.

CHAPTER TEN   *An Island All Their Own*

Gorham Gilman on Niihau: Gilman, "Rustications on Kauai and Niihau."
Arrival of the *Bessie: Honolulu Advertiser,* 24 September 1863.
Reverend Damon's observations: Bird, 184.
History of the Sinclairs prior to Hawaii: von Holt, 1–25; Andersen, 160–166.
Offer of land on Oahu: von Holt, 31.
Niihau a greener place: Conversation with Roland Gay, 9 October 1975.
"The whole island is now owned": Luther Gulick to Rufus Anderson, 28 April 1865. ABCFM.
Valdemar Knudsen: von Holt, 41–61.
Purchase of Makaweli lands by Elizabeth Sinclair: Bureau of Conveyances, Record Book 19, 29 June 1865, 416–417.
Waldemar Muller: Holograph Letters, 28 March through 6 April 1873, Isabella Lucy (Bird) Bishop.
Muller in Honolulu: *Hawaiian Gazette,* 11 October 1871.
Muller at Koloa: Grove Farm Account Book 1864–1883. See years 1875–1883 in general. Grove Farm Homestead.
A. Kaukau on affairs on Niihau: Niihau Church and Statistical Reports, HEA Archives.
"Higher far I hold my birthright": Francis Sinclair, 8.
Mann and Brigham: MacCaughey, 27–28; von Holt, 57.
Heinrich Wawra: von Holt, 57; Wilcox; MacCaughey, 28.
Jules Remy: MacCaughey, 26–27.
John C. Jones trades in California: Davis, 2.
Price of beef at Lihue: Mary Agnes Rice.
Estimate of the number of cattle: Mr. Wyllie's answers to questions put by M. Dudoit, Consul of France, 22 April 1846, F.O. & Ex.; 1852 estimate, RHAS *Transactions,* 1852, 91.
Duncan McBryde: 12 October 1857, Int. Dept.
Gerrit P. Judd buys horses: 21 July 1851, Int. Dept.
Importation of animals: Henke.
Joseph Gardner: *Hawaiian Annual* 1903, 169.
Kalakaua and Knudsen: Kalakaua to Valdemar Knudsen, 14 February and 1 March 1877. Valdemar Knudsen Collection.
Hui Kawaihau: Charles Dole.
Emma on Kauai: Forbes; Eric A. Knudsen and Gurre Noble, 135–141.
Emma at the Alakai Swamp: Hulme.
Early years of rice-growing: Coulter and Chun; Kuykendall, vol. 2, 150–151, and vol. 3, 47–48; *Hawaiian Annual* 1877, 45–49.
Leong Pah On: Wong, 18–22.
Chulan and Company: Kuykendall, vol. 3, 48.
Rice birds: Letter to Hon. G. Rhodes, 3 July 1876, Int. Dept.
"Gunny sack wives": Tin-Yuke Char and Wai Jane Char, 12–13.

Wyllie on steam transportation: *The Friend,* 4 September 1844.
Akamai: Kemble, 12–13.
Kalama: The Polynesian, 12 January 1856.
Kilauea: Kemble, 16–24.
Annie Laurie: Hawaiian Gazette, 17 February 1866; *Hawaiian Annual* 1889, 70–81.
Saginaw: Head; *Honolulu Advertiser,* 28 December 1870, 4, 7, and 21 January 1871; *Hawaiian Gazette,* 28 December 1870.
Stripping of the bodies at Kalihiwai: Lydgate, "The Wreck of the *Saginaw.*"

CHAPTER ELEVEN   *Kauai Could Excel at This Enterprise*

The Gap: Mary Agnes Rice.
Time-consuming difficulties of field work: Krauss and Alexander, 145–146, 232.
Oxen at Kilauea plantation: *The Hawaiian Kingdom Statistical and Commercial Directory,* 403.
Hawaiian Sugar Company irrigation system: *Hawaiian Annual* 1892, 72–75; Kuykendall, vol. 3, 66.
Kilauea celebration: *Honolulu Star-Bulletin,* 25 May 1935.
Railroad at Kilauea: Conde and Best, 150–152; *Honolulu Star-Bulletin,* 25 May 1935; *Honolulu Advertiser,* 8 October 1881.
James Tuthill at Kekaha: Tuthill.
"A large part of our machinery": C. R. Bishop to E. A. Allen, 14 February 1880. Elisha H. Allen Papers.
Robert Macfie and Kilauea: Private Collection.
Agencies representing Kauai plantations: *Hawaiian Annual* 1897, 159–160.
Lihue plantation expansion: *Evening Bulletin Industrial Edition,* November 1901.
Grove Farm expansion: Krauss and Alexander, 181–234.
McBryde expansion: Dean; *Ampersand,* Summer 1979.
"In my opinion": W. Hillebrand to Minister of Interior, 6 June 1877, Int. Dept.
Arrival of Portuguese: Kuykendall, vol. 3, 122–126; *Planters' Monthly,* 2(1883), 149–150, 153.
Reverend Joel Mahoe and Gilbertese: Eastman, 17–22; Gilbert Islands Mission in Hawaiian Islands 1880–1890, Micronesian Mission, HEA Archives.
German immigrant workers: Hormann, 62–77; Kuykendall, vol. 3, 133–135; Schweizer, 110–144.
Contract of Louis Depken: Private Collection.
Lutheran Church at Lihue: Hormann, 91–98; Lo.
Anton Cropp: Arthur Alexander, 85–86.
Dunnotter Castle: Hawaiian Gazette, 14 and 21 September 1886; *Honolulu Advertiser,* 14, 15, and 17 September 1886.
Planter: Hawaiian Gazette, 2 February 1886; *Honolulu Advertiser,* 1 February 1886.
Kalakaua on Kauai: *Honolulu Advertiser,* 28 March 1874; *Hawaiian Gazette,* 29 April 1874.
Difficulties of Kalakaua: Kuykendall, vol. 3, 4–5; Joesting, 208–232; Damon, *Sanford Ballard Dole,* 196–220.
Mass meeting and speech of William Hyde Rice: *Hawaiian Gazette,* 1 July 1887.

Leprous persons in Kalalau Valley: Marshal of the Kingdom, from the Sheriff of Kauai, 16, 23, 29, and 30 June 1888; also 29 March 1889.

Judge Kauai: *Hawaiian Gazette,* 4 July 1893; Kalalau Expedition 1893, F.O. & Ex.

Troubles at Waimea: Marshal of the Kingdom, from the Sheriff of Kauai, 8 June 1888.

Louis Stolz: Stolz to Hitchcock with Marshal of the Republic, from the Sheriff of Kauai, 17 May 1893.

Shooting of Stolz: Mouritz, 73–74.

Expedition to Kalalau: Kalalau Expedition 1893, F.O. & Ex.; *Hawaiian Gazette,* 4, 11, and 18 July 1893.

Death of Dr. Jared Smith: Mouritz, 75–76; draft of a letter from Juliette Smith to Anna Farley regarding brother Jared's death, 1897, Smith Papers; *Forty-Sixth Annual Report of the Hawaiian Mission Children's Society,* 24–25; Marshal of the Republic, from the Sheriff of Kauai, 25 September 1897.

Christian Bertelmann: A conversation with Juliet Rice Wichman, 15 April 1982.

CHAPTER TWELVE   *In Favor of Maintaining the Monarchy*

Chinese arrivals of 1880–1881: Kuykendall, vol. 3, 135–141; Coman, 35–42; *Hawaiian Annual* 1894, 70–78.

Smallpox on Kauai: Marshal of the Kingdom, from the Sheriff of Kauai, 11, 18, and 24 February, 4, 11, 19, and 26 March, and 8 and 29 April 1881; *Hawaiian Gazette,* 16 February and 2 March 1881.

Japanese immigration organized: Conroy, 54–80; Kuykendall, vol. 3, 155–172.

Controls on Chinese: Kuykendall, vol. 3, 174–185; *Hawaiian Annual* 1890, 81–90, and 1894, 70–78.

Statistics on workers on Kauai plantations: See the annual *Report of the President of the Bureau of Immigration;* also the *Hawaiian Annual* for the years concerned.

Strike at Kilauea: *Hawaiian Gazette,* 26 January and 2 February 1881; Marshal of the Kingdom, from the Sheriff of Kauai, 21 and 28 January and 11 February 1881.

Court case between Macfie and Moniz: R. A. Macfie v. Jacintho Moniz et al.

Disturbance at Princeville: Marshal of the Kingdom, from the Sheriff of Kauai, 7 November 1865.

Trouble at Koloa: Lorrin A. Thurston, Minister of Interior and President, Board of Immigration, to H. Hackfeld & Co., 8 February 1889, Bureau of Immigration Letter Book.

Raid at Kilauea: Marshal of the Kingdom, from the Sheriff of Kauai, 24 December 1889, and 4 and 9 January 1890.

Kauai police: The history of the Kauai police can best be traced in the files of the Marshal of the Kingdom, from the Sheriff of Kauai.

Fairview Hotel: *Directory and Hand-Book,* advertisement opposite 365.

Shifting of population: Handy, *The Hawaiian Planter,* 58–73; Coulter, 14–16.

Liliuokalani's visit to Kauai: *Honolulu Advertiser,* 13, 20, and 21 July 1891; Damon, *Koamalu,* 833.

Kauai Industrial School at Malumalu: "A Statement Concerning the Kauai Industrial School. Its Design, Resources and Needs," 20 June 1891, HEA Archives.

Sacred spring at Kipukai: William Hyde Rice, 74; Damon, *Koamalu,* 385.

Prince Jonah Kuhio Kalanianaole: *Hawaiian Annual* 1923, 43–47; Damon, *Koamalu*, 785.

Wilcox cabinet: Kuykendall, vol. 3, 558–559, and 580–581; Krauss and Alexander, 243–259.

"I think he [Wilcox]": *Daily Bulletin*, 17 September 1892.

Deposing Liliuokalani: Kuykendall, vol. 3, 582–605; Liliuokalani; Joesting, 233–240.

Paul Isenberg on the overthrow of the monarchy: Damon, *Koamalu*, 839–841, quotes a letter to William Castle from Paul Isenberg dated 18 April 1893.

Kauaians in the legislature: Lydecker, 182.

Survey of Kauai's leaders concerning the monarchy: See the *Hawaiian Annual* 1893 for a list of the plantation managers on Kauai. Men of British and German descent formed the majority of managers or owners and they were pro-monarchy, although anti-Liliuokalani. The few managers of American descent were, at best, reluctant supporters of overthrowing the monarchy.

Juliette Smith fears for her brother: Juliette Smith journal, 1 February 1893.

George P. Ewart: Comments on Ewart are in Marshal of the Republic, from the Sheriff of Kauai, 27 July 1895.

Citizens' Guard: Marshal of the Republic, from the Sheriff of Kauai, 16 November, 7 December 1895, and 11 January 1896.

George Dole correspondence: George Dole to Sanford Dole, 24 January 1896, Sanford Dole Papers.

Epilogue

Organic Act: *Organic Act of the Territory of Hawaii.*
Taxes collected on Kauai and Niihau: *Territory of Hawaii—Report of the Treasurer*, 94.
Ports of Kauai: Cajski in general.
Ahukini: Cajski, 69–71.
Port Allen: Cajski, 90–94.
Nawiliwili: Cajski, 76–87.
Sanford Dole: "Hawaii Under Annexation." Dole Collection.

Bibliography

Names of authors, editors, committees, periodicals, and collections of documents are in alphabetical order. The list of references consists basically of the sources cited in the notes. Primary and secondary sources are listed together. If a source is located outside Hawaii, the Hawaii location of a copy of the document is listed. Abbreviations used in the bibliography are listed preceding the notes.

Alexander, Arthur C. *Koloa Plantation, 1835–1935.* Honolulu: Honolulu Star-Bulletin, 1937.

Alexander, Mary Charlotte, comp. *William Patterson Alexander in Kentucky, The Marquesas, Hawaii.* Honolulu: n.p., 1934.

Alexander, Mary C., and Charlotte P. Dodge. *Punahou 1841–1941.* Berkeley and Los Angeles: University of California Press, 1941.

Alexander, William D. "Early Visitors to the Hawaiian Islands." *Hawaiian Annual,* 1890. 37–43.

———. "Private Journal of a Tour of Kauai." Journal Collection, 1849. HMCS. Typescript.

———. "The Proceedings of the Russians on Kauai 1814–1816." HHS *Papers* No. 6, 1894. 1–17.

———. "The Story of Cleopatra's Barge." HHS *Papers* No. 13, 1906. 24–31.

Allen, Elisha H. Papers. UH. Microfilm.

American Board of Commissioners for Foreign Missions (ABCFM). Hawaii Papers, Houghton Library (Harvard), 1820–1900. HMCS.

Ampersand. Magazine. Alexander & Baldwin, Inc. Honolulu.

Andersen, Johannes C. *Place Names of Banks Peninsula: A Topographical History.* Wellington, New Zealand: W. A. G. Skinner, Government Printer, 1927.

Anderson, Rufus. *Hawaiian Islands: Their Progress and Condition Under Missionary Labors.* Boston: Gould and Lincoln, 1864.

Arthaud, John B. "Doctor Afield: Egor Scheffer—Russia's Hawaiian Interloper." *New England Journal of Medicine* 281 (October 2, 1969): 778–780.

Bates, George Washington. *Sandwich Island Notes by A Haole.* New York: Harper & Brothers, 1854.

Beaglehole, J. C. *The Life of Captain James Cook.* Stanford, California: Stanford University Press, 1974.

Beaglehole, J. C., ed. *The Journals of Captain James Cook on His Voyages of Discovery.* 3 vols. Cambridge: Printed for the Hakluyt Society at the University Press, 1955–1967.

Beckwith, Martha. *Hawaiian Mythology.* Honolulu: University of Hawaii Press, 1970. (Originally published in 1940.)

Beechey, F. W. *Narrative of a Voyage to the Pacific and Bering's Strait . . . .* 2 vols. New York: Da Capo Press, 1973. (Reprinted from 1831 edition.)

Bellwood, Peter. *The Polynesians: Prehistory of an Island People.* London: Thames and Hudson, 1978.

Bennett, Wendall C. *Archaeology of Kauai.* Honolulu: BPBM Bulletin 80, 1931.

Berger, Andrew. *Hawaiian Birdlife.* Honolulu: The University Press of Hawaii, 1972.

Bills, Robert W. *Citizen.* Anchorage, Alaska: O. W. Frost, 1978.

Bingham, Hiram. *A Residence of Twenty-One Years in the Sandwich Islands . . . .* Hartford: Hezekiah Huntington; New York: Sherman Converse, 1848.

Bird, Isabella L. Intro. and notes by Alfons L. Korn. *Six Months in the Sandwich Islands.* Honolulu: University of Hawaii Press for Friends of the Library of Hawaii, 1964. (First printed in 1875.)

Bishop, Charles. *The Journal and Letters of Captain Charles Bishop on the North-West Coast of America, in the Pacific and in New South Wales 1794–1799.* Ed. Michael Roe. Cambridge: Published for the Hakluyt Society at the University Press, 1967.

Bishop, Isabella Lucy (Bird). Holograph letters written to her sister from the Sandwich Islands between 19 February and 15 June 1873. Transcribed by Alfons L. Korn, 1975. UH. Typescript.

Boit, John. *The Journal of a Voyage Round the Globe, 1795 & 1796.* Consists of the 22 pages dealing with Hawaii. HMCS. Typescript.

Bolkhovitinov, N. W. "The Adventures of Doctor Schaffer in Hawaii, 1815–1819." Trans. from the Russian by Igor V. Vorobyoff. *The Hawaiian Journal of History* 7 (1973): 55–78.

Boston Recorder. Newspaper.

Bradley, Harold W. *The American Frontier in Hawaii, 1789–1843.* Palo Alto: Stanford University Press, 1942.

Broughton, William R. *A Voyage of Discovery to the North Pacific Ocean . . . Performed in His Majesty's Sloop* Providence, *and Her Tender, in the Years 1795, 1796, 1797, 1798.* London: T. Cadell and W. Davies, 1804.

Brown, Malcolm. *Reminiscences of a Pioneer Kauai Family.* Honolulu: Thos. McVeagh, 1918.

Brown, Mervyn. *Madagascar Rediscovered—A History from Early Times to Independence.* Hamden, Connecticut: Archon Books, 1979.

Buck, Peter H. (Te Rangi Hiroa). *Arts and Crafts of Hawaii.* Honolulu: BPBM Special Publication 45, 1957.

———. *Explorers of the Pacific.* Honolulu: BPBM Special Publication 43, 1953.

———. *Vikings of the Sunrise.* Philadelphia and New York: J. B. Lippincott, 1938.

Burbank, Mary A. "The Koloa School." KHS Papers. Typescript.

Bureau of Conveyances. Department of Land and Natural Resources. State of Hawaii. Honolulu.

Bureau of Immigration Letter Books. AH.

Cajski, Thomas Anthony. "The Ports of Kauai." Master's thesis, Univ. Hawaii, 1964.

Campbell, Archibald. *A Voyage Round the World, from 1806 to 1812 . . . .* Honolulu: University of Hawaii Press, 1967. (Facsimile reproduction of the third American edition of 1822.)

Carter, Sybil A. *Kaahumanu.* Honolulu: R. Grieve, 1893.

Chamberlain, Levi. Journal. HMCS. Typescript.

Char, Tin-Yuke, ed. and comp. *The Sandalwood Mountains.* Honolulu: The University Press of Hawaii, 1975.

Char, Tin-Yuke, and Wai Jane Char, eds. and comps. *Chinese Historic Sites and Pioneer Families of Kauai.* Honolulu: A Local History Project of Hawaii Chinese History Center, Inc., 1979.

Chevigny, Hector. *Lord of Alaska.* New York: The Viking Press, 1942.

Cleveland, Richard J. *A Narrative of Voyages and Commercial Enterprises.* 2 vols. Cambridge: John Owen, 1842.

Colcord, John N. Journal. AH. Typescript.

Collector General of Customs, Ports of Entry. Waimea and Koloa, Kauai, Account Book. AH.

Collinson, Richard. *Journal of H.M.S.* Enterprise . . . *in 1850–1855.* London: Sampson Low, Marston, Searle & Rivington, 1889.

Coman, Katharine. *The History of Contract Labor in the Hawaiian Islands.* New York: Macmillan Company for the American Economic Association, 1903.

Conde, Jesse C., and Gerald M. Best. *Sugar Trains.* Felton, California: Glenwood Publishers, 1973.

Conroy, Hilary. *The Japanese Frontier in Hawaii, 1868–1898.* Berkeley and Los Angeles: University of California Press, 1953.

Cook, James, and James King. *A Voyage to the Pacific Islands.* 3 vols. Dublin: Printed for H. Chamberlaine, W. Watson . . . , 1784.

Cook, John. *Reminiscences of John Cook.* Honolulu: The New Freedom Press, 1927.

Coulter, John W. *Population and Utilization of Land and Sea in Hawaii, 1853.* Honolulu: BPBM Bulletin 88, 1931.

Coulter, John, and Chee Kwon Chun. *Chinese Rice Farmers in Hawaii.* University of Hawaii Research Publication No. 16. Honolulu: University of Hawaii, 1937.

Daily Bulletin. Honolulu newspaper.

Damon, Ethel M. *The Heiau at Wailua.* Lihue: KHS, 1934.

———. *Koamalu.* 2 vols. Honolulu: Privately printed at the Star-Bulletin Press, 1931.

———. *Sanford Ballard Dole and His Hawaii.* Palo Alto: Pacific Books. Published for the Hawaiian Historical Society, 1957.

Davies, Theo. H. "Personal Recollections of Hawaii." N.p., n.d. Mimeographed.

Davis, William Heath. *Seventy-Five Years in California.* San Francisco: John Howell, 1929.

Daws, Gavan. *Shoal of Time: A History of the Hawaiian Islands.* New York: The Macmillan Company, 1968.

Daws, Gavan, and Timothy Head. "Niihau: A Shoal of Time." *American Heritage* 14 (October 1963): 48–51, 81–85.

Dean, Arthur Lyman. *The Story of McBryde 1899–1949.* N.p., n.d.

Degener, Otto. *Ferns and Flowering Plants of Hawaii National Park.* Honolulu: Honolulu Star-Bulletin, Ltd., 1930.

Delano, Amasa. *A Narrative of Voyages and Travels, in the Northern and Southern Hemispheres. . . .* New York: Praeger Publishers, 1970. (Reprint of 1817 edition.)

Dickey, Lyle A. "Stories of Wailua, Kauai." HHS *Report* 25, 1916. 14–36.

Directory and Hand-Book of Honolulu and the Hawaiian Islands, 1894–95. San Francisco: F. M. Husted, n.d.

Dixon, George. *A Voyage Round the World: But More Particularly to the North-West Coast of America. . . .* London: Geo. Goulding, 1789.

Dobel, Pierre. *Sept années en Chine. Nouvelles observations sur cet empire, l'Archipel Indo-Chinois, les Philippines et les Iles Sandwich.* Paris: Gide, 1838.

Dole, Charles S. "The Hui Kawaihau." HHS *Papers* No. 16, 1929. 8–15.

Dole, Daniel. Journal. Journal of the Reverend Daniel Dole, Koloa Academy, 1858–1870. Journal Collection. HMCS. Manuscript.

Dole, George, "The Ascent of Waialeale (1874)." KHS Papers. Typescript.

Dole (Sanford) Collection. AH.

Dole, Sanford. "Hawaii Under Annexation." Dole Collection. n.d. AH. Manuscript.

———. *Memoirs of the Hawaiian Revolution.* Ed. Andrew Farrell. Honolulu: Advertiser Publishing Co., Ltd., 1936.

———. *Papers, 1840–1926.* HMCS.

Dwight, Edwin. *Memoirs of Henry Obookiah, A Native of Owhyee. . . .* Honolulu: Women's Board of Missions for the Pacific Islands and Hawaii Conference, the United Church of Christ, Honolulu, 1968. (Reprint of 1818 edition.)

Eastman, Frances. *Pioneer Hawaiian Christians.* New York: Frontier Books, 1948.

Ellis, [Surgeon] William. *An Authentic Narrative of a Voyage Performed by Captain Cook and Captain Clerke . . . During the Years 1777, 1778, 1779, and 1780 . . .* 2 vols. London: Printed for G. Robinson, J. Sewell, and J. Deberett, 1792.

Ellis, [Rev.] William. *Journal of William Ellis.* Honolulu: Advertiser Publishing Company, 1963. (Reprint of London edition of 1827 and Hawaii edition of 1917.)

Emerson, Nathaniel B. "The Long Voyages of the Ancient Hawaiians." HHS *Papers* No. 5, 1893. 1–28.

———. *Pele and Hiiaka.* Honolulu: Honolulu Star-Bulletin, Ltd., 1915.

———. *Unwritten Literature of Hawaii.* Washington: Smithsonian Institution, Bureau of American Ethnology Bulletin 38, 1909.

Emory, Kenneth P. *Archaeology of Nihoa and Necker Islands.* Honolulu: BPBM Bulletin 53, 1928.

———. "Ruins at Kee, Haena, Kauai." *Hawaiian Annual,* 1929. 88–94.

Estate of R. C. Wyllie Junr., First Circuit Court, Probate 2327. AH.

Evening Bulletin Industrial Edition. A special edition of the *Evening Bulletin,* November 1901. Honolulu newspaper.

Feher, Joseph, with Edward Joesting and O. A. Bushnell. *Hawaii: A Pictorial History.* Honolulu: BPBM Special Publication No. 58, 1969.

Forbes, David. *Queen Emma and Lawai.* Lihue: KHS, 1970.

Foreign Office and Executive (F.O. & Ex.) AH.

Fornander, Abraham. *An Account of the Polynesian Race: Its Origins and Migrations, and the Ancient History of the Hawaiian People to the Times of Kamehameha I.* 3 vols. London: Trubner & Co., 1878–1885.

———. *Fornander Collection of Hawaiian Antiquities and Folk-Lore.* Revised translations and notes by Thomas G. Thrum. Honolulu: Memoirs of the BPBM, Vols. 4, 5, and 6, 1916–1919.

Forty-Sixth Annual Report of the Hawaiian Mission Children's Society Presented July 2, 1898 with the Constitution and By-Laws and List of Members. Honolulu: Press Publishing Company Print, 1898.

Franklin, Jane (Lady), Collection. Microfilm 213. UH.

The Friend. Honolulu newspaper.

Gallaudet, Thomas H. *An Address, Delivered at a Meeting for Prayer, with References to the Sandwich Mission.* Hartford: Lincoln & Stone, Printers, 1819.

Garden Island. Lihue newspaper.

Gast, Ross H., and Agnes C. Conrad. *Don Francisco de Paula Marin.* Honolulu: The University Press of Hawaii for the Hawaiian Historical Society, 1973.

Gay, Lawrence K. *Tales of the Forbidden Island of Niihau.* Honolulu: Topgallant Publishing Co., Ltd., 1981.

Gilman, Gorham. "Journal of a Canoe Voyage Along the Kauai Palis, Made in 1845." HHS *Papers* No. 14, 1908. 3–8.

———. (Makaikai). "Rustications on Kauai and Niihau in the Summer of 1845." HHS. Manuscript.

Golder, Frank A. *Bering's Voyages.* 2 vols. New York: American Geographical Society, 1925.

———. "Proposals for Russian Occupation of the Hawaiian Islands." In *Hawaiian Islands,* Albert P. Taylor and Ralph S. Kuykendall, eds. Honolulu: Captain Cook Sesquicentennial Commission and the Archives of Hawaii Commission, 1930.

Golson, Jack, ed. *Polynesian Navigation—A Symposium on Andrew Sharp's Theory of Accidental Voyages.* Wellington and Sydney: A. H. & A. W. Reed, 1972.

Gordon, Arthur. "The Great Stone Fleet—Calculated Catastrophe." *The United States Naval Institute Proceedings* 94 (December 1968): 72–82.

Gould, Rupert T. "Some Unpublished Accounts of Cook's Death." *The Mariner's Mirror* 4 (1928): 301–319.

Grove Farm Account Book, 1864–1883. Grove Farm Homestead.

Gruening, Ernest. *The State of Alaska.* New York: Random House, 1954.

Gulick, Rev. and Mrs. Orramel Hinckley. *The Pilgrims of Hawaii.* New York and London: Fleming H. Revell Company, 1918.

Haddon, A. C., and James Hornell. *Canoes of Oceania.* 3 vols. Honolulu: BPBM Special Publications 27, 28, and 29, 1936–1938.

Halford, Francis John. *9 Doctors & God.* Honolulu: University of Hawaii Press, 1954.

Handy, E. S. Craighill. *The Hawaiian Planter.* Vol. 1. Honolulu: BPBM Bulletin 161, 1940.

———. *History and Culture in the Society Islands.* Honolulu: BPBM Bulletin 79, 1930.

———. *The Native Culture in the Marquesas.* Honolulu: BPBM Bulletin No. 9, 1923.

Hawaiian Annual. Periodical published in Honolulu by Thomas G. Thrum.

Hawaiian Evangelical Association (HEA) Archives, 1853–1947. AH.

Hawaiian Gazette. Honolulu newspaper.

The Hawaiian Kingdom: Statistical and Commercial Directory and Tourists' Guide, 1880–1881. Honolulu and San Francisco: George Bowser & Co., 1880.

Head, George H. *The Last Cruise of the Saginaw.* Boston and New York: Houghton Mifflin Company, 1912.

Henke, Louis A. *A Survey of Livestock in Hawaii.* University of Hawaii Research Publication No. 5. Honolulu: University of Hawaii, August 1929.

Hillebrand, William F. *Flora of the Hawaiian Islands.* London: Williams & Norgate; New York: B. Westernmann & Co.; Heidelberg: University Bookseller, 1888.

Hind, Norman E. A. *The Geology of Kauai and Niihau.* Honolulu: BPBM Bulletin 71, 1930.

Hiroa, Te Rangi. See Peter H. Buck.

History of American Missions to the Heathen. . . . Worcester: Spooner & Howland, 1840.

Hobbs, Jean. *Hawaii: A Pageant of the Soil.* Stanford: Stanford University Press, 1935.

Hohman, Elmo P. *The American Whaleman.* New York: Longmans, Green and Co., 1928.

Holman, Lucia Ruggles. *Journal of Lucia Ruggles Holman.* Honolulu: BPBM Special Publication 17, 1931.

Holt, Elizabeth Knudsen von. See von Holt.

Honolulu Advertiser. Newspaper.

Honolulu Star-Bulletin. Newspaper.

Hooper, William N. Diaries in the handwriting of William N. Hooper. Leases and other documents. 1835–1846. Unpaged. UH. Photocopies.

Hopkins, Manly. *Hawaii: The Past, Present and Future of Its Island Kingdom.* New York: D. Appleton and Co., 1869.

Hormann, Bernhard L. "The Germans In Hawaii." Master's thesis, Univ. Hawaii, 1931.

Hotimsky, C. M. *The Death of Captain James Cook.* Sydney: Wentworth Books, 1962.

Howay, F. W. "The Last Days of the Atahualpa, Alias Behring." HHS *Report* 41, 1933. 70–80.

Hulme, Kathryn C. "The Timeless Kauai Swamp." *The Atlantic Monthly* 215 (January 1965): 68–71.

Hunt, Cornelius. *The Shenandoah.* New York: G. W. Carleton & Co., 1867.

Ii, John Papa. *Fragments of Hawaiian History.* Ed. Dorothy B. Barrère. BPBM Special Publication 70, 1959.

Indices of Awards Made by the Board of Commissioners to Quiet Land Titles in the Hawaiian Islands. Territory of Hawaii. Honolulu: Star-Bulletin Press, 1929. AH.

Ingraham, Joseph. *Extracts From the Log of the Brig* Hope *Among the Sandwich Islands.* 20 May–12 October 1791. From the original manuscript in the Library of Congress. HHS Reprint No. 3, 1921.

Instructions of the Prudential Committee of the American Board of Commissioners for Foreign Missions to the Sandwich Islands Mission. Lahainaluna: Press of the Mission Seminary, 1838.

Interior Department (Int. Dept.). AH.

Iwai, Charles K. "The Rice Industry in Hawaii." Master's thesis, Univ. Hawaii, 1933.

Jackson, Francis O. "Koloa Plantation Under Ladd and Company, 1835–1845." Master's thesis, Univ. Hawaii, 1958.

Jarves, James J. *History of the Hawaiian or Sandwich Islands.* Boston: Tappan Dennet, 1843.

———. *Scenes and Scenery in the Sandwich Islands and a Trip Through Central America 1837–1842.* Boston: James Munroe and Company, 1844.

———. "Sketches of Kauai." *The Hawaiian Spectator* 1 (1838): 66–86.

Joesting, Edward. *Hawaii: An Uncommon History.* New York: W. W. Norton & Company, 1972.

Johannessen, Edward. *The Hawaiian Labor Movement—A Brief History.* Boston: Bruce Humphries, Inc., 1956.

Johnson, Rubellite Kinney, ed. *Kukini 'Aha'ilona.* Honolulu: Topgallant Publishing Co., 1976.

Judd, Bernice. "Koloa: A Sketch of its Development." HHS *Report* 44, 1935. 51–85.

———. *Voyages to Hawaii Before 1860.* Ed. and enl. by Helen Y. Lind. Honolulu: The University Press of Hawaii for the Hawaiian Mission Children's Society, 1974.

Judd, C. S. "Niihau." *The Hawaiian Forester and Agriculturalist* XXIX (1932): 5–9.

———. "The Parasitic Habit of the Sandalwood Tree." Board of Commissioners of Agriculture and Forestry, Territory of Hawaii, 1932. UH. Mimeographed.

Kalakaua Papers. AH.

Kamakau, Samuel Manaiakalani. *Ka Po'e Kahiko (The People of Old).* Trans. Mary Kawena Pukui. Ed. and arr. Dorothy B. Barrère. Honolulu: BPBM Special Publication 51, 1964.

———. *Ruling Chiefs of Hawaii.* Honolulu: The Kamehameha Schools, 1961.

———. *The Works of the People of Old (Na Hana a ka Po'e Kahiko).* Trans. Mary Kawena Pukui. Ed. and arr. Dorothy B. Barrère. Honolulu: BPBM Special Publication 61, 1976.

Kelly, Marion. "*Hālau Hula* and Adjacent Sites at Kē'ē, Kaua'i." In *Hula: Historical Perspectives,* Dorothy B. Barrère, Mary Kawena Pukui, and Marion Kelly. Honolulu: Pacific Anthropological Records No. 30. Honolulu: Department of Anthropology, BPBM, 1980.

Kemble, John H. "Pioneer Hawaiian Steamers, 1852–1877." HHS *Report* 53, 1944. 6–25.

Khlebnikov, K. T. *Baranov—Chief Manager of the Russian Colonies in America.* Trans. Colin Bearne. Ed. Richard A. Pierce. Kingston, Ontario: The Limestone Press, 1973.

King, Josephine Wundenberg. "Queen Emma on Kauai." KHS Papers. Typescript.

King, William. "Arctic Whaling Fleet Disaster." HHS *Report* 63, 1954. 19–28.

Knapp, Horton. Journal. Journal Collection. HMCS. Manuscript.

Knudsen, Eric. "Waialeale." KHS Papers. Typescript.

Knudsen, Eric A., and Gurre P. Noble. *Kanuka of Kauai.* Honolulu: Tongg Publishing Company, 1944.

Knudsen, Valdemar, Collection. 1867–1884. AH.

Korn, Alfons L. *The Victorian Visitors.* Honolulu: University of Hawaii Press, 1958.

Kotzebue, Otto von. *A Voyage of Discovery into the South Sea and Beering's Straits . . .*

in the Years 1815–1818. . . . 3 vols. London: Longman, Hurst, Rees, Orme, and Brown, 1821.

Krauss, Bob, and William P. Alexander. *Grove Farm Plantation.* Palo Alto: Pacific Books, Publishers, 1965.

Krout, Mary Hannah. *Reminiscences of Mary S. Rice.* Honolulu: The Hawaiian Gazette Co., Ltd., 1908.

Krusenstern, Adam John von. *Voyage Round the World in the Years 1803, 1804, 1805 & 1806* . . . . Trans. from the German by Richard B. Hoppner. 2 vols. London: John Murray, 1813.

Kuokoa, Ka Nupepa. Honolulu newspaper.

Kuykendall Collection. UH.

Kuykendall, Ralph S. *The Hawaiian Kingdom.* 3 vols. Honolulu: University of Hawaii Press, 1938–1967.

Lafon, Thomas. *The Great Obstruction to the Conversion of Souls at Home and Abroad.* New York: Union Missionary Society, 1843.

Land Commission Awards. AH.

Langdon, Robert, ed. *Thar She Went.* An interim index to the Pacific ports and islands visited by American whalers and traders in the 19th century, being a supplement to *American Whalers and Traders in the Pacific: A Guide to Records on Microfilm.* Canberra: Pacific Manuscripts Bureau, Research School of Pacific Studies, Australian National University, 1979.

Langsdorff, G. H. von. *Voyages and Travels in Various Parts of the World.* Carlisle: Printed by George Philips, 1817.

Lewis, David. *We, the Navigators.* Honolulu: University of Hawaii Press, 1972.

Liliuokalani. *Hawaii's Story by Hawaii's Queen.* Boston: Lee and Shepard, 1898.

Lisiansky, Urey. *A Voyage Round the World in the Years 1803, 4, 5, & 6* . . . . London: Printed by J. Booth, 1814.

Lo, Catherine Pascual. *Lihue Lutheran Church.* Lihue: Lihue Lutheran Church, 1981.

Lomax, Alfred L. "Geographic Factors in Early Sheep Husbandry in the Hawaiian Islands (1791–1870)." HHS *Report* 48, 1939. 29–54.

Luomala, Katharine. "Creative Processes in Hawaiian Use of Place Names in Chants." *Laographia* 22 (1965): 234–247.

———. *The Menehune of Polynesia and Other Mythical Little People of Oceania.* Honolulu: BPBM Bulletin 203, 1951.

———. *Voices on the Wind.* Honolulu: BPBM, 1955.

Lydecker, Robert Colfax. *Roster Legislatures of Hawaii, 1841–1918.* Honolulu: The Hawaiian Gazette Co., Ltd., 1918.

Lydgate, John M. "The Affairs of the Wainiha Hui." *Hawaiian Annual* 39, 1913. 125–137.

———. "Kaumualii, The Last King of Kauai." HHS *Report* 24, 1915. 21–43.

———. "Sandalwood Days." *Hawaiian Annual* 42, 1916. 50–56.

———. "Wailua—The Home of Kings." *The Garden Island,* 16 March 1920.

———. "The Wreck of the *Saginaw*: Notes on Halford's Story." KHS Papers. Typescript.

Lyman, Chester. *Around the Horn to the Sandwich Islands and California, 1845–1850.* New Haven: Yale University Press, 1924.

MacCaughey, Vaughan. "History of Botanical Exploration in Hawaii." *The Hawaiian Forester and Agriculturalist* XVI (1919): 25–54.

McCoy, Patrick C. *Archaeological Research at Fort Elizabeth, Waimea, Kauai, Hawaiian Islands. Phase 1.* Departmental Report Series 72-7. Honolulu: Department of Anthropology, BPBM, 1972.

Macdonald, Gordon A., and Agatin T. Abbott. *Volcanoes in the Sea.* Honolulu: University of Hawaii Press, 1970.

Macfie, R. A. v. Jacintho Moniz et al. Fifth Circuit Court, Special Proceedings. No. 93. 1881. AH.

Macrae, James. *With Lord Byron at the Sandwich Islands in 1825, Being Extracts from the MS Diary of James Macrae, Scottish Botanist.* Ed. Willard F. Wilson. Honolulu: n.p., 1922.

Malo, David. *Hawaiian Antiquities* (Moolelo Hawaii). Trans. Nathaniel B. Emerson. Honolulu: BPBM Special Publication 2, 1951. (Originally published 1903.)

Marshal of the Kingdom, from the Sheriff of Kauai, 1849–1900. AH.

Mazour, Anatole G. "Doctor Yegor Scheffer: Dreamer of a Russian Empire in the Pacific." *The Pacific Historical Review* VI (March 1937): 15–20.

Meares, John. *Voyages Made in the Years 1788 and 1789 . . . to Which are Prefixed . . . a Voyage Performed in 1786 . . . in the Ship* Nootka . . . . London: Logographic Press, 1790.

Medcalf, Donald, and Ronald Russell. *Hawaiian Money Standard Catalog.* Honolulu: Medcalf and Russell, 1978.

Micronesian Mission—HEA. Hawaiian Evangelical Association, Papers. HMCS.

Missionary Album. Honolulu: Hawaiian Mission Children's Society, 1969.

Missionary Herald 1805–1934. Boston. Periodical.

Missionary Letters, 1820–1900. HMCS.

Mission Station Reports, 1822–1865. HMCS. Typescript.

Morgan, Theodore. *Hawaii: A Century of Economic Change, 1778–1876.* Cambridge: Harvard University Press, 1948.

Morison, Samuel Eliot. "Boston Traders in the Hawaiian Islands." *Massachusetts Historical Society* LIV (October-November 1920): 9–47.

Mouritz, Albert A. *The Path of the Destroyer.* Honolulu: Honolulu Star-Bulletin, 1916.

Native Register. AH.

Neal, Marie C. *In Gardens of Hawaii.* Honolulu: BPBM Special Publication 50, 1978.

Nellist, George F., ed. *Men of Hawaii.* Honolulu: Honolulu Star-Bulletin, 1925.

Oliver, Douglas. *Ancient Tahitian Society.* 3 vols. Honolulu: The University Press of Hawaii, 1974.

Organic Act of the Territory of Hawaii (As Amended). Honolulu: Bulletin Publishing Co., Ltd., 1 July 1911.

Pacific Coast Commercial Record. San Francisco newspaper.

Pacific Manuscripts Bureau—Guide to Collections of Manuscripts Relating to the Pacific Islands. Canberra: Pacific Manuscripts Bureau (PMB), The Australian National University, 1968. (Also see Langdon.)

Parke, William C. *Personal Reminiscences of William Parke.* Rewritten and arr. by his son, William C. Parke. Cambridge: Printed at the University Press, 1891.

Penal Code of the Hawaiian Islands, Passed by the House of Nobles and Representatives on the 21st of June, A.D. 1850. Honolulu: Printed by Henry M. Whitney, Government Press, 1850.

Phillips, James Tice. "Report of the President." HHS *Report* 53, 1944. 50–52.

Pierce, Richard A. *Russia's Hawaiian Adventure, 1815–1817.* Berkeley and Los Angeles: University of California Press, 1965.

Planters' Monthly. Periodical. Published for the Hawaiian Sugar Planters' Association.

Plews. Edith Rice. "Poetry." In *Ancient Hawaiian Civilization.* E. S. Craighill Handy et al. Rutland, Vermont and Tokyo: Charles E. Tuttle Co., Publishers, 1965. (Revised edition.)

The Polynesian. Honolulu newspaper.

Portlock, Nathaniel. *A Voyage Round the World . . . in 1785, 1786, 1787, and 1788 . . . .* London: Printed for John Stockdale and George Goulding, 1789.

The Public Statutes at Large of the United States of America . . . . Boston: Charles C. Little and James Brown, 1845.

Pukui, Mary Kawena. "The Hula, Hawaii's Own Dance." *Hawaiian Annual,* 1943. 115–118.

Pukui, Mary Kawena, and Samuel H. Elbert. *Hawaiian Dictionary.* Honolulu: University of Hawaii Press, 1971.

Pukui, Mary Kawena, Samuel Elbert, and Esther T. Mookini. *Place Names of Hawaii.* Honolulu: The University Press of Hawaii, 1974.

Queen Emma Collection. AH.

Report of the President of the Bureau of Immigration to the Legislature. Annual reports.

Report of the Proceedings and Evidence in the Arbitration Between the King and Government of the Hawaiian Islands and Messrs. Ladd and Co. . . . . Honolulu: Charles E. Hitchcock, Government Press, 1846.

Reynolds, Stephen. Journal. HHS. Microfilm.

Rice, Mary Agnes. "The History of Lihue." KHS Papers. Typescript.

Rice, Mary S. "Life and Work at Punahou." In *Jubilee Celebration of the Arrival of the Missionary Reinforcement of 1837.* Honolulu: Daily Bulletin Steam Print, 1887.

Rice, William Hyde. *Hawaiian Legends.* Honolulu: BPBM Special Publication 63, 1977.

Rock, Joseph F. *The Indigenous Trees of the Hawaiian Islands.* Lawai, Hawaii: Pacific Tropical Botanical Garden; Rutland, Vermont & Tokyo: Charles E. Tuttle Company, 1974. (Originally published 1913.)

Royal Hawaiian Agricultural Society (RHAS) *Transactions.* Annual reports, 1850–1856.

Ruggles, Samuel, and Nancy Ruggles. Journal. Portions of the journal appeared in the *Boston Recorder,* Boston, Massachusetts, 21 and 28 April 1821.

Rush, B. F. *History of Construction and Development of Honolulu Harbor, Hilo Harbor, Kawaihae Harbor, Kahului Harbor, Kaunakakai Harbor, Nawiliwili Harbor, Port Allen Harbor.* N.p., 1957.

Sailor's Magazine and Naval Journal. Periodical. New York.

Salisbury, Mary. "Wailua Valley of Kauai, Kings and Priests, Rich in Splendor." *Honolulu Star-Bulletin,* 5 September 1936.

Sandwich Island Mirror. Honolulu newspaper.

Schmitt, Robert C. *Historic Statistics of Hawaii.* Honolulu: The University Press of Hawaii, 1977.

Schweizer, Niklaus R. *Hawaii and the German Speaking Peoples.* Honolulu: Topgallant Publishing Co., Ltd., 1982.

Shaler, William. *Journal of a Voyage Between China and the Northwestern Coast of America Made in 1804.* Claremont, California: Saunders Studio Press, 1935.

Shepard, Francis P. *The Earth Beneath the Sea.* Baltimore: The Johns Hopkins Press, 1959.

Simpson, George (Sir). *Narrative of a Journey Round the World, During the Years 1841 and 1842.* 2 vols. London: Henry Colburn, 1847.

Sinclair, Francis. *Ballads and Poems from the Pacific.* London: Sampson Low, Marston, Searle, & Rivington, 1889.

Sinclair, Isabella. *Indigenous Flowers of the Hawaiian Islands.* London: Sampson Low, Marston, Searle, & Rivington, 1885.

Sinoto, Yosihiko H. "An Archaeologically Based Assessment of the Marquesas Islands as a Dispersal Center in East Polynesia." In *Studies in Oceanic Culture History,* Vol. I, R. C. Green and M. Kelly, eds. Pacific Anthropological Records No. 11. Honolulu: Department of Anthropology, BPBM, 1970.

――――. "The Marquesas." In *The Prehistory of Polynesia,* Jesse D. Jennings, ed. Canberra: Australian National University Press, 1979.

Smith, James W. Journal. Journal Collection. HMCS. Manuscript.

Smith, Juliette. Journal. Journal Collection. HMCS. Manuscript.

Smith Papers, Koloa, Kauai, 1865–1900. HMCS.

Smith, Walter. *Legends of Wailua.* Lihue: Garden Island Publishing Co., 1955.

Spaulding, T. M. "The Adoption of the Hawaiian Alphabet." HHS *Papers* No. 17, 1930. 28–33.

Spoehr, Anne H. "George Prince Tamoree: Heir Apparent of Kauai and Niihau." *The Hawaiian Journal of History* XV (1981): 31–49.

Starbuck, Alexander. *History of the American Whale Fleet.* 2 vols. New York: Argosy-Antiquarian, 1864.

Stauder, Catherine. "George, Prince of Hawaii." *The Hawaiian Journal of History* VI (1972): 28–44.

――――. "A Study of the Two Sites at Wailua, Kauai, from Oral Documentation and Historical Records." *Archaeology of Kauai* 5 (December 1976): 1–27. Mimeographed.

Stearns, Harold T. *Geology of the Hawaiian Islands.* Division of Hydrography Bulletin 8. Honolulu: Territory of Hawaii, 1946.

Stejneger, Leonhard. *Georg Wilhelm Steller.* Cambridge, Mass.: Harvard University Press, 1936.

Stewart, Charles. *Journal of a Residence in the Sandwich Islands.* Honolulu: University of Hawaii Press, 1970. (Originally published 1828.)

Stokes, John F. C. "New Bases for Hawaiian Chronology." HHS *Report* 41, 1932. 23–65.

――――. "Whence Paao?" HHS *Papers* No. 15, 1927. 40–45.

Stroup, Elaine Fogg, ed. *The Ports of Hawaii.* Honolulu: Honolulu Port No. 67, Propeller Club of the United States, 1959.

Sullivan, Josephine. *A History of C. Brewer & Company Limited—One Hundred Years in the Hawaiian Islands 1826-1926.* K. C. Leebreck, ed. Boston: Walton Advertising & Printing Company, 1926.

Territory of Hawaii—Report of the Treasurer for the Year Ended December 31st 1900. Honolulu: Hawaiian Gazette Co., Ltd., 1900.

Thompson, Virginia, and Richard Adloff. *The Malagasy Republic—Madagascar Today.* Stanford: Stanford University Press, 1965.

Thrum, Thos. G. "Notes on the History of Coffee Culture in the Hawaiian Islands." *Hawaiian Annual,* 1876. 46–51.

———. "Notes on the History of the Sugar Industry of the Hawaiian Islands." *Hawaiian Annual,* 1875. 34–42.

———. "Tales from the Temples." *Hawaiian Annual,* 1907. 49–69.

Turnbull, John. *A Voyage Round the World.* 3 vols. London: Printed for Richard Phillips, 1805.

Tuthill, James A. "A Visit to a Sugar Plantation—1898." *Hawaii Historical Review.* April 1965. Mimeographed.

Vancouver, George. *A Voyage of Discovery to the North Pacific Ocean . . . in the Years 1790, 1791, 1792, 1793, 1794, and 1795. . . .* 3 vols. London: Printed for G. G. and J. Robinson and J. Edwards, 1798.

von Holt, Elizabeth Knudsen. *Stories of Long Ago.* Honolulu: Star-Bulletin Printing Company, 1968.

Wakukawa, Ernest K. *History of the Japanese People in Hawaii.* Honolulu: The Toyo shoin, 1938.

Walsh, Arsenius. Journal. KM. Typescript.

"Whalemen's Shipping Papers." See Pacific Manuscripts Bureau.

White, Henry. "Sugar Industry and Plantation Agencies." In *The 13th New Americans Conference.* Honolulu: n.p., 1939.

Whitney, Mercy. Journal. Journal Collection. HMCS. Also KM. Typescript.

Whitney, Samuel. Journal. Journal Collection. HMCS. Manuscript.

Wilcox, George N. "Notes on Two Trips to Waialeale." KHS. Typescript.

Wilkes, Charles. *Narrative of the United States Exploring Expedition. During the Years 1838, 1839, 1840, 1841, 1842.* 5 vols. Philadelphia: Lea and Blanchard, 1845.

Wong, Christie Lee. "Kauai's Rice King, Leong Pah On (1848–1924)." In *Chinese Historic Sites and Pioneer Families of Kauai,* Tin-Yuke Char and Wai Jane Char, eds. and comps. Honolulu: A Local History Project of Hawaii Chinese History Center, Inc., 1979.

Woodward, Frances J. *Portrait of Jane.* London: Hodder and Stoughton, 1951.

Wright, Anna W. "Reminiscences of Lihue and Koloa, Kauai." KHS Papers. Typescript.

Yzendoorn, Reginald. *History of the Catholic Mission in the Hawaiian Islands.* Honolulu: Honolulu Star-Bulletin, Ltd., 1927.

Index

About the Author

Edward Joesting was born in St. Paul, Minnesota in 1925. His early years were spent in Southern California where he received his education, graduating from Pomona College in 1948.

Three years later Edward Joesting came to Hawaii. For the next twenty years he worked in the corporate world, serving as an officer in two of Hawaii's largest companies.

In 1972 *Hawaii—An Uncommon History* was published. Since then several editions have appeared and the book is considered an authoritative history of the Islands. In 1974 he started devoting full time to writing and in that year began work on *Kauai: The Separate Kingdom*.

Joesting was a former trustee and a past president of the Hawaiian Historical Society, and he served as a lecturer at the University of Hawaii.

In 1969 he received an Award of Merit from the American Association for State and Local History for his part in *Hawaii—A Pictorial History*. In addition to his books, Joesting wrote many newspaper and magazine articles about Hawaii and the Pacific.

Major works by Edward Joesting include: *The Islands of Hawaii*, with photographs by Ansel Adams, 1958, (privately printed); *An Introduction to Hawaii*, with photographs by Ansel Adams, 1964, (5 Associates); *Hawaii—A Pictorial History*, with Joseph Feher and O. A. Bushnell, 1969, (Bishop Museum Press); *Hawaii—An Uncommon History*, 1972, (W. W. Norton & Co.); "Hawaii—A Revolution in Law and Land," an essay in *Land and the Pursuit of Happiness*, 1975, (University of California Press); *Eternal Hawaii*, with photographs by Aaron Dygart, 1976, (Graphic Arts Center); *Tides of Commerce*, 1983, (privately printed); and *Kauai: The Separate Kingdom*, 1984, (University of Hawaii Press).